NUMBER THREE:
Texas A&M University Economics Series

LIBERTY AND THE RULE OF LAW

Liberty and the Rule of Law

EDITED WITH AN INTRODUCTION BY

Robert L. Cunningham

TEXAS A&M UNIVERSITY PRESS

College Station and London

Library of Congress Cataloging in Publication Data
Main entry under title:
Liberty and the rule of law.

(The Texas A&M University economics series; no. 3)
Papers from a conference held in San Francisco in 1976.
Includes index.
1. Rule of law—Congresses.   2. Liberty—Congresses.
3. Hayek, Friedrich August von, 1899–   —Congresses.
I. Cunningham, Robert L., 1926–   II. Series: Texas. A&M
University, College Station. Texas A&M University eco-
nomics series; no. 3.

K3171.A3L5   340.1'1   78-6366
ISBN 0-89096-056-9 (cloth) ISBN 1-58544-020-5 (pbk.)

Manufactured in the United States of America
FIRST PAPERBACK EDITION

Contents

Introduction

IN 1859 J. S. Mill traced in *On Liberty* the history of what he called civil or social liberty: the nature and limits of the power that can legitimately be exercised by society over the individual. A time came, he tells us, when a great many people began to believe that there was a way to ensure that the powers of government would never be abused to the people's disadvantage. That way was self-government via representative democracy. The rulers are identified with the people, and since any power given the rulers was but the concentrated form of the nation's own power, it would hardly be necessary to protect the nation against its own will. But, Mill went on to say, those who exercise the power are not always the same as those over whom it is exercised; the "will of the people" means the will of the majority, and so the tyranny of the majority must be guarded against.

A hundred years later Friedrich A. Hayek in *The Constitution of Liberty* restated and clarified the traditional doctrine of liberal constitutionalism, making explicit the principles which, in his view, governments would have to follow if they wished to preserve freedom. The central part of that book is titled "Freedom and the Law" and is devoted to an examination and analysis of the institutional arrangements, most notably the rule of law, that Western man has developed to secure individual liberty. John Locke had written that "the end of law is, not to abolish or restrain, but to preserve and enlarge freedom." Hayek developed a modern restatement of how law was, or could be, instrumental in the "taming of power."

The issues and problems Hayek dealt with under the aegis of liberty and the rule of law, notably the problem of how law can constrain government from interfering with legitimate liberty, certainly are in the forefront of both practical and scholarly interest today. But has the "rule of law, not of men" failed to provide an adequate defense of liberty? Those who had placed their faith in "self-government" and, earlier, in Montesquieu's constitutional "separation of powers," as sufficient institutional safeguards of individual freedom, clearly had their expectations disappointed; governments everywhere succeeded in obtaining powers that men had by these means attempted to deny them. And it would appear that the rule of law, at least as it operates today, has proved inefficacious in stopping the growth and extension of the scope of government, a government many are coming to see increasingly as Leviathan.

The following questions are typical of the suspicion many have expressed that perhaps law has failed to make its expected contribution to a free, tolerably stable, and efficient society. Has law served to constrain state action, or is it rather the case that the working of our democratic institutions offer strong incentives to invest resources in using the state for private ends? Is it not true that law is used in the service of interest-group politics, with the result that more of individuals' resources are demanded than can be justified by the need to fill the gaps left by the operations of the market mechanism? How can law be made better to serve as a stable and safe basis for individual planning, serving to promote human dignity by giving people a wide range of options for the autonomous planning of their own futures? Since modern technology, increased mobility, and population density make for increasing interdependence—and so increasing areas of conflict of interests—does the preservation of individual freedom call for more, or less, formal law? Can less formal law, and regulation, be justified on the basis of confidence in the evolutionary powers of common law, making recourse to the legislature unnecessary? Can one trust the evolution of the common law to "select" conflict-reducing laws without supplementation by positive legislation? The age of democracy is the age of legislation: what are the dangers that legislation poses for the rule of law? Are there limits to the scope of legislation implied by the rule of law? Is the rule of law merely formal, "justice as regularity" in Rawls' expression, so that any conduct is legal if it conforms to authoritative rules? Or, is the rule of law, properly understood, also substantive in the sense that there are constraints on the rules that can rightly be enacted?

Are tradeoffs between liberty and order and the principle of equal consideration necessary, and, if so, on the basis of what principles should such tradeoffs be made?

A group of scholars interested in such questions concerning the nature and limitations of the rule of law, and in how law can contribute to fostering and protecting individual liberty—particularly in how governments can and should be ruled by law—met in San Francisco in 1976 to discuss these issues together. A number of disciplines were represented, including jurisprudence, philosophy, history, economics, and political science. All of the participants were interested in Hayek's approach to such issues, both as represented in *The Constitution of Liberty* and his later writings, particularly his newest major work, *Law, Legislation and Liberty*; the first volume of the latter work, subtitled "Rules and Order" deals explicitly with some of the crucial problems faced by one who attempts to see how law can enlarge, or diminish, freedom. The conference was intended to honor Hayek, and it did so by focusing on themes that most deeply concern him, by critical analysis of his own views, such as his preference for "spontaneous order" over organization, and by attempts to evaluate the adequacy of the jurisprudential and philosophical foundations that underlie his views.

ROBERT L. CUNNINGHAM

Liberty and the Rule of Law

The papers in this book were delivered at a conference held in honor of F. A. Hayek, January 14–18, 1976, in San Francisco. Cosponsors of the conference were Liberty Fund, Inc., and the University of San Francisco. Liberty Fund, Inc., is a foundation established to encourage study of the ideal of a society of free and responsible individuals.

1.

The Rule of Law and Its Virtue

JOSEPH RAZ

F. A. HAYEK has provided one of the clearest and most powerful formulations of the ideal of the rule of law: "Stripped of all technicalities this means that government in all its actions is bound by rules fixed and announced beforehand—rules which make it possible to foresee with fair certainty how the authority will use its coercive powers in given circumstances, and to plan one's individual affairs on the basis of this knowledge."[1] At the same time, Hayek draws certain conclusions from this ideal that illustrate one of the two main fallacies in the contemporary treatment of the doctrine of the rule of law: the assumption of its overriding importance. My purpose is to analyze the ideal of the rule of law in the spirit of Hayek's statement of it and to show why some of his conclusions cannot be thus supported. But first, let us consider the other common fallacy concerning the rule of law.

Not uncommonly when a political ideal captures the imagination of large numbers of people, it becomes a slogan used by supporters of ideals that bear little or no relation to the original. The fate of "democracy" not long ago and that of "privacy" today are only two examples of this familiar process. In 1959 the International Congress of Jurists meeting in New Delhi gave official blessing to a similar perversion of the doctrine of the rule of law: "The function of the legislature in a free society under the rule of law is to create

This is a revised version of the paper presented at the Conference. I am grateful to Professor Rolf Sartorius and Mr. David Libling for useful suggestions on ways to improve on an early draft of the paper.
    [1] F. A. Hayek, *The Road to Serfdom* (Chicago: University of Chicago Press, 1944), p. 54.

and maintain the conditions which will uphold the dignity of man as an individual. This dignity requires not only the recognition of his civil and political rights but also the establishment of the social, economic, educational, and cultural conditions which are essential to the full development of his personality."[2] The report goes on to mention almost every political ideal that has found support in any part of the globe during the postwar years.

If the rule of law is the rule of the good law, then to explain its nature is to propound a complete social philosophy. But then the term lacks any useful function. We have no need to be converted to the rule of law in order to discover that to believe in it is to believe that good should triumph. The rule of law is a political ideal that a legal system may lack or may possess to a greater or lesser degree. That much is common ground. The rule of law, however, is only one of the virtues that a legal system may possess and by which it is to be judged. The rule of law is not to be confused with democracy, justice, equality (before the law or otherwise), human rights of any kind, or respect for persons or for the dignity of man. A nondemocratic legal system, based on the denial of human rights, on extensive poverty, on racial segregation, sexual inequalities, and religious persecution may, in principle, conform to the requirements of the rule of law better than any of the legal systems of the more enlightened Western democracies. This does not mean that the nondemocratic system will be better than those Western democracies. It will be an immeasurably worse legal system, but it may excel in one respect: in its conformity to the rule of law.

Given the promiscuous use made in recent years of the expression "the rule of law," it is hardly surprising that my claim will alarm many. We have reached the stage in which no purist can assert that truth is on his side and blame others for distorting the notion of the rule of law. All that I can claim for my position is, first, that it presents a coherent view of one important virtue which legal systems should possess and, second, that it is not original, that I am following in the footsteps of Hayek and of many others who understood "the rule of law" in similar ways.

2 Clause 1 of the report of Committee I of the International Congress of Jurists, New Delhi, 1959.

THE BASIC IDEA

"The rule of law" means literally what it says: the rule of the law. Taken in its broadest sense, this mean that people should obey the law and be ruled by it.[3] In political and legal theory, however, it has come to be read in a narrower sense, that the government shall be ruled by the law and subject to it. The ideal of the rule of law in this sense is often expressed by the phrase "government by law and not by men." No sooner does one use this formula than its vagueness becomes evident. Surely government must be both by law and by men. It is said that the rule of law means that all government action must have foundation in law, must be authorized by law. But is not that a tautology? Actions not authorized by law cannot be the actions of the government as a government. They would be without legal effect and, often, unlawful.

It is true that we can elaborate a political notion of government that is different from the legal one: government as the location of real power in the society. It is in this sense that one can say that Britain is governed by the City or by the trade unions. In this sense of government it is not a tautology to say that government should be based on law. If the trade union ruling a country breaks an industrial-relations law in order to impose its will on the Parliament, or if the president or the FBI authorizes burglaries and conspires to pervert justice, it is, one can say, violating the rule of law. But here the rule of law is used in its original sense of obedience to law. Like anybody else, powerful people and the people in government should obey the law. This is no doubt correct, and yet does it exhaust the meaning of the rule of law? There is more to the rule of law than the law-and-order interpretation allows. It means more even than law and order applied to the government. I shall proceed on the assumption that we are concerned with government in the legal sense and with the conception of the rule of law that applies to government and to law and is no mere application of the law-and-order conception.

Now we seem to return to our initial puzzle. If government is,

[3] See, on this sense of the phrase, Jennings, *The Law and the Constitution* (London: University of London Press, 1933), pp. 42–45.

by definition, government authorized by law, the rule of law seems to amount to an empty tautology, not a political ideal.

The solution to this riddle lies in the difference between the professional and the lay sense of law. For the lawyer anything is the law if it meets the conditions of validity laid down in the system's rules of recognition or in other rules of the system.[4] Such rules include the constitution, parliamentary legislation, ministerial regulations, policemen's orders, the regulations of limited companies, and conditions imposed in trading licenses. To the layman the law consists only of a subclass of these. To him the law is essentially a set of open, general, and relatively stable laws. "Government by law and not by men" is not a tautology if *law* means general, open, and relatively stable law. In fact, the danger of this interpretation is that the rule of law might set too high a requirement, one which no legal system can meet and which embodies very little virtue. It is humanly inconceivable that law can consist only of general rules, and it is very undesirable that it should. Just as we need government both by laws and by men, so we need both general and particular laws to carry out the purposes for which the law is intended.

The doctrine of the rule of law does not deny that every legal system should consist of both general, open, and stable rules (the popular conception of law) and particular laws (legal orders), which are an essential tool in the hands of the executive and the judiciary alike. As we shall see, what the doctrine requires is the subjection of particular laws to general, open, and stable ones. It is one of the important principles of the doctrine that the making of particular laws should be guided by open and relatively stable general rules.

This principle shows how the slogan Rule of Law and Not of Men can be read as a meaningful political ideal. The principle does not, however, exhaust the meaning of the rule of law and does not by itself illuminate the reasons for its alleged importance. Let us, therefore, return to the literal sense of the "rule of law." It has two aspects: (1) people should be ruled by the law and obey it, and (2) the law should be such that people will be able to be guided by it. As was noted above, it is with the second aspect that we are concerned: the law must be capable of being obeyed. A person conforms

---

[4] I am here following Hart, *The Concept of Law* (Oxford: Oxford University Press, 1961), pp. 97–107.

to the law to the extent that he does not break the law, but he obeys the law only if part of his reason for conforming is his knowledge of the law. Therefore, if the law is to be obeyed it must be capable of guiding the behavior of its subjects. It must be such that they can find out what it is and act on it.

This is the basic intuition from which the doctrine of the rule of law derives: the law must be capable of guiding the behavior of its subjects. It is evident that this conception of the rule of law is a formal one. It says nothing about how the law is to be made: by tyrants, democratic majorities, or any other power. It says nothing about fundamental rights, equality, or justice. It may even be thought that this version of the doctrine is so formal that it is almost devoid of content. This is far from the truth. Most of the requirements that were associated with the rule of law before it came to signify all the virtues of the state can be derived from this one basic idea.

SOME PRINCIPLES

Many of the principles that can be derived from the basic idea of the rule of law depend for their validity or importance on the particular circumstances of different societies. There is little point in trying to enumerate them all, but some of the more important ones might be mentioned:

1. *All laws should be prospective, open, and clear.* One cannot be guided by a retroactive law that does not exist at the time of action. Sometimes it is known for certain that a retroactive law will be enacted, and when this happens retroactivity does not conflict with the rule of law (though it may be objected to on other grounds). The law must be open and adequately publicized. If it is to guide people, they must be able to find out what it is. For the same reason its meaning must be clear. An ambiguous, vague, obscure, or imprecise law is likely to mislead or confuse at least some of those who desire to be guided by it.

2. *Laws should be relatively stable.* If laws are frequently changed, people will find it difficult to find out what the law is at any given moment and will be constantly in fear that the law has been changed since they last learned what it was. But more important

still is the fact that people need to know the law not only for short-term decisions (where to park one's car, how much duty-free alcohol is allowed), but also for long-term planning. Knowledge of at least the general outlines, and sometimes even the details, of tax law and company law is often important for business plans that will bear fruit only years later. Stability is essential if people are to be guided by law in their long-term decisions. Of course, uncertainty generated by instability of law also affects people's planning and action. If it did not, neither then would stability have an impact. The point is that only if the law is stable are people guided by their knowledge of the content of the law.

Three important points are illustrated by this principle. First, conformity to the rule of law is often a matter of degree not only when the conformity of the legal system as a whole is at stake, but also with respect to single laws. A law is either retroactive or not, but it can be more or less clear or more or less stable. It should be remembered, however, that by asserting that conformity to the principles is a matter of degree, it is not meant that the degree of conformity can be quantitatively measured by counting the number of infringements or by some similar method. Some infringements are worse than others. Some violate the principles in a formal way only, a way that does not offend against the spirit of the doctrine.

Second, the principles of the rule of law affect primarily, although not only, the content and the form of the law; for example, the law should be prospective and clear. The principles also affect the manner of government beyond what is or can usefully be prescribed by law. The requirement of stability cannot be usefully subjected to complete legal regulation. It is largely a matter for wise governmental policy.

Third, though the rule of law concerns primarily private citizens as subject to duties and governmental agencies in the exercise of their powers, it is also concerned with the exercise of private powers. Power-conferring rules are designed to guide behavior and should conform to the doctrine of the rule of law if they are to function effectively.

3. *The making of particular laws (particular legal orders) should be guided by open, stable, clear, and general rules.* It is sometimes

assumed that the requirement of generality is the essence of the rule of law. This notion derives from the literal interpretation of "the rule of law," where "law" is read in its lay connotations as being restricted to general, stable, and open law. It is also reinforced by a belief that the rule of law is particularly relevant to the protection of equality and that equality is related to the generality of law. The last belief is, as has been often noted before, mistaken. All manner of discrimination is not only compatible with, but often institutionalized by, general rules.

The formal conception of the rule of law that I am defending does not object to particular legal orders as long as they are stable and clear. But, of course, particular legal orders are mostly used by government agencies to introduce flexibility into the law. For example, the orders given by a policeman regulating traffic or a license granted by a licensing authority under certain conditions are among the more ephemeral parts of the law. As such they run counter to the basic idea of the rule of law. They make it difficult for people to plan ahead on the basis of their knowledge of the law. This difficulty is overcome to a large extent if particular laws of an ephemeral status are enacted only within a framework set by general laws, which are more durable and which impose limits on the unpredictability introduced by the particular orders.

Two kinds of general rules create the framework for the enactment of particular laws: those conferring the necessary powers for making valid orders and those imposing duties instructing the powerholders in the exercise of their powers. Both have equal importance in creating a stable framework for the creation of particular legal orders.

Clearly, similar considerations apply to general legal regulations that do not meet the requirement of stability. They too should be circumscribed to conform to a stable framework. Hence the requirement that much of the subordinate administrative lawmaking should be made to conform to detailed ground rules laid down in framework laws. It is essential, however, not to confuse this argument with democratic arguments for the close supervision by nonelected bodies over lawmaking by popularly elected bodies. These further arguments may be valid but have nothing to do with the rule of law;

though sometimes they reinforce rule-of-law arguments, on other occasions they support different and even conflicting conclusions.

4. *The independence of the judiciary must be guaranteed.* It is of the essence of municipal legal systems that they institute judicial bodies charged, among other things, with the duty of applying the law to cases brought before them, and the judgments and conclusions of these legal bodies as to the legal merits of those cases are to be final. Since almost any matter arising under any law can be subject to a conclusive court judgment, it is obviously futile to guide one's action on the basis of the law if, when the matter is adjudicated, the court will not apply the law but acts for other reasons. The point can be put even more strongly: since the court's judgment establishes conclusively what is the law in the case before it, the litigants can be guided by law only if the judge applies the law correctly. Otherwise people will be able to be guided only by their guesses as to what the courts are likely to do—and these guesses will be based not on the law but on other considerations. The courts, to be sure, also make law. This fourth principle of the rule of law applies to them primarily in their duty to apply the law; as lawmakers they are subject to the same principles as all lawmakers.

The rules concerning the independence of the judiciary—the method of appointing judges, their security of tenure, the way of fixing their salaries and other conditions of service—are designed to guarantee that the judiciary will be free from extraneous pressures and independent of all authority save that of the law. These rules are, therefore, essential for the preservation of the rule of law.

5. *The principles of natural justice must be observed.* Such principles as open and fair hearings and absence of bias are obviously essential for the correct application of the law and thus, through the same considerations mentioned above, essential to its ability to guide action.

6. *The courts should have review powers over the implementation of the other principles.* This includes review of both subordinate and parliamentary legislation and of administrative action, but in itself it should be very limited review—merely to ensure conformity to the rule of law.

7. *The courts should be easily accessible.* Given the central position of the courts in ensuring the rule of law (see principles 4 and

6), it is obvious that their accessibility is of paramount importance. Long delays or excessive costs may effectively turn the most enlightened law into a dead letter and frustrate one's ability effectively to guide oneself by the law.

8. *The discretion of crime-preventing agencies should not be allowed to pervert the law.* Not only the courts but also the actions of the police and the prosecuting authorities can subvert the law. The prosecution should not be allowed, say, to decide not to prosecute for commission of certain crimes, or for crimes committed by certain classes of offenders. The police should not be allowed to allocate their resources in ways that allow avoidance of efforts to prevent and detect certain crimes or to prosecute certain classes of criminals.

This list of principles is incomplete; other principles could be mentioned. Those that have been mentioned need further elaboration and justification (why—as required by my sixth principle—should the courts and not some other body be in charge of reviewing conformity to the rule of law?).[5] The purpose of this list is merely to illustrate the power and fruitfulness of the formal conception of the rule of law. It should, however, be remembered that in the final analysis the doctrine rests on its basic idea that the law should be capable of providing effective guidance. The principles do not stand on their own but must be constantly interpreted in light of the basic idea.

The eight principles listed fall into two groups. Principles 1 to 3 require that the law should conform to standards designed to enable it effectively to guide action. Principles 4 to 8 are designed to ensure that the legal machinery of enforcing the law should not, through distorted enforcement, deprive the law of its ability to guide and that the legal machinery shall be capable of supervising conformity to the rule of law and providing effective remedies in cases of deviation from it. All the principles directly concern the system and method of government in matters directly relevant to the rule

---

[5] Similar tests have been discussed by various authors. English writers have been mesmerized by Dicey's unfortunate doctrine too long. For a list similar to mine, see Lon Fuller, *The Morality of Law*, 2d ed. (New Haven: Yale University Press, 1969), ch. 2. His discussion of many of the principles is full of good sense. My main reason for abandoning some of his principles derives from a difference of views on conflicts between the laws of one system.

of law. Needless to say, many other aspects in the life of a community may, in more indirect ways, either strengthen or weaken the rule of law. A free press run by people anxious to defend the rule of law is of great assistance in preserving it, just as a gagged press or one run by people wishing to undermine the rule of law is a threat to it. However, these more indirect influences are beyond the scope of this discussion.

THE VALUE OF THE RULE OF LAW

One of the merits of the doctrine of the rule of law I am defending is that there are so many values it does not serve. Conformity to the rule of law is a virtue, but only one of the many virtues a legal system should possess. This makes it all the more important to clarify the values that the rule of law does serve.

The rule of law is often rightly contrasted with arbitrary power. Arbitrary power is broader than the rule of law. Many forms of arbitrary rule are compatible with the rule of law. A ruler can promote general rules based on whim or self-interest without offending against the rule of law, but certainly many of the more common manifestations of arbitrary power run afoul of the rule of law. A government subjected to the rule of law is prevented from changing the law retroactively or abruptly or secretly whenever this would suit its purposes. The one area where the rule of law excludes all forms of arbitrary power is in the law-applying function of the judiciary: the courts are required to be subject only to the law and to conform to fairly strict procedures. (The rule of law itself does not exclude all possibilities of arbitrary lawmaking by the courts.) No less important is the restraint imposed by the rule of law on the making of particular laws and thus on the powers of the executive. The arbitrary use of power for personal gain, out of vengeance or favoritism, is most commonly manifested in the making of particular legal orders. These possibilities are drastically restricted by close adherence to the rule of law.

"Arbitrary power" is a difficult notion, and a detailed analysis of it is not required here. It seems, however, that an act which is the exercise of power is arbitrary only if it was done either with indifference to serving the purposes that alone justify use of such power, or with belief that it will not serve them. The nature of the purposes alluded to varies with the nature of the power. This condition represents arbitrary power as a subjective concept. It all depends on the state of mind of the men in power. As such the rule of law does not bear directly on the extent of arbitrary power. But around its subjective core the notion of arbitrary power has grown a hard objective edge. Since it is universally believed that it is wrong to use public powers for private ends, any such use is in itself an instance of arbitrary use of power. As we have seen, the rule of law does help to curb such forms of arbitrary power.

There are other reasons for valuing the rule of law. We value the ability to choose styles and forms of life, to fix long-term goals and effectively direct our lives toward them. The ability to do so depends on the existence of a stable, secure framework for action. The law can help to secure such fixed points of reference in two ways: (1) by stabilizing social relationships which, but for the law, may disintegrate or develop in erratic and unpredictable ways; (2) by a policy of self-restraint designed to make the law itself a stable and safe basis for individual planning. This latter aspect is the concern of the rule of law.

This second virtue of the rule of law is often, as by Hayek, identified as the protection of individual freedom. This is right if the sense of freedom is identified with an effective ability to choose between as many options as possible. Predictability in one's environment does increase one's power of action. But then welfare law and governmental manipulation of the economy also increase freedom by increasing—if successful—people's welfare. If the rule of law is defended as the bulwark of freedom in this sense, it can hardly be used to oppose in principle governmental management of the economy. The important thing to remember is that this sense of freedom differs from what is commonly meant by political freedom. Political freedom consists of (1) the prohibition of certain forms of behavior that interfere with personal freedom, and (2) the limits imposed on the powers of public authorities in order to minimize interference with personal freedom. The prohibition of criminal offenses against the person is an example of the first mode of protecting personal freedom; the disability of the government to restrict freedom of movement, an example of the second. It is in connection with political freedom in this sense that constitutionally guaranteed rights are of great importance and that the rule of law may be yet another mode of protecting personal freedom. But the rule of law has no bearing on the existence of spheres of activity free from governmental interference, and it is compatible with gross violations of human rights.

More important than both these considerations is the fact that observance of the rule of law is necessary if the law is to respect human dignity. Respecting human dignity entails treating humans as persons capable of planning and plotting their future. Thus, respecting people's dignity includes respecting their autonomy, their right to control their future. A person's control over his life, which is never complete, can be incomplete in any one of several respects. The person may be ignorant of his options, unable to decide what to do, incapable of realizing his choices or frustrated in his attempts to do so, or have no choice at all (at least none worth having). All these failures can occur through natural causes or through the limitations of the person's own character and abilities.

Naturally, there are many ways in which one person's action may affect the life of another. Only some of these interferences will amount to an offense to the dignity or a violation of the autonomy of the person thus affected. Such offenses can be divided into three classes: insults, enslavement, and manipulation (I am using the last two terms in a somewhat special sense). An insult offends a person's dignity if it consists of or implies a denial that he is an autonomous person and deserves to be treated as one. An action enslaves another if it intentionally and practically denies him, through changing his external environment, all options of acting in ways other than that mandated by the enslaver. (Though it may be for a length of time— as in real slavery—I mean to include here also coercing another to act in a certain way on a single occasion.) One manipulates a person by intentionally changing his tastes, his beliefs, or his ability to act or decide. Manipulation, in other words, is manipulation of the person, of those factors relevant to his autonomy that are internal to him. Enslavement is the elimination of self-control by changing factors external to the person.

The law can violate people's dignity in many ways. Observing the rule of law by no means guarantees that such violations do not occur, but it is clear that deliberate disregard for the rule of law violates human dignity. It is the business of law to guide human action by affecting people's options. But, as we saw, not every interference with the external circumstances of one's life, however unjustified, is a violation of one's dignity. Deliberate violation of the rule of law affects not only the external circumstances but also one's very ability to decide, act, or form beliefs about the future. A legal system that in general observes the rule of law treats people as persons at least in the sense that it attempts to guide their behavior through affecting the circumstances of their action. It thus presupposes that they are rational, autonomous creatures and attempts to affect their actions and habits by affecting their deliberations. (However, the law, if it institutes slavery or confers powers on officials enabling them to manipulate people, can violate people's dignity even when observing the rule of law. It may also do so by sanctioning insults or in various other ways.) Violations of the rule of law affect one's fate by frustrating deliberations, by making it impossible to plan the future or to decide on actions on the basis of a rational assessment of their outcome. The rule of law provides the foundation for the legal respect for human dignity.

THE RULE OF LAW AND ITS ESSENCE

Lon Fuller has claimed that the principles of the rule of law which he enumerated are essential for the existence of law.[6] This claim if true is crucial to our understanding not only of the rule of law but also of the relation of law and morality. I have been treating the rule of law as an ideal, as a standard to which the law ought to conform but which it can and sometimes does violate most radically and systematically. Fuller, while allowing that deviations from the ideal of the rule of law can occur, denies that they can be radical or total. A legal system must of necessity conform to the rule of law to a certain degree, he asserts. From this assertion he concludes that

---

[6] In *The Morality of Law* Fuller's argument is complex and his claims are numerous and hard to disentangle. Many of his claims are weak and insupportable; others suggestive and useful. It is not my purpose to analyze or evaluate them. For a sympathetic discussion, see R. E. Sartorius, *Individual Conduct and Social Norms* (Encino, Calif.: Dickinson, 1975), ch. 9.

there is an essential link between law and morality. Law is necessarily moral in at least some respects.

It is, of course, true that most of the principles enumerated above cannot be violated altogether by any legal system.[7] Legal systems are based on judicial institutions. There could not be institutions of any kind without general rules to establish them. A particular norm can authorize adjudication in a particular dispute, but no number of particular norms can set up an institution. Similarly, retroactive laws can exist only because there are institutions enforcing them. This entails that there must be prospective laws instructing those institutions to apply the retroactive laws if the retroactive laws are to be valid. In the terminology of H. L. A. Hart's theory one can say that at least some of the rules of recognition and of adjudication of every system must be general and prospective. Naturally they must also be relatively clear if they are to make any sense at all.

Clearly, the extent to which generality, clarity, or prospectivity is essential to the law is minimal and is consistent with gross violations of the rule of law. But are not considerations of the kind mentioned sufficient to establish that there is necessarily at least some moral value in every legal system? I think not. The rule of law is essentially a negative value. The law inevitably creates a great danger of arbitrary power—the rule of law is designed to minimize the danger created by the law itself. Similarly, the law may be unstable, obscure, or retrospective, and thus infringe people's freedom and dignity. The rule of law is designed to prevent this danger as well. Thus the rule of law is a negative virtue in two senses: conformity to it does not cause good except through avoiding evil, and the evil avoided is evil that could only have been caused by the law itself. It is thus somewhat analogous to honesty when this virtue is narrowly interpreted as the avoidance of deceit. (I do not deny that honesty is normally conceived more broadly to incorporate other virtuous acts and inclinations.) The good of honesty does not include the good of communication between people, for honesty is consistent with a

---

[7] I am here not adopting Fuller's own conception of the law but following my own adaptation of Hart's conception. See Hart's *The Concept of Law* and my *Practical Reason and Norms* (London: Hutchinson, 1975), pp. 132–54. Therefore, the discussion that follows is not a direct assessment of Fuller's own claims.

refusal to communicate. Its good is exclusively in the avoidance of the harm of deceit—and not deceit by others but by the honest person himself. Therefore, only a person who can deceive can be honest. A person who cannot communicate cannot claim any moral merit for being honest. A person who through ignorance or inability cannot kill another by poison deserves no credit for it. Similarly, that the law cannot sanction arbitrary force or violations of freedom and dignity through total absence of generality, prospectivity, or clarity is no moral credit to the law. It means only that there are some kinds of evil that cannot be brought about by the law. But this is no virtue in the law, just as it is no virtue in the law that it cannot rape or murder (all it can do is sanction such actions).

Fuller's attempt to establish a necessary connection between law and morality fails. Insofar as conformity to the rule of law is a moral virtue, it is an ideal that should, but may fail to, become a reality. There is another argument, however, which establishes an essential connection between the law and the rule of law, though it guarantees no virtue to the law. Conformity to the rule of law is essential for securing whatever purposes the law is designed to achieve. This statement should be qualified. We could divide the purposes a law is intended to serve into two kinds: those which are secured by conformity with the law in itself, and those further consequences of conformity with the law or of knowledge of its existence which the law is intended to secure.[8] Thus a law prohibiting racial discrimination in government employment has as its direct purpose the establishment of racial equality in the hiring, promotions, and conditions of service of government employees (since discriminatory action is a breach of law). Its indirect purposes may well be to improve race relations in the country in general, prevent a threat of a strike by some trade unions, or halt the decline in popularity of the government.

Conformity to the rule of law does not always facilitate realization of the indirect purposes of the law, but it is essential to the realization of its direct purposes. These are achieved by conformity with the law that is secured (unless accidentally) by people taking

---

[8] See further on this distinction, J. Raz, "The Functions of Law," *Oxford Essays in Jurisprudence*, 2d series, ed. A. W. B. Simpson (Oxford: Oxford University Press, 1973).

note of the law and guiding themselves accordingly. Therefore, if the direct purposes of the law are not to be frustrated, the law must be capable of guiding human behavior, and the more it conforms to the principles of the rule of law the better it can do so.

It has been stated above that conformity to the rule of law is one among many moral virtues the law should possess. The present consideration shows that the rule of law is not merely a moral virtue, it is a necessary condition if the law is to serve directly any good purpose at all. Of course, conformity to the rule of law also enables the law to serve bad purposes. That does not show that it is not a virtue, just as the fact that a sharp knife can be used to harm does not show that being sharp is not a good for knives. At most it shows that from the point of view of the present consideration, it is not a moral good. Being sharp is an inherent good of knives. A good knife is, among other things, a sharp knife. Similarly, conformity to the rule of law is an inherent value of laws; indeed, it is their most important inherent value. It is of the essence of law to guide behavior through rules, and through courts in charge of their application. Therefore, the rule of law is the specific excellence of the law. Since conformity to the rule of law is the virtue of law in itself—law as law regardless of the purposes it serves—it is understandable and right that the rule of law is viewed as among the few virtues of law that are the special responsibility of the courts and the legal profession.

Regarding the rule of law as the inherent or specific virtue of law is a result of an instrumental conception of law. The law is not just a fact of life, it is a form of social organization that should be used properly and for the proper ends. It is a tool in the hands of men differing from many other tools in being versatile and capable of being used for a large variety of proper purposes. As with other tools, machines, and instruments, a thing is not of the kind unless it has at least some ability to perform its function. A knife is not a knife unless it has some ability to cut. The law to be law must be capable of guilding behavior, however inefficiently. Like other instruments, the law has a specific virtue that is morally neutral concerning the end to which the instrument is put. It is the virtue of efficiency, the virtue of the instrument as an instrument. For the law this virtue is the rule of law. Thus the rule of law is an inherent virtue of the law, but not a moral virtue.

The special status of the rule of law does not mean that conformity with it is of no moral importance. Quite apart from the fact that conformity to the rule of law is also a moral virtue, it is a moral requirement when necessary to enable the law to perform useful social functions. Similarly, it may be of moral importance to produce a sharp knife when it is required for a moral purpose. In the case of the rule of law this means that it is virtually always of great moral value.

SOME PITFALLS

The undoubted value of conformity to the rule of law should not lead one to exaggerate its importance. We saw how Hayek noted correctly its relevance for the protection of freedom. We also saw that the rule of law itself does not provide sufficient protection of freedom. Consider, however, Hayek's position. He begins with a statement that inevitably leads to exaggerated expectations:

> The conception of freedom under the law that is the chief concern of this book rests on the contention that when we obey laws, in the sense of general abstract rules laid down irrespective of their application to us, we are not subject to another man's will and are therefore free. It is because the judge who applies them has no choice in drawing the conclusions that follow from the existing body of rules and the particular facts of the case, that it can be said that laws and not men rule. . . . As a true law should not name any particulars, so it should especially not single out any specific persons or group of persons.[9]

Then, aware of the absurdity to which this passage leads, he modifies his line, still trying to present the rule of law as the supreme guarantor of freedom:

> The requirement that the rules of true law be general does not mean that sometimes special rules may not apply to different classes of people if they refer to properties that only some people possess. There may be rules that can apply only to women or to the blind or to persons above a

[9] F. A. Hayek, *The Constitution of Liberty* (Chicago: University of Chicago Press, 1960), pp. 153–54.

certain age. (In most instances it would not even be necessary to name the class of people to whom the rule applies: only a woman, for example, can be raped or got with child.) Such distinctions will not be arbitrary, will not subject one group to the will of others, if they are equally recognized as justified by those inside and those outside the group. This does not mean that there must be unanimity as to the desirability of the distinction, but merely that individual views will not depend on whether the individual is in the group or not.[10]

Here the rule of law is transformed to encompass a form of government by consent, and it is this which is alleged to guarantee freedom. This is the slippery slope leading to the identification of the rule of law with the rule of the good law.

Hayek's main objection is to governmental interference with the economy:

> We must now turn to the kinds of governmental measures which the rule of law excludes in principle because they cannot be achieved by merely enforcing general rules but, of necessity, involve arbitrary discrimination between persons. The most important among them are decisions as to who is to be allowed to provide different services or commodities, at what prices or in what quantities—in other words, measures designed to control the access to different trades and occupations, the terms of sale, and the amounts to be produced or sold.
>
> There are several reasons why all direct control of prices by government is irreconcilable with a functioning free system, whether the government actually fixes prices or merely lays down rules by which the permissible prices are to be determined. In the first place, it is impossible to fix prices according to long-term rules which will effectively guide production. Appropriate prices depend on circumstances which are constantly changing and must be continually adjusted to them. On the other hand, prices which are not fixed outright but determined by some rule (such as that they must be in a certain relation to cost) will not be the same for all sellers and, for this reason, will prevent the market from functioning. A still more important consideration is that, with prices different from those that would form on a free market, demand and supply will not be equal, and if the price control is to be effective, some method must be found for deciding who is to be allowed to buy or sell. This would necessarily be discretionary and must consist of *ad hoc* decisions that discriminate between persons on essentially arbitrary grounds.[11]

Here again it is clear that arguments which at best show that

10 Ibid., p. 154.
11 Ibid., pp. 227–28.

certain policies are wrong for economic reasons are said to show that they infringe the rule of law, and the making of supposedly misguided but subjectively principled particular orders is condemned as arbitrary exercise of power.

Since the rule of law is only one of the virtues the law should possess, it is to be expected that it possesses no more than prima-facie force. It has always to be balanced against competing claims of other values. Hence Hayek's arguments, to the extent that they show no more than that some other goals inevitably conflict with the rule of law, are not the sort of arguments which could, in principle, show that pursuit of such goals by means of law is inappropriate. Conflict between the rule of law and other values is just what is to be expected. Conformity to the rule of law is a matter of degree. When other things are equal, the greater the conformity the better. But other things are rarely equal. A lesser degree of conformity is often to be preferred precisely because it helps to realize other goals.

In considering the relation between the rule of law and other values the law should serve, one must particularly remember that the rule of law is essentially a negative value. It is merely designed to minimize the harm to freedom and dignity which the law may cause in pursuit of its goals, however laudable these may be. Finally, regarding the rule of law as the inherent excellence of the law means that it fulfills essentially a subservient role. Conformity to it makes the law a good instrument for achieving certain goals, but conformity to the rule of law is not itself an ultimate goal. This subservient role of the doctrine shows both its power and its limitations. On the other hand, if the pursuit of certain goals is entirely incompatible with the rule of law, then these goals should not be pursued by legal means. On the other hand, one should be wary of disqualifying the legal pursuit of major social goals in the name of the rule of law. After all, the rule of law is meant to enable the law to promote social good and should not be lightly used to show that it should not do so. Sacrificing too many social goals on the altar of the rule of law may make the law barren and empty.

2.

Economic Due Process in the American Constitution and the Rule of Law

WILLIAM LETWIN

THE rule of law, the idea that men should be governed by reason-able general laws rather than by the arbitrary will of rulers, appeals immediately to the intuition of people brought up in a free society. Nevertheless, it is a difficult idea, hard to translate into practical limitations on the power of government and easily forgotten in the fray of political engagements. The general precept, that the rule of law is a pillar of free society, therefore needs constantly to be re-emphasized and its practical implications reexplored. No one in our time has done so as devotedly as Professor Hayek, whose voluminous writings (excluding those on economics) have mainly centered on this issue and have much enriched a theoretical conversation that began some two thousand years ago.

One of the most important arenas in which the rule of law has been discussed during the past two centuries is the Supreme Court of the United States, which regularly encounters the question when interpreting the American Constitution. The Constitution does not mention the rule of law in so many words, yet the idea is implicitly present in the concept of "enumerated powers," which concept lim-its the federal government's powers to those expressly conferred by the Constitution. It is implicitly present also in those passages in the Constitution that expressly deny certain powers to the federal gov-ernment or the state governments. And, finally, it is expressed in the formula "due process of law." The Fifth and Fourteenth Amendments prohibit American governments from depriving any person of "life, liberty or property without due process of law." The due-process clauses are the ultimate guardians of the rule of law in America; or, better, since ultimately it is men rather than words that must do the guarding, due process is, as it were, the compass needle that shows the course.

In practice the due-process clauses have served more or less well to protect Americans found to have been treated arbitrarily— by judges or juries, prosecutors or police, officials of various sorts, or even private persons exercising powers delegated by government. An accumulated catalogue, long and varied, of actions invalidated by the courts on such grounds testifies to the power that Americans have breathed into the phrase *due process.*

On the other hand, the catalogue of rights protected by due process is flawed by two curious gaps. First, although due process has defended "life" and "liberty" often, it has defended "property" seldom—and since 1937, practically never. Second, although due process has been invoked to correct unfair actions by judicial and executive persons, it has far less often annulled unfair actions by legislatures. The notion that a legislature might deprive a person contrary to due process of law was rare among American judges before about 1900, and the view that a legislature might deprive a person of property in a manner that justified redress in accordance with the due-process clause has been explicitly rejected by the Supreme Court since 1937. "Substantive economic due process" was ruled out, I believe, for unconvincing and indeed dangerous reasons. It ought to be restored. Although it probably will not be restored deliberately, there are indications that it may be rejuvenated, by indirection, under a different name.

I

To understand the exceptional and threatening immunity of legislatures from control by due process, especially when the legislature is acting so as to affect "property rights," it is useful to review a series of leading decisions that shaped today's judicial doctrines on this subject.

Fletcher v. Peck[1]

In 1795 the legislature of Georgia passed a law whereby the state sold much of its land for a great deal of money to four private companies. Accusations were made that many of the legislators had been bribed. A new legislature, elected the next year, concluded that bribes had indeed been offered and accepted; it thereupon repealed the act of sale, ordering that a copy be burned at a public ceremony to the sound of appropriate imprecations. In the meantime, however, the original buyers had sold some of the land, which sooner or later was resold, and so on. Because the legislature's act of sale had been repealed, doubts naturally began to arise whether any of the purchasers had good title, and doubt inspired litigation. The issue came into the federal courts in 1803, when Fletcher sued Peck, maintaining that a contract by which Peck sold some of that land was invalid. After much delay, the Supreme Court decided unanimously that, despite the repeal act of 1796, Peck had acquired good title which had been properly conveyed to Fletcher.

If a legislature could possibly violate the requirement of due process, as that phrase would be understood by a sensible layman, then the legislature of Georgia did it when passing the act of sale in 1795. Should a strained imagination suggest the possibility that legislators could act consistently with due process while taking bribes, it might be answered that bribery of public officials is a crime in many civilized places. Yet a man may commit a crime without interfering with due process. To which it may be answered that a bribed legislator is like a bribed judge, and that legislation like adjudication is part of law; since a bribed judge cannot act in accord with due process, neither can a bribed legislator. In any event, the question of due process was raised, by implication even if not squarely, by Fletcher, who maintained in his pleadings before the Supreme Court that the legislature's act of sale was null because the legislators had been "unduly influenced."[2]

Chief Justice Marshall, in his opinion for a unanimous court, did

---

[1] 6 Cranch 87 (1810). The facts and arguments surrounding the case are thoroughly analyzed in C. P. Magrath, *Yazoo* (Providence, R.I.: Brown University Press, 1966).

[2] 2d count.

not evade the issue. He and they might have taken the line adopted in later decisions, that though the federal government was restrained by the Fifth Amendment, state governments were not. Instead he conceded, though in carefully guarded, hypothetical terms, that a federal court might be justified in nullifying a statute of a state on the ground that it had been passed improperly—though only after he expressed doubt "how far the validity of a law depends upon the motives of its framers," and how far those motives "are examinable in a court." But the principle, even if conceded, would be extremely difficult to apply, he said. Must the improper means, adequate for invalidation, "be direct corruption, or would interest or undue influence of any kind be sufficient? Must the vitiating cause operate on a majority, or on what number of the members?" (130). These questions and related ones posed by Marshall are undoubtedly difficult, though not distinctively more difficult than many others that courts compel themselves to answer.

Marshall held that in the circumstances of *Fletcher* v. *Peck* the Court need not decide such difficult questions as how much corruption would be needed to invalidate an act. Had the state of Georgia instituted proceedings to annul a contract consequent to a law which it alleged to be invalid, the Court would have faced the problem, though "with much circumspection." But in this case the solemn question of whether an act should be declared invalid had been brought before the Court "collaterally and incidentally." "It would be indecent, in the extreme, upon a private contract, between two individuals, to enter into an inquiry respecting the corruption of the sovereign power of a State" (131). So the due-process question was set aside on procedural grounds.

The case was decided, as Marshall went on to say, on the principle that rights to property acquired by purchasers having no knowledge of defects in the legislature's act of sale could not be annulled by any subsequent act of the legislature, since that would violate the constitutional guarantees against *ex post facto* laws and laws impairing the obligation of contracts. Marshall's opinion has been interpreted ever since as the rock on which was erected the conservative power of the contract clause.

The opinion has, with less reason, been interpreted as precedent

for the rule that courts must not inquire into the motives of legislatures. It is by no means certain that the courts have applied that
rule consistently and severely, but it is certain that Marshall's opinion in *Fletcher* v. *Peck* was far from decisive on this point. Everything he says about what we may classify as legislative due process
is hedged by expressions such as "it may well be doubted," "is not
clearly discerned," and "is a question which the Court would approach with much circumspection." Marshall's opinion certainly left
room for a later Court to annul an act on the grounds that it had
been passed by improper means, if the case did not involve rights
which had vested in innocent private persons as a result of the corrupt act; but despite the apparent meaning of the words, closely
read, it was generally interpreted as discouraging, if not forbidding,
judicial scrutiny of legislative motives.

There is another way to construe the opinion, which seems more
in keeping with the circumstances of the case. The issue was not
whether a *court* could annul a statute but whether a *legislature*
could. Nobody could doubt that a subsequent legislature has power
to repeal, but Marshall denied that it could annul, at least, not so as
to extinguish rights vested by the earlier statute (135). Johnson, in
his concurring opinion, pointed out the inconveniences that would
arise if courts were to give effect to annulling statutes: "The absurdity in this case would have been strikingly perceived, could the
party who passed the act of cession have got again into power, and
declared themselves pure, and the intermediate legislature corrupt"
(144). Persuasive as this argument appears, it is not conclusive. A
court might regard itself as authorized to review the later legislature's finding of fact, and some such power is implicitly recognized
in Marshall's comment, "In this case the legislature may have had
ample proof that the original grant was obtained by [corrupt] practices . . ., which would have justified its abrogation so far as respected those to whom crime was imputable" (134). All of which
suggests that *Fletcher* v. *Peck* ought to be read not as foreclosing
the Court's power to scrutinize the action of legislatures, but, on the
contrary, as asserting the Court's power to declare that certain actions of legislatures—in this instance, the annulling statute—are void
insofar as they would deprive persons of constitutional rights.

Wynehamer v. People[3]

Although a certain number of state courts scrutinized legislation under the lens of due process during the first half of the nineteenth century, the earliest occasion on which an authoritative court ruled on this sort of issue was in 1856, when the highest court of New York State decided the *Wynehamer* case. Despite the high esteem in which this court was held, no doubt for the best of reasons, a degree of puzzlement must have been engendered by this decision, which was explained by a large number of opinions, diverse in scope, and variable in expression.

The affair began in 1855, when the legislature of New York passed an "act for the prevention of intemperance, pauperism and crime," which act was, to put it bluntly, a prohibition law, making it a crime to sell hard drink or, for that matter, even to possess it, unless one kept it in his own house. It hit hard at dealers who held stocks, and was intended to. In general, nobody could have doubted that a legislature had power to prohibit dealing in such a commodity, for, although corn whisky had been a staple of the American diet, sumptuary legislation of all types was well within a tradition still quite alive in the nineteenth century, especially in the near neighborhood of New England.

Shortly after the act came into effect, Wynehamer was convicted for selling liquor. So, quite independently, was Toynbee. On final appeal the two cases were decided together because both defendants questioned the constitutionality of the act from the standpoint of due process. In other respects, however, Wynehamer's case and Toynbee's case raised quite different questions of law. What resulted was a bewildering array of opinions, six for the majority (of which two dealt with both cases and four with Toynbee's alone), and three for the minority (of which two were by a single justice dealing with each of the cases separately). What makes matters worse, when one tries to clear a path through this thicket, is that the opinion of Comstock, which enjoys pride of place—though it bears no other mark of speaking for the majority—is far less clear than those of the others.

[3] 13 N.Y. 378 (1856).

In the pursuit of light we do well to start from the briefest and most pointed opinion, by Chief Justice Denio, who was of the majority. What he found to be the fatal flaw, making the act inconsistent with the due-process clause, was that it prohibited any use by the owners of liquor which they possessed lawfully at the time the act took effect. In other words, the failure of due process consisted simply and exclusively in the retroactive operation of the statute. This was emphasized when Denio added that, although it would be "competent for the legislature to pass an act containing the provisions embraced in this statute, to operate only upon intoxicating liquors *hereafter* to be imported or manufactured, the act referred to does not discriminate between existing property and that which may *hereafter* be acquired or created" (459). This defect, he held, could not be remedied by judicial interpretation, and he therefore concluded that the act was invalid because it violated the due-process clause of the constitution of New York.

The chief justice's view—that the retroactive character of the act, as it applied to Wynehamer and Toynbee and all others whom it deprived of property acquired before the act, constituted a denial of due process—was confirmed in other opinions. Mitchell, dissenting, argued that insofar as the act might apply retroactively the court would be bound "to pronounce only such parts of the law void as were unconstitutional," giving effect to the law in prospective operation while voiding it only when it acted retrospectively (480). A. S. Johnson, concurring, said—among a good deal else—that though the legislature could control and indeed prohibit "future acquisitions" of liquor, the act was invalid "at least in respect to property which had been acquired while there was no prohibition against the acquisition of such property" (424). Again Selden, of the majority, conceded (at least for the sake of the argument), that the legislature could make it unlawful to acquire such liquor in the future, from which it would seem to follow that the act "may be enforced as to all rights not shown to have existed when the law took effect," an implication he dismissed because he regarded the constitutional and unconstitutional provisions of the act as indivisible (440–42). Hubbard made the same distinction, though he felt that the failure of due process arose from the fact that the deprivation of property owned at the time the law took effect could take place without a trial (453–54, 456).

In most of the opinions, then, the Court seems clearly to have meant that, insofar as the statute deprived persons of property rights lawfully acquired prior to its passage, it was acting retroactively and that retroactive legislation is contrary to due process. This sense of clarity is bound to be shaken, however, as one reads the opinion of Comstock, which, as it happens, stands first in the report, goes on longer than the other opinions, and insists repeatedly that property is inviolable. Despite which, the core of his opinion is direct enough: "It is certain that the legislature cannot totally annihilate commerce in any species of property, and so condemn the property itself to extinction. It is equally certain that the legislature can regulate trade in property of all kinds" (339). Regulation of property is constitutional, destruction is not; therefore, the court's task was to determine on which side of the line the act in question fell.

Comstock maintained at some length that "the act is one of fierce and intolerant proscription. . . . On the day the law took effect, it was criminal to be in possession of intoxicating liquors, however innocently acquired the day before . . . No alternative was left to the owner but their immediate destruction" (385–89). To what extent the notion of impermissible annihilation of property is linked with retroactive operation ("however innocently acquired the day before"), Comstock did not make clear.

Nor did Comstock clarify just why, in his view, the outright destruction of property, when ordered by a statute, runs contrary to due process of law. After all, there was no suggestion whatsoever in *Wynehamer* (unlike *Fletcher*) that the legislature had been bribed, so no doubt arose as to whether the legislative "process" which produced the act fell short of "due." Neither could it be held that the act denied due process by blocking an accused person's access to fair trial in the courts, though Comstock seemed at one point to suggest this possibility (388). To be sure, Toynbee complained that the act had denied him trial by jury, and the court of appeals held that in that respect the statute did violate a specific right guaranteed by the constitution of New York. This contention was therefore resolved without reference to due process, and certainly Wynehamer and Toynbee did get their day in court, or rather many days in many courts. Evidently, then, the failure of due process, in Comstock's eyes, consisted exclusively in this, that the act "destroyed" property rather than regulated it. To put it more generally, he had no doubt due process could be violated as much by a legislature as by a court, even when the process or procedure the legislature followed in adopting the act was faultless. As to this general conclusion the rest of the majority obviously agreed. But, as I have shown, the opinion of the Court, as distinct from the opinion of Comstock, found the denial of due process in retroactivity.

It would be less necessary to insist on the distinction between Comstock's principle and the Court's principle had not Professor Corwin, in his immensely influential writings on due process, based his interpretation of the decision almost exclusively on Comstock's opinion, which, moreover, he interpreted as deleting the words *due process* from the due-process clause, leaving only the bald prohibition: "No person shall be *deprived* of life, liberty or property."[4] This seems to me to be a totally untenable view, inasmuch as all the justices, including Comstock, agreed that the legislature could constitutionally regulate property. To regulate property certainly deprives owners of some part of its previous or potential value, but such deprivation the Court regarded as constitutional, as long as it did not operate retroactively.

Retroactivity is not, of course, an unambiguous idea. Long after the *Wynehamer* decision courts were still trying to clear their minds about whether a law changing the ways people may use property which they already possess—a law which thereby confounds their previous expectations—must accordingly be regarded as fatally retroactive.

Slaughterhouse Cases[5]

The Fifth Amendment prohibits the federal government from depriving any person of life, liberty, or property without due process of law. The constitutions of some states set an equivalent or identical limit on the power of state government, and this limit was ex-

---

[4] E. S. Corwin, *Liberty against Government* (Baton Rouge: Louisiana State University Press, 1948), p. 103 and *passim*.
[5] 16 Wall. 36 (1873).

tended to all the states by the Fourteenth Amendment, ratified in 1868.

The first case which brought the due-process clause of the Fourteenth Amendment before the Supreme Court arose from a law passed in 1869 by the state of Louisiana, bearing the title, "An Act to Protect the Health of the City of New Orleans . . ." It closed down all slaughterhouses in New Orleans, designated a single area outside the city in which all slaughtering must thereafter take place, and established a private company as the sole authorized operator of slaughterhouses in the area. Numerous butchers and stock dealers of New Orleans, thus prevented from doing business as usual, attacked the statute in the courts. One argument they advanced before the Supreme Court was that the statute deprived them of property contrary to the Fourteenth Amendment.

The Supreme Court's opinion, delivered by Justice Miller, made short work of the plaintiff's arguments along this line. Certainly, Miller said, nobody could doubt that a legislature had a right and duty to prescribe how slaughtering should be done, this being part of the traditional and unquestioned "police power" (61). Whether the legislature had acted wisely when it established a monopoly as an instrument for carrying out its purpose of protecting health might be questioned, but it was not, in any event, a monopoly that deprived butchers of their work. The company had been given the exclusive privilege of operating a slaughterhouse, not the exclusive privilege of slaughtering, for in fact it was sternly obliged by the statute to offer its facilities at a reasonable charge to anyone who wished to use them. In short, Miller held, the statutory monopoly could not be said "to destroy the business of the butcher, or seriously interfere with its pursuit" (61). Miller seems here to echo Comstock's distinction between destroying property and regulating it, though his opinion does not mention the *Wynehamer* decision—nor, on the other hand, is the distinction so idiosyncratic as to be traceable to any single inventor. When Miller then turned to the due-process clause, there was little left to say. The due-process argument, he remarked, had "not been much pressed" by the butchers. In any event, as the due-process clause of the Fourteenth Amendment repeated the familiar words of the Fifth Amendment and of many state constitutions, its meaning had been often explored by courts—although,

curiously enough, Miller cited no precedents on this score. He simply brushed the argument aside, saying that the statute of Louisiana
did not violate due process under any "construction of that provision
that we have ever seen, or any that we deem admissible" (81).

The *Slaughterhouse* cases are one of a series distinguished by
the dissenting opinions of Justice Field. Though powerful and ele-
gant arguments in favor of laissez-faire, they could more accurately
be called constitutional objections to excessive regulation of economic activity, for to portray Field as a doctrinaire opponent of all regulation is radically to distort the truth.[6] Indeed, one of the foundations
of his reasoning in this case was the broad scope that he attributed
to the police power: "That power undoubtedly extends to all regulations affecting the health, good order, morals, peace and safety of
society, and is exercised on a great variety of subjects, and in almost
numberless ways" (87). But the power could be misused, and it had
been, he maintained, because the statute in question only pretended
to be, as its title declared, a health measure. Had it truly been that,
Field said, it could certainly have excluded slaughtering from the
city, but it could not and would not have done so "for the benefit of
a single corporation." If health were protected by having one slaughterhouse outside the city, then it would have been equally well protected by allowing many, and as, in fact, one had been given the
exclusive privilege, "the pretense of sanitary regulations . . . is a
shallow one" (88). This motif, of impermissible intent masquerading
behind a proper avowed power, has of course become very familiar
in desegregation cases during the past twenty years.

It was left to Justice Bradley, who concurred in Field's dissent,
to connect their objections to the statute with the due-process clause.
His argument, whose thrust is less pointed than one would wish,
seems to aim at the unreasonableness of the statute. To be a butcher
is to follow an "ordinary occupation," a "lawful employment," and
slaughtering is part of that trade. "To compel a butcher, or rather
all the butchers of a large city and an extensive district, to slaughter

[6] See, for instance, H. N. Scheiber, "The Road to *Munn*," *Perspectives in
American History* ed. D. Fleming and B. Bailyn (Harvard University: Center
for Studies in American History) 5 (1971): 348–49. Scheiber describes Field as
the "paragon of judicial activism on behalf of laissez-faire doctrine" and a
"champion of inviolable property rights." See also the various commentators
cited by Scheiber.

their cattle in another person's slaughterhouse and to pay him a toll therefore, is such a restriction upon the trade as materially to interfere with its prosecution. It is onerous, unreasonable, arbitrary and unjust" (119). Those faults, we may conclude, constituted in his eyes the violation of due process.

The disagreement between majority and minority of the Court hinged largely on whether the statute was an authentic exercise of the police power, carrying with it an incidental, questionable, but not unconstitutional grant of monopoly, or a pretended exercise of the police power, a mere subterfuge for an unconstitutional grant of monopoly, which excluded a thousand men from part of their trade in order to benefit the seventeen incorporators of the company. There is an epilogue which casts some, if flickering, light on the facts. In 1879 Louisiana adopted a new constitution which withdrew the power of regulating slaughtering from the state legislature, transferred it to local authorities, prohibited the creation of any monopolies of slaughtering, and abolished all existing statutory monopolies. The company whose monopoly had been vindicated in the *Slaughterhouse* decision now appeared as plaintiff before the Supreme Court, maintaining that its constitutional rights were denied by an act which abrogated the rights of contract. The Court held unanimously that, although in general a legislature could not act so as to abrogate the rights of contract, this limitation did not operate with respect to the police power.[7] Field strongly concurred that a state could not by contract "restrain, diminish or surrender its power to enact laws for the preservation of the public health or the protection of the public morals" (590).

The provisions of the Louisiana Constitution of 1879 might be interpreted as bearing out the accusation made by plaintiffs in the *Slaughterhouse Cases,* that the legislature prior to 1872 had been openhanded with grants of monopoly: "Prodigal expenditures and jobs innumerable form only a portion of the mischiefs of a government destitute of any sense of moral responsibility" (83 U.S. 398). Whatever the truth is about that, whether Field was right or wrong to believe that the health regulation was a mere pretext for giving a valuable monopoly to favorites of the legislature, he and all the justices agreed that the police power did not generally or necessarily

[7] *Crescent City* v. *Butchers' Union,* 111 U.S. 585 (1884).

come into conflict with the due-process clause. At no time, not in 1873 or 1905 or 1922, did the Supreme Court subscribe to the dogma, often ascribed to it, that the Fourteenth Amendment made property immune to all regulation.

Munn v. Illinois [8]

In 1871 the legislature of Illinois, responding to the wishes of farmers, merchants and others and using powers newly conferred by the state constitution of 1870, passed a law to regulate charges made by railroads and warehouses. Several other states passed similar laws at that time, which were spoken of as "Granger Laws" to betoken the influence of the Grange, a farmers' organization which rapidly if briefly acquired a good deal of political power just after the Civil War.

Munn and other owners of grain elevators in Chicago refused to take out the licenses required by the Illinois statute, arguing that the act was invalid under the U.S. Constitution, partly because it denied due process.

Chief Justice Waite, for the Court, opened his discussion by announcing a principle of the greatest importance: "Every statute is presumed to be constitutional" (123). It ought not to be invalidated unless it is "clearly" unconstitutional; any doubt should be resolved in its favor. This was neither a novel nor an unreasonable view. It places a burden of proof on the person who wishes to undo the "expressed will of the legislature" (123), which can be presumed to represent the will of the majority of the people. It places an obligation of self-restraint on the courts, in accordance with the constitutional doctrine of separation of powers. On the other hand, it is certainly a contestable view. A society which puts a high value on the freedom of individuals, and which seeks to safeguard that freedom by a considerable array of constitutional bulwarks, might be thought to have erected a presumption against legislation, at least against any which directly limits the freedom of individuals. And as to the self-

[8] 94 U.S. 113 (1877). A lively account of the background is given by C. P. Magrath, "The Case of the Unscrupulous Warehouseman," in J. A. Garraty, ed., *Quarrels That Have Shaped the Constitution* (New York: Harper & Row, 1962). The authoritative analysis of the case is Charles Fairman, "The So-Called Granger Cases, Lord Hale, and Justice Bradley," *Stanford Law Review* 5 (1953): 587. A recent illuminating study is Scheiber, "The Road to *Munn*."

restraint that courts should exercise, so as not to usurp the proper functions of the legislature, it might properly be subordinated to a self-restraint which government—in all its branches, the judiciary included—ought to regard as incumbent on it whenever its actions might limit the freedoms of the governed. For every argument that supports the presumption in favor of the legislature, it is easy enough to supply a serious argument tending in the opposite direction. Be that as it may, the presumption in favor of the legislature—whether there should be any at all, and if so how far—has been a pivotal issue in the field of due process. When the presumption became practically absolute in the field of economic legislation, "substantive" due process was expelled from that field.

Next, Waite turned to the meaning of "deprive," or as the context shows, "deprive without due process." As the Constitution does not define it, recourse must be had to usage (123). One branch of usage is general constitutional law, from which Waite elicited that the "very essence of government" is its power to establish laws "requiring each citizen to so conduct himself, and so use his own property as not unnecessarily to injure another" (124). A second branch of usage is English and American statute law, in which Waite found numerous instances showing that "down to the time of the adoption of the Fourteenth Amendment, it was not supposed that statutes regulating the use, or even the price of the use, of private property necessarily deprived an owner of his property without due process of law" (125). These considerations may be regarded as reasons fortifying the presumption in favor of a statute.

To say, as Waite did, that every regulatory act is *not necessarily* unconstitutional led him to distinguish between valid and invalid regulations; to do so he carried over from the common law the notion of property "affected with a public interest," which the legislature could constitutionally regulate (126). That phrase and doctrine Waite rightly attributed to a treatise by Lord Chief Justice Hale, written about 1670; it has been regarded since as "an artificial and basically extraneous concept conjured up by the Court, thoroughly alien to historic American juridical consideration of the issues in Munn."[9] It has been shown recently, however, that the common-law

[9] Scheiber, "The Road to *Munn*," p. 333.

doctrine summarized by Hale continued to be followed by American courts right down to the time of the *Munn* decision.[10] Its scope was, however, narrow, confined to the question of when a river could be owned privately and when, though owned privately, the owner's rights were subject to legal limitation in behalf of others, the "public"; the answer given by common law was that unqualified private rights of a river could apply only to that part of it which is unnavigable, whereas the navigable part of a river, while capable of being owned privately, could not be used by its owner in a manner which interfered with public use or public rights. From the common-law rule that government could regulate the use of private property on the navigable stretch of a river because such property is "affected with a public interest," Justice Bradley generalized to the broader view that "the public authorities ought to have entire control of the great passageways of commerce and navigation."[11] Or perhaps he found warrant for it in a passage from another book by Hale: "The common good requires that all public ways be under the control of the public authorities."[12] Still another jump was needed to get from the metaphorical "great passageway" to the grain elevators in Chicago. In any event, Justice Bradley apparently persuaded Chief Justice Waite that this was the line of argument to follow.[13]

The chief justice had no trouble establishing that grain produced in the Midwest was shipped to Chicago, where for a time some or much of it was stored in the defendants' elevators, before being transhipped to the East Coast. So the "passageway" was there and the elevators were part of it, a sort of door, or, in the phrase that Waite adopted, the "gateway of commerce" (130–32). If any private property is affected with the public interest, in Waite's view a "gateway" in a "passageway" must be, and it could therefore be regulated constitutionally, that is, without depriving, or at least improperly depriving, the owners of their property.

Two other considerations were apparently connected, in Waite's mind, with this one, though he did not spell out the connections. The first was that the Chicago elevators were "public" inasmuch as

10 Ibid., pp. 334–55.
11 Ibid., p. 354.
12 Hale, *De Juris Maris*, quoted in *Munn v. Illinois*, p. 126.
13 Scheiber, "The Road to *Munn*," pp. 334–35.

they did not store only wheat belonging to their owners. But "public" could not have meant "affected with a public interest." For, if it had meant that, a private pastrymaker, unless he consumed all his own product, would also own property affected with a public interest, as would every other businessman, and all private property used in business would be properly subject to regulation. This view surely was not espoused by Waite, who asserted that "the legislature has no control over"—meaning no legitimate power to control—"mere private contracts, relating to members in which the public has no interest" (134)—meaning property not part of a great passageway. The second interwoven theme was monopoly. Munn and his colleagues had maintained a price-fixing cartel or, in Waite's term, a "virtual monopoly" (131), a term which, to judge by an authority whom he cited (128), meant a de facto monopoly as distinct from a statutory monopoly. And this, of course, raises the possibility that Waite meant to rule that regulation of private property was only justified or even more justified by the presence of a monopoly. Probably rather the latter, though he does not help us to discern which he means.

Waite also disposed of the question of retrospectivity in the statute. It had not operated backward in time because the defendants had always been subject to regulation. "They entered upon their business and provided themselves with the means to carry it on subject to this condition" (133). Whether this is correct factually about the defendants' knowledge or state of mind when they entered the business is not known. Had the defendants maintained that they had not realized that their business was subject to regulation, Waite would no doubt have answered that they should have known and could have known because the principle had existed in common law from time immemorial. Retroactivity, on this view, can only be posited of novel legislation. And so Waite disposed of the last doubt about due process. Indeed he went so far as to say that "rights of property which have been created by the common law cannot be taken away without due process; but the law itself, as a rule of conduct, may be changed at the will, or even the whim of the legislature, unless prevented by constitutional limitations" (134). The last phrase seems to be a token qualification, given the flavor of "will, or even the whim," and seems to be confirmed as such by a passage which follows almost at once: "For protection against abuses by legislatures the people must resort to the polls, not to the courts." In some instances, the polls undoubtedly, but in others, the Constitution perhaps might be the right protector—and if the Constitution, then necessarily the courts. Waite, in short, went very much further than the Court's decision required.

In the *Munn* case, Justice Field again wrote a powerful dissent. But, contrary to the common view of recent commentators, Field was not automatically repeating an unthinking objection to all regulatory statutes. Whereas in the *Slaughterhouse* cases he had objected to the legislature's creation of a private monopoly on the pretext that it was regulating health, in the *Munn* case his complaint was that the legislature asserted a power to regulate private firms on the pretext that their business was "public."

Recognizing that the majority's opinion pivoted on the question whether the grain elevators were "private" or "public," Field explored the distinction at greater length and rather more critically than Waite. Respects in which Field asserted that the elevators were private were these. The defendants had built them, with "their own means," on land which they themselves leased and where they themselves did business (136). Moreover, their business had always been treated as private by the common law, "and is so in its nature"—in that the business of operating warehouses of any sort (including grain elevators) had never been regarded as part of the "prerogative or privilege" of the sovereign (154). On the other hand, Field undertook to rebut every ground on which the majority held or might have held that the elevators were public. First there was a provision of the Illinois Constitution of 1870 that "all elevators or storehouses where grain or other property is stored for a compensation, whether the property stored be kept separate or not, are declared to be public warehouses" (136). To this provision Field retorted that calling a private thing "public" does not change its character: "One might as well attempt to change the nature of colors, by giving them a new designation" (138). In drafting the statute of 1871, legislators had followed the constitutional declaration and added, as Field implied, another respect in which the elevators might be deemed public, that the grain of different owners "was mixed together and stored in such a manner that the identity of different lots or parcels could not be accurately preserved" (136–37). This meaning of "public" Field did not scrutinize or question; it would have been possible for him to maintain that such mixing is the sign not of a public storehouse but of a fungible commodity. In any event, Field did not face determined opposition on this point, as Waite conceded that the elevator business "may not be made [public] by the operation of the constitution of Illinois or this statute" (132).

If not made public by legal declaration, added Waite, the elevators were public as a matter of fact: "Property does become clothed with a public interest when used in a manner to make it of public consequence, and affect the community at large" (126). This argument Field characterized as saying that when property is used as a matter of fact, "in such a way as to be generally useful," it becomes public (139), and he answered the argument by indicating that all property used in business would in this sense of the term be public, since all businessmen sell goods to "the public," that is, many persons (140–41). And if someone were to accept this implication, Field could have maintained that it directly contradicted the assumption of the constitution, legislature, and Court, that only *some* businesses were public.

Further the Court propounded a third criterion of a public business, resting on the theory of a constructive grant. "When, therefore, one devotes his property to a use in which the public has an interest, he, in effect, grants to the public an interest in that use, and must submit to be controlled by the public for the common good, to the extent of the interest he has thus created" (126). Field obviously rejected the imputation of a constructive grant, though he did not hesitate to admit that a person might "dedicate" his private property to public use, in which event that property would become subject at once to the common-law rule that charges must be reasonable (150). This distinction between whether the owner has implicitly "devoted" his property to public use or "dedicated" it, a distinction crucial to Field's argument, he does not explain in so many words. Its content is suggested by analogies he used, such as that of a person dedicating his private property to the public when he opens a street through his own land or a park on it (149, 150). And the essence of such dedication is suggested by a passage that Field quotes from Ellenborough: dedication has taken place if as a result, "for a particular purpose, the public have a right to resort to his premises and make use of them" (151). In short, Field's view seems to have been that if one uses property in the course of business, selling it or its services to many people, that does not make it public, unless one does something intentional that signifies the owner's desire to give the public, that is, everyone and anyone, the *right* to use the property, a right which he may subject to a reasonable charge but which he cannot otherwise qualify.

In Field's view the prototype of private property having a public use or a public interest attached is that where the value of the property derives from some special privilege or right conferred by the state. This is the respect in which courts had properly treated as public the business of "public ferries, bridges and turnpikes, of wharfingers, hackmen and draymen" (148) in precedents which Waite invoked. However, whereas Waite identified the grain elevators with those public businesses, Field insisted that this was unwarranted because "no right or privilege is conferred by the government upon" the owners of the grain elevators (149).

For all these reasons, then, Field insisted that the grain elevators were in fact private business, not in any material sense public.

This conclusion, it should be emphasized, did not lead Field to the implication, on simpleminded laissez-faire lines regularly attributed to him, that the grain elevators should not be regulated by law. On the contrary, he reiterated that a range of well-defined regulatory powers was compatible with the due-process clause. Private property may be taken for public use, on payment of just compensation; part of it may be taken by taxation; and its use may be controlled by law "so far as may be necessary for the protection of the rights of others, and to secure to them the equal use and enjoyment of their property" (145). But none of these acknowledged powers was involved in the *Munn* case. Eminent domain was not being asserted, the statute levied no tax, and the regulation was not founded on injuries that the grain elevators might do to others, for they were not dangerous or in any sense nuisances (148).

The question raised by the *Munn* case, as Field understood it, was whether a legislature could regulate the price, rather than the use, of private property or of services rendered by its owners. He concluded that it could not. All the precedents on which Waite depended showed, according to Field, that a "public" business—one created by a grant of privilege from the state or by the owner's own act of dedicating his property to a public use—could be compelled to charge only such rates as were reasonable (146–49). Reasonable rates might be constitutionally determined by a legislative act, when the legislature in giving a privilege "prescribes the conditions upon which such privilege should be enjoyed," and when the grantee's acceptance of the privilege "implies an assent to the regulation of its use and the compensation for it" (149). Alternatively, in an exchange involving private property, where compensation has not been arranged by contract, reasonable rates must be determined by courts, since "what is a reasonable price in any case will depend on a variety of considerations, and is not a matter for legislative determination" (153). But as to the category of purely private property, where the price of use has been arranged between the parties—and this was in Field's view the category to which the Chicago grain elevators belonged—he denied "the power of any legislature under our government to fix the price which one shall receive." (152). That denial, if quoted out of context, sounds absolute and categorical; understood as the final term of a syllogism, it states that while legislatures may constitutionally regulate the price which owners ask for the use of private property that is public in character, they may not regulate the price of a business which is purely "private" in his sense.

If a statute (or for that matter a judicial decree) regulated the price at which purely private property or its use could be transferred, then it deprived persons without due process. Field rejected the "doctrine of the state court, that no one is deprived of his property, within the meaning of the constitutional inhibition, so long as he retains its title and possession," as a view which would empty the due-process clause of all substantive effect, rendering it a mere formality, powerless to protect anyone (141).

The *Munn* decision gave rise to a host of cases in which the Court upheld regulation by legislatures on the ground that the business in question was "clothed with a public interest." In a much deeper sense its legacy altered the relations between legislature and Court. This came about because of the emphatic approval which Waite gave to the presumption in favor of a statute, nowhere more clearly indicated than in the somewhat cryptic dictum, "For our pur-

poses we must assume that, if a state of facts could exist that would
justify such legislation, it actually did exist when the statute now
under consideration was passed" (132). This was generosity on a
large scale.

Holden v. Hardy [14]

Once again, in this case the issue was a statute exercising the
state's police power on the theory that the private property being
regulated was dangerous. Alcoholic drinks, in the *Wynehamer* case,
had been held to endanger the health and morals of consumers;
slaughterhouses, in the *Slaughterhouse Cases*, the health of people
living near them in a crowded city; and mines, in this case, the
health of people working in them. And indeed, had the grain elevators in the *Munn* case been peculiarly dangerous in fact, or had the
legislature seen fit and been able to present the statute as a measure
aimed at health or safety, the majority of the Court would not have
needed to invoke the theory of a business affected with a public interest, and Field—if we may infer his position from his dissents in
Slaughterhouse and *Munn*—would have upheld the statute, at least
if it had struck him as an authentic health measure. Throughout the
nineteenth century, the Supreme Court, and American courts in general, gave unwavering assent to the rule that a genuine exercise of
the police power did not improperly deprive persons of property
and would be presumed valid unless it interfered with some other
constitutional protection, such as the contract clause or the equal-
protection clause.

The *Holden* decision hewed to this line so closely as to be quite
unremarkable. It is not the decision but the opinion which gives the
case its persistent interest. It was one of those systematizing opinions
wherein the court rehearses all its decisions over many years about a
number of related subjects in order to clarify or reformulate the
rules of law in that field.

The statute in question, adopted by Utah in 1896, limited mine
workers to eight hours of work per day. Holden, a mine owner who
violated the law, challenged its validity on grounds that it violated
the Fourteenth Amendment in three respects: by abridging the priv-

14 169 U.S. 366 (1898).

ileges or immunities of citizens of the United States, by depriving employers and employees of property without due process of law, and by denying them the equal protection of the laws. Justice Brown, writing the opinion for the majority of seven (Brewer and Peckham dissented without opinion), held at the outset that these three grounds, resting on separate clauses of the amendment, were so interconnected as to warrant treating them together (381–82). He then set out to summarize all the Court's decisions on the Fourteenth Amendment since the first one, in the *Slaughterhouse Cases*, twenty-five years earlier.

Brown divided the decisions into two great classes: first, those in which a state's legislature or courts were alleged to have "unjustly discriminated" against some person or class of persons or to have denied them due process; and second, those in which a state changed its methods of trial. The first class comprehended five subclasses: unjust discriminations against blacks, against Chinese, against women, against particular individuals denied due process contrary to the statutes of the state, and, finally, against persons deprived by a "state legislature charged with having transcended its proper police power" (383).

In dealing with both classes, the Court had recognized "the fact that the law is to a certain extent a progressive science" (385), by which Brown meant that as circumstances changed men deemed it useful to change their laws, which he demonstrated by listing a long series of reforms in substance and procedures of law (386). Such changes would continue and were not necessarily antipathetic to the "immutable principles of justice" or to the Constitution, which "should not be so construed as to deprive the states of the power to so amend their laws as to make them conform to the wishes of the citizens as they may deem best for the public welfare" (387). On the other hand, that power of the states, though not prohibited, was certainly limited by the Constitution, particularly by the Fourteenth Amendment (389).

The exact scope of the Fourteenth Amendment had not been defined in general terms, nor did the Court do so on this occasion, but Brown did not doubt that it implied these four commands: law must conform with "natural and inherent principles of justice"; one man's property may not be taken for the benefit of another; a person's property may not be taken for the state without compensation; and nobody "shall be condemned in his person or property" without opportunity of defending himself (390–91). Moreover, since to say that persons cannot be deprived of property in certain ways necessarily implies that they must be free to acquire property in some ways, the Fourteenth Amendment must be understood to rule out any law depriving anybody "of the general power to acquire property" and, as an immediate consequence, to rule out a law generally prohibiting persons from entering into contracts (391).

Nevertheless, the general right of persons to make contracts could constitutionally be restricted by the state in the exercise of its police powers. This power applied especially to "occupations which are dangerous, or so far detrimental to the health of employees as to demand special precaution for their well-being and protection, or the safety of adjoining property" (391–92). Brown then amply catalogued such police measures, including many directed to safety and health in mining, which courts had often upheld as constitutional (393–95). Moving thus to the Utah statute, Brown held that to limit hours of work in mines was reasonable in view of the special dangers to health in that occupation, and he concurred with the view of the supreme court of Utah that once the legislature deemed eight hours to be a reasonable limit, a court must resolve any disagreement as to the most suitable concrete limit in favor of the legislature (395–97).

The court's decision to uphold the Utah statute might appear, Brown concluded, to contradict the proposition advanced "by many authorities"—whom the Court declined to criticize—that a statute restricting the hours of labor in all employments would be unconstitutional. But the present statute of Utah did not impose such a general limitation. In any event, Brown seemed to say, such limitations were constitutional whenever the legislature regarded them as necessary to preserve health, provided "there are reasonable grounds for believing that such determination is supported by the facts," and that the purported objective of preserving health is not "a mere excuse for an unjust discrimination, or the oppression, or spoilation of a particular class" (397–98).

On this view, the Court, when reviewing legislation under the Fourteenth Amendment, would confine itself to two questions. First, is there reasonable ground for believing that the legislature's determination was supported by facts? It is instructive to watch just how Brown handled this question in the *Holden* setting. The grounds, so far as he was concerned, for believing that the legislature's decision was supported by facts were these: legislatures and courts of many other states had reached similar conclusions about mining (393–95); "the general experience of mankind," though recognizing that ordinary laborers could remain healthy while working longer than eight hours a day, did not militate against the likelihood that working in mines was different (395–96); and the supreme court of Utah, giving judgment on the *Holden* case, had found that "there can be no doubt that prolonged effort day after day" in smelting works (which, with mines, were regulated by the Utah statute) "will produce morbid, noxious, and often deadly effects in the human system" (396).

Brown's way of stating and using the test shows how far it differed from the view pronounced in the *Munn* decision, in which Waite had said: "For our purposes we must assume that, if a state of facts could exist that would justify such legislation, it actually did exist when the statute now under consideration was passed" (94 U.S. 132). The difference is between an absolute presumption and a plausible showing.

The second question left open to the Court by Brown's codification was whether the purported health regulation was a mere excuse for unjust discrimination. This he answered implicitly when he concluded that the special treatment of miners, which gave the statute a discriminatory effect, was not unjust, being amply justified by the special circumstances of mining. He added a further consideration on this score. In rehearsing valid exercises of the police power he had mentioned laws limiting the hours of work of women and children, about which he commented that "while their constitutionality, at least as applied to women, has been doubted in some of the states, they have been generally upheld" (395). Presumably he believed that the police power could be invoked rightly to protect persons too weak to protect themselves. But presumably the mine workers, being men, "of full age and competent to contract," did not need to be protected against themselves (397). Was the regulation therefore unjustly discriminatory? No, answered Brown. The legislature of Utah had "recognized the fact . . . that the proprietors of these establishments and their operatives do not stand upon an equality.

. . . In other words, the proprietors lay down the rules and the laborers are practically constrained to obey them" (397). This being so, the statute's protection of these workers, though discriminatory, was justified by their exposure to coercive treatment.

But suppose the miners had complained that the statute unjustly discriminated by preventing them alone among male workers in that state from working more than eight hours a day even though they freely wished to do so. Of course the question was hypothetical in one sense, since no mine worker was a party to this case. But in another sense it was present, because Holden's attorneys had maintained that the act was discriminatory in its effect upon "but one of many classes of employers and employees," and Brown accepted in his statement of the case (367) as well as in his opinion (381) that Holden's attack was directed against the damage to mine workers as well as mine owners. But in the end Brown seems to have forgotten this, for he said that Holden's "defense is not so much that his right to contract has been infringed upon, but that the act works a peculiar hardship to his employees, whose right to labor as long as they please is alleged thereby to be violated." After misrepresenting this defense, Brown brushed it aside: "The argument would certainly come with better grace and greater cogency from the latter class" (397). Perhaps so, but it is well to recall that since the time of *Holden,* the movement for an eight-hour day—which at that time pressed for statutory prohibition of anything over eight hours—came to favor the present eight-hour day, which while requiring the employer to pay overtime rates after eight hours permits the worker to continue as long as he pleases. So perhaps, despite Brown's caustic comment, mine workers could reasonably have regarded the eight-hour rule as unwarranted interference with their freedom.

Brown's opinion ordered and greatly clarified the approach which the Court had been taking to Fourteenth Amendment cases. It identified two criteria which regulations would have to meet: a reasonable showing that the legislature had acted in accordance with facts, and the requirement that legislation be intended genuinely to police rather than covertly to discriminate. Any thought that these criteria excessively constrained the Court's power was dispelled just a few years later by the *Lochner* decision.

Yick Wo v. Hopkins[15]

As the opinion in *Holden* v. *Hardy* pointed out, the Supreme Court had by 1898 invalidated a number of statutes (or nullified certain of their effects) on the grounds that they produced unjust discrimination. Perhaps the clearest illustration was the case brought by Yick Wo, a Chinese laundryman in San Francisco. The ordinance that he called into question had been passed, presumably, in recollection of the San Francisco fire. While permitting laundries to operate in brick or stone buildings, it excluded them from wooden buildings except those approved for the purpose by a board of supervisors. Yick Wo had operated a laundry in defiance of the ordinance and had been duly convicted of an offense.

According to the Supreme Court, the ordinance was suspect in itself. It established "an arbitrary line" between those wooden buildings which would be approved for laundries and those not approved, approval depending on the "mere will and pleasure" of the supervisors. Whereas ordinary license laws, which also lodged discretion in public officers, required them to determine whether the applicant was "fit" for the privilege, thus limiting their discretion to a quasi-judicial inquiry into facts concerning fitness, the San Francisco ordinance did not require the supervisors to inquire into the "personal character and qualifications for the business" of applicants (366). The supervisors therefore enjoyed a "purely personal and arbitrary power" contrary to the principles of the Constitution (366–68). Nevertheless, although the discretionary power thus given was untrammeled and prone to abuse, the Court displayed some reluctance to invalidate the ordinance merely on its judgment of the possibility or even probability of misuse (372–73). To invalidate on this ground would have been to override a presumption in favor of the municipal authorities, administrative as well as legislative, a presumption firmly lodged in the Court's view of its constitutional role.

But, the Court held, the facts of the case enabled it to bypass questions about the legislative intent or probable tendency of the ordinance, and indeed those facts evidently were sufficient to rebut any presumption that the public officials had executed their offices

[15] 118 U.S. 356 (1886).

properly.[16] The record established that the supervisors had withheld consent from some two hundred applicants, "all of whom happened to be Chinese subjects," while granting consent to eighty persons who were not Chinese. While conceding this fact, the supervisors gave no reason for it, "and the conclusion cannot be resisted that no reason for it exists except hostility to the race and nationality to which the petitioners belong." This constituted unjust discrimination, contrary to the Fourteenth Amendment (374).

Toward the end of the opinion the Court particularly stressed equal protection of the laws as the constitutional requirement violated by the ordinance as administered. Elsewhere, and especially while examining the words of the ordinance, the Court seemed to be concerned with due process, the probable denial of which would arise from the fact that the supervisors were not obliged to reach an objective judgment on the applicant's merits. But these two clauses of the Fourteenth Amendment the Court had begun to read as more or less the same, as was made explicit in the *Holden* opinion. Unjust discrimination might be thought of as denying due process by applying laws unequally or as denying equal protection by improprieties of process; the Court did not insist on one of these lines in preference to the other, though it seemed to find the link between discrimination and equal protection intuitively easier to grasp or at least easier to explain. It was not, however, until about fifty years after *Yick Wo* that the Court sharply sundered the two clauses, with the intention of restricting due-process considerations to the operation of judicial and executive branches and invoking equal protection chiefly or only when actions of legislatures were at issue.

Lochner v. *New York*[17]

This, the most famous instance in which the court invalidated a regulatory statute, has regularly been attacked as a high watermark of conservatism, not to mention reaction. The statute, part of the Labor Law of New York, limited the hours of work in a bakery to ten hours a day and sixty hours a week. Lochner, owner of a small bakery, broke the law and fought repeated appeals until he reached the Supreme Court.

---

[16] Cf. *Neal* v. *Delaware*, 103 U.S. 370 (1881).
[17] 198 U.S. 45 (1905).

The majority of the Court, speaking through Justice Peckham, started from the hallowed premises: individuals enjoy a general right, guaranteed by the Fourteenth Amendment, to enter into voluntary contracts including those concerning employment (52–53), and states have police powers to regulate contracts, with which powers the Fourteenth Amendment "was not designed to interfere" (53). The question in this case then is whether the right of individuals or the right of the state shall prevail (54). The question, put another way, is whether the statute is "a fair, reasonable, and appropriate exercise of the police power of the state, or . . . an unreasonable, unnecessary, and arbitrary interference" with the individual's right to make contracts (56).

Considered as an exercise of the police power, the statute would be justified if bakers needed special protection because they were unable to look after themselves, because the occupation threatened their health, or because the conditions of their work threatened the public health. The first of these possibilities Peckham dismissed at the outset. Bakers are "equal in intelligence and capacity" to other workers; they can "assert their rights and care for themselves"; they are "in no sense wards of the state" (57). The third possibility he dispatched in few words: "Clean and wholesome bread does not depend upon whether the baker works but ten hours per day or only sixty hours a week" (57, 62). And so the only remaining ground that might justify the regulation was the health of bakers.

The Court must judge whether the work of a baker endangered his health. This question, Peckham reported, had provoked disagreement in the high court of New York. One of the judges had said that they could sustain the regulation only if they could say "from common knowledge" that the trade was unhealthy, and despite some conflict of evidence he had found himself able to say so; however, three dissenters thought that it "was not to such an extent unhealthy" as to warrant the regulation (58). The majority of the Supreme Court shared the latter view. As Peckham put it, in a paragraph which displays some of his habitual jauntiness:

We think that there can be no fair doubt that the trade of a baker, in and of itself, is not an unhealthy one to that degree which would authorize the legislature to interfere with the right to labor. . . . In looking through statistics regarding all trades and occupations, it may be true that the trade of a baker does not appear to be as healthy as some other trades, and is also vastly more healthy than still others. To the common understanding the trade of a baker has never been regarded as an unhealthy one. Very likely physicians would not recommend the exercise of that or of any other trade as a remedy for ill health. . . . It might be safely affirmed that almost all occupations more or less affect the health. (59)

If the fact that any number of things that people do voluntarily are more or less unhealthy were to justify regulation, then there would be no practical limit to health laws, in which case the Fourteenth Amendment would have been in effect nullified. A statute limiting the hours of work of "grown and intelligent men" could stand under the Fourteenth Amendment only if "there be some fair ground, reasonable in and of itself, to say that there is material danger to the public health, or to the health of the employees, if the hours of labor are not curtailed" (61). Such fair and reasonable ground for asserting a "material danger" did not exist; it was negated by the evidence that baking was neither absolutely nor relatively perilous.

Since the New York statute could not rationally have been intended to protect the health of bakers, it must have been aimed at some other objective. Likening it to other recent statutes, among which were instanced a number to regulate and license the trade of horseshoeing, Peckham said that while purporting to be health laws these were "in reality, passed from other motives." Stepping carefully through a terrain declared out of bounds by *Fletcher* v. *Peck*, Peckham offered the excuse that his inference about legislative motives derived from the purpose of such statutes, which must be determined from their "natural effect . . . when put into operation, and not from their proclaimed purpose," a rule for which he cited the *Yick Wo* decision as a leading precedent (64).

What were the suspect legislative motives that Peckham (and presumably his colleagues in the majority) detected? If we are to understand well why they reached the decision they did in this pivotal case, we must go behind the opinion.

Justice Peckham had been appointed to the Supreme Court in 1895, shortly before the Court decided *Holden* v. *Hardy*, a decision from which he dissented, though without opinion. Earlier Peckham had been a judge of the New York Court of Appeals, where he had made clear his views on regulatory exercises of the police power.

For instance, in the case of *Budd* v. *People*, involving a New York statute of 1888 to regulate charges of grain elevators, while the court upheld the law on the principles laid down in *Munn* v. *Illinois*, Peckham dissented, referring to his dissent in a related case which characterized a similar statute as "vicious in its nature and communistic in its tendencies."[18] However strong his language, Peckham's dissent in the *Budd* case was not as tendentious as might seem at first sight. If the case had quite obviously fallen within the rule of *Munn* v. *Illinois*, it is hardly believable that the New York Court of Appeals and the Supreme Court would have allowed appeal. The reasons why they did, it seems, were that the complex factors of the case permitted the inference that elevator operators might be paid nothing at all for part of their services, and that, according to three justices at least, the Supreme Court had in effect overruled *Munn* v. *Illinois* by their decision in *Chicago, Milwaukee and St. Paul Railroad* v. *Minnesota*.[19] In the end the courts upheld the New York statute, and Peckham persisted in believing that contracts voluntarily agreed upon by mature men should be left alone by the laws.

Just a few years before the *Budd* case, Peckham had written the opinion of the New York Court of Appeals in *People* v. *Gillson*[20] concerning a statute that prohibited sellers of food from offering a premium or reward to buyers. The court held the act to be invalid as a health regulation concerning food, on the ground that there was no "fair and reasonable relation of means to end, which courts can see and admit the force of" (403). It is interesting to note that Peckham virtually repeated that language in the *Lochner* opinion, but, whereas in the latter he referred only cryptically to the improper motives of the legislature, in his *Gillson* opinion he was more forthright. The statute there under consideration he described "as evidently that kind which has been so frequent of late, a kind which is meant to protect some class in that community against the fair, free, and full competition of some other class, the members of the former

[18] *Budd* v. *People*, 117 N.Y. 1 (1889). *Budd* v. *New York*, 143 U.S. 517 (1892). Contrary to Corwin, *Liberty against Government*, p. 139 n, the comment by Peckham is from his opinion in *People* v. *Walsh*, 117 N.Y. 34 (1889), p. 47.

[19] 134 U.S. 418 (1890), p. 461; dissent by Bradley J. See *Budd* v. *New York*, 143 U.S. 517, p. 538.

[20] 109 N.Y. 389 (1888).

class thinking it impossible to hold their own against such competition, and therefore flying to the legislature to secure some enactment which shall operate favorably to them or unfavorably to their competitors" (399). The improper motive of the legislation in such instances was its intention to help some competitors to the disadvantage of others.

Now Peckham, it is true, was passionately committed to the view that competition is the best way to order an economy, and he believed that the right of persons to enter into voluntary contracts is the legal precondition of competitive markets.[21] One need not share his approval of competition in order to understand the force of his complaint against legislative intervention as in the *Gillson* case. For him the legislature and all government is properly a protector only with respect to persons who cannot help themselves, who are naturally "wards"; however, with respect to intelligent and able persons, the legislature must act as a fair umpire, and it betrays its responsibilities as umpire when it throws the power of the state behind some of the players in the competitive contest.

How does this apply to the facts of the *Lochner* case? An answer is suggested by the brief for Lochner, which incidentally quoted from Peckham's opinion in the *Gillson* case.[22] Lochner's attorneys maintained that the statute "was never intended as a health provision but was purely a labor law" (40). Among the evidence they produced was a good deal to show, not surprisingly, that the ten-hour day had been demanded by bakers, that a bill had been promoted in the New York legislature by the secretary of the Journeymen's Bakers Union, and that the union continued to work for it until the act was passed in 1896 (41–42). Then when the legislature was consolidating the statutes in 1897, it "determined that this act was a labor measure and that its passage was so intended," whereupon it included its provisions not in the consolidated Public Health Act but in the Labor Law (42). The hidden motive of the legislature then was revealed inasmuch as the statute proclaimed itself to be a labor law rather than a health law; in other words, in Peckham's

---

[21] W. Letwin, *Law and Economic Policy in America* (New York: Random House, 1965), pp. 180–81 and *passim.*
[22] *Lochner* v. *New York. Brief for Plaintiff in Error,* pp. 29–30.

view, not a legitimate exercise of the police power. Given this background, the ten-hour day had no "fair and reasonable" relation to health because it had never been wanted for the sake of health. Restricting all bakers to ten hours a day was a regulation by which the legislature tipped the scales against bakers who wanted to work more than ten hours—and this, I would suggest, is the way Peckham saw the matter—and which constitutionally amounted to unjust discrimination if not outright unfairness.

The dissents in the *Lochner* case, on behalf of a minority of four, attracted a great deal of attention and have in the long run been more influential than the majority opinion, though not, in my view, entirely influential for the good.

Harlan, while accepting fundamentally the basic premises of the majority, stressed that when a statute is attacked as invalid because its means have "no real or substantial relation" to its purported end as a health measure, the burden of proof is on the attacker (68). He himself could not see that, "in view of common experience," he could find this fault (69–70). He quoted medical authority and statistics on the unhealthfulness of the baker's work; he noted as a matter of judicial knowledge that Congress and nearly all the states had regulated the hours of work in particular occupations; and he observed that this was a sort of question "about which there is room for debate and for an honest difference of opinion" (70–72). That being so, the court must sustain the statute as not obviously invalid, not "plainly and palpably" unconstitutional.

We are not to presume that the state of New York has acted in bad faith. Nor can we assume that its legislature acted without due deliberation, or that it did not determine this question upon the fullest available information and for the common good. We cannot say that the state has acted without reason, nor ought we to proceed upon the theory that its action is a mere sham. (73)

His difference with the majority, then, rested entirely on the question of how strong ought to be the Court's presumption in favor of the legislature.

Holmes' separate dissent is renowned of course for the quip, "The Fourteenth Amendment does not enact Mr. Herbert Spencer's *Social Statics*" (75). It is gratuitous. Herbert Spencer was not cited as authority by anyone in the case, and *Social Statics* had no direct bearing on it. Spencer was of course recognized as exponent of the doctrine that the state ought not to protect the weak because to do so would interfere with the evolutionary process of natural selection, whereas the majority of the Court insisted that to protect the weak was well within the police power. It might equally well have been said that the Fourteenth Amendment did not enact Plato's *Republic* or the platform of the Populist Party, or, as Holmes went on to say, any "particular economic theory." It missed the point to suppose, as Holmes did, that "this case is decided upon an economic theory which a large part of the country does not entertain." It was decided, no doubt, by justices who held economic views, but they decided the case on a well-established constitutional principle that a health law would be constitutional where there was a danger to health and unconstitutional where the danger to health was insubstantial. What could well be argued was the point presented by Harlan about presumptions and burdens of proof—again a point of constitutional law and not economics. Holmes' witticism amounted nearly to an ad hominem attack.

On the question of presumptions, Holmes shared and restated Harlan's view. The test for him was whether "a rational and fair man necessarily would admit that the statute proposed would infringe fundamental principles as they have been understood by the traditions of our people and our law." No research was necessary in order to deny such an infringement in this case. "A reasonable man might think it a proper measure on the score of health" (76).

The last two sentences of the opinion, which follow on immediately, are of great interest: "Men whom I certainly could not pronounce unreasonable would uphold it as a first instalment of a general regulation of the hours of work. Whether in the latter aspect it would be open to the charge of inequality I think it unnecessary to discuss" (76). From the standpoint of the majority, a general regulation of the hours of work would have been even more invalid than the baker's statute, since it would obstruct the rights of the people in occupations much less dangerous than that of a baker. The last sentence suggests that Holmes misunderstood or otherwise was deliberately misrepresenting the majority's view, as though they invalidated the statute because it treated bakers differently from other

sorts of workers. Certainly Lochner had argued that bakers and bakery owners ought not to be "singled out." But the majority had declined to follow the line of unjust discrimination, basing themselves
instead on the doctrine that the means and ostensible purpose of an
act must be reasonable and fairly related.

Although Holmes was rather cavalier in debate, although he did
not join issue with Peckham in the frankest manner, it would be a
mistake to underestimate the cogency of his own political theory or
the deep seriousness which underlay his sometimes flippant rhetoric.
He held that American laws would always be shaped by the settled
opinions of the majority, which must be allowed by the courts to
have its way unless that obviously flouted the basic principles of
justice; these principles were the spirit of the Constitution but could
not be discerned by any literal reading of the Constitution, nor by
extrapolating from such a term as *liberty* to Peckham's idea of free
contract, nor by regarding the Constitution as a set of rules fixed
over time in its concrete applications. As conditions changed, men's
opinions would change, so would the laws, and so must the Constitution. For those reasons, then, the courts must always go a long way
toward assuming that legislation is valid.

This of course was precisely the opposite of Peckham's view,
since it appeared to him that legislatures might often be swayed (or
even corrupted) to not act in accordance with the settled opinions of
the majority but to satisfy the sharply asserted interests of minorities. Moreover, if one wanted to detect the really stable and profound principles of the majority, one must look at the Constitution.
Whenever statute collided with Constitution, whenever passing fash-
ions of the many or, more likely, selfish motives of the few confronted the long-held principles of the whole, there was then no
doubt where a court's duty would lie.

In the history of American government, the debate between
Peckham and Holmes echoed the debate between Jefferson and
Hamilton and is echoed today in every court which reviews the actions of public officials. Although the view that Peckham represented was in some sense overthrown in 1937, the notion that it was
slain once and for all is a mistake, and the notion that it needed to
be destroyed root and branch is a much more serious mistake.

The Heritage of Lochner

Before the *Lochner* decision, the Supreme Court had upheld state legislation in the leading cases which we have considered and had voided it in a number of others, and so had the state courts and lower courts—the batting record on both sides is recited fully in the *Lochner* pleadings and opinions. During the thirty years after the *Lochner* decision, a brief summary of how well regulatory statutes fared in the courts would have to use almost the same words. This is not to say that the courts wavered inconsistently but, rather, that the rules of law which had been established in the field of so-called economic due process, and which the courts slowly modified, were highly differentiated, relatively specialized, and accordingly resistant to broad summary. However, a number of contemporary critics—prominent among whom were Corwin, Brandeis, and Frankfurter—were not reluctant to summarize them broadly.

The earliest of these cases to become inscribed in the list of leading precedents was *Muller v. Oregon,* decided by the Supreme Court in 1908.[23] It arose under an Oregon statute prohibiting the employment of women in factories or laundries for more than ten hours a day. In view of the *Lochner* rule it would seem that the questions to be considered were whether such employment materially threatened the health of the employees, whether the limitation in the statute was fairly and rationally adjusted to the danger, and whether the particular condition of women would sufficiently distinguish the Oregon law from the New York law. The question of danger to health was examined in detail by the brief of Brandeis for the state, in which he first catalogued the acts by which at least nineteen other states between about 1870 and 1905, as well as many foreign nations, had restricted the hours of work of women, acts whose constitutionality had been upheld by a number of state courts. He then quoted from over ninety official reports, American and foreign, on the medical effects of long working hours on women. All this greatly impressed the unanimous Court, speaking by Justice Brewer, who has been described as "its most conservative member."[24] Brewer summarized Brandeis' evidence as signifying "a wide-

[23] 208 U.S. 412 (1908).
[24] Corwin, *Liberty against Government,* p. 152.

spread belief that woman's physical structure, and the functions she performs in consequence therefore, justify special legislation" to regulate conditions of work. And though he went on to emphasize, presumably with a sideways glance at Holmes, that "a consensus of present public opinion" does not settle constitutional questions, he did accept that it authorized the Court to take judicial cognizance of the facts (419–21). It followed that as women are "not upon an equality" with men (a criterion carried over from *Holden* v. *Hardy*), and as they had always been regarded by the courts "as needing especial care," the statute of Oregon was justified as a measure to protect the private interests of women (421–23). Moreover, it served the public interest as well, because "healthy mothers are essential to vigorous offspring" and thus essential "to preserve the strength and vigor of the race" (421). Therefore the court upheld the statute, "without questioning in any respect the decision in *Lochner* v. *New York*" (423).

In fact, the *Muller* decision might be said to have been a direct corollary of the *Lochner* decision, even if not a logically inevitable corollary. It has been said that the decisions are fundamentally different in that the Brandeis brief was given credence by the Court, whereas medical evidence cited by Harlan in his dissent had been set aside by Peckham and the majority—in other words, between 1905 and 1908 the majority changed its mind about whether it ought to take judicial cognizance of scientific evidence. There is a simpler explanation for the court's different reactions in the two cases. Brandeis' evidence pointed overwhelmingly in one direction, and, as far as the record shows, no counterevidence was introduced (nor, for all we know, could any have been introduced, though that seems unlikely, women being strong and evidence of all sorts plentiful). By contrast, evidence about the health of bakers in the *Lochner* case was decidedly mixed. Lochner's counsel, Frank Harvey Field and Henry Weismann, appended to their brief a section of medical statistics and findings which supported the conclusion that baking was less dangerous than the average occupation[25]—and they may therefore be said to have invented the "Brandeis brief" before Brandeis

[25] *Lochner* v. *New York. Brief for Plaintiff in Error*, pp. 50–61.

did. And it was to this material that Peckham referred when he said, "In looking through statistics regarding all trades and occupations" baking seemed not especially unhealthy (198 U.S. at 59). On the other hand, Harlan referred to conflicting medical opinion and evidence —it is not clear how this came before the court—to the effect that baking was an extremely unhealthy occupation (198 U.S. at 70). I would say then that the same principle of judicial cognizance was at work in both cases, and that in one case the majority had to apply it to seriously conflicting and ambiguous evidence, whereas in the other the evidence was abundant and uncontested.

A new and important variant on the *Lochner* theme arose in review of another Oregon statute, passed in 1913, to establish a ten-hour day for all factory workers, male as well as female. Great care had apparently been taken in drafting the act so as to avoid the pit-falls mapped out by the *Lochner* decision. The act was labeled a health measure in order to avoid the imputation of being a labor law. It made exceptions to the ten-hour rule in case of emergencies, as had the Utah statute in *Holden* v. *Hardy*, but as the New York baker's statute had not, for which narrow technical reason (one is tempted to say frivolous reason) the Court had held that "there is nothing in *Holden* v. *Hardy* which covers the case now before us" (198 U.S. at 55). And finally the Oregon statute did not absolutely prohibit workers from going beyond ten hours a day; it provided that they could work as much as three hours overtime, provided they were paid for overtime at a rate of time and one half. Since circum-navigating known perils exposes one to unknown perils, the careful-ly drafted statute raised a problem possibly unanticipated by the draftsmen: perhaps the overtime proviso transformed it from a regu-lation of hours, which might reasonably be linked to the state's po-lice power relative to health, into a regulation of wages, whose link to health would be sure to be questioned.

The statute came before the Supreme Court in *Bunting* v. *Ore-gon*,[26] Bunting having been convicted for employing a worker thir-teen hours a day without paying the prescribed overtime rate. Jus-tice McKenna, for the majority of five, posed two questions: whether

[26] 243 U.S. 426 (1917).

the statute was a wage law or an "hours-of-service" law; and if the latter, whether it had "equality of operation," in defect of which it would violate due process (435). As to what sort of law it was, there was the evidence of a declaration of legislative policy in the statute itself and a finding by the Oregon Supreme Court that the statute's object was health and hours, not wages, since it left wages to be negotiated freely between employer and employee. Against this Bunting contended that the overtime rule was the paramount feature of the act. To assent to Bunting's contention, McKenna declared, would be "to ascribe to the legislation such improvidence of expression as to intend one thing and effect another; or artfulness of expression to disguise illegal purpose." The Court was reluctant to impute either fault and did not regard the facts as compelling it to do so (435–36). If the act were interpreted as *permitting* laborers to work thirteen hours, then it would not stand up as much of a health law, but appear as a wage law giving fourteen and a half hours worth of wages for thirteen hours of work; that is, raising average wage rate by 11.5 percent. The Court, however, interpreted the overtime provision as deterrent rather than permissive: the overtime rate was a burden or penalty on the employer, intended to dissuade him from keeping anyone at work for more than ten hours. Why did the legislature arrange things so indirectly? McKenna answered rather coyly: "It might not have been possible, it might not have been wise, to make a rigid prohibition" (437). In fact, a rigid prohibition would have run directly afoul of the *Lochner* rule. That much settled, McKenna emphasized that the Court was upholding the statute as a regulation of hours; it would not consider the state's argument that the act would be valid even if a wage law.

Turning now to the second question, whether as a regulation of hours the act was unreasonable or arbitrary, McKenna dealt summarily with Bunting's attack. Bunting had supplied no facts to support the contention. The legislature and the state supreme court had denied it "in view of the well-known fact that the custom in our industries does not sanction a longer service than ten hours per day." And, added McKenna, referring to the Brandeis brief filed by Felix Frankfurter (Brandeis himself having by now joined the Court, though absenting himself from this case): "Statistics show that the average daily working time" in various countries ranged from eight to twelve hours, though what this was supposed to prove about the legitimacy of a ten-hour act he did not explain. In any event, statistics were there to support presumption, which ought especially to favor a statute measured to match the *Lochner* pattern. There was only one point at which the match was imperfect: if the health of bakers did not reasonably justify a statutory limit of ten hours, how could the health of all factory workers justify it, as the work of about half of them was safer than that of bakers? But then again, curiously enough, the Court failed in the *Bunting* opinion to mention even once the *Lochner* decision, though it had been urged on it as precedent by counsel for both parties. So in the end, the Court left behind some reason to wonder whether the *Bunting* decision affirmed or overruled the *Lochner* decision.

As *Muller* v. *Oregon* established that conditions of work for women could be regulated, and as *Bunting* v. *Oregon* upheld a regulation that some called a wage law, together they set the stage for a case in which a frankly intended wage law claimed validity because its beneficiaries were women, or better still, as it happened, women and children. Any shrewd observer could have predicted the main course of the contest: one champion would declaim that all wage laws are bad including this one, his opposite number that all laws protecting women are valid, including this one. The issue came to Court in *Adkins* v. *Children's Hospital*,[27] which arose under an act of Congress in its capacity as municipal legislature of the District of Columbia. The act created a system for establishing minimum-wage rates for women and children subsequent to administrative determination that existing wage rates were "inadequate to supply them with the necessary cost of living, maintain them in health, and protect their morals" (540)—so asserting a link between wages and the recognized police-power objectives of health and morals.

Justice Sutherland, for the Court, neatly systematized all the decisions in the long line which by this time had grown up from *Holden* v. *Hardy*, in the course of which he spent two pages quoting from *Lochner* v. *New York*. Then, coming to the crux of the case

[27] 261 U.S. 525 (1923).

before him, he observed that, though women were still physically weaker than men—a difference which would continue to justify special legislation concerning the conditions and hours of their work—they were, since the changes culminating in the Nineteenth Amendment, no longer unequal in any other way and so could not be thought to need their liberty of contract restricted except in ways constitutional if applied to men (553). Since laws fixing the wages of men would not be upheld by the Court, this law could not be upheld as to women now equal to men (554). Sutherland added a further argument: the procedure for determining the minimum wage, and the standard furnished by the statute, were "so vague as to be impossible of practical application with any reasonable degree of accuracy" (555). As a result, the act and its consequences were fatally "uncertain" and "arbitrary," they responded only to the hypothetical "need" of employees on the average, while overlooking the right of the employer to arrange a fair bargain for himself (555–59). In addition to aiming at an impermissible end, the statute used unacceptable means.

Once again there was a Frankfurter-Brandeis brief on hand, but this time it carried no conviction. It pointed to the fact that several states had adopted similar statutes; opposing counsel, who may have learned by example how to display their facts, showed that "three times as many states, presumably as well informed and as anxious to promote the health and morals of their people, have refrained from enacting such legislation" (559). The brief further quoted a large number of writings in which minimum-wage laws were endorsed, to which McKenna retorted that the Court's "own reading disclosed a large number to the contrary." All that was beside the point, however, since the question of the act's validity could not be elucidated "by counting heads" (560).

Chief Justice Taft wrote one of the two dissenting opinions. The Court had firmly established, he maintained, that states could regulate hours of work; as he could not reconcile the *Bunting* decision with the *Lochner* decision, he had "always supposed that the *Lochner* case was thus overruled sub silentio" (564). That being so, the majority's decision in the present case must rest on the distinction between maximum hours and minimum wages. But to him that distinction was formal rather than real. Maximum hours and minimum wages interfered equally with absolute freedom of contract. And if it were said that "long hours of labor have a more direct effect upon the health of the employee than the low wage, there is very respectable authority . . . that they are equally harmful in this regard" (564). In any event, he argued, the passage of the Nineteenth Amendment did not change the fact that women are physically weaker than men and so remained eligible for special protection, which, as he saw it, could not rationally exclude minimum wages while including maximum hours (566–67). He concluded by saying that he would merely have concurred in Holmes' "forcible" dissenting opinion, had it not been for certain "general observations" with which he could not agree—so bequeathing to historians an attractive minor puzzle. Certainly Holmes was at his most amusing, ironic, caustic, and wisest in this dissent, which is accordingly heavily studded with "general observations." One of the finest shows his constant insistence on the dividing line between legislature and court. If a legislature were to empower courts to fix minimum wages, he would not be able to say that the statute was based on opinions "impossible to be held by reasonable men." "I should have my doubts, as I have them about this statute; but they would be whether the bill that has to be paid for every gain, although hidden as interstitial detriments, was not greater than the gain was worth—a matter that is not for me to decide" (571).

The doctrine of *Adkins* was tested and upheld in the Court on three subsequent occasions, of which the last was *Morehead* v. *New York*, decided in 1936.[28] The opinion in that case is unremarkable except for one curious turn in Justice Butler's opinion. He emphasized at some length that Morehead, in applying for review, had asserted that the statute of New York was distinguishable from the statute in the *Adkins* case. He had not asked "to be heard upon the question whether the *Adkins* case should be overruled" and therefore the Court would not entertain that question (605). It was a rather broad hint that the Court might deal with that question should anybody apply for review on that basis. At least three of the justices felt, as Stone said in dissent (636), that the Court had already virtually overruled *Adkins* when it upheld in *Nebbia* v. *New*

28 *Morehead* v. *New York ex. rel. Tipaldo*, 298 U.S. 587 (1936).

York,[29] a statute fixing the minimum price of milk. The Court did not have to wait long for an opportunity to undo *Adkins.*

West Coast Hotel v. Parrish[30]

This decision formally closed the reign of *Lochner,* which as we have seen had begun to crumble some twenty years earlier, and can thus be appreciated, in the longer view, as a fleeting episode. More, this decision, coupled with others made by the Supreme Court during the New Deal period, put an end to "economic due process." These effects, however, were outside the technical limits of the case, which concerned the narrower question whether the rule of the *Adkins* decision could continue to stand.

It was not thanks to counsel for Parrish that the Court was able to use the occasion to reconsider the *Adkins* rule. In their brief they maintained that a decision upholding the Washington minimum-wage law would not conflict with the *Adkins* rule, and in oral argument they amplified this by pointing out that as Parrish had been employed by a hotel, a business affected with a public interest and hence constitutionally regulable, the Washington statute was constitutional so far as concerned Parrish.[31] But as Chief Justice Hughes remarked for the Court, with possibly a touch of irritation, the hotel argument was "obviously futile," since one of the parties in the *Adkins* case had worked in a hotel, so that the *Adkins* rule applied *a fortiori* to hotel employees (388). Nevertheless, the Court discovered a different ground on which the *Adkins* rule could be reconsidered. It was that the supreme court of Washington had upheld the statute in this case, maintaining that other decisions of the Supreme Court both before and after *Adkins* supported the statute's constitutionality. In so ruling, the state court had suggested that the *Adkins* rule was inconsistent with others in the field; it had, in effect, taken it upon itself to overrule *Adkins.* This was sufficient to muster the Supreme Court to a duty it was eager to perform—all the more so because the Court had reached the *Adkins* decision by a bare majority—because since the *Adkins* decision many states had passed

29 291 U.S. 502 (1934).
30 300 U.S. 379 (1937).
31 81 *L. ed.,* p. 705.

similar laws, and because of the "economic conditions which have supervened," a reference to the Great Depression (389–90).

Moving now to the substantive issue, Hughes identified its crux as the assertion that minimum-wage laws for women deprived them of freedom of contract. But the Constitution, said Hughes, following a favorite line of Holmes, does not speak of freedom of contract. The asserted right to freedom of contract must derive from liberty, which is guaranteed by the Fourteenth Amendment.

This brought Hughes to the enunciation of the familiar first principles. The Constitution "prohibits the deprivation of liberty without due process of law." That liberty exists within "a social organization," or, as one might say, a community. The community needs laws to protect it against "the evils which menace the health, safety, morals, and welfare of the people." Up to this point, all is in order in Hughes' statement; it accords with what had been said many times before about due process and the police power, though his choice of words reveals subtle changes of emphasis. Hughes omitted to mention that the letter of the due-process clause protects property as well as liberty; he spoke of "social organization," a turn of phrase less congenial to Lockeans than, say, to Hegelians; and he added to the normal list of the police power's objectives the catchall, welfare. Still, his meaning up to this point is easily followed.

Hughes' next sentence, which concludes the syllogism, is totally baffling: "Liberty under the Constitution is thus necessarily subject to the restraints of due process, and regulation which is reasonable in relation to its subject and is adopted in the interests of the community is due process" (391). Those words as they stand in the report are totally confusing. The restraints of due process were intended to restrain not the liberty of the subject but the power of the government. And the implication of the second clause, that regulation of a certain sort is due process, contradicts the implication of the Fourteenth Amendment that regulation might conceivably operate with or without due process and therefore cannot possibly be identical with due process. As it stands, the sentence is practically meaningless.

I believe the passage to be corrupt. The Court was extraordinarily busy just then and working under the stress of heavier hostile criticism than it had ever experienced before. Hughes was busy enough and perhaps at seventy-five tired enough to have made a mistake. Or maybe it was a typist. In any event, I would suggest that somewhere between Hughes' mind and the printed opinion, two slips occurred. The garbled passage, suitably emended, would read: "Liberty under the Constitution is thus necessarily subject to the restraints of *regulation*, and regulation which is reasonable in relation to its subject and is adopted in the interests of the community *conforms to* due process." If this is a reasonable approximation of Hughes' thoughts, then it brings to a logical conclusion an argument the whole of which departs little, though a significant little, from the tradition that flowered on the *Slaughterhouse* decision.

That freedom of contract is not an absolute right Hughes was able to show by listing a large number of restrictions that had been upheld. That freedom of contract may be limited validly in circumstances such as the present, where the contracting parties were "unequal," he showed by reference to *Holden* v. *Hardy* and *Muller* v. *Oregon*. And that minimum-wage laws were as legitimate as maximum-hour laws he showed as well as he could, which was by quoting from and endorsing the dissenting opinions in the *Adkins* and *Morehead* cases. Besides, decisions since *Adkins*, such as *Nebbia*, showed that the Court would regard statutes regulating the use of private property as satisfying the due-process requirement if they have "a reasonable relation to a proper legislative purpose, and are neither arbitrary nor discriminatory." From all of which he concluded that the *Adkins* ruling could not be reconciled with the "well-considered declarations" in all the other cases.

Finally, almost as an afterthought, Hughes referred to "recent economic experience" as bearing on this case. Even though no "factual brief" had been presented in this case, the Court would take judicial notice of "the unparalleled demands for relief which arose during the recent period of depression." If employers were not forced to pay a decent minimum wage, taxpayers would have to make up the deficit. "The community is not bound to provide what is in effect a subsidy for unconscionable employers. The community may direct its lawmaking power to correct the abuse which springs from their selfish disregard of the public interest" (399–400).

Four justices—Sutherland, Van Devanter, McReynolds, and Butler—joined in a dissent which recapitulated the argument for the

Adkins rule and insisted on its constitutional soundness despite subsequent decisions and supervening economic events. "If the Constitution, intelligently and reasonably construed in the light of these principles, stands in the way of desirable legislation . . . the remedy in that situation—and the only true remedy—is to amend the Constitution" (404).

Surrounding circumstances gave the decision interest far beyond the relatively insignificant fact that it overruled the *Adkins* decision. The *West Coast Hotel* case was argued before the Court in December 1936. Since President Roosevelt assumed office in 1933, the Court had invalidated a number of New Deal measures, though it is often forgotten or treated as wholly exceptional that it upheld others. After Roosevelt was massively reelected in November 1936, he turned his attention to reforming the Court so as to prevent it from undoing his legislative program. He announced his plan on February 5, 1937, after the *West Coast Hotel* case had been heard by the Court and, some say, after it had been decided but before the Court announced its decision on March 29. Casual observers noticed that Justice Roberts, who had been with the majority in the *Morehead* case in June 1936, was with the majority in *West Coast Hotel* eight months later, and they took this to mean that Roberts had changed his mind. As this rather sudden change coincided with the announcement of the court-packing plan, it was labeled "the switch in time that saved nine."[32]

In a memorandum released for publication posthumously, Roberts explained that he voted as he did because he was convinced that the *Morehead* statute did fall under the *Adkins* rule but that the rule itself ought to be abandoned and, in short, that he had not "switched" in any but the most superficial sense of the word.[33] All of which had little bearing on the story of economic due process.

And so it seemed had the *West Coast Hotel* decision, for as far as anyone could tell at the time it only changed one rule, thus adding to the list of permissible regulatory statutes the one small item of wage fixing. But of course other things were happening as well. Be-

---

[32] C. Herman Pritchett, *The Roosevelt Court* (Chicago: Quadrangle Books, 1969), pp. 2–9.

[33] F. Frankfurter, "Mr. Justice Roberts," *University of Pennsylvania Law Review* 104 (1956): 311.

tween 1934 and 1936 the Court had upheld a few departures from
the traditional line, and after 1937 it began regularly to uphold a
new breed of regulations on the use of private property. In those
cases substantive due process was not so much deliberately overruled as quietly abandoned. If there was a formal death knell, it was
sounded in an obscure place, a footnote in a relatively uninteresting
case.

In 1938 the Court upheld a federal statute prohibiting interstate
trade in a milk substitute, in *U.S. v. Carolene Products.*[34] The defense hinged in part on denial of due process. Justice Stone, in the
majority's opinion, dismissed this argument with a pungent statement of the doctrine of presumption in favor of the legislature:
"regulatory legislation affecting ordinary commercial transactions is
not to be pronounced unconstitutional unless in the light of the facts
made known or generally assumed it is of such a character as to preclude the assumption that it rests upon some rational basis within
the knowledge and experience of the legislators" (152). Though
blunt, nothing very shocking could be detected in this. But to this
statement Stone attached a footnote, famous since as "Footnote 4,"
of which the first paragraph is said to have been drafted by Hughes
and the second and third by Stone's law clerk.[35] According to the
footnote, "There may be narrowed scope for operation of the presumption of constitutionality" as to legislation which appears on its
face to contravene specific provisions of the Constitution "such as
those of the first ten amendments"; such legislation might be subjected to "more exacting judicial scrutiny." That the separate paragraphs of the footnote are not perfectly dovetailed may be due to
mixed authorship, and certainly the whole is distinctly *obiter dictum,*
despite which it is the source from which has grown the doctrine
that political and personal rights enjoy a "preferred position."

II

Many have said that the Supreme Court in 1937 did away with
substantive due process, that the Court announced a new rule, a

[34] 304 U.S. 144 (1938).
[35] W. F. Murphy and C. H. Pritchett, *Courts, Judges, and Politics* (New
York: Random House, 1961), p. 635.

revolutionary departure from its previous tradition, according to which it would thereafter refrain from invalidating legislation except in instances where statutes could be demonstrated to be contrary to some specific constitutional guarantee—other than due process.

Anybody who reads the *West Coast Hotel* and *Carolene Products* decisions with the slightest care must conclude from the words (excluding *obiter dicta*) that the Court was deciding nothing more than the validity of the particular, narrow sorts of statutes before them at the time. But within the next ten or fifteen years the justices began to attribute a much wider significance to those decisions and some few others that followed. In 1951 Justice Douglas made a general pronouncement which has become famous with repetition: "Our recent decisions make plain that we do not sit as superlegislature to weigh the wisdom of legislation."[36] Such is the power of historical reconstruction that any number of judges and scholars accepted this as an accurate account of judicial history. Before 1937 the Court had willingly reviewed the wisdom (rather than as earlier justices fondly imagined, only the constitutionality) of statutes. From 1937 they rejected this role. In other words, they had abandoned substantive due process.

Even so keen and precise a scholar as Robert McCloskey misspoke himself about the character of the great change of 1937. In his justly famous article on "economic due process," he slipped into saying that "the whole doctrine of substantive due process was scheduled for destruction."[37] Other writers less careful than he have regularly spoken as though what went was the whole of substantive due process rather than only one part of it, which must be referred to either by the unbearably clumsy title of "economic substantive due process" or by the intolerable one of "substantive due process concerning property rights." Better to avoid confusing ourselves with such wads of adjectives. What the Supreme Court did was to stop overruling statutes regulating "property"—that is, the use of one's goods or one's labor. The Court did so little by little, until, after about ten years, all the justices began saying that they had done it

---

[36] 342 U.S. 421 (1951), p. 423.

[37] R. G. McCloskey, "Economic Due Process and the Supreme Court," in P. B. Kurland, ed., *The Supreme Court and the Constitution* (Chicago: University of Chicago Press, 1965), p. 161.

in a great sweep. They have tended ever since to say that of course they do not mean to sustain every exercise whatsoever of the legislative power, even in the economic realm, but so far their deeds have mainly belied their words. It would be rash to doubt that for the time being the Court will continue along the path taken in 1937.

If the Court had demolished economic due process in a great reversal, documented by an opinion arguing out its position in general terms, its subsequent stance could be better understood. As things happened otherwise, one is bound to wonder how the Court overcame one huge logical gap in its position on economic due process.

Substantive due process still stands. What this means is that the Court continues to maintain in force one of its oldest traditions of interpretation, namely, that the due-process clause may be offended against just as readily by a legislature as by a court or an executive official, and may be offended against even though the statute in question does not interfere with procedural due process, as for instance by establishing a presumption of guilt on arbitrary or unreasonable grounds.[38] In other words, the Court will invalidate statutes that deprive persons of "life or liberty" without due process of law. On what logical ground, then, was the Court able effectively to delete property from the literal text of the due-process clause?

Before trying to solve this puzzle, we should note a logical irregularity, not to say flaw, in the due-process clause itself. Life, liberty, and property are not mutually exclusive categories, nor are they of equal degrees of generality. Any person deprived of life is thereby deprived of all liberties and if deprived of property is deprived of one liberty or one set of related liberties. Liberty, therefore, comprehends life and property, and the last two terms are therefore redundant. But this does not justify excluding property from the total catalogue of liberties.

Stone's argument, in the *Carolene* footnote, suggests that "political rights" are more important than others because they "can ordinarily be expected to bring about repeal of undesirable legislation" (152–53). Imagination would not need to be stretched to say that property rights matter in "political processes"; it seems to be com-

---

[38] See, for instance, *Tot* v. *U.S.*, 319 U.S. 463 (1942).

mon ground that campaign contributions can influence the repeal of "undesirable legislation." On this ground a man's right to use his property ought to be recognized as a "political right." But that is an unnecessarily specialized argument. Why should a person's liberty to use goods be more subject to undue restriction than any other of his liberties? Who steals my purse steals not trash but in most cases something vital.

It would seem that the Court based its decision, so far as logic goes, on the distinction frequently made between "property rights" and "human rights." Every decent person naturally acknowledges that people should take precedence over things, and therefore that the rights of property must bow to the rights of human beings. The totally transparent vacuity of this argument has been summarized by Justice Stewart, for the Court, in a recent decision, wherein he said that the "dichotomy between personal liberties and property rights is a false one. Property does not have rights. People have rights. The right to enjoy property without unlawful deprivation, no less than the right to speak or the right to travel, is, in truth, a 'personal' right."[39] In other words, the Court's virtual deletion of property from the due-process clause stands on no defensible logical ground.

The revolution in economic due process must be explained by history. During the whole time, 1905 to 1937, when the Court was invalidating some state regulations of hours, wages, and the like, states were increasingly passing such regulations. This wave of economic legislation can be accounted for in many different ways, ranging from the extreme view that such legislation was imposed by objective needs to the opposite extreme that these laws were a pure expression of political theories. I believe the most accurate way to summarize the case is that from about 1870 Americans increasingly came to regard it as legitimate for government to further the interests of any and every interest group that could lawfully persuade a majority of the legislature to act in its favor. This is often described as "the democratic process," though one could make out an equally compelling case for the thesis that a democratic process should restrict its aims to furthering the common interest rather than special interests.

[39] *Lynch* v. *Household Finance*, 405 U.S. 538 (1972).

Be that as it may, legislatures did devote themselves with increasing fervor after 1870 to passing laws some of which the Court regarded as going beyond the limts of the police power. Especially after the great crash of 1929 and during the Great Depression, the Court felt itself to be in the midst of a constitutional crisis and gave way. Or, to be more precise, five of the nine old men thought it wise to give way, and, it should be added, did so because they were deeply convinced that the better legal and constitutional arguments were ranged on the side of giving ampler scope to legislatures. "Popular will" was presumed to infuse any action of a legislative majority —at least where "the channels of the democratic process remained unobstructed"—and was given full sway as to economic regulations, even though this necessarily meant that some few, and often indeed quite a few, individuals were deprived by it.

Since the outbreak of World War II, "popular will" has fallen into some disrepute, whereas the rights of individuals and minorities who suffer from the popular will have found an increasingly sympathetic hearing in the courts, as indeed they should. So it came about that in the *Gobitis* case, which concerned children of Jehovah's Witnesses who violated a law requiring them to salute the flag, Justice Stone—who had been a strong advocate of abandoning economic due process—wrote in dissent that to uphold that law seemed to him "no more than the surrender of the constitutional protection of the liberty of small minorities to the popular will."[40] Not long after, *Brown v. Board of Education* laid the foundation for a long series of decisions asserting the constitutional right of minorities as against statutes expressing the popular will, and other decisions such as *Griswold, Gideon,* and *Miranda* did the same in respect of other constitutional rights.

Despite which, when the Court encountered a case falling more or less squarely within the scope of economic due process, it tended still to presume heavily in favor of the legislature. In the *Day-Bright Lighting* case,[41] for instance, it upheld a Missouri statute providing that an employee could leave his work for four hours in order to vote in an election and that the employer must pay his normal wages for this interval just as though he had been at work. Justice Douglas for

[40] 310 U.S. 589 (1939), pp. 605–6.
[41] 342 U.S. 421 (1952).

the majority conceded that "the judgment of the legislature that time out for voting should cost the employee nothing may be a debatable one," but he held that the Court's refusal to act as a superlegislature meant that the Court would "leave debatable issues as respects business, economic, and social affairs to legislative decisions" (425). Justice Jackson, dissenting sharply, maintained that "there must be some limit to the power to shift the whole voting burden from the voter to someone else who happens to stand in some economic relation to him" (427). A similar decision was reached in the *Lee Optical* case in 1955.[42] In a few cases since then, though cases involving rather specialized tax questions, the Court has nevertheless held that statutes, despite the fact that they bore on property rights, were invalid for want of due process.[43]

Is there any ground for hope that economic due process may be revived, if only tacitly? There are a few slight signs that something of this sort may have begun. In 1957 the Court reversed a decision below excluding one Rudolph Schware from the Missouri bar on the grounds that having once been a Communist he was not of good moral character.[44] The court held that inasmuch as the standards applied by the bar examiners were arbitrary, they contravened the due-process clause. In a subsequent opinion, Justice Goldberg interpreted the *Schware* decision as meaning that "the Fourteenth Amendment protects from arbitrary state action the right to pursue an occupation, such as the practice of law."[45]

As the "right to pursue an occupation" or "a common calling" was one of the traditional components of economic due process, it may be that the *Schware* decision was a first step toward recovering the old principle. And of course one might suppose that when in 1948 the Court struck down restrictive covenants insofar as they prevented blacks from acquiring houses, it was striking a blow for property rights and "freedom of contract," even though it did not refer to the *Lochner* precedent or even to the Fourteenth Amendment as authority for that decision.[46] Again, in 1965, when declaring

42 348 U.S. 483 (1955).
43 *National Bellas Hess* v. *Department of Revenue*, 386 U.S. 753 (1967).
44 *Schware* v. *Board of Bar Examiners*, 353 U.S. 232 (1957).
45 381 U.S. 479, n. 1.
46 *Shelley* v. *Kraemer*, 334 U.S. 1 (1948).

unconstitutional a Connecticut birth-control statute, the Court went out of its way to emphasize that it did not rely on the *Lochner* rule —though in fact that precedent must still come unbidden into the mind of the Court whenever it invalidates a state law under the Fourteenth Amendment, even one such as the Virginia miscegenation act.[47] The fact is that the *Lochner* decision supplies the most natural, the most obviously logical, argument for invalidating arbitrary state laws, whatever their subject matter, and now that the Court knows itself to be ready to invalidate arbitrary state laws, and knows that evading the *Lochner* rule requires it to engage in quite extraordinary feats of circumnavigation, I believe that the spirit of the *Lochner* rule may be revived under some different name.

To suggest a hopeful possibility is pleasant. But the point of my review has been rather to show that while substantive due process remains in effect, economic due process does not; to indicate how and why it was dismantled; and to show that its destruction was justified not by any compelling constitutional argument but by a political theory that the Court itself has begun to question. Whether economic due process will be restored we cannot foretell, but it could be and should be.

The rule of law requires something more than rule by statutes rather than fiat; it requires that the statutes themselves should be rational and general, not arbitrary, capricious, whimsical, or discriminatory. To this general proposition American courts have always assented, although in the field of economic regulation they seem to have forgotten it.

[47] *Griswold* v. *Connecticut*, 381 U.S. 479 (1965); *Loving* v. *Virginia*, 388 U.S. 1 (1967).

3.

The Necessity of State Law

GOTTFRIED DIETZE

F. A. HAYEK's skepticism toward legislation must not conceal the fact that he attributes important functions to it. Since legislation constitutes part of state law, or *Staatsrecht*, as understood in a broad sense, Hayek, who as an "unrepentant Old Whig" never tires of emphasizing the danger of state law to the law state, or Staatsrecht to the *Rechtsstaat*, thus admits the importance of the former for the latter. Clearly distinguishing between *diritto, droit, Recht*, or (right) law, and *legge, loi, Gesetz*, or (not necessarily right) law, he goes out of his way to stress that the latter might not be identical, and might be indeed incompatible, with the former.[1] On the other hand, he also makes clear that the two may well be in harmony.

This is evident already in *The Road to Serfdom*: "The Rule of Law . . . implies limits to the scope of legislation: it restricts it to the kind of general rules known as formal law and excludes legislation directly aimed either at particular people or at enabling anybody to use the coercive power of the state for the purpose of such discrimination. It means, not that everything is regulated by law, but, on the contrary, that the coercive power of the state can be used only in cases defined in advance by the law and in such a way that it can be foreseen how it will be used. A particular enactment can thus infringe upon the Rule of Law."[2] It must not do so. As long as legislation establishes general rules known as formal law and is not directly aimed either at particular people or at enabling anybody to use the

---

This paper is part of a larger work, "Hayek on the Rule of Law," published in *Essays on Hayek* (New York: New York University Press, 1976).

[1] *Law, Legislation and Liberty* (Chicago: University of Chicago Press, 1973), vol. 1, *Rules and Order*, p. 94.

[2] *The Road to Serfdom* (Chicago: University of Chicago Press, 1944), pp. 83–84.

coercive power of the state for the purpose of such discrimination, it is compatible with the rule of law.

In his Cairo lectures, Hayek again attributes an important place to legislation. Together with adjudication, it will tend to approach the ideal of the rule of law "more and more."[3] This is evident when he discusses the generality, equality, and certainty of the law, the separation of powers, administrative discretion, legislation, and policy. He describes legislative acts "which decide about the use of the means which are put at the state's disposal" and "are in effect orders to its servants." He indicates regret that such acts "are also called laws" because they are not generally valid for everybody. On the other hand, some legislative acts constitute general rules and are "true laws in the specific sense in which we distinguish laws from orders." This kind of legislation is in conformity with the rule of law and is conducive to the freedom of the individual.[4]

The same applies to legislation that binds the administration: "It would certainly not be compatible with the Rule of Law if this was interpreted to mean that in its dealings with the private citizen the administration is not always subject to the law laid down by the legislature and applied by independent courts." The legislature may delegate powers to make rules for the protection of the individual from the administration to some other body. In that case, that body would act according to legislation which corresponds to the rule of law.[5] Finally, Hayek regrets that in current usage the distinction between legislation and policy is often obscured, writing that "there is good sense in it where the two concepts are deliberately contrasted." While he admits that in a certain sense legislation always involves policy, namely, long-run policy, he points to the danger of short-term policy, which is to be contrasted with legislation.[6]

In *The Constitution of Liberty* these remarks are repeated.[7] In a way that is reminiscent of Sir Edward Coke when he talks about the artificial reason of the law that has been built up over the ages

[3] *The Political Ideal of the Rule of Law* (Cairo: National Bank of Egypt, 1955), p. 33.

[4] Ibid., p. 35.

[5] Ibid., p. 38.

[6] Ibid., pp. 42–43.

[7] *The Constitution of Liberty* (Chicago: University of Chicago Press, 1960), pp. 211, 214–15.

by great jurists, Hayek writes that legislation has the important function of adding the contributions of speculative thinkers, after they
have passed through a long process of selection and modification in
the course of time, to the body of the law. He quotes at length
Dicey's classical description of lawmaking, according to which legislation reflects more than the desires of the day:

The opinion which changes the law is in one sense the opinion of the
time when the law is actually altered; in another sense it has often been
in England the opinion prevalent some twenty or thirty years before that
time; it has been as often as not in reality the opinion not of today but of
yesterday. . . . Legislative opinion must be the opinion of the day, because, when laws are altered, the alteration is of necessity carried into
effect by legislators who act under the belief that the change is an amendment; but this lawmaking opinion is also the opinion of yesterday, because
the beliefs which have at last gained such hold on the legislature as to
produce an alteration in the law have generally been created by thinkers
or writers, who exerted their influence long before the change in the law
took place. Thus it may well happen that an innovation is carried through
at a time when the teachers who supplied the arguments in its favor are
in their graves, or even—and this is well worth noting—when in the
world of speculation a movement has already set in against ideas which
are exerting their full effect in the world of action and of legislation.[8]

Legislation reveals the opinion of yesterday and can be recorded as
an amendment of the laws as they have existed for ages. Legislation
can be in the mainstream of the evolution of the rule of law and
make an important contribution to that rule.[9]

The title *Law, Legislation and Liberty* shows a fundamental
distinction between law and legislation. The first volume, *Rules and
Order*, devotes a chapter to "Nomos: The Law of Liberty" and one
to "Thesis: The Law of Legislation." The former is good. The latter,
bad, or at least dubious and quite possibly and probably at variance
with the law of liberty. This is the gist of these chapters. Yet in spite
of all emphasis upon the threat of legislation to the rule of law and
freedom, Hayek, in a chapter on the changing concept of the law,
shows why "grown law requires correction by legislation." He thus
admits the value of legislation in a way that reminds us of the ad-

[8] Quoted in ibid., p. 445, n. 15.
[9] Ibid., p. 113.

mission, centuries ago, of the value of equity as a corrective of the common law. He concedes that the "case for relying even in modern times for the development of law on the gradual process of judicial precedent and scholarly interpretation has been persuasively argued by the late Bruno Leoni, *Liberty and the Law* [Princeton, 1961]." Yet he does not agree with his friend Leoni, writing that "although his argument is an effective antidote to the prevailing orthodoxy which believes that only legislation can or ought to alter the law, it has not convinced me that we can dispense with legislation even in the field of private law with which it is chiefly concerned."[10]

Even the good law, arising out of the spontaneous endeavor to articulate rules of conduct, may "develop in very undesirable directions." And "when this happens correction by deliberate legislation may . . . be the only practicable way out." The spontaneous growth of the law "may lead into an impasse from which it cannot extricate itself by its own forces or which it will at least not correct quickly enough." He adds, "The development of case law is in some respects a sort of one-way street: when it has already moved a considerable distance in one direction, it often cannot retrace its steps when some implications of earlier decisions are seen to be clearly undesirable. The fact that law that has evolved in this way has certain desirable properties does not prove that it will always be good law or even that some of its rules may not be very bad. It therefore does not mean that we can altogether dispense with legislation." Hayek even goes so far as to admit the necessity of "radical changes of particular rules" by legislation.[11] He thus seems to come close to the idea of a "motorized lawmaker."[12]

The need for legislation follows from various considerations. One is the slow and gradual process of judicial development, which precludes a rapid adaptation of the law to wholly new circumstances, something Hayek considers desirable. The legislature must become active here, because the judges should use restraint in reversing "a development, which has already taken place and is then seen to have

[10] *Rules and Order*, p. 168, n. 35.
[11] Ibid., pp. 88–89.
[12] Compare the author's *In Defense of Property* (Chicago: Henry Regnery, 1963), p. 152.

undesirable consequences or to be downright wrong. . . . The judge
is not performing his function if he disappoints reasonable expectations created by earlier decisions." The judge ought to develop the
law, not to alter it, at least not rapidly. Although the judge "may
clearly recognize that another rule would be better, or more just, it
would evidently be unjust to apply it to transactions which had
taken place when a different rule was regarded as valid." Therefore,
a new rule should be made known through legislation, fulfilling the
proper function of all law, that of guiding expectations.

Hayek reveals himself as a liberal rather than a conservative
when he stresses the liberating effect of legislation. More effectively
than judicial decisions, legislation may do away with injustices
caused by the fact that "the development of the law has lain in the
hands of members of a particular class whose traditional views made
them regard as just what could not meet the more general requirements of justice." In an obvious agreement with Marx, the honorary
president of the Mont Pelerin Society writes that the law on the relations between master and servant, landlord and tenant, creditor
and debtor, organized business and its customers, has been shaped
in large measure by the views of the parties and their particular interests, especially in the first two instances, with masters and land-
lords almost exclusively supplying the judges. While he takes issue
with Kelsen's assertion that "justice is an irrational ideal" and that
"from the point of rational cognition there are only interests of human beings and hence conflicts of interests," Hayek admits that the
interests of ruling groups may bring about law that, incompatible
with justice and not measuring up to the ideal of the rule of law,
should be quickly replaced by legislation that corresponds to that
ideal.[13]

The age of democracy is an age of legislation because legislation
makes up the bulk of democratic law. It constitutes an important
part of modern state law and, as Hayek pointed out again and again,
a great threat to freedom and the rule of law.[14] However, as he has
also shown, legislation can be an essential support of liberalism and
the Rechtsstaat. Hayek praises legislation while he condemns it. This
is not surprising. Although Hayek distinguishes *isonomia* or the rule

[13] *Rules and Order*, pp. 88–89.
[14] See ibid., pp. 121–22, 129–33.

of law and liberalism from democracy[15] and emphasizes that democratic development can be and has been a threat to the rule of law and to freedom, he also leaves no doubt that democratic development can be and has been an important part of the evolution of liberty and the rule of law. Stressing that "democracy is a means rather than an end," Hayek sees

three chief arguments by which democracy can be justified, each of which may be regarded as conclusive. . . . The first is that, whenever it is necessary that one of several conflicting opinions should prevail and when one would have to be made to prevail by force if need be, it is less wasteful to determine which has the stronger support by counting numbers than by fighting. Democracy is the only method of peaceful change that man has yet discovered.[16]

The second argument is that "democracy is an important safeguard of individual liberty" and that "the prospects of individual liberty are better in a democracy than under other forms of government." The third, and to Hayek the most powerful, argument is that the existence of democratic institutions will improve the general level of understanding of public affairs. Agreeing with Tocqueville's "great work, *Democracy in America*," he writes that "democracy is the only effective method of educating the majority." The liberal who rejects conservatism because it is static feels that democracy as a process of forming opinion must be given preference over a government by an elite which may be all too static, that the value of democracy proves itself in its dynamic aspects. At the end of his chief arguments in favor of democracy, Hayek ties up that form of government with liberty: "As is true of liberty, the benefits of democracy will show themselves only in the long run, while its more immediate achievements may well be inferior to those of other forms of government."[17]

To Hayek, then, democracy may well be conducive to freedom and the rule of law. In other words, the state law (Staatsrecht) of liberal democracy, irrespective of whether it has grown slowly through custom or judicial decisions or been enacted by legislatures,

[15] *The Political Ideal of the Rule of Law; The Constitution of Liberty*, esp. pp. 54–56, 103–4, 106, 162–219; "The Principles of a Liberal Social Order," in *Studies in Philosophy, Politics and Economics* (Chicago: University of Chicago Press, 1967), p. 161.
[16] *The Constitution of Liberty*, p. 107.
[17] Ibid., pp. 107–9.

can favor the law state, or Rechtsstaat, and its far-reaching realization of freedom.

Hayek goes further than maintaining that the law of the state can aid the rule of law. To him, Staatsrecht is a prerequisite for the Rechtsstaat.

One concept is a sine qua non for the other: its tangible, concrete aspect is necessary for the realization of the ideal or part of it. The rule of law implies not merely a restriction of the government for the sake of the individual through the law. Law, as distinguished from ethics and morals, implies sanction by the government vis-a-vis individuals. So does "rule." Law being an ethical minimum,[18] it is the very essence of that minimum that it is enforceable. In view of the fact that all law in one way or another measures and restricts, law implies the absence of license. Although freedom is the predominant value in Hayek's social thought,[19] Hayek is not inclined toward anarchy. The latter word does not appear in the index to *The Road to Serfdom* or in that to *The Constitution of Liberty*.[20] Hayek wants freedom under law. True freedom must be something tangible that cannot really exist without the protection of the laws. While the rule of the law of the state, just as the empire of men of which James Harrington spoke,[21] can and does infringe the freedom of the individual, that freedom—that is, what remains of it in society—is protected by virtue of the law. It is the law that transforms parts of the general, vague, and intangible concept of freedom into specific and clearly defined tangible rights the individual can claim. As the title of his book shows, Hayek does not believe only in liberty. He believes in the constitution of liberty. He prefers a constituted liberty to a nonconstituted one, even though the former may not be a transmutation into the reality of freedom in its totality. Hayek favors a liberal constitution, a liberal order. To him, order is the prerequisite for freedom. While freedom is the great ideal that hovers over the legal order and always prompts that order to become more free, the legal order is the realization, if only partial, of the ideal. Hayek, per-

---

[18] See Georg Jellinek, *Die sozialethische Bedeutung von Recht, Unrecht und Strafe*, 2d ed. (Berlin: D. Häring, 1908), p. 45.

[19] See *The Constitution of Liberty*, pp. 107–11.

[20] *Rules and Order* contains an index of names only.

[21] James Harrington, *The Commonwealth of Oceana* (London, 1656), p. 2.

haps in Hegelian measure, deems the real the rational.[22] The genuine liberal realizes that it is reasonable to accept the authority of the state, while always being wary of its power. *Potestas* is dangerous. *Auctoritas* is necessary.

Different as they are, authority and power will usually coexist. Even the most powerful government will possess some legitimate authority, just as even under the most liberal regimes there will be some aspects of power. The liberal aristocrat Friedrich August von Hayek expresses his kinship to liberals such as Burke and de Tocqueville.[23] These men expressed serious misgivings about the French Revolution, an event that challenged royal absolutism and monarchical power. It is an interesting question whether Hayek resents revolution as a means for absolutely destroying an existing legal order for the sake of freedom. He shows his admiration for Schiller, author of *Die Räuber* and *Wilhelm Tell*, dramas in which legal orders based upon men's law are challenged by an appeal to the immutable rights of men that are, as it says in *Wilhelm Tell*, "hanging in heaven."[24] At the same time, Hayek often quotes Schiller's friend Goethe, who, while he confessed that he could imagine having committed every crime, observed when he saw innocent people hurt by the police in a riot that it was better having injustice than disorder. Hayek mentions revolutions against regimes in which power and abuses of power were more obvious than authority, such as the revolutions against Charles I and Louis XVI.[25] Yet, although he seems to be sympathetic to such revolutions, he seems not to come out with a plain statement proposing a right of revolution.

This is obvious also from what he writes at the end of *The Constitution of Liberty*, in the chapter "Why I Am Not a Conservative," under the subtitle "A New Appeal to the Old Whigs." He agrees with Lord Acton that "the notion of a higher law above municipal codes, with which Whiggism began, is the supreme achievement of Englishmen and their bequest to the nation," and, Hayek adds, "to the world." He writes that in "its pure form it is represented in the

22 The liberalism of Hegel is brought out in Carl J. Friedrich's introduction to his edition of *The Philosophy of Hegel* (New York: Modern Library, 1954).

23 *The Constitution of Liberty*, p. 407.

24 *Wilhelm Tell*, act 2, sc. 2.

25 *The Constitution of Liberty*, pp. 168, 194–95.

United States, not by the radicalism of Jefferson, nor by the conservatism of Hamilton or even John Adams, but by the ideas of
James Madison, the 'father of the Constitution.' "[26] From this statement it can be concluded that Hayek, while he believes in higher
law as a constant guide for the improvement of municipal law and
believes change according to higher law justified for the sake of freedom, is reluctant to accept radical change. This is not surprising in
a man who believes that the large body of the law of an existing
legal order has grown gradually.

Difficult as it is to answer the question whether Hayek favors
revolution as a means for the absolute destruction of an order characterized by the abuse of power and the absence of the freedom of
the individual, there is not much doubt that his admission of the
necessity of authority in a liberal state, his emphasis upon the constitution of liberty, makes him reluctant to want radical change in a
society that is predominantly liberal. He favors Madison, the great
compromiser,[27] over Jefferson, Hamilton, and John Adams. For the
sake of order, he is willing to make compromises at the cost of liberty, realizing that liberty, to be useful to men, must be protected by
a legal order.

In *The Road to Serfdom*, Hayek stated: "Within the known
rules of the game the individual is free to pursue his personal ends
and desires."[28] Known rules can restrict freedom. In 1953 Hayek
voiced approval of Louis Philippe's formulation of an idea of Benjamin Constant's, according to which liberty exists only under the
law, and everybody must do what the law requires.[29] His third Cairo
lecture, entitled "The Safeguards of Individual Liberty," was a lecture under Ortega's motto, "Order is not a pressure imposed upon
society from without, but an equilibrium which is set up from with-

[26] Ibid., p. 409.

[27] Compare Alpheus T. Mason, *Free Government in the Making* 3d ed.
(New York: Oxford University Press, 1965), pp. 189, 250–51, 312–13.

[28] *The Road to Serfdom*, p. 73.

[29] "Entstehung und Verfall des Rechtsstaatsideales," in Albert Hunold, ed.,
Wirtschaft ohne Wunder (Zurich: E. Rentsch, 1953), p. 49: "La liberté ne con-
siste que dans le règne des lois. Que chacun ne puisse être tenu de faire autre
chose que ce que la loi exige de lui, et qu'il puisse faire tout ce que la loi
n'interdit pas, telle est la liberté. C'est vouloir la detruire de vouloir autre
chose."

in." Here he first discusses "Law and Order" as a prerequisite for liberty, making plain that order exists not merely as a result of human design, but also as a result of human action.[30]

In *The Constitution of Liberty* Hayek devotes a chapter to "Responsibility and Freedom," writing:

Liberty and responsibility are inseparable. A free society will not function or maintain itself unless its members regard it as right that each individual occupy the position that results from his action and accept it as due to his own action. Though it can offer to the individual only chances and though the outcome of his efforts will depend on innumerable accidents, it *forcefully directs* his attention to those circumstances that he can control as if they were the only ones that mattered.[31]

He continues with regret: "This belief in individual responsibility, which has always been strong when people firmly believed in individual freedom, has markedly declined, together with the esteem for freedom. Responsibility has become an unpopular concept, a word that experienced speakers or writers avoid because of the obvious boredom or animosity with which it is received by a generation that dislikes all moralizing." While responsibility "means an unceasing task, a discipline that man must impose upon himself if he is to achieve his aims,"[32] it also implies responsibility toward others. It means obedience to the laws. The latter idea is elaborated in the chapter "Coercion and the State."[33] Finally, of his last work Hayek says: "The central concept around which the discussion of this book will turn is that of order. . . . Order is an indispensable concept. . . . We cannot do without it."[34]

The concessions the responsible unrepentant Old Whig is willing to make to the liberal order at the expense of freedom are manifold. They can be found with respect to individual rights and various concepts he believes to be conducive to liberty. They range from permitting the state to control weights and measures, to prevent fraud, deception, and violence, and to make building regulations and

[30] *The Political Ideal of the Rule of Law*, pp. 29–32. Compare Hayek's essay, "The Results of Human Action but not of Human Design," in *Studies in Philosophy, Politics and Economics.*
[31] *The Constitution of Liberty*, p. 71. (Emphasis supplied.)
[32] Ibid., pp. 71–72.
[33] Ibid., pp. 133–147.
[34] *Rules and Order*, p. 35.

factory laws,[35] to allowing the state to tax individuals and require them to do military service, and to the general right of the government to build up an organization in order to preserve internal peace and to keep out external enemies.[36]

Hayek believes that a spontaneous order is more conducive to liberty than an imposed one. Yet, for the sake of order, he refrains from denying that the latter and its laws should be complied with.[37] The same applies to the law that comes about through evolution and one that is the result of "reason": the law produced by human action and the law produced by human design.[38] Hayek laments that during the last generation, private law has been increasingly replaced by public law, the former aiding, the latter threatening, liberty.[39] Yet he does not urge disobedience to public law. He complains that law in the sense of general rules is being challenged by law in the sense of organizational orders.[40] Yet, while he sees the latter as a danger to liberty, he does not want it disobeyed. He feels that law based upon just principles is better for freedom than law based upon expediency.[41] However, the latter must be obeyed. He distinguishes between *nomos*, the law of liberty, and *thesis*, the law of legislation. There is no doubt about the greater liberal content of the former,[42] but Hayek wants the latter to be complied with all the same.

The willingness to compromise at the cost of freedom does not necessarily compromise freedom. On the contrary, it serves liberty by securing its protection through laws that reflect reason. "Though the sentiments which are expressed in such terms as the 'dignity of man' and the 'beauty of liberty' are noble and praiseworthy, they can have no place in an attempt at rational persuasion," he writes in the

---

[35] *The Road to Serfdom*, p. 81.

[36] *The Constitution of Liberty*, p. 143; *Rules and Order*, p. 124.

[37] *The Political Ideal of the Rule of Law*, pp. 29–32; *The Constitution of Liberty*, pp. 148–61; "Principles of a Liberal Social Order."

[38] "Principles of a Liberal Social Order"; *Rules and Order*, pp. 8–34; "The Results of Human Action but not of Human Design."

[39] *The Constitution of Liberty*, pp. 205–49; "Principles of a Liberal Social Order."

[40] *The Road to Serfdom*, pp. 72–87; *The Constitution of Liberty*, pp. 148–61; "Principles of a Liberal Social Order"; *Rules and Order*, pp. 94–144.

[41] *Rules and Order*, pp. 55–71.

[42] Ibid., pp. 94–144.

introduction to *The Constitution of Liberty*.[43] He wants to promote freedom rationally—through the law, the law of the state, the *Staatsrecht*. In doing so, the unrepentant Old Whig is an adamant advocate of law and order. He follows those who before him believed in the *Rechtsstaat* with its maximal realization of liberty. To Hayek, freedom ought to be the spirit of the laws, which alone can transform that spirit into true rights of man.

Hayek's ideas on the rule of law reveal him as a man of measure.

As we are close to the bicentennial of the publication of that seminal work, *The Wealth of Nations*, Hayek's thoughts on legality remind us of Adam Smith as well as Montesquieu. The measure implied in the balance of powers made the great Frenchman, often considered the father of constitutionalism, famous. Measure is also characteristic of the great Scotsman, in whom many see the founder of political economy and economic liberalism. Like Hayek, Smith saw, and Montesquieu before him, in the rule of law a means for the promotion of freedom. For Smith, justice implied the liberation of man from private as well as public oppression. Yet, despite his emphasis upon liberty, Smith is careful not to lean toward anarchy. He is convinced that the wealth of nations can be increased by the freedom of the individual rather than by his regulation and regimentation. At the same time, he admits controls here and there for what he deems the good of the society and its members. And he leaves no doubt that justice implies the protection of citizens from their fellow men through the government's enforcement of the laws.

Both Montesquieu and Smith had a great impact upon the development of the United States. The American Revolution was a continuation of the Whig revolution and was characterized by measure. Independence was declared on account of the excesses of monarchy. The Constitution was a reaction to democratic extremes. The founders' ideal was free government, a popular government under which the majority, while ruling, was for the sake of the individual limited by law which, for the citizen's safety, had to be strictly enforced. This was constitutionalism, which Hayek regards as "The American Contribution."

[43] *The Constitution of Liberty*, p. 6.

Hayek, in recognition of the lawful principle *in dubio pro reo*, has always given with *noblesse* and in good scholarly fashion, his opponents the benefit of the doubt: he has given to his works mottoes drawn from that man of measure, Goethe; he addressed *The Road to Serfdom* to the socialists of all parties. In addressing *The Constitution of Liberty* to the unknown civilization now arising in America, that liberal aristocrat hoped that men would not once more lose that sense of measure but again respect the rule of law.

4.

The Limits of Libertarianism

ROLF SARTORIUS

ROBERT NOZICK's *Anarchy, State, and Utopia*[1] is surely the most provocative defense of a libertarian political philosophy to appear since F. A. Hayek's masterful *The Constitution of Liberty*.[2] The conception of the state defended by Nozick is that of a voluntary association which would protect the liberty of all within a given geographical territory by exercising an effective monopoly of the use of coercive force. The extent of governmental interference with individual liberty which this would itself require, Nozick argues, might be kept to such a minimum that nobody's moral rights would be violated in the process. Such a minimal state, precluded in particular from engaging in the forms of compulsory redistribution required to finance the programs of the modern welfare state, is meant, on the one hand, to overcome the anarchist's objections to government and, on the other hand, to provide the framework within which a variety of utopian conceptions might be freely experimented with. Nozick's vision of a free society, achieving social progress by depending upon private market mechanisms protected by government rather than upon paternalistic policies funded through compulsory taxation, is strikingly similar to Hayek's model of a civilization free to develop under the rule of law. Although Nozick acknowledges his considerable intellectual debt to Hayek in numerous places, there is an equally striking and fundamental difference between their versions of a free society. For Nozick, there are no exceptions to the principle that the state may employ coercion only to prevent coercion.[3]

---

[1] New York: Basic Books, 1974.

[2] Chicago: University of Chicago Press, 1960.

[3] This is a bit too simplistic to capture Nozick's views; it is meant merely to reflect the character of the difference in their positions in a sharp way.

Hayek, although not without reservations, concedes the necessity of government's resorting to compulsory taxation in order to finance the provision of essential social services that will not appear in the palm of the invisible hand which guides the operation of private market mechanisms.

The noncoercive or purely service activities that government undertakes are usually financed by coercive means. The medieval state, which financed its activities mainly with the income from its property, might have provided services without resorting to coercion. Under modern conditions, however, it seems hardly practicable that government should provide such services . . . without relying on its coercive powers to finance them.[4]

To this . . . group belong all those services which are clearly desirable but which will not be provided by competitive enterprises because it would be either impossible or difficult to charge the individual beneficiary for them.[5]

It is not to be expected that there will ever be complete unanimity on the desirability of the extent of such services, and it is at least not obvious that coercing people to contribute to the achievement of ends in which they are not interested can be morally justified.[6]

Hayek's own reservations might be taken to indicate the only stance that can be taken by the consistent libertarian, one which reflects Nozick's view that compulsory taxation is a form of theft in that it is a morally impermissible violation of people's rights not to be deprived of their property without their consent. Must not the libertarian position be that such services must either be provided by private market mechanisms, whatever the difficulties, or—if this is impossible—be forgone by the people, however regrettable that may be, unless the services are made available through private philanthropy? The difficulty with this approach, I suggest, is this: among the services of which Hayek is speaking is the provision of public goods that are not only desirable but essential, yet some of them are services that no rationally self-interested and moral individuals would have a motive to contribute to. They are services of a kind which, if they are available to some, are available to all free of

4 Hayek, *The Constitution of Liberty*, p. 144.
5 Ibid., p. 223.
6 Ibid., p. 144.

charge. Each, attempting to go for a free ride, will find that there is no ride to be taken at all. Might not Nozick "bite the bullet" in such cases and simply admit that there are certain public goods, no matter how "essential," which libertarians must do without for the sake of liberty? Only, I shall argue, if libertarians are to remain anarchists in the state of nature, for among the public goods in question is the provision of protection, the very function in terms of which Nozick's minimal state is defined!

Let me begin by describing the public-goods problem in full generality, and in a manner which I hope will be of some independent interest. I shall then turn to a sketch of Nozick's overall argument, and next indicate where and why I believe free-rider problems arise within his theory of the minimal state. I shall conclude with some remarks concerning the ways in which his views might be modified in order to meet these difficulties.

There are numerous instances in which voluntary cooperation among a number of individuals would be sufficient, and might be necessary, to achieve shared social goals. Some familiar and important examples are prevention of inflation, preservation of scarce natural resources, control of population growth, and widespread political participation in a democratic society.

In spite of the important differences among them, these examples share the following significant features: (1) Properly coordinated actions by some but not all of the members of a group are sufficient to provide each member of the group with a social good which each desires. (2) If the good in question is actually produced, its availability to some assures its availability to all, even those who did not contribute to providing it (jointness of supply). (3) It is either practically impossible or not worth the costs to exclude free riders (non-excludability), and in some cases those who would prefer not to go for the ride at all cannot even exclude themselves. The last two features are usually taken to define the class of public goods, as opposed to private goods, which individuals may purchase and enjoy to the exclusion of others. Contrary to what is often implied by writers on the subject, the possibility of voluntary collective action leading to the provision of a public good does not necessarily create a free-rider problem; as in the case of conventions that represent solutions to pure coordination problems, each individual might prefer to co-operate contingently upon others doing so.[7] Indeed, unless coupled with the first feature, these two features do not even assure us that a public good is not a public evil; polluted as well as unpolluted air exhibits jointness and nonexcludability. The problematic aspect shared by our examples arises only when we add the following. (4) The required form of social cooperation is burdensome; it represents the assumption of real costs by the individuals in question. (5) The potential value of the collective benefit to each individual is greater than his fair share of the total costs of the cooperation required to provide it. Our question is this: What constitutes rational and moral voluntary individual behavior in social situations in which all of these features are present?

First let us consider how the rationally self-interested individual, calculating only his own costs and benefits and motivated by moral considerations only to the extent that he will act so as not to violate the rights of others, would view the choice between coopera-tion and noncooperation. If a collective benefit that is also a public good is available within a given group, it is available to any par-ticular member free of charge. No significant further benefit would accrue to an individual by his voluntarily sharing in the costs of pro-viding it; the costs of cooperation, on the other hand, would be sig-nificant. Where a public good is available to an individual, rational self-interest dictates that he be a free rider. If the public good is not available, and the individual is not in a position to provide it by act-ing unilaterally (either because this is impossible or because the costs of doing so would outweigh the benefits), acting cooperatively would simply be a wasted effort. Thus, either way, rational self-interest calls for noncooperation. Each individual reasoning in this way of course leads to none cooperating and the good not being pro-vided at all, even though this means that all members of the group are worse off than they would have been had they acted otherwise. The individual members of a group that fails to provide itself with a collective benefit in this way are in an n-person prisoners' dilemma.

The choice situation for each individual may be represented in terms of the possible outcomes of the alternative decisions to coop-

[7] See David Lewis, *Convention* (Cambridge, Mass.: Harvard University Press, 1969).

erate or not to cooperate, where it is assumed that others' cooperation is sufficient to assure the production of the public good in question and their noncooperation its nonproduction:

OTHERS

	Cooperate	*Do Not Cooperate*
Cooperate	Benefits of G	Costs of cooperation
	Costs of cooperation	No benefits
INDIVIDUAL		
Do Not Cooperate	Benefits of G	No costs
	No costs	No benefits

Given the facts that the benefits of the public good (G) are of positive value for the individual, and that the costs of cooperation are of
negative value, the rationally self-interested maximizer of expected
value must have the following preferences over the possible outcomes (expressed in descending rank order):

OTHERS

	Cooperate	*Do Not Cooperate*
Cooperate	2	4
INDIVIDUAL		
Do Not Cooperate	1	3

In the parlance of the decision theorist, the point is that, for
each individual, noncooperation strictly dominates cooperation; regardless of how others are behaving, noncooperation is that which
maximizes expected value. The situation in which all choose not to
cooperate (the lower righthand cell in the matrix) is a strongly stable
equilibrium point; it is the best strategy choice for each individual
against whatever choices are made by others. But as there is a situation (the upper lefthand cell in the matrix) that each would prefer
to it and that could have been brought about by appropriately coordinated individual choices, the outcome is not Pareto-optimal. This
matrix, as defined by the order of preferences represented within it,
has been shown to be the only two-by-two matrix having this unfor-

tunate combination of properties; that is, a strongly stable equilibrium point which is not Pareto-optimal.[8] All can realize that each
will be worse off than he might otherwise be, but this will not provide any individual with a reason to change his choice from noncooperation to cooperation. They must, much like Hobbesian individuals unable rationally to contract themselves out of a state of nature
and into civil society, forgo the benefits of those public goods whose
creation depends upon their mutual cooperation.

Having mentioned the notion of a contract, we should pause
here to consider what difference, if any, would result if the individuals in question were in a position to enter into binding agreements,
either because of the existence of some reliable mechanism for the
enforcement of promises or because of their recognition of a moral
obligation to keep promises. Might not each agree to cooperate contingently upon others doing likewise? Not if each reasons that either
enough others so agree and the public good thus becomes available
to him free of charge, or enough others do not and thus there would
have been no point to agreeing in the first place. Agreement to cooperate in providing a public good is itself, in short, a public good,
and the dilemma of collective action can arise with respect to it. As
Nozick himself notes:

It will be in the interests of any individual to refrain from otherwise
unanimous agreements in the state of nature: for example, the agreement
to set up a state. . . . Any contract which really needs almost unanimity,
any contract which is essentially joint, will serve its purpose whether or
not a given individual participates; so it will be in his interests not to bind
himself to participate.[9]

Does not this dilemma depend upon people acting selfishly? And
might not we (including Nozick) consider what the situation would
be like if people were morally required to act benevolently (at least
as long as this would not violate anyone's rights)? In *The Logic of
Collective Action*, Mancur Olson states what I believe has come to
be the prevailing view: "Even if the member of a large group were
to neglect his own interests entirely, he would still not rationally

---

[8] See the references in Russell Hardin, "Collective Action as an Agreeable
n-Person Prisoners' Dilemma," *Behavioral Science* 16 (September 1971).

[9] Nozick, *Anarchy, State, and Utopia*, pp. 90, 472–81.

contribute toward the provision of any collective or public good, since his own contribution would not be perceptible."[10]

Brian Barry has called attention to a difficulty with this position: "If each contribution is literally 'imperceptible' how can all the contributions together add up to anything?"[11] Barry's point, I take it, is that benevolent men, moved by a sense of community, would calculate the benefits of a public good in terms of the entire group to which it would be available. Although the difference that any individual's contribution would make with respect to the level at which the good was provided might be very small, it must nonetheless make a difference, and since the number of people to whom it would make such a difference would be very large, cooperation would be called for on the basis of a calculation of expected utility.

The disagreement between Olson and Barry may, I believe, be resolved along the following lines: Cooperation in providing a public good will be required of benevolent men when, and only when, no strong threshold effects are involved, threshold effects being those consequences of individual action which arise or fail to arise depending upon whether or not a sufficient number of others are acting in the appropriate way. Consider, for example, two public-goods aspects of the problems surrounding fuel consumption: price inflation and the possibility of the imposition of gasoline rationing. If we assumed that our monetary unit was infinitely divisible, price theory would tell us that, with supply held constant, price will vary continuously with demand. An individual's decision to refrain from consuming those extra gallons of fuel oil per month required to heat his home to a very comfortable seventy degrees Fahrenheit rather than a merely comfortable sixty-eight degrees would thus (in theory) make a small difference, to be sure, but one which would extend to millions of people. So, perhaps, as benevolent men, we are morally required to turn our thermostats down two degrees this winter. Let us also suppose that there is some point at which high levels of consumption would produce such scarcity that the government would impose gasoline rationing. Is this also a reason why I should turn my

[10] Cambridge, Mass.: Harvard University Press, 1965, p. 64.
[11] *Sociologists, Economists and Democracy* (London: Collier-Macmillan, 1970), p. 32.

thermostat down? I think not. Whatever the threshold point which would have to be crossed before rationing would be imposed, the likelihood of my level of consumption determining whether or not it is crossed is virtually nil. If this were the only aspect of the problem, each consumer would quite rightly reason that either enough others were "cooperating" so as to avoid rationing or that they were not; either way, the rational and "noncooperative" decision must be to wait and see, and remain very comfortable at seventy degrees in the meantime.[12] Where strong threshold effects are involved, even those motivated by considerations of benevolence may have no reason to cooperate in providing public goods. (And I of course plan to argue that strong threshold effects are of overriding significance with respect to those public goods which are associated with the functions of Nozick's minimal state.)

As suggested earlier, in some situations a particular individual might be in a position to produce a given public good all by himself. The self-interested individual will do so where the benefits to him outweigh the costs; the benevolent man will do so when the benefits to the entire group outweigh his private costs. Both sorts of cases do arise, although we are of course often in no position to know whether the actions of a public benefactor are selfishly motivated or represent an instance of genuine philanthropy. (Such institutional mechanisms as tax deductions for charitable contributions muddy the waters, and may, perhaps, be understood as deliberately designed to do so.)

It must also be noted that behind the construction of the matrix representing the dilemma of collective action lies the assumption that the cooperation of a sufficient number of others to produce the public good in question exists or does not exist independently of the decision of the individual to cooperate or not to cooperate. Although this is typically the case, especially with regard to the kinds of cases with which we are primarily concerned, it surely need not be.[13] A particular individual may be in a position to set an example that

---

[12] On the threshold involved with an individual's likelihood of casting a swing vote in a national election, see Paul Meehl, "The Selfish Voter Paradox and the Throw-Away Vote Argument," *The American Political Science Review* 71, No. 1 (March 1977): 11–30.

[13] This point is elaborated upon in James Buchanan, "Ethical Rules, Expected Values, and Large Numbers," *Ethics* 76, No. 1 (October 1965): 1–13.

others, for whatever reasons, will be inclined to follow. In theory, a given individual might be able to attach specific values to the probabilities of his cooperation or noncooperation setting an example that would be followed by a sufficient number of others so as to lead to the production of a particular public good. Taking into account the costs of cooperation, the value of the public good, and the probabilities of others following the examples of cooperation or noncooperation, cooperation might be called for as that which would maximize expected utility. On the assumptions that the value of the public good would outweigh the cost to the individual of contributing to its production, and that others would in fact follow whatever he set by way of an example, cooperation would be required of either the self-interested or the benevolent individual, for his choice would be tantamount to one between the upper lefthand cell of the matrix and the cell in the lower right, and it is the former that ranks higher in his order of preferences. Examples in which the cooperation or noncooperation of some is likely to influence the behavior of others do abound, but they surely do not typify those cases in which large numbers of people are involved.

Although more controversial, there are other candidates for moral principles that might suffice to motivate voluntary cooperation in the production of public goods and that might be acceptable to Nozick as long as they did not require individuals to act in a way which would violate anyone's rights. Three such principles (or families of principles) merit serious attention: those of universalization, fair play, and justice.

The criticism and justification of action from a moral point of view often seem to rely upon the rhetorical thrust of this question, But what if everyone did that? The implication is that an individual ought to recognize good reasons for or against a particular action simply upon the basis of a consideration of what the consequences would be if others were to act in a similar way. A principle of utilitarian universalization or generalization might be put as follows: An act, X, is morally right, other things being equal, if it is a kind of act that, done by everyone under similar circumstances, would have consequences at least as good as those resulting from everyone's performing any alternative act under those circumstances.

Principles such as this, including variants of Kant's categorical imperative,[14] could be invoked to require cooperation in producing public goods because they do not permit the individual to argue that his contribution to such production would be insignificant, or that the benefits in question would be available to him (if at all) whether or not he cooperated in the production. The modes of reasoning that produce the dilemma of collective action are blocked by these principles because they do not require the individual to determine the rightness or wrongness of a particular act of cooperation or noncooperation on the basis of its likely consequences, whether assessed from a self-interested or from a benevolent point of view or not. Rather, these principles require the agent to consider what the consequences would be if everyone acted in a certain way. An individual who accepted such principles would have quite different preferences over the outcomes representing the possible results of cooperation or noncooperation in producing a public good from what the self-interested or benevolent man would have. Individual preferences again expressed in descending rank order, cooperation would now strictly dominate noncooperation rather than vice versa:

OTHERS

	Cooperate	*Do Not Cooperate*
Cooperate	1	2
INDIVIDUAL		
Do Not Cooperate	3	4

In spite of their initial appeal and their ability to provide a basis for requiring cooperation of the sort that would lead to the production of public goods, generalization principles of the kind under consideration have, I believe, inescapable difficulties of the most general sort.

The principles base the morality of any specific act on an evaluation of the consequences of everyone's performing similar acts under similar circumstances. But when are acts and circumstances relevantly similar? In particular, in describing acts and distinguishing them for the purposes of these principles, is it permissible to in-

---

[14] Attempts to defend Kantian versions of universalization principles continue to be made, but have yet to meet with any success.

clude in the description of the act or its surrounding circumstances a specification of the way in which others are behaving or are likely to behave? If the answer is in the affirmative, it may be demonstrated that the principles generate the same dilemma of collective action as do those which simply require the direct maximization of welfare. If in the negative, it may be shown that the principles have absurd consequences because the rightness or wrongness of particular acts often does hinge upon the manner in which others are behaving.[15]

Suppose the principles do permit one to consider how others are behaving, and that it is cooperation, C, in producing a public good, G, that is in question. Suppose one contemplates noncooperation, NC, and is met with the rhetorical question, But what if everyone did that? The appropriate reply must then be, Did what? For either enough others are C-ing so as to produce G or they are not; I may not know which is the case, but where it is a virtual certainty that my potential contribution is so small as to make no real difference, I do know that one of these descriptions does apply. If not enough others are C-ing to produce G, then the proper description of my act is not simply "not C-ing"; it is, rather, "not C-ing when not enough others are C-ing so as to produce G regardless of how one behaves." Surely the generalized consequences of everyone's acting that way are not undesirable; just consider all the wasted effort avoided by everyone's acting that way (in similar circumstances) rather than otherwise. On the other hand, if enough others are C-ing to produce G, then the proper description of my act is not simply "not C-ing"; it is, rather, "not C-ing when enough others are C-ing so as to produce G." Again, the generalized consequences of everyone who is similarly situated acting that way are not undesirable; the benefits of G are available to all and some save the costs of cooperation. So if these principles do allow one to take into account the way in which others are behaving, the dilemma of collective action with respect to the provision of public goods remains.

If the principles do not permit one to consider how others are in fact behaving, they have consequences that are clearly morally unacceptable, for there are many acts whose consequences, and thus

---

[15] I follow fairly closely here (in outline) an argument which is elaborated with great care and in considerable detail by David Lyons, *Forms and Limits of Utilitarianism* (Oxford: Oxford University Press, 1965).

morality, depend very heavily—sometimes almost exclusively—upon their coordination or lack thereof with the ways in which others are acting. Indeed, many of the requirements of social morality may be understood as representing conventions that constitute solutions to problems of the coordination of individual action, where what is central is not what the consequences of one's acts would be if others were acting in certain sorts of ways, but what their consequences are likely to be given the way others are behaving or are likely to behave in fact.[16] As in the case of collective action of the sort that may produce or fail to produce public goods, there are many kinds of acts that will only have good or bad consequences once a certain threshold is reached with respect to the number of people performing them. My doing X may have very good consequences if enough others act in a similar way but very bad consequences if enough others do Y. The consequences of everyone's driving on the right-hand side of the road are, let us assume, just fine, but the consequences of everyone's driving on the left would be equally desirable. This does not imply, I trust, indifference to which side of the road I drive on, for what is important in such a case is clearly not what the consequences of my act would be if . . ., but what they will be given the way in which others are in fact behaving. Ostensible solutions to such difficulties have been unconvincing and to a considerable degree ad hoc.[17]

Our rules-of-the-road example suggests a closely related difficulty. There will often be different kinds of acts the general performance of which would have equally good consequences, although the general performance of one kind of act would preclude the general performance of the other kinds. In the case of public goods, everyone acting in manner C might produce G, while everyone acting in manner C' might produce G', where G and G' would be equally beneficial and C and C' equally costly. But if no one can do both C and C', or if some doing C and others doing C' would have very bad consequences, what is required by the principle? Although the clear intent of such a principle is to require convergence on similar

[16] See Lewis, *Convention*.

[17] The most sustained recent treatment is Marcus Singer, *Generalization in Ethics* (New York: Alfred A. Knopf, 1961). Singer's position is criticized in Lyons, *Forms and Limits of Utilitarianism*, pp. 198–216.

courses of conduct in such cases, it would appear to be unable to do so. Even if some such principle might be elaborated in a manner that would require conformity to an ongoing scheme of mutually beneficial social cooperation, this would by no means guarantee that it provided a way of handling those cases where there is no general practice for the individual to grasp, and where the overriding social problem is to generate some appropriate mode of coordinated collective action. The public-goods problems with which we are concerned are typically of just this sort. And where there is in fact some existing cooperative practice to which generalization principles would require compliance, independent principles of fair play or justice might do so as well.

The principle of fair play is this: If one has voluntarily and intentionally accepted the benefits that arise from others doing their (fair) share by way of contributing what is required of them by the rules of a just scheme of social cooperation, then one has an obligation (of fair play) to do one's fair share of assuming the burdens of cooperation when one's turn comes. Failing to assume one's fair share of the burdens while accepting the benefits that exist only because of others' willingness to do their part is to be a free rider; it is to take unfair advantage of those whose compliance with the rules of the practice renders freeloading possible (which it always will be when it is public goods that are in question).[18]

There are surely good grounds for claiming that some such principle of fair play receives universal recognition by many or most members of those social groups which in fact enjoy the benefits of advanced forms of voluntary social cooperation. And it is clear that considerations of fair play do provide a basis for requiring individual cooperation in the production of public goods in those circumstances in which others' cooperation has already brought the goods into existence and one has voluntarily and intentionally availed oneself of them. What such a principle would require would yield a considerable modification of the matrix originally used to represent the dilemma of collective action. With the individual's preferences over

---

[18] See H. L. A. Hart, "Are There Any Natural Rights?" *Philosophical Review* 64 (1955): 175–91; John Rawls, "Justice as Fairness," *Philosophical Review* 67 (1958): 164–94; Rawls, *A Theory of Justice* (Cambridge, Mass.: Harvard University Press, 1971), esp. sec. 18, 52.

the various possible outcomes again expressed in descending rank order, the principle of fair play would generate the following:

OTHERS

	Cooperate	Do Not Cooperate
Cooperate	1	3
INDIVIDUAL		
Do Not Cooperate	4	2

What is important to note here is that the principle of fair play requires cooperation when enough others have cooperated so as to produce a public good whose benefits one has enjoyed and which one will be able (because of others' continued cooperation) to continue to enjoy, but that fair play does not require cooperation which would be fruitless because of others' noncooperation (past or future). Fair play would thus seem to have at least some of the virtues of principles of moral generalization while avoiding their defects.

The limitations of the fair-play principle are obvious. While it may require cooperation within an ongoing practice of mutual cooperation and the past acceptance of common benefits, it provides no basis for generating such cooperation in the first place. Yet this is precisely what is needed with respect to many serious social problems having to do with the production of public goods, including those associated with the functions of Nozick's minimal state. Furthermore, the principle may be invoked against an individual only when it may be claimed that his acceptance of the benefits in question has been intentional and fully voluntary, a claim which is quite dubious when what are at issue are public goods that are available to all within a large community, including those who have little option with regard to the question of continued membership.[19] The principle is surely unacceptable if it permits some to foist obligations upon others by providing them with benefits that they have not freely chosen and in whose production they had no intent of cooperating. Although one can incur obligations of fair play by the voluntary acceptance of benefits provided by others, the cases in which he can do so are much more limited than is usually recognized. What

---

[19] Even Rawls, *A Theory of Justice*, pp. 336–37, now admits this.

is typically required is that an individual join a small group activity and that the benefits from cooperation in the group could have (and usually would have) been denied him had it not been assumed that he would shoulder his share of the burdens involved when it came his turn. Indeed, it may be that the only defensible version of the principle of fair play is one which requires such clearly voluntary and intentional acceptance of the benefits of social cooperation that the satisfaction of these requirements might equally well be taken to argue the individual's tacit agreement to do his share when it comes his turn. This is surely the position of Nozick, who raises grave difficulties for the fair-play principle that are only partially reflected in the above remarks. Nozick writes: "Even if the principle could be formulated so that it was no longer open to objection, it would not serve to obviate the need for other persons' *consenting* to cooperate and limit their own activities."[20]

The principle of fair play looks to the past and the present and relies upon the acceptance of benefits already available; what I shall call principles of justice look to the future and require cooperation in the production of social goods not yet existing. Although problematic, I shall consider two recent attempts to formulate such principles, ones which have been quite explicitly developed with an eye to the dilemma of collective action and the provision of public goods.

In *A Theory of Justice*, John Rawls has argued from the standpoint of a modern social-contract theory that there is a natural duty of justice to support, further, and help establish just institutions and social practices.[21] Now the notion of "helping" here cannot usually be taken literally; when the cooperation of vast numbers of individuals is in question, and strong threshold effects also are involved, the magnitude of any one individual's contribution reaches the vanishing point, and it cannot be said that his cooperation or lack thereof is really helping to achieve anything.[22] What must be meant is that the individual is in a position to help produce a public good in the sense that he is a member of a group that would make the good available if a sufficient number of its members cooperated in the good's pro-

---

[20] Nozick, *Anarchy, State, and Utopia*, p. 95.
[21] Secs. 19, 51.
[22] This point is well made in some detail in Meehl, "The Selfish Voter Paradox."

duction. Rawls avoids the absurdities of principles of moral generalization which also employ this formula by holding that justice
requires cooperation in the establishment of just institutions and social practices only when the individual has reasonable grounds for
believing that enough others will in fact cooperate so as actually to
produce the benefits in question. With respect to the provision of
public goods, Rawls suggests that government regulation is typically
required as the basis for such an assurance that others will so cooperate.[23] The choice matrix that would be yielded by Rawls' principle of justice is thus the same as that based on the principle of fair
play; the important difference between them is in their range of application.

It might be thought that once government regulation is introduced as a way of manipulating individual incentive structures and
providing a reasonable assurance of widespread cooperation, the
problem has been reduced to one of considering only what self-
interest requires. But this is not the case; the magnitude of the incentives that government would need to introduce to motivate individuals sensitive to considerations of justice might be considerably
less than that needed to motivate the rationally self-interested. In
the United States, for instance, the personal income-tax system seems
to rely very heavily on the assumption that most individuals will
honestly report their taxable incomes rather out of a sense of duty
than because of a fear of the legal penalties attached to not doing so.
It is not unreasonable to suggest that the legal sanctions associated
with noncompliance with the tax laws primarily serve the function
of providing the individual with the kinds of assurances concerning
others' cooperation that Rawls has in mind and that the primary
motive behind compliance is a sense of justice (and perhaps fair play
as well) rather than pure self-interest.[24] If this were not so it would
seem that the tax laws would have to be backed up with much more
severe penalties and enforced through a greatly more elaborate and
costly mechanism.[25]

[23] A Theory of Justice, sec. 42.
[24] See Karen Johnson, "A Note on the Applicability of Olson's Logic of
Collective Action to the State," Ethics 85, no. 2 (January 1975): esp. 173.
[25] The cost of collection of personal income taxes in the United States is
reportedly amongst the lowest in the world—about 5¢ per dollar.

A moral principle similar to that defended by Rawls has been discussed by Colin Strang in a paper appropriately titled, "What If Everyone Did That?"[26] What this principle would require with respect to the kind of cooperation necessary to lead to the production of public goods is that individuals be prepared, and present themselves as being prepared, to cooperate if—but only if—others are willing to do so as well. With Rawls' principle, actual cooperation is required of the individual only where there is reasonable assurance of others' cooperation, but Strang's principle seems to call for more initial efforts of the kind that, at least sometimes, might produce such assurances. Just precisely what this might come to in particular cases is not so easy to say, but sometimes, it is clear, steps toward cooperation may be taken that do not represent a firm commitment from which one cannot withdraw. In some cases, cooperation can be offered with an eye to how others are in fact behaving; sometimes, for instance, one's share of the costs of cooperation can be doled out in small bits contingent upon others continuing to contribute.[27] And where there is some vehicle, moral or legal, for making one's promises binding, cooperation may be pledged contingent on others making and carrying out similar pledges.

Although Strang's principle is both appealing and plausible, it has the limitation, as does Rawls' principle, of requiring assurances of others' cooperation before the cooperation of the individual would actually be called for. In the absence of the sort of assurances provided by effective government regulation, such principles of justice would seem to have their greatest potential application in small-group contexts where it is possible for individuals to provide one another with convincing assurances of mutual cooperation in a manner that may simply be impossible within large groups.

I have now completed my review of what forms of social cooperation, if any, would be required in the production of public goods by rational considerations of self-interest, benevolence, fair play, and justice. Individuals motivated to cooperate or not cooperate solely

[26] *Durham University Journal* 53 (1960): 5–10. Reprinted in Judith Thomson and Gerald Dworkin eds., *Ethics* (New York: Harper & Row, 1968), pp. 151–62.
[27] As suggested by Thomas Schelling, *The Strategy of Conflict* (Cambridge, Mass.: Harvard University Press, 1960), p. 45.

upon the basis of considerations having to do with the maximization of welfare, whether their own or that of others, may find themselves in a dilemma: they may fail to provide themselves with a collective benefit when there are strong threshold effects and the number of people whose cooperation is required is so large as to render negligible the contribution that any particular individual is in a position to make. The acceptance of principles of fair play and justice may provide a way out of such a dilemma only when there is a reasonable basis for the individual to believe that enough others have in the past done or will in the future do their fair share in cooperating in a manner that will indeed lead to the production of a public good. But sometimes such beliefs are not reasonable, especially when, as with inflation or population growth, there is an ongoing practice of noncooperation. Yet the principles that I have considered seem to me the only plausible candidates worth considering as possible bases for the type of social cooperation in question, since I hold that independent principles of moral generalization, which could deal with such cases directly, are indefensible. Must we then conclude that there are genuine cases in which moral and rational individuals will be unable to provide themselves with collective benefits in spite of the fact that those benefits could be obtained if a sufficient number of individuals were to act in obvious ways and no one is prevented from acting in those ways? Is it only groups of irrational individuals that will be able to extract themselves from the kind of dilemma of collective action that I have described?

The traditional solution to the dilemma of collective action that has been offered by economists and political theorists lies in the notion of regulation, especially governmental regulation. Whereas individual economic decisions will in theory lead to a supply of private goods adequate to meet collective demand in a free market, the theory of public goods has been seen as a demonstration of the need for mechanisms which will control individual decisions by restructuring the incentives that determine the manner in which people will behave. Even the most dedicated proponents of laissez-faire economics have admitted that there is no "invisible hand" which will guarantee the provision of public goods, and that the strong guiding hand of government will typically be required to lead individuals to make decisions whose collective effects will be mutually advantageous rather than mutually detrimental.[28] The power to tax is, in this view, the power to compel individuals to contribute to the purchase of public goods that they would not be motivated to purchase for themselves. The power to make and enforce laws backed by legal sanctions is, in this view, the power to provide individuals with reasons to act in ways not otherwise in their interest, namely, those ways that satisfy the general schema "If everyone (or a sufficiently large number of people) acted that way, everyone would be better off." On this account, it is not only government at all levels, but also many other kinds of organization, such as labor unions, which have as their primary function the furthering of the common interests of individuals who are incapable, acting solely as individuals, of helping themselves. Although some form of compulsion is typically involved—"compulsory" dues, union membership (the closed shop), or taxation—it may be viewed as rationally self-imposed upon those to whom it is applied. In other words, rational individuals, understanding that they are in a dilemma of collective action because of their inability to provide themselves with a specific public good, would voluntarily seek to create and to join organizations which would compel them to cooperate with others—by giving them private incentives to do so—in ways which would otherwise not be rational for them. Although we may find here a nonrepulsive interpretation of Rousseau's notion of men forcing themselves to be free, some significant limitations on a resort to direct regulation as a means of assuring cooperation in providing public goods must be noted.

An obvious constraint on resort to direct regulation as a solution to the dilemma of collective action lies in the fact that the costs involved in restructuring individual incentives in order to motivate cooperation in the provision of public goods may exceed or largely cancel out the benefits. Government regulation in all forms, not only the criminalization of conduct, is costly in a variety of ways, not the least of which is its necessary interference with human freedom. Some solace is to be found here in the prospect that, at least accord-

28 All of this was understood well, and clearly argued, by John Stuart Mill in his *Principles of Political Economy* (ed. David Winch [Harmondsworth, Eng.: Penguin Books, 1970], bk. 4, pt. 11, sec. 12). For an extensive recent treatment, see William H. Riker and Peter C. Ordeshook, *An Introduction to Positive Political Theory* (Englewood Cliffs, N.J.: Prentice-Hall, 1973).

ing to my analysis, regulatory measures that may initially be required to compel individual compliance with a scheme of social cooperation may no longer be needed, or be needed to only a much lesser degree, once a cooperative practice is off the ground and moral principles of justice and fair play become legitimate grounds upon which to require continued cooperation. Although laws and regulatory agencies do have a tendency to develop a life of their own, surviving long after their need has passed, there is no reason why they must do so. Coordinated forms of individual action that lead to the provision of public goods are social phenomena which also develop an inertia of their own; sometimes, at least, the sort of "pump priming" which is necessary to generate them in the first place may be safely withdrawn after they become well established.

Organizations are themselves public goods for those whose interests they are capable of promoting by compelling or providing new incentives for cooperation that will lead to the availability of specific collective benefits. To create and support organizations may be quite costly ("organization costs"), even where the potential benefits outweigh the costs to the individual. Thus the dilemma of collective action may arise at the level of creating and sustaining organizations capable of solving the dilemma of collective action with respect to specific public goods. Either the organization exists, in which case the individual may avail himself of the benefits it produces without sharing in the costs of supporting it, or it does not, in which case contributing to its support would simply be wasted effort. A worker, for instance, may enjoy the benefits of unionization—good wages, safe working conditions, short hours—without (in the absence of a closed shop) being a union member. The moral indignation that is apt to be felt toward such "freeloaders" lends support to the view that moral principles of justice and fair play may provide a basis for requiring cooperation within an already existing scheme of social cooperation. Also, most organizations attract support by providing their members with private goods that are available only to those who pay their dues and by using most of the money collected to purchase public goods for members. Thus the professional organization provides its members with private goods such as an academic journal and attractive insurance programs and uses membership dues primarily to support costly lobbying efforts which, if successful, will result in legislation favorable to all members of the profession, even those who do not belong to the organization.

But what of creating such organizations in the first place? Cooperation toward this end cannot be required by a principle of fair play, and considerations of justice may have little effect if there is little reason for individuals to believe that others are willing to assume the costs of organization. And of course the organization cannot provide private incentives that will lead to its support if it does not exist. Here, perhaps, the best that can be said is that the individuals who stand to benefit by being organized into an interest group capable of providing its members with public goods must wait upon the advent of some individual (or group of individuals) both able and willing, whether for selfish or benevolent reasons, to bear the entire costs of organization. The union organizer, political leader, and consumer-group advocate do on this account have an important role to play, whatever may be the reasons which lead them to play it.[29]

There is yet a final difficulty. A public good might be provided in a number of different ways, and each individual might prefer that it be provided in any one of those ways to its not being provided at all. But if the support of a majority is required in order that it be provided in any particular way, it may fail to be provided should a number of competing organizations arise and each promote its own pet scheme, no one of which is capable of winning majority support.

Essentially the same difficulty arises for both the fair-play principle and the ostensible duty to support and help establish just institutions. Suppose I have voluntarily accepted the benefits of others doing their fair share within a just scheme of social cooperation, C, but that I would vastly prefer that all be rather engaged in a quite different practice, C'. Even if I view the benefits to me of C as outweighing the costs of cooperation, it would appear strange to argue that I have an obligation to contribute where I barely prefer the existence of C to no scheme of cooperation at all.[30] The problem is even more pressing with respect to the duty to support and help establish just institutions. If all agree that some given (just) practice is

[29] See Riker and Ordeshook, *Introduction to Positive Political Theory,* pp. 75–77.
[30] As noted by Nozick, *Anarchy, State, and Utopia,* p. 94.

the most desirable way to achieve some shared social goal, all is well. But where a number of quite different and equally just practices are possible, the natural duty to help establish a just scheme of cooperation would appear to amount to little more than the duty to resist the establishment of an unjust one. And once some practice is established, with the assurance problem where public goods are involved perhaps being solved through the use of the coercive mechanisms of government, it would be odd to argue that even those who had resisted its establishment have a moral duty to support it. We have already seen that Hayek is sensitive to this problem; it is worth noting that Nozick is as well:

> Though everyone might favor some compulsory scheme over a voluntary one, there need be no one compulsory scheme that each person favors most, or even one that each person favors over the voluntary one. Funds can be raised by a proportional tax, or by any number of different progressive taxes. So it is not clear how unanimous agreement to one particular scheme is supposed to arise.[31]

Does not Hayek indicate the obvious solution when he notes that "most of us find it expedient . . . to make . . . contributions on the understanding that we will in turn profit from similar contributions of others toward the realization of our own ends"?[32] What is suggested here is that such considerations of reciprocity would produce unanimous consent to the adoption of a social-decision procedure based on majority rule for deciding which public goods would be provided and how they would be financed. Each would agree because each would see himself as gaining in the long run. Rather than finding the moral grounds which require cooperation in the support of specific projects of which one might not approve in dubious principles of fair play or justice, why not base cooperation simply upon hypothetical consent to a general social-decision procedure? The problem is that there is no more reason to expect unanimous agreement at the constitutional level than to expect it in the provision of particular public goods. Even were majority rule unanimously preferred, it might take a number of different forms. Quite different conceptions of the legitimate sphere of governmental activity are possible even within the domain limited (as it would be for liber-

---

[31] Ibid., p. 267 n.
[32] Hayek, *The Constitution of Liberty*, p. 144.

tarians) by the provision of public goods, and, as Nozick notes, quite different schemes of compulsory taxation might be employed to finance the provision of public goods. The existence of the state itself, it would seem, is just as elusive a public good as the specific public goods which many have claimed the state is necessary to assure the provision of.[33] Within a just constitutional framework, compulsory taxation may be justified on utilitarian grounds as a means of financing social services that are genuinely desirable and that will not be provided by the operation of private market mechanisms. But since there appear to be no grounds for arguing the existence of even hypothetical consent to any specific set of constitutional procedures, it would seem that resort to government regulation in this area must constitute direct violation of the libertarian principle that people may not be deprived of their property without their consent. Let us now turn, finally, to the argument by which Nozick seeks to avoid this conclusion.

Whereas Hayek bases his position on rule-utilitarianism,[34] Nozick's libertarianism has its moral foundation in a theory of natural rights akin to Locke's. There are first-order substantive rights to property in the broad Lockean sense of life, liberty, and estate, and there are second-order procedural rights to punish violations of rights and to exact reparation for damages. Such rights are viewed as setting inviolable constraints on individual and social action; whatever one's goals, one may not in the course of pursuing them violate the rights of others. In particular, one may not deprive others of their property without their consent. Not much is said by Nozick about the specific contours of such rights, nor about their epistemological foundation. Yet I agree with Nozick that enough is said to place his position in sharp contrast with that of competing views; I believe he is right that important consequences for political philosophy follow if anything like his position is correct.[35]

The fundamental question of political philosophy is this: What, if anything, is the legitimate sphere of governmental activity? Answers to this question range from the no-holds-barred position of the uto-

[33] David Braybrooke, "The Social Contract Returns, This Time as an Elusive Public Good," forthcoming.
[34] Hayek, *The Constitution of Liberty*, p. 159.
[35] Nozick, *Anarchy, State, and Utopia*, pp. 202–3.

pian who would accept governmental activity in virtually any area as long as it was a means to realizing his pet vision of the good society to the anarchist's claim that there is no legitimate sphere for interference, governmental or other, with individual liberty at all. Although Nozick has no sympathy with the utopian who would impose his particular vision of the good life upon others, he is in favor of creating a social climate that would be conducive to the widest variety of "experiments in living" by voluntary associations. Nozick takes the anarchist seriously on two scores: (1) There is sufficient historical evidence of the abuse of power to warrant one who places great value upon human freedom in viewing with considerable trepidation the likely consequences of investing anyone with political power. (2) If even a minimal state must exercise an effective monopoly of the use of coercive force within its territory, how can it possibly avoid violating individual rights? In enforcing its virtual monopoly, must not it violate individuals' procedural rights to punish and exact compensation? Given that some individuals will be either unable or unwilling to pay for the protection they receive, must not the minimal state protecting all within its territory mean that some must be required to pay for the protection of others? Does this not involve compulsory redistribution, which violates the principle that no one may be deprived of his property without his consent?

Nozick argues that a minimal state could arise in a manner which need not involve a violation of anyone's rights but that anything more than the minimal state would involve morally impermissible forms of redistribution. Rationally self-interested individuals, he also contends, would prefer the minimal state to the nonstate situation. Even if more than the minimal state were morally permissible, Nozick argues that the minimal state would be preferred by those who understood the way in which it provides a framework within which a variety of utopian conceptions would be free to develop. So from either end—both from the standpoint of the anarchist with his reservations about any state at all and from the perspective of the utopian concerned lest his pet conception of the ideal state not be realized—Nozick argues to the middle ground of the minimal state on the basis of (1) the moral principle that no one may be deprived of his property without his prior consent, and (2) consequentialist considerations. Following Nozick's own emphasis, I shall be primarily concerned with tracing the implications of the view that there are inviolable natural rights to property, both substantive and procedural, which define the sphere of legitimate government activity.

Although the question whether the minimal state is morally permissible is in one sense prior to the question whether it is desirable, the latter question takes precedence in the sense that only if it is answered in the affirmative is the former question of any practical significance. But by way of comparison, against what nonstate situation is the desirability of the minimal state to be determined? On the one hand, if the state of nature is conceived of as a war of all against all, Hobbes is surely right that virtually any effective political power, no matter how evil, is preferable. On the other hand, if the state of nature is depicted as a Garden of Eden in which each pursues his own ends while dutifully respecting the rights of others, anarchy and utopia would appear to be one, and even the best of governments would appear as less desirable than no government at all. Following Locke, Nozick characterizes the nonstate situation in terms which would seem to be the best that the anarchist (to whom the argument is initially directed) could hope for: the state of nature is an essentially peaceable one in which rationally self-interested individuals pursue their own ends while by and large recognizing and observing the requirements of morality.[36] Violations of rights will of course occur, and individuals will have nothing other than self-help to resort to in order to enforce their rights to punish and exact reparation. The "inconveniences" of such a situation (as Locke called them) are numerous: honest disagreements may arise as to what is in principle right, as well as to the proper application of commonly held principles of right to the facts of particular cases, and matters are made worse by the fact that men are notoriously biased when it comes to judging what justice requires in their own cases. Enforcement of justice and the bringing of disputes to final termination pose such serious problems that at one point Locke writes that in a state of nature "even the least difference is apt to end" in a "state of war."[37]

Why does not Nozick simply follow Locke here too and argue

---

[36] Ibid., pp. 4–5.
[37] John Locke, *The Second Treatise on Government* (New York: Macmillan, 1956), sec. 21.

that in order to remedy these inconveniences in the state of nature men would naturally turn over the "umpirage of the law of nature" to some government to be elected by a majority? As the picture is painted by Locke and Nozick, a government exercising the executive, judicial, and legislative functions as a means of protecting the natural rights of its subjects would be preferable to the nonstate situation, and if based on unanimous consent to an original contract, its protecting all by monopolizing the use of coercive force would not violate anyone's rights. Nozick cannot take the contract theorist's way out, because according to him unanimous consent, hypothetical or other, would not be given to any such contract for the two reasons already noted: (1) Even if each preferred to enter into some unanimous agreement, it is not reasonable to expect that each would prefer to enter into the same agreement; indeed, there might not even be some one form of the original contract that each would prefer to no contract at all (that is, to remaining in a state of nature). (2) Even if there were some form of the original contract which each preferred, it would be in the rational self-interest of each to attempt to be a free rider by refraining from agreeing to it.

Nozick's explanation of how the minimal state would arise from a state of nature is an invisible-hand explanation in that it depicts the state as arising, not as the result of the intentional designs of a number of individuals seeking to coordinate their activities in pursuit of a common goal, but as the result of the uncoordinated actions of a number of individuals seeking other (and quite private) ends. Nozick expresses a strong preference for invisible-hand explanations in general and for such explanations of the political realm in particular. At least with respect to the political realm, I believe there are a variety of reasons for this: (1) Nozick's concern is to show how the state could arise without anyone's rights being violated. Thus one cannot resort, a la Hume, to explanation in terms of usurpation or conquest.[38] Explanation in terms of an original contract of government is ruled out for the reasons given above. What possibility remains but that of an invisible-hand explanation? (2) An invisible-hand explanation of the political realm is fundamental in that the explanation does not appeal to concepts by which what is to be ex-

[38] David Hume, *Of the Original Contract* (New York: Macmillan, 1956).

plained must itself be described.[39] (3) The invisible-hand explanation of the state (at least the ultraminimal state) simply traces out the implications of rationally self-interested (but moral) individuals attempting to further their own particular interests. (4) The invisible-hand process which ostensibly leads to the emergence of the state is a competitive one in which private market mechanisms are at work. I am sure that Nozick, like Hayek and other libertarians, believes that such mechanisms will typically produce better results than will deliberate attempts to design the details of social institutions in advance. What, then, is Nozick's account of the manner in which invisible-hand processes will lead from a state of nature to a minimal state?

Although all have the right to punish a perpetrator of injustice (while only the injured party has the right to exact compensation), individuals acting alone in the state of nature, receiving whatever aid in punishing violations of their rights is volunteered by others, are very much alone indeed. Their ability to enforce their rights against others is severely limited in a number of respects, and it will soon be apparent to them that their powers may be augmented by joining together into voluntary protective associations, where each member is pledged to come to the aid (upon request) of any other member whose rights have been violated. Although an improvement, such a situation is still defective in a number of ways: (1) each is always on call by each and thus liable to have valuable personal activities interrupted at any time; (2) the less troublesome members of the association will find themselves investing a disproportionate amount of time and energy aiding their more troublesome associates; (3) it is not clear how disputes among members of the same association are to be handled. The existence of such problems, the availability of different ways of dealing with them, the obvious advantage of division of labor and economies of scale—these and other factors will lead voluntary associations to present themselves on the open market as private protection agencies performing the "functions of detection, apprehension, judicial determination of guilt, punishment, and exaction of compensation"[40] for all (and only) those who purchase their services. From the initial situation in which there are a

[39] Nozick, *Anarchy, State, and Utopia*, p. 19.
[40] Ibid., p. 13.

number of agencies competing to provide protection, a dominant agency (or federation of such agencies) will emerge in a given geographical territory. For competing agencies will come into conflict, and their attractiveness to actual and potential customers will depend largely upon the extent of their ability to win such conflicts. Weaker agencies will thus for the most part disappear because of a lack of customers. In any given area, either a dominant agency will emerge or a group of competitors of roughly equal strength will see that it is in their interest to agree on some peaceful procedure for resolving their disputes (those strong agencies that did not see this would be at a competitive disadvantage as against agencies that had federated, and thus would be driven out of business at this stage). What we have here, according to Nozick, is the unusual case in which the invisible hand that guides the operation of private market mechanisms will lead to the emergence of a virtual monopoly.[41]

Note that we do not yet have a minimal state, for only those who pay for protection get protected, and the monopoly enjoyed by the dominant agency is only a market monopoly—it does not exercise a monopoly over the use of coercive force in the sense of prohibiting noncustomers from resorting to self-help against its members. (Of course it may require its members to refrain from self-help except in cases of self-defense as a condition of membership.) The ultraminimal state, on the other hand, would prohibit nonmembers from using their own enforcement procedures against its members. The minimal state is one which would, in addition, protect all within the territory it dominates. Let us first see how, according to Nozick, invisible-hand processes would transform a dominant protective agency into an ultraminimal state.

Some independents and members of small associations will fail to avail themselves of the services offered by the dominant agency. Given the considerable advantages that membership in the dominant agency offers, why, outside of pacifists and the like,[42] would anyone choose to remain an independent member of a relatively weak association? A number of possibilities come to mind: some might be virtual hermits or very strong and clever—considering themselves, for

[41] Ibid., p. 17.
[42] Ibid., p. 131.

whatever reasons, unlikely victims of assault, and so on; others might have so little property worth protecting that they do not deem the costs of a protection policy worth the benefits; still others simply will not be able to afford protection.[43] Finally there is that group of independents not explicitly recognized by Nozick at all, but which is perhaps the most important to consider: those who refuse to join the dominant agency because they object, on moral grounds, either to the enforcement procedures it employs or to the substantive conception of justice which the rules it enforces embody. I shall return to this group shortly.

Nozick suggests that with disputes among independents themselves, the dominant agency will have little concern. But this is to ignore the significant spillover effects that independents and their associates doing battle with one another may have on members of the dominant agency—just consider the stray bullets and flying barstools of the old Wild West. So the actions of at least some independents in enforcing their rights against other independents will impose risks, sometimes quite considerable and undue risks, upon members of the dominant agency. But what will be of even greater concern are those instances in which independents seek to enforce their rights against members of the dominant agency. This need give rise to no difficulty when the independent's enforcement procedures are viewed as just and reliable by the dominant agency and its clients. But those independents who employ procedures that the dominant agency judges unjust or unreliable will be seen as imposing considerable risks upon its members. And Nozick admits what is surely obvious: "There will be a strong tendency for it to deem all other procedures, or even the 'same' procedures run by others, either unreliable or unfair."[44]

Central to Nozick's position is the view that the state is to acquire no new rights; even the minimal state is still an agency exercising merely those rights which its citizen-clients had in a state of nature and have voluntarily chosen to transfer to it. An individual in a state of nature has the right forcibly to prevent others from imposing upon him undue risks which, if realized, would violate his rights. In particular, each has the right to prevent others from employing

---

[43] These are the ones which Nozick seems to have foremost in mind; see ibid., p. 112.

[44] Ibid., p. 108.

unjust or unreliable enforcement procedures against him. Acting as its client's agent, the dominant agency may thus prohibit independents from employing enforcement procedures which it views as unjust or unreliable; given its dominant position, it will have the power effectively to enforce this prohibition. As Nozick admits, it will most likely prohibit virtually all independents from enforcing their rights against its members and, I have suggested, even prevent them from enforcing their rights against other independents. Enforcing such prohibitions, the dominant protective agency (which enjoyed only a market monopoly) is transformed into an ultraminimal state exercising a monopoly, in the full sense, of the use of coercive force within its territory.

Prohibited from enforcing their rights against members of the dominant agency, independents are put at the obvious disadvantage of being unable credibly to threaten retaliation against members for violations of the independents' rights. Those who benefit from placing the independents at such a disadvantage are morally required to compensate them for the losses they sustain as a result of their disadvantage. The right to prevent others from imposing undue risks upon oneself is correlative to an obligation to compensate others for risks which one imposes upon them. Either by providing them with money sufficient to purchase protection, or simply by giving them a free protection policy, the dominant agency must in essence protect independents as well as members. The costs of compensating independents will be reflected in the premiums paid by members; some will be paying for the protection of others. Such redistribution, not being for the sake of redistribution,[45] is not only unobjectionable, but morally required. Thus has the ultraminimal state been transformed into the minimal state, an association protecting the rights of all within a given territory by exercising an effective monopoly of the use of coercive force. In the process, nobody's rights have been violated, and the anarchist's objections have supposedly been met.

(I cannot resist noting, in passing, the following difficulty: What of those who choose to remain independents because they object on moral grounds to the substantive rules that the state enforces or to

---

[45] Ibid., p. 27.

the enforcement procedures that it employs? Will they view themselves as being compensated by being given free protection under such rules and procedures?)

The minimal state is to provide the framework within which a wide variety of different utopian conceptions might be realized, not through government's imposing some particular pattern of life, but, rather, by way of protecting people's freedom to form voluntary associations within which various lifestyles might be freely experimented with. Individuals fired with the humanitarian ideals that may be claimed to lie behind many of the programs of the modern welfare state would thus be free to join communities dedicated to such ends; outside such communities, individuals would of course remain free to engage in acts of private philanthropy. What no government may justifiably compel people to do, individuals, acting either alone or as members of communities which they have voluntarily joined, may choose to do for themselves. In the minimal state, theft—in the form of compulsory taxation—would be replaced by charity.

With this brief sketch of Nozick's libertarian theory before us, and against the background of my general account of what rationality and morality require by way of voluntary cooperation in providing public goods, let us turn to the question whether Nozick has succeeded in avoiding the need for the kinds of limitations upon libertarianism that Hayek has recognized. My contention is that there are three central places where Nozick's theory relies on voluntary individual action to produce essential public goods which would not be produced under the conditions which he sets out. In each of these cases, I shall argue, the obvious remedy is a resort to government regulation of a kind that would violate individual property rights as they are conceived of by Nozick.

1. The substantive rights to acquire and transfer property on which Nozick's theory is based are constrained by what he calls "the Lockeian proviso," meant to prevent some from acquiring the total supply of something essential to the lives of others: "A process normally giving rise to a permanent bequeathable property right in a previously unowned thing will not do so if the position of others no longer at liberty to use the thing is thereby worsened."[46]

46 Ibid., p. 178.

The preservation of certain natural resources clearly represents the provision of extremely important public goods. With respect to many of them, overconsumption is to be understood not as a process of continuous depletion but as consumption reaching certain critical levels beyond which natural processes of replacement will be incapable of assuring a continued supply of the resource in question. Natural processes of reproduction, for example, will keep the population of a herd of wild animals or of a fishery relatively constant as long as consumption does not reach the point where reproductive mechanisms cannot keep up with it. Overconsumption in such cases, in short, may involve strong threshold effects. Now consider any particular individual's decision as to whether he should exercise his right to acquire property in such a thing. The Lockean proviso tells him that he may do so as long as he does not thereby worsen the position of others with respect to their ability to do likewise. That is to say, he may do so as long as his act of acquisition will not be responsible for the crucial threshold being crossed. But the probability of his act of consumption being responsible for crossing the threshold is virtually nil, and so he may exercise his right of acquisition. Each reasoning this way, the threshold is crossed; yet no one has violated the Lockean proviso. In such cases a genuine prisoner's dilemma-type situation exists, and the only way out would appear to be by resorting to government regulation that would keep consumption below the threshold through the use of coercive mechanisms. But since no one individual could violate the Lockean proviso, this would mean that some individuals would be prohibited from doing that which they had a right to do.[47]

If I am correct in claiming that the Lockean proviso must be enforced at the institutional level, it would appear that principles of distributive justice not included within Nozick's entitlement theory must be available as a basis for determining who is to be permitted to exercise his rights of acquisition and who is not. Locke, in arguing that there is a right to acquisition even where it would not leave enough and as good for others, appealed to what sounds like Rawls'

---

[47] Cf. Nozick's own discussion of the thresholds involved with the fear one might have of being harmed because a large number of individuals are engaging in activities each of which is risky but not very risky (ibid., pp. 73–74).

difference principle.[48] How ironical it would be if it turned out that Nozick had to do the same.

2. The provision of national security has been taken by many writers to be the paradigm case of a public good that would not be provided by voluntary contributions and that must be financed by compulsory taxation. One might also mention here certain public health programs, ranging from sanitation measures to the prevention of contagious lethal diseases. While in either case one is concerned with the protection of life, it is only in the former case that it might be claimed that the threat to life is based on a threatened invasion of individual property rights. As I do not know how Nozick would handle the public health cases, I shall confine myself to a discussion of the protection the state may (must?) offer against external aggression.

With respect to at least certain forms of external aggression, if some within the boundaries of a given territory are protected against it, all others within the same boundaries will be as well, even those who do not contribute to its provision. There is no effective way of excluding noncontributors from the enjoyment of the benefits of protection; indeed, they could not even exclude themselves if they wished to do so. (In many other cases where the free-rider problem arises, one can at least decline to go for the ride.) And the protection enjoyed by all is enjoyed by each to approximately the same degree. The provision of (at least some forms of) national security is thus a collective benefit which is as "pure" an example of a public good as one is likely to find. With respect to many forms or aspects of it, strong threshold effects are clearly involved. This is especially so where security is achieved by the state's posing a credible deterrent threat of retaliation against aggression; both the credibility and the effectiveness of the threat will depend on the potential aggressor's perceiving certain values as having reached certain orders of magnitude.[49]

It is clear that the rationally self-interested individual, if given the choice of whether or not to contribute to the financing of a system of national defense, will choose to be a free rider. Even a sub-

[48] Locke, *The Second Treatise on Government*, sec. 41.
[49] On deterrent threats, see Schelling, *Strategy of Conflict*.

ordinate utilitarian principle, constraining only those acts that promote the general welfare without violating anyone's rights, will not
provide a basis for requiring cooperation to the extent that strong
threshold effects are involved. Even if an acceptable version of the
principle of fair play were available to Nozick, it could not suffice to
generate a scheme of voluntary cooperation in providing national
defense, and it would not be applicable even within an existing
scheme of voluntary cooperation, because the acceptance of the
benefits in question is anything but fully voluntary (they are unavoidable). One can point out the disastrous consequences that
would stem from everyone's failing to cooperate, or speak of the im-
possibility of anyone's desiring that the maxim of the act of noncooperation become a universal law. However, given the absence of
any acceptable principle of moral generalization, utilitarian or Kantian, this must be seen as merely a restatement of the problem, not a
solution to it. What of the ostensible duty to support and help establish just schemes of social cooperation? Leaving aside the question
whether the strong threshold effects involved militate against viewing any single individual's contribution as helping to accomplish
anything, the problem here is that the principle requires cooperation
only when there are reasonable grounds for believing that others will
cooperate. Note that this requires assurance that others will act both
in a cooperative manner and in support of the same practice or institution (this being important here because there may be a number
of different ways of protecting against external aggression). Rawls,
we have seen, adopts the prevailing view that government regulation is required to solve the assurance problem and to ensure the
provision of public goods. Within a community whose members
recognized a moral obligation to keep promises, it could be solved in
another way: each could promise to contribute conditionally upon
(enough) others doing so as well. The duty to help establish just
institutions would then operate in conjunction with the obligation to
keep promises as a reason for cooperating in the provision of public
goods.

    This way out is surely one that must be considered seriously
within the framework of Nozick's theory—a view which, like Hayek's, relies heavily at a number of points on what can be accom-
plished through voluntary contractual arrangements. In the case of

financing a system of national defense, the conditional agreement contemplated might be either very general or quite specific; one might agree to contribute to whatever scheme a majority favored or to some quite specific proposal (bombers versus battleships). But we have already seen that Nozick himself argues—I believe correctly—that such agreement would not be forthcoming. First, it is not reasonable to expect that everyone, or even a majority, would prefer some particular form of agreement, and this would not seem to depend on whether or not the agreement were couched in generalities or made quite specific. Second, even if there were some form of the agreement which each preferred, it would be in the rational self-interest of each to refrain from agreeing to it. A contract to contribute to the provision of national security, like the hypothetical social contract of government, is an elusive public good. For the same reasons that one would not voluntarily contribute to the provision of national security, one would not voluntarily agree to contribute to it.

Some might say that this represents no real problem for Nozick, because in the political realm which he is considering there would be no need for national defense. Just as competing and equally powerful protective agencies within a given territory will quickly see the advantages of agreeing upon some peaceful means of resolving their disputes, so will minimal nation states agree on some form of federation or world government. Indeed, Nozick's argument is so general that it might be understood, to begin with, in terms of the emergence of a dominant protective agency that would be transformed into a minimal world state within the territory Planet Earth. Well and good, but my point is this: Any such federation, whatever its geographical extent, would be one within which each member would be well advised to protect itself against possible aggression by fellow members. Indeed, the stability of such a federation might depend on each member's being able to pose a credible deterrent threat of retaliation against aggression by any other member. Any assumptions that would be strong enough to imply the denial of this would, I suspect, also imply that individuals in a state of nature could protect their rights against other individuals simply by entering into the appropriate kinds of agreements with them, which is just another way of saying that the situation would remain one of political anarchy.

But perhaps my argument against Nozick on this score can be turned against itself. The only need for a system of national defense is to protect against the threat of external aggression. I have contended that individuals would not voluntarily cooperate toward that end and that observing the principle that no one may be deprived of his property without his consent would prevent the state from compelling him to do so, either by way of compulsory taxation or conscription. Thus no state, so my argument runs, will have a system of national defense. But does not the very same sort of argument imply that no state will be able to develop as a potential aggressor? Financing weapons systems and standing armies must be just as difficult, if my argument is correct, whether they are intended for defensive or offensive use. But if no state poses a threat of aggression against another, there is no need for any state to have a system of national defense. Indeed, since any state having such a system would pose an aggressive threat to its neighbors, which would lead them to arm in self-defense if they could, have we not discovered a virtue rather than a defect in Nozick's theory? Peace on earth, if only all states would recognize libertarian principles. Needless to say, I do not think that this point should provide much consolation to the libertarian who is concerned that his theory have a bearing on the real world.

3. Very early on in his book Nozick writes:

[Apart from spillover effects] only those paying for protection get protected. . . . External economies again to the side, no one pays for the protection of others except as they choose to. . . . Protection and enforcement of people's rights is treated as an economic good to be provided by the market, as are other important goods such as food and clothing.[50]

Whereas Nozick goes on virtually to ignore the spillover effects to which he here alludes, I shall argue that they are so great as to render the protection and enforcement of individual rights against violations by other individuals a public rather than a private good. Rationally self-interested individuals, hoping to free-ride on a general state of peace and security that others would be responsible for, would remain independents rather than join a dominant protective

---

[50] Nozick, *Anarchy, State, and Utopia*, p. 24.

agency. Each, hoping to go for a free ride, would find that there is no ride to be taken at all. The invisible hand, in short, would not lead them beyond anarchy. I shall first argue that private protection is a public good and, second, that the free-rider problem exists with respect to it.

It was with good reason that Hobbes, for instance, spoke of a general condition of peace and security, and that Locke (followed by Nozick) distinguished the right of all to punish from the right of only the injured party to exact compensation. The distinction is reflected in our own legal system, which in a number of different ways treats criminal liability quite differently from the way in which it treats liability in tort or contract. Assault, murder, fraud, and crimes against property are all viewed as crimes against society at large; public agencies are charged with their detection and prosecution, and public funds pay for the support of the criminal justice system. The public's interest in preventing crime is brought into sharp focus by considering the following distinction: a criminal prosecution must be initiated by a prosecutor acting as a government official and cannot be brought to an end by the complainant requesting it; the plaintiff in a civil action, on the other hand, must initiate the suit, may bring the action to a halt at any stage of the proceedings, and will not find the court enforcing a final judgment unless he requests it to. The underlying notion, it would appear, is this, and I believe that it is well founded: those who commit serious crimes are violating moral principles in a manner which shows that they lack due respect for the persons and property of others. As such, they are dangerous and pose a threat to society at large. Their apprehension and punishment is in the public interest, both as a means of bringing a halt to their dangerous activities and as a way of deterring potential offenders. Nozick's theory, like Locke's, takes the view that such individuals, even in a state of nature, are few in number. Apprehending and punishing a sufficient number of them will produce a general level of peace and security of person and property which all may enjoy, even those who do not pay for protection. The protection and enforcement of those rights with which the criminal law is concerned are public goods with which strong threshold effects are associated. What Nozick himself asserts about the fear of being harmed by others' risky actions applies equally well, I contend, to the fear of being harmed by dangerous persons.

A risky action might present too low a probability of harm to any given person to cause him worry or fear. But he might fear a large number of such acts being performed. Each individual act's probability of causing harm falls below the threshold necessary for apprehension, but the combined totality of the acts may present a significant probability of harm.[51]

A rationally self-interested individual would regard the existence of a dominant agency as an assurance of a general level of peace and security, the availability of which would not depend upon his membership and which he might enjoy free of charge. He will thus have good reason to remain an independent. Once he understands that should a dominant agency emerge it will be morally required to compensate him by providing him with a free protection policy against its members, he will have even more reason to remain independent. Each viewing the matter in this way, all will remain in a nonstate situation of political anarchy; the minimal state will not emerge. This does not depend upon people acting selfishly. Because of the strong threshold effects involved, benevolent men would act no differently. And, as we have seen in other cases, appeals to considerations of justice and fair play would be to no avail. Nor would agreement to join contingent upon others doing so be more rational than joining without any such agreement. If people are to pay for private protection, it would seem, it will only be because they are compelled to do so.

Nozick explicitly considers the question whether the provision of protection to independents by way of compensation will "lead people to leave the agency in order to receive its services without paying."[52] His reply is that

the agency protects these independents it compensates only against its own paying clients on whom the independents are forbidden to use self-help enforcement. The more free riders there are, the more desirable it is to be a client always protected by the agency. This factor, along with . . . others, acts to reduce the number of free riders and to move the equilibrium toward almost universal participation.[53]

[51] Ibid., p. 73.
[52] Ibid., p. 113.
[53] Ibid.

The suggestion here seems to be that as independents would be unprotected against other independents, the larger their number the greater the risk of being an independent. But this ignores the fact that the existence of an effective dominant agency would reduce the number of active criminals and the threat which they pose to independents and members alike to a tolerable level. And independents need not rely solely upon individual self-help to protect and enforce their rights against one another; the state will not prohibit them from forming voluntary protective associations to that end. The original assumption that individuals in a nonstate situation, although self-interested, are by and large peaceable implies that those inclined to engage in serious violations of the rights of others are few in number. The emergence of a dominant agency would seem to imply that most violators would sooner or later be identified and their dangerous activities put to an end or else that they would simply be deterred for fear of being apprehended and punished. Note also that to the extent to which the number of independents is large and the outbreaks of violence among them frequent, the spillover effects on members of the dominant agency will be more severe. To protect its members, the dominant agency will have to step in, prohibiting self-help enforcement of the rights of independents against other independents and compensating them for the disadvantages to which they are thereby put by offering them free protection. So I persist in my claim that the equilibrium situation is the anarchist one in which everyone attempts to go for a free ride.

Would not clever criminal types choose to remain independents and prey only upon their fellow independents, carefully avoiding imposing the risks of spillover effects on nonindependents and thus avoiding the wrath of the dominant agency? Would not remaining an independent thus be tantamount to inviting a violation of one's rights? But how are our (unrealistically hyperrational) criminal types to know who is an independent and who is not? Independents do not live in isolation and identify themselves as such; they live on the same blocks, travel the same roads, shop in the same stores, send their children to the same schools as members of the dominant agency. (Note also that such facilities would all be private in a libertarian society and would attempt to win customers away from competitors by offering better services. Would not an important attraction be the security within which they could assure their customers that their services might be enjoyed?) Could not members of the dominant agency identify themselves as such ("Don't you dare attempt to rob me; I'm no defenseless independent")? Surely, but what is to prevent independents from saying that they are members of the dominant agency? In doing so they would be lying, of course, but to whom would they be lying? In effect, only to potential aggressors against their rights. This would be justifiable self-defense. To mark independents and distinguish them from its members, the dominant agency would have to take strong steps—perhaps announcing their names and addresses nightly over the state radio station. But if successful, this would substantially increase the risk of independents' having their rights violated. Nozick's principle of compensation would then require that they be compensated for this, just as it is required that they be compensated for the disadvantages thrust upon them by being prohibited from enforcing their rights against members of the dominant agency. Whether by being offered free protection against other independents or by being compensated in some other way, the fact that independents were compensated would mean that their rights were being protected—free of charge—to virtually the same degree as that of members of the dominant agency. Almost all would choose to remain independents.

Although I am confident that there are some interesting things to be said on the matter, I shall not here consider the question whether a similar argument might be pressed against Nozick with respect to the protection and enforcement of those rights whose violation gives rise to liability in tort or contract. Nor shall I explore the question whether a serious free-rider problem exists at the "other end" of the theory because of the organization costs associated with the formation of voluntary associations designed to realize particular utopian vision (which would clearly be public goods to their potential members). I shall rest my assertion that a resort to government regulation in a manner which violates the principle that no one may be deprived of liberty or property without consent is required because of the unavoidable free-rider problems involved with the public goods associated with (1) the Lockean proviso, (2) national defense, and (3) private protection against crime. Nozick's libertarianism will have to be qualified or limited in serious ways if I am right on any one of these scores.

How might Nozick's position be qualified? I have been able to think of only two ways. Both of them are highly problematic in themselves, and neither of them, I suspect, would be happily accepted by Nozick. (I think that either of them might be given a place within Hayek's rule-utilitarian theory, thus removing the source of his expressed discomfort with the need for regulation in such cases.)

The first way out would be to formulate a subordinate moral principle designed to require cooperation in the provision of public goods; this principle should avoid the difficulties of principles of moral generalization (ignoring the threshold effects connected with the way in which others are in fact behaving) while at the same time solving the assurance problem involved with the ostensible duty to help establish just institutions. Such a principle is suggested by reflection on the position of Colin Strang, briefly discussed, and perhaps too quickly dismissed, above. Like Rawls' natural duty of justice, it would require cooperation in providing public goods when there was assurance that others would cooperate as well, but it would go further by also requiring that one give such assurances. Assuming that most individuals recognize moral obligations to keep promises and not to lie, each individual—perceiving himself to be in a prisoner's dilemma situation with respect to some public good which he and others desired—might be required by such a principle to make a conditional promise based on an unconditional declaration of his desires and intentions. Something like this does not strike me as too unnatural: "I prefer that state of affairs G obtain and intend to do my fair share of cooperating in its provision if, but only if, I have reasonable grounds for believing that enough others will also cooperate so that it will actually be provided. I thus promise to take initial steps toward cooperation and promise to carry them through, if I receive similar assurances from enough others."

A principle of the sort suggested might suffice to generate cooperation, and by such means a dominant protective agency might emerge. Unanimity is not required. Only the number of individuals required to form a dominant coalition need make and carry through on such a conditional agreement. Once they have an effective monopoly of the use of coercive force, they will of course be required to compensate those independents whom they prohibit from resorting to self-help. (At least those who choose to remain independents on moral grounds or because they cannot afford to join up must be compensated; those who simply wish to go for a free ride might be disqualified from receiving compensation because they would be viewed as violating our new moral principle.) But the need for compensation of independents has been with us all along and thus presents no new difficulty for Nozick's theory.

Now an old problem returns to haunt us. What if most or all desire that some public good obtain, but only under some very general description (such as "protection")? What if no dominant coalition is able to form around any particular conception of how it is to be realized? Perhaps a sufficient number would prefer having the question decided by a specific voting procedure to having the public good not provided at all; they would be able to form a dominant coalition. Adoption of such a social-decision procedure would itself be a public good, and our modified principle of justice would require that individuals give the appropriate assurances of cooperating in its provision. But our old problem can be raised here too: What if not enough can agree upon some particular procedure to produce a dominant coalition? At this point, one might say that there is some procedure, such as simple majority rule, which is the "natural solution" to what now may have become a simple coordination problem.[54] Or one might contend that his favorite candidate for the natural solution is the morally required one. Locke, it seems to me, may be viewed as making both claims for simple majority rule, and perhaps the same can be said for Rousseau.[55]

The general problem concerning collective action and the provision of public goods has proved so recalcitrant to other principled solutions that some such principle as I have hinted at above perhaps deserves serious consideration. Were Nozick to resort to such a principle, it would be incumbent upon him to detail it, and to indicate

---

[54] On conventions as solutions to problems of pure coordination, see Lewis, *Convention.*

[55] Locke, *Second Treatise*, secs. 96, 97; Jean-Jacques Rousseau, *The Social Contract* (Chicago: H. Regnery Co., 1954), bk. 3, ch. 17.

the manner in which it related to his conception of substantive and procedural rights and the overarching principle that no one may be deprived of his liberty or property without his consent. Basing Nozick's theory on any such moral principle would mean that the explanation of the emergence of the ultraminimal state, like that of the minimal state, could not be an invisible-hand explanation. Given Nozick's expressed unhappiness[56] at having to appeal to moral principles of compensation to explain how the ultraminimal state would be transformed into a minimal state, this result, I take it, would make him very unhappy. It might be, though, that Nozick's theory modified along these lines would still succeed in answering the anarchist's objections by showing how the state could arise through morally permissible means without anyone's rights being violated in the process.

The second kind of general solution to the problems I have raised for Nozick is not likely to meet the anarchist's objections, at least as Nozick understands them. Nonetheless, it would appear to be consonant with a libertarian perspective, and it is one which gives prominence to the notion of natural rights, both substantive and procedural. It does not provide the basis for an invisible-hand explanation of the origin of government either, for it does not provide any explanation of the origin of the state at all. As does a utilitarian view like Hume's or Mill's, it takes the state as given, and asks the question of what it is morally permitted to do by way of interfering with the liberty of those over whom it exercises coercive power. Although it may of course address itself to the question of what individuals may and ought to do in a nonstate situation, it begins with something like Nozick's ultraminimal state and asks what, morally, may happen from there. Following Hayek, the principle I have in mind would permit individuals to be deprived of their liberty or property without their consent (through compulsory taxation or other forms of coercive government regulation) in order to assure the provision of essential public goods that would not be provided by the operation of private market mechanisms. Essential public goods would be defined as those whose availability is necessary for the meaningful exercise of individual rights. Suggested by the first principle of justice

---

[56] Nozick, *Anarchy, State, and Utopia*, p. 119.

defended in Rawls' *A Theory of Justice*, my principle would restrict interferences with individual liberty to those required to preserve liberty itself.[57] Such a principle would require a specification of original rights and liberties, both substantive and procedural, but this Nozick owes us anyway. (It is at least clear that he would exclude ostensible rights to such things as adequate food, shelter, and education[58] and include those rights which come into play where the Lockean proviso, national security, and private protection are involved.) What Nozick would further owe us, were he to accept such a modification of his theory, is some account of how tradeoffs between different rights would be understood and the consequences of making them measurable in principle.

As originally formulated, Nozick's theory permitted two different kinds of cases in which the boundary set by an individual's moral rights might be crossed without his consent. First, there was the case in which one knew that another person's boundary would be crossed by one's engaging in a vital but, say, dangerous activity, yet could not in advance identify that other person. Such activities were deemed permissible as long as compensation was paid afterward to the injured parties. Second, there was the case of prohibiting others from engaging in activities that imposed unjustifiable risks, even risks which might not eventuate in actual harm to anyone. Here, too, compensation was required. So the notion of a morally justified interference with another's rights without his consent would not be new to Nozick's theory. What would be new, and contrary to one of Nozick's central contentions, is this: the state, in justifiably coercing individuals with a view toward producing a system of maximal equal liberty, would be exercising a right that no one had in the state of nature. In Nozick's original view, the state is an agency which exercises only those rights delegated to it by those who voluntarily join it. The principles which permit crossing others' boundaries as long as compensation is paid exist already, and apply to individuals, in a state of nature. But I see no way of understanding how the right of the state to create and impose a system of maximal equal liberty could be viewed as a right which an individual could have in a state of nature. As already suggested in my discussion of the Lockean

---

[57] See *A Theory of Justice*, esp. ch. 4.
[58] *Anarchy, State, and Utopia*, p. 238.

proviso, it would seem that a theory built upon a conception of natural rights will have to recognize institutional as well as individual rights. I shall not speculate here on the difficulties this might involve for a tradition already beset by enough other problems.

Perhaps there are other solutions to the public-goods problem that are available to Nozick and that I have failed to consider. I strongly suspect, though, that any plausible answer to the questions I have raised will show that Nozick's libertarianism must be qualified in a manner that will bring it much closer to Hayek's position than it is at present.[59]

[59] Hayek makes the important point that the need for government regulation as a means of assuring the provision of certain public goods does not imply that it should exercise a monopoly in the areas in question (*The Constitution of Liberty*, p. 261).

5.

Courts as Legislatures

GORDON TULLOCK

MOST conventionally trained Anglo-Saxon lawyers believe that one of the most important functions of the courts is writing new law. Indeed, Anglo-Saxon training in law consists very largely of reading judicial decisions rather than the legal codes enacted by the legislatures. That this is a bizarre characteristic of Anglo-Saxon law is not emphasized in American law schools. Although as far as I know the Anglo-Saxon emphasis upon the courts as lawmaking bodies is unique, it is not true that common-law-type developments were found only in the Anglo-Saxon countries. Both the Roman law and the highly elaborate Muhammadan law were essentially extralegislative, having been developed by legal scholars rather than by formal lawmaking bodies.

In the case of the Romans, these were essentially the jurisconsults who had a good deal of practical experience in actual litigation, but whose writings were, in essence, interpretive essays on various legal problems. In Muhammadan countries, the learned doctors of the Koran and the Hadith developed the law. They too might well have had a good deal of practical experience as judges, but their contribution to the law took the form of books and articles on general topics rather than on individual cases.

In most of the world, the lawmaking body, whether a legislature or a king, and the law-applying organization (that is, the courts) have been kept conceptually distinct, except insofar as ultimate appeal might go to the king or, in Rome, to the Senate. It is likely that in all legal systems, specific decisions on specific cases have at least some effect on future decisions of a similar nature, but the effect can be very small indeed. Anglo-Saxon law, although not unique in permitting courts to make binding rules for future cases, nevertheless carries this system to a much higher level than is found anywhere else. Further, most lawyers trained in our tradition seem to feel there is some kind of natural law that makes it impossible to avoid doing this. Indeed, they are very surprised to discover that in most of the world's judicial systems, the Anglo-Saxon custom is not followed.[1]

In Anglo-Saxon law, three separate possible functions are characteristically intermingled. First, the judges may find themselves confronted in many cases with a situation not exactly in accord with the existing law—that is, the existing law is unclear with respect to it—and they make a decision as to what shall be done in this particular case. Second, they lay down a rule for cases that will be brought in the future. Note that I have said cases that will be *brought* in the future, not cases dealing with incidents that will *occur* in the future. In almost all cases (recently some exceptions have been created), the decision setting down a new rule by the courts has retroactive effect. Third, the judges write an essay about the case that is intended to explain to all and sundry why they have done what they have done. It is the third part, the essay, which makes Anglo-Saxon law libraries so voluminous. If the courts confined themselves to making decisions on existing cases and laying down the rules for future cases, the West Publishing Company would have an immensely shorter list of publications. Indeed, I would imagine this would eliminate something like 95 percent of all present Anglo-Saxon law libraries.

The habit of writing an essay explaining the decision, which is characteristic of Anglo-Saxon law, is perhaps more widespread in world judicial systems than are some other aspects of Anglo-Saxon law. Nevertheless, it is by no means universal. A great many courts throughout history have simply made a decision, as is true with many today. Indeed, a great many Anglo-Saxon courts simply make a decision without discussing it. Nevertheless, the common Anglo-Saxon custom is to produce a rather long essay, and the rule for future cases has to be distilled by the lawyers from that essay, rather than that rule being presented in its simplest and clearest form. This makes our law immensely voluminous and less clear than it could be. However, the habit of writing essays is, I think, something of not much

---

[1] For some other areas where Anglo-Saxon procedure departs from the world norm, see Gordon Tullock, *The Logic of the Law* (New York: Basic Books, 1971).

importance, and I propose to discuss it no further here. Presumably it developed from the problems of the appeal process, but it is clear that one could have an appellate system (as the Romans did) which did not produce such essays.

We thus have two functions remaining, one of which is making a decision in the case in which the existing law does not perfectly fit, and the second is the laying down of law for other cases. Note that the retroactive aspect of the second function is not only unnecessary, but, as far as I can see, positively undesirable. In general, laws should have only future effect, and individuals should not be punished for actions not contrary to the law at the time the actions occurred. The retroactive effect in our law comes from a fact that the judges in mythology were attempting rather to find out what the law actually was than to create new law; hence, when the Supreme Court ruled as to what the law was, this did not create a new rule—it simply made manifest what had already been true. I think this myth is not much longer believed. Unfortunately, the consequence of it— that is, retroactive effect of court decisions—is still with us.

In the late Middle Ages when legislatures first began making laws, they thought of their task not as one of writing laws, but as one of simply presenting the existing law in a clearer, more definite form. In a sense, their activity in their own view was one of publicity rather than legislation. With time, they began to realize that they were not simply restating the law or writing down something that existed somehow in the air, but were creating new law. With this realization, they began to make their laws prospective instead of retroactive. Eventually, it became the rule that all laws affect only things that happen after the time the laws are enacted.[2]

The desirability of making new law prospective rather than retroactive is, I suppose, fairly obvious. The point of the law, after all, is to control behavior and it is impossible to control past behavior. The only argument for making the law retroactive would be a desire that people attempt to figure out what the law is going to be at some future time and obey that. If one did have strong natural-

---

[2] There are a few special exceptions to this; for example, in Western (as distinguished from Communist) law, if the legislature lowers the sentence for a particular crime, then the new lower sentence will apply also to crimes committed before the date of the enactment.

law ideas—that is, believed that the real law is something somehow in existence that the legal entities simply make concrete—then it might be rational to give people the duty of investigating the real nature of the law themselves, even before it has been proclaimed. However, this view of the law is rarely held today.

Unfortunately, although legislatures realized a long time ago that they were writing new law, the courts have only very, very gradually come to the realization that they are doing the same thing. Further, when they did realize sometime in the nineteenth century, that they were writing new law, they continued making their decisions retroactive. It is only in the past ten years that the U.S. Supreme Court has begun to act as if it realized it was making retroactive decisions. Up to that time, the Court had always acted as if any decision was the discovery of a preexisting law rather than the formulation of new law, although surely judges were aware of the hypocrisy of this position for at least a hundred years.

Recently the Supreme Court has incorporated the realization that it is making law into its behavior and has provided that such laws, at least sometimes, will not be retroactive. Sometimes it makes decisions making its law partially prospective. Suppose Smith sues Jones about something that happened in 1965, and in 1974 the suit reached the Supreme Court. In the past, the Court would have reached a decision about the case, and this decision would be law with respect to all cases that came before the courts, even if the actions involved had occurred before 1965, to say nothing of before 1974. The Court now sometimes changes this procedure, and specifies that its new decision will apply only to cases after a certain date. Sometimes the date to which the new decision applies is the date of the original case, and sometimes it is the date on which the Court reaches its decision; in some cases the decision has been made effective at a date in the near future, in order to give administrative authorities time to make the necessary provisions. The latter is normal for legislative laws.

An interesting and paradoxical characteristic of this system, however, is that the original case—*Smith* v. *Jones*—is decided by the new law, even though the case clearly arose before the new law was written and even though the Court says that in all other cases the law will be prospective rather than retroactive. Apparently, the

Court is not yet completely free from the myth that it is simply applying a preexisting law rather than writing a new law.

However, leaving aside the problem of retroactivity of legal decisions, it is obvious that the Court, if presented with a case in which the law is not clear, must make a decision. In my opinion, this decision should be made quickly and without much investment of resources.[3] The argument is simply that this is a rule which the parties before the Court cannot have known before the Court made its decision; hence, of necessity, it is arbitrary and there is, therefore, no need to invest a great many resources in determining which arbitrary rule will be used. We should hope to have our law as clear as possible, that is, written in such a way that the parties can readily determine what the law is and then have their behavior influenced by their knowledge of the law.

If we are in an area where behavior could not be influenced by the law because the law did not say anything, or, alternatively, where behavior could only be sort of stochastically influenced by the law because the law said something that was very unclear, there is little to be gained from great care in making the decision. In a sense, the law has already failed by not informing the parties in advance what their legal rights were, and there is nothing we can do now which, from the standpoint of the parties at the time they took the action now under litigation, is not arbitrary. One arbitrary rule is probably very nearly as good as another.

The only known method of reducing the likelihood that the Court will find itself confronted with cases which do not fit the law perfectly is to make the law more lengthy and detailed. Unfortunately, although making the law more lengthy and detailed will reduce the number of cases the law fails to fit clearly, it does not reduce them to zero. There will always be some cases that require interpretation of the law coming before the courts no matter how long the law or how carefully it is drafted.

The question of how much detail we want in the law itself is a difficult one to answer. The advantage of having the law extremely detailed, that is, making a serious effort to anticipate as many possible future contingencies as one can, is that it is possible for people

---

[3] The following line of reasoning will be developed much more fully in a forthcoming book.

to determine in advance what the law is for a vast range of contingencies. The disadvantage is that it leads to very large investments of mutually canceling legal research by the parties. If you have a very large number of rules, then the party with the best lawyers or the largest investment in researching rules will have an advantage over the other party. Hence, a great many resources will have to be invested by both parties in determining the details of the law. Since there surely will still be a great many cases which the law does not fit, the gain may not counterbalance the cost. Further, if the law is expressed in the form of lengthy essays on each case, there is still a large random component. The question is really how much we wish to add to legal costs in order to reduce the random component of decisions that have to be made under circumstances where the law is not clear. In my opinion, our present law is much more detailed than it should be, but I must admit that this is merely an opinion and I should like to see the results of some empirical investigation of the matter.

There is another problem with a detailed legal system, particularly one like ours in which most of the details take the form of lengthy essays on specific cases and hence are communicated to the student in a very inefficient way. The problem is that an additional rule may not increase the certainty of the law at all. Anyone who has had anything to do with computers knows that very long programs have many unexpected interactions, with the result that the outcome is very hard to predict. Adding more instructions to such long programs is apt only to change the nature of the unexpected interactions, not reduce them. The same may well be true of the law; it may be that each additional rule added to the law—whether by the Supreme Court or by some European administrative tribunal—has unexpected interactions with other parts of the immense mass of legal rules, with the result that it does not reduce the degree of uncertainty of the law as a whole. If this is so, then there is no gain from increasing the number of rules. Empirical research is needed to determine the effects of increasing the number of rules.

In any event, the decision on the desired degree of detail in the law should not turn on the accidental question of which cases come to court. That a particular type of case has come up several times is, I suppose, fairly good evidence that the questions they raise are of some importance, and hence perhaps argues that a special rule should be drawn up. If a case comes up once, it indicates nothing of the sort. Further, the fact that a case has not yet reached an appellate tribunal does not indicate that it is an unimportant case. There are very large numbers of areas in our law in which most of the problems that arise involve small amounts of money (or very minor penalties if they are criminal law), and hence never get to the higher courts. It is clear to anyone who has any knowledge of the way the law functions that, in these cases, there frequently is no clear rule, but nothing is done about it, unless the legislature eventually gets around to enacting a law.

I suspect that the reason for the present scheme comes from the view (which used to be the prevalent myth) that the courts do not write the law but find it. To repeat, a similar myth existed for the legislatures for a long time, and it was only gradually realized that legislatures were creating new laws. Unfortunately, in the case of the courts, the realization that they were creating new law came even later and is not well integrated into our scheme of thought.

In a more general sense, there is no intrinsic reason why the body that makes decisions with respect to cases which have arisen and the body that decides what rules will apply in future cases must be the same. For an American example, consider the method the federal government now uses to make its decisions on parole. For people in prison, this is an immensely important decision, since it can change the actual time served over an immense range. It used to be that the parole board could cut any sentence by two-thirds, but now the range is even larger than that. Thus, the decision by the parole board as to how long a person serves is, in most cases, more important to him than the original decision by the judge, although the judge's decision puts limits on the amount of change the parole board can impose.

Currently, the National Parole Board makes policies that are issued to its subordinates, who actually make the individual decisions on parole. Individual parole decisions can be appealed. Interestingly enough, they are mainly appealed by minorities of the committees who make the decisions, rather than by the prisoners. As a matter of fact, however, either the prisoner or the minority may appeal, and this appeal can eventually get to the National Parole Board. The parole board's instructions to its inferiors, however, are made primarily by changes in its policy guidelines. Such changes are prospective rather than retroactive, of course, although in the particular case of the parole decision, this may not be a very important matter. Presumably the National Parole Board makes changes in its general guidelines in part because of information about decisions actually made in the lower-ranking committees, which it receives through the appellate process, but, unless the board is totally incompetent, it does not depend solely upon that source of information in searching for defects in its existing rules.

Note that this procedure is both less tedious for the National Parole Board (which does not have to write lengthy opinions every time, although it is free to do so if it wishes) and simpler from the standpoint both of the parties and of the subordinate bodies which make decisions in individual cases. The amount of material they must read is massively less, and, presumably, a good deal clearer because it is written *not* to explain the decision in some case in the past, but to control decisions made in the future.[4]

Note that in this case we have the basic law set by the legislature,[5] and the administrative body merely makes the detailed interstitial laws. The making of interstitial laws is characteristically the rationalization for the lawmaking activity of our court system, although the rationalization is now becoming a little thin, granted the activist role of the courts in recent years. It is hard to argue that *Brown* v. *Board of Education* was an interstitial decision.

The parole law, then, consists of the basic legislation, a gloss upon it by the court system, and a further gloss on these two segments by the administrative board; these three parts of the law cover, basically, most cases. Of course, some cases will not fit the law as it is written, and it will be necessary for the lower-level committees to make decisions, just as lower-level courts periodically find cases where the law is not clear. Just as in the case of the lower-level court decision, these lower-level decisions do not become part of the

---

[4] The discussion is based on Peter B. Hoffman and Lucille K. DeGostin, "Parole Decision-Making: Structuring Discretion," *Federal Probation* 38 (December 1974): 7–15.

[5] And also by the courts, which in our system are able to act as a sort of legislature or constitutional convention, controlling behavior of administrative bodies.

law, but they may have influence, particularly if they are appealed, on the higher-level agencies who might change the law.

In most European countries, the legal system is similar to the U.S. system, but with one exception: the power of the courts, on appeal of given cases, literally to change the law or to produce additional detail normally does not exist. The courts, including the appellate courts, deal with the particular cases brought before them, and only to a very minor extent do they make law for future cases.

To explain a legal system, in a very idealized form, assume that some country has a legislature that makes laws. There is also a professional commission that produces glosses upon the law as the legislature writes it. Thus, when the legislature produces a new law, if this commission feels that it is unclear or requires further detailed specification in some area or another, it will produce such a detailed gloss. In a way, this is rather like the activities of that anonymous group of lawyers who produce the annotations for the federal code. Indeed, in our system this role is, to a large extent, carried on by fairly low-level groups such as the civil servants who produce annotations, or the private employees who produce the West Publishing Company works, the various loose-leaf services, and other guides to the law.

In the European system I am describing, this type of activity would be little developed because there would be an official agency that produced detailed glosses. These glosses are sometimes very detailed. For example, in France they had laws against "indecent exhibitions" on the stage. About ten years ago, when the French were more puritanical than they are now, the central commission responsible for these things reached a decision that there was an indecent exhibition if the girl on the stage wore a *cache sexe* which was less than two inches wide and four inches long, and not if she wore one of the appropriate size. The legislature had, of course, not specified matters in this detail.

The board that produces these glosses is not compelled to provide detailed regulations if it feels the law is reasonably clear already, and it is free to change such regulations; the changes are prospective rather than retroactive in their effect. Further, the legislature if it does not like the interpretation put upon the law by the commission, may at any time change the basic law.

Unlike the situation in the United States where the deliberations either of the people who produce the federal code annotated or of the higher courts are unrecorded and, in fact, deeply secret, the commissions I am referring to in European countries normally operate in public, and a record of their deliberations is kept. This, together with the fact that their decisions are prospective rather than retroactive in character, means that aggrieved parties have an opportunity to complain about interpretations before they find themselves bound by them. The complaint would characteristically go to the legislature.

Another advantage of this system is that the degree of detail of the law is consciously decided upon. Under the Anglo-Saxon system, the decision as to the amount of detail the law will have is essentially an accidental byproduct of lawsuits brought by private parties and then appealed. If a highly unusual case succeeds in getting into the appellate court because the parties have much to gain or lose, the case makes law and the law becomes somewhat longer than it otherwise would be. In the idealized system I am describing, this would not be true. The appeal on this particular case would go to higher courts but would become "law" only if the commission preparing the gloss on the basic law thought the matter was important enough to make it worthwhile to put something about it into the law. Further, if it did become law, it would become law not by way of a fifty-page opinion but probably by way of a sentence, or perhaps a paragraph, with the basic law being changed only a little so that its application to this particular issue was clarified.

As a result of this technique of providing the detailed interstitial part of the law, the law is briefer, easier to find, and the result of a conscious decision by a specialized commission as to the appropriate degree of detail to put into the law. Further, the decision made by this commission in making a change in its gloss on the law is the result of consideration of the social consequences of a change in the law, rather than the result of consideration of the effect upon the two parties to some particular action which arose under the previous law.

The importance of the last point is probably a little difficult for Anglo-Saxon lawyers to understand. Consider a situation that can readily arise in any court system. A and B come into conflict over some matter on which it is not clear what the law is. The matter goes to court and the court, of necessity, must reach a decision. Since parties A and B were operating under an unclear law, this decision will necessarily have an element of arbitrariness, perhaps a large one. Nevertheless, it seems fairly sensible to decide in terms of what A and B would have thought the law was. There seems to be no reason, in deciding the rights between A and B, for inquiring what the law should be rather than what it in fact was. A and B are, after all, held responsible for knowing only what the law is, not what the law should be.

Of course, it can be said that the court will make a better decision as to what the law should be than a legislature would. Bruno Leoni and Richard Posner take this position.[6] The argument apparently is that the parties have the strongest possible motives to offer strong arguments for their respective positions, and the problem is necessarily a concrete one. Leoni, who was schooled in the Roman law, emphasizes that both under the Roman law and under the common law as it existed at the time of Blackstone, an individual decision was not binding on future courts. The same issue had to arise and be decided by the courts in the same way several times before it was thought to be a valid precedent. Clearly this reconsideration of the same issue several times provided a higher assurance that the outcome was socially desirable than does consideration of the single case, which is the method we now use and which is endorsed by Posner.

In essence, the argument for this point of view has to take roughly the following form. With respect to the issue between A and B, the law is not clear, and hence any decision is necessarily arbitrary. Making the arbitrary decision in the way which is best not for A and B but for the future of society is not particularly bad for A and B, because the decision between them will be arbitrary in any event. Thus, compelling them to present evidence as to the social effect of any given decision in order to win their cases may be a good way of getting a good social decision by providing a well-motivated debate. The problem here is, first, that this method seems to put an undue burden on A and B. Second, the courts are almost certain to

---

[6] Bruno Leoni, *Freedom and the Law* (Princeton: Van Nostrand Press, 1961); Richard A. Posner, *Economic Analysis of Law* (Boston: Little, Brown & Co., 1972).

take into account the concrete situation of A and B, as well as possible future social effects of their rule, when making their decision; as a result, their rule is not likely to be optimal from the standpoint of future effects.

To interject a note here, it has always seemed to me rather unfair to imprison a man for violating a law if the law is so unclear that four members of the Supreme Court think it did not cover his act. On the other hand, there is, clearly, nothing unfair—whatever else one can say about it—about setting rules for future behavior by a decision of five to four, as long as those rules are given adequate publicity.

The system I have described above as the European system divides the social from the private decision. Suppose, again, that in the European system the issue comes up between A and B where the law is not clear. The court must make a decision between them in an unclear state of the law. It makes this decision in terms of the concrete situation of A and B, without much concern for the future social consequences of this decision, because there are not going to be many future social consequences. The fact that the case between A and B has come up, however, alerts the gloss-preparing commission to the fact that the law is not clear. If this seems to be of sufficient importance to require clarification (and if a number of cases come up, this would almost obviously be true), it can provide a change in its interpretive gloss. If this interpretation is contrary to the desires of the legislature, the legislature is free to change it.

Note that in all of this I have not discussed constitutional issues. This is because these issues are essentially separate. Any constitution must be so designed that it has some kind of self-enforcing mechanism. Whether the courts are a suitable mechanism or a suitable portion of such a mechanism is a matter which I should like to put aside until my next book on political science. In our procedure, that is, American procedure, the courts are deeply involved in this issue. In England they are not. There seems to be no reason why the American variant of the Anglo-Saxon court system is inevitable.

People rationalizing Anglo-Saxon legal customs have tended to mix up two issues. First, it is clear that no legal code will always fit exactly every case that comes up. When the law does not fit, it is necessary for the deciding authority to decide what will be done. It does not follow from that, however, that it is necessary that this decision be enshrined and regarded as controlling all further cases of a similar nature. Indeed, in the United States, as in other Anglo-Saxon systems, it is not regarded as a precedent in most cases because most cases never get into the appellate tribunal and hence never become part of the literature from which the law is distilled. There is, further, no law of nature which says that appellate tribunals' decisions must become law, and an institutional structure was described above under which they would not. It is no doubt depressing that individuals will find themselves confronted with a state of law in which they do not know exactly what their responsibilities are, but nevertheless they may find a court reaching a decision against them. Unfortunately, we know of no way to draw up a law which does not present that particular problem. It does not follow therefrom, however, that we must have the individual judicial decision also set the law for the future.

It will not have escaped the reader that I believe our present system of having the details of our legal system generated as a sort of byproduct of judicial decisions to be an extremely poor one. It developed rather by accident in Anglo-Saxon law at a time when the judges thought they were not making new law, but finding or interpreting the existing law. Its continuance now is simply a matter of tradition. The tradition is, of course, very deeply ingrained in the legal profession, and it must be said they have not only a very deep belief in it but also the strongest of material motives for favoring it. A switch to a system in which the bulk of the law is a code and there is a central body which produces detailed glosses upon it, the whole thing being relatively short and compact, would reduce immense amounts of legal human capital to worthlessness. Thus, the lawyers have the combination of very strong feeling with which they have been indoctrinated, even stronger material grounds for wanting their present position to remain stable, and practically a monopoly of all decision-making posts in our present system. Under the circumstances, I doubt very much if my arguments here will have any policy effect.

I suspect the same will be true of my earlier arguments that fewer resources should be invested in the judicial problem of determining what the law actually is. Once again, this would be hard on lawyers and a drastic change in tradition. However, there seems to be little or no reason for investing many resources in determining the meaning of the law if the law is not reasonably clear on its face. If it is not reasonably clear on its face, it certainly cannot have fulfilled its social function. At best, it should have acted as a sort of warning to potential criminals or the parties before a civil suit that the law in this area is unclear and that they should proceed at their own risk. If the law is unclear, it is unclear, and retrospectively—that is, after whatever has happened has happened—we can do absolutely nothing to change the state of the law as it was when the parties undertook the action that now leads to legal proceeding. Once the moving finger has written, not all the efforts of expensive lawyers and appellate courts can change one fact!

6.

Liberty, Morality, and Justice

J. R. LUCAS

Thou shalt have no other gods than me: for
I am a jealous god.

I had not loved thee half so well
Loved I not honor more.

PROFESSOR HAYEK is jealous for liberty. Not only does he argue, trenchantly and convincingly, that liberty is a great good, but he often argues also that no other good is to be compared with it, and that in any case of conflict other goods must always be compromised in order that the overriding claims of liberty may not be in any way abated. I think this is a mistake. It distorts Hayek's analysis of our legal and economic institutions and weakens his defense of the free society. Critics can justly complain that he concentrates on one aspect of our social relationships to the exclusion of everything else, and the ill-disposed are enabled to evade the force of his arguments because he has refused to countenance considerations that evidently carry some weight and ought not to be brusquely dismissed. I shall comment briefly, as a logician, on the pattern of some of Hayek's typical arguments and then attempt to sketch an account of economic transactions and the rule of law that will accommodate the fact that the state is necessarily committed to other values besides liberty, and inescapably to justice.

A common argument of Hayek's is the denial of the third alternative. It is central to *The Road to Serfdom*. If we do not resolutely embrace the market economy with all its capitalist implications, we shall be inevitably edged toward totalitarian collectivism. As a practical argument it was undoubtedly valid at the time it was put forward, and has been substantially accepted. When it comes to the crunch, however much we dislike various aspects of the American way of life, we find Russia quite revolting, and are prepared to fight on the American side rather than become Soviet slaves in a Siberian salt mine. But this practical argument does not still theoretical doubts. Many liberal intellectuals have persisted in the hope that there is a third way, a mixed economy, which will preserve the essential freedoms valued by the West, while avoiding some of the unattractive features of capitalism. No Briton can argue that Hayek has been proved wrong by events. The sad decline of our country all too accurately bears out his gloomy prophecies of what would befall us if we were to falter in our love of freedom.[1] But often his arguments rely uncomfortably much on the assumption that if it is false that all As are B, then the only alternative is that no As are B. Thus in chapter six of *The Constitution of Liberty*, he argues, as I think Aristotle did earlier,[2] that total meritocracy is impossible because no state is completely of one mind about all values, and thus no state can make authoritative assessments of what each person ought in justice to be paid. But from the fact that distributive justice cannot be the sole criterion, he concludes that it cannot be any criterion at all, although he allows that actually it often is, for instance in large organizations where the contribution of each man cannot really be assessed in market terms. Such cases are common, not only in large private organizations like General Motors, but in the state as well. How much should British members of Parliament be paid? Although we cannot ignore market considerations, often we do not have to, and sometimes cannot, rely on them alone, and on occasion, as Hayek himself later concedes,[3] it is important that differentials should be felt to be just. Nevertheless, he is at pains to exclude justice as even one consideration among many. "Hayek's view," as H. B. Acton summarizes it,[4] is that "the pursuit of distributive justice tends to become *total*,

[1] F. A. Hayek, *The Constitution of Liberty* (Chicago: University of Chicago Press, 1960), pp. 47–48.

[2] Aristotle, *Politics*, III, esp. 1282b 30–1283a 16 (my interpretation is open to dispute).

[3] Hayek, *Constitution of Liberty*, p. 276.

[4] Arthur Seldon, ed., *Agenda for a Free Society* (London: Hutchinson, 1961), p. 82.

and does this not only in practice, but as a matter of logic," and since total distributive justice is impossible, distributive justice ought not to be pursued at all.

Various assumptions would legitimate Hayek's inference. I shall pick out three. First, the inference from not all to none is valid in a one-object universe, and totalitarianism makes the state the only object of concern. If we deify the state, then we address all our prayers and queries to it, and the question Why should I be paid less than that pop-singer, or stockbroker? becomes one which the state cannot refuse to answer.[5] And the state can answer only in terms of a complete system of distributive justice based on a monolithic set of values, which takes everything into account and assigns every factor a definitive value. In an age in which many people find it hard to believe in God, there is a strong tendency to worship the state—or society—as a God-substitute and to refer all our demands and duties to it alone, and then the demand for distributive justice will manifest totalitarian tendencies. The mistake lies in thinking too much of the state, not in seeking justice in our dealings with our fellow men. Hayek has argued admirably against our looking to the state for everything, and once we recognize that we cannot hope to have from it every sort of justice, there is no objection on this score in allowing some considerations of distributive justice to enter some of our calculations of prices and incomes.

A second assumption is more modal in character. Although not every decision of an arbitrator is bound to be bad, we cannot trust anyone not to make bad decisions sometimes, so the only safe rule is not to vest any discretion in state officials at all. Hayek argues against price-and-income boards on these grounds, and it is essentially the same argument that underlies his attack on administrative tribunals and his formulation of the rule of law. We must have cast-iron guarantees against the state's abusing its power, and therefore we must prevent it from doing various things it might sometimes do well but could possibly do ill. On one view of the first-order predicate calculus the effect of a modal operator, for example, is very like that of confining it to a universe of one member. If we use modal operators, we shall construe questions in all-or-nothing terms. If we cannot be

[5] F. A. Hayek, *Law, Legislation and Liberty* (Chicago: University of Chicago Press, 1973), pp. 143–44.

sure that a power will always be exercised well, we should not allow it to be exercised ever. It is an appealing argument. Nobody who knows what states have done in this century will dismiss it. We need, we desperately need, security against the state. But I think Hayek has chosen the wrong line of defense. His imputations of possible abuse are too sweeping to be plausible to those who have had the good fortune to live under relatively good governments, his prohibitions too wide to be practicable. His ideal rule of law is confessedly only an ideal, and therefore vulnerable as a practical safeguard. We need to discriminate between different dangers—a bumbling bureaucrat is bad, but should be checked in a way quite different from that needed to restrain a would-be commissar from taking over the ministry of the interior. If we make too much of Hume's dictum that in politics every man must be supposed a knave,[6] we shall fail to man the defenses against the more insidious danger of the well-meaning, but insensitive, administrator who is anxious to do his best for society but is not imbued with a sense of freedom or a respect for the rights of the individual citizen.

A third, very different argument can be adduced against the intellectuals' claim that other alternatives are in principle available. In politics we are concerned with large-scale institutions involving large numbers of men, many of whom lack either the intelligence or the interest to think very deeply about possibilities. Their discriminations are therefore blunt. Many possibilities that are conceivable are not practicable, because people would not understand them well enough to distinguish them from other, superficially similar, ones and operate them aright. It is a fair criticism of the welfare state in Britain that it is too complicated for most people to understand. Hayek can argue that the market economy and the slave economy are alike intelligible to the majority of mankind but that most of the mixed economies will not work because they will not be understood by those who work them. This argument, however, is not conclusive. The market economy also is too difficult for most people to understand. Moreover, the market economy never accounts for all our transactions with our fellow men. People can find their way through

6 David Hume, *Essays, Moral, Political and Literary*, ed. T. H. Green and T. H. Grose (London, 1875), vol. 1, p. 118; quoted in Hayek, *Constitution of Liberty*, p. 435.

a variety of social and legal transactions, and we cannot rule out all mixed economies a priori. Nevertheless, some weight remains in Hayek's contention that mixed economies may generate confusion in the minds of many and may therefore degenerate into a slave economy or revert to a market one.

Hayek relies on the inference from not all to none in one of his commendations of the market economy, or *catallaxy* as he calls it. "The defense of the free society," he writes, "must therefore show that it is due to the fact that we do not enforce a unitary scale of concrete ends, nor attempt to secure that some particular view about what is more and what is less important governs the whole of society, that the members of such a free society have as good a chance successfully to use their individual knowledge for the achievement of their individual purposes as they in fact have."[7] The premise is the entirely acceptable one of nontotalitarianism, that we do not have all our values in common. The conclusion Hayek often extracts from this is that we need not, and ought not to expect to, have values in common, and that it is vitally important that our institutions should be, as indeed the market economy can be, entirely neutral as regards ends, being merely the vehicle whereby each man is enabled to use other men's services for his own ends. I believe that here is a fundamental ambiguity which seriously weakens the whole of Hayek's argument. Sometimes he is what I might call a moral Whig and is at pains to point out that a love of freedom is, at the very least, not incompatible with religious beliefs.[8] Similarly he argues elsewhere against the thesis that all laws must be made by some human agency: "Rather, a group of men can form a society capable of making laws because they already share common beliefs which make discussion and persuasion possible and to which the articulated rules must conform in order to be accepted as legitimate."[9] At other times, however, he comes perilously close to a position of moral indifferentism and makes a great virtue of the market's unconcern with moral merit. But this is, I shall argue, to expose free institutions quite gratuitously

[7] F. A. Hayek, *Studies in Philosophy, Politics and Economics* (Chicago: University of Chicago Press, 1967), pp. 164–65.

[8] Ibid., p. 161.

[9] *Constitution of Liberty*, p. 181; see also Hayek, *Law, Legislation and Liberty*, chs. 4 and 5, esp. p. 95.

to the moral censure of moral men. The reason why the West has become increasingly critical of its economic arrangements is not that it has failed to deliver the goods—on the contrary, it has been spectacularly successful in doing that—but that the *theory* of them has failed to accord with our moral sentiments about society and has sometimes affronted our sense of justice. Hayek the economic individualist has walked away in the Whig Hayek's clothing, and the public washing of the dirty linen of the one has led people to suppose that the moral outfit of the other is equally blotchy and full of holes.

The market has received a bad moral press. Although we are keenly aware of its advantages as soon as we are deprived of it—a short visit to countries beyond the iron curtain or in the third world will make most westerners misty-eyed even about Madison Avenue —we find it difficult to love Mammon or preach the profit motive with total conviction. Although we read and fully accept the testimony of the victims of the Soviet system, the great bulk of the literature of dissent in the West has been protesting at the impersonality and institutionalized selfishness of market economics. It is a charge which Hayek indignantly rejects. He urges that the market gives us freedom, which we may, but do not have to, use for selfish ends. "It is part of the ordinary nature of men (and perhaps still more of women)," he says, "and one of the main conditions of their happiness that they make the welfare of other people their chief aim."[10] True, but it does not quite meet the points being made in moral criticism of the market system. These are essentially two, one a strict accusation of selfishness, which applies only to the strong doctrine of economic individualism, the other, which I shall call "non-tuism,"[11] which applies to most market systems as currently expounded by political economists.

If liberty is the only value we can be sure of, then social esteem will collapse into respect for pecuniary success. Hayek notices that this often has been the case in parts of America, but does not see why. Although liberty by itself is a great value, and one which refu-

---

[10] *Constitution of Liberty*, p. 78; see also Hayek, *Law, Legislation and Liberty*, p. 56; and *The Road to Serfdom*, p. 66.

[11] I borrow this useful term from Philip H. Wickstead, *The Common Sense of Political Economy* (London: Macmillan and Co., 1910), p. 174.

gees from European tyranny in the past century were only too thank-
ful to enjoy, it does not give guidance either to me individually or to
us collectively about how it is to be used. If I, or we, already have a
set of values, well and good. The Jew could breathe freely in New
York, the Irishman in Boston. But as the children and grandchildren
of the immigrants become more integrated into American society,
the problem of social success begins to arise. It is no longer enough
for me, as it was for my grandfather, that there are no pogroms, and
that I can ply my trade as a tailor and keep the law and the prophets
without fear or hindrance; I want to get on. In other societies, where
there are many shared values, there are nonpecuniary standards of
success; the Jew could become an intellectual in France or a gentle-
man in England. But if we are insistent that liberty is the only interpersonal value, then pecuniary advancement is the only available
interpersonal standard of success, and people who are ambitious and
anxious to do well in society will find their ambitions naturally taking financial form.

We thus need to distinguish two theses, one claiming that liberty is the only value we can be sure of, the other that it is only one
among many we are committed to. The former thesis can be defended at a theoretical level by skeptical arguments[12] and at a practical level by consideration of available alternatives. In an age of
positivism and agnosticism, it has become increasingly attractive to
cast doubt on any value held to be self-evidently valid and to pare
down the range of shared values to this sole remaining one as an
irreducible minimum. I notice a shift among friends of freedom over
the past three centuries from the high metaphysical line of liberal
Protestantism—which defends freedom because it has a special view
of human nature and regards freedom as a necessary condition of a
man's being able to be authentic and enter into a right relationship
with God—to the low profile of agnostic humanism, which finds the
claims of all illiberal doctrines unconvincing and therefore is left
with liberty as the one undoubted good. But I think that this line of
defense, although sometimes tactically effective, is strategically disastrous. It may ward off some assaults but can offer no defense
against nihilism; bullies often obtain power and will not be deflected

[12] As in Hayek, *Road to Serfdom*, p. 44.

by the skeptic unconvinced of their having an adequate justification for their actions. Moreover, inasmuch as this line of defense provides no outlet for men's moral sentiments, it renders liberty open to attacks from a moral point of view. Much as we may regard the American system as far less to be detested than the Russian, the American way of life, as expounded by commentators and as seen on TV, has not worn a sufficiently attractive aspect to be generally acceptable.

If we argue that liberty is only one among many values, albeit a cardinal one, we shall have a more defensible system, although a much less clear-cut one. For example, Hayek's skeptical argument about the use of funds raised by taxation for ends that some people are not interested in would then be invalid.[13] It was an argument much canvassed in Victorian England over the levying of church rates and is now over foreign aid. Enoch Powell argues that it is wrong for governments to aid foreign nations for idealistic reasons, which many individuals may not approve of, and that such monies should be raised by voluntary subscription from those individuals who are minded to contribute. But once we allow that a society may in general esteem values which not all its members are interested in, then we cannot rule out collective action on its part to realize them or insist that if they are to be realized at all it must be only by individual efforts. Hayek does the cause of individual liberty no good by setting it in stark contrast to collective activity. What we need to do is not to discountenance collectivist sentiments or ban collective action, but to ensure that individual liberties are nonetheless observed. Provided taxes are not excessive—and I entirely concur with Hayek's strictures on modern fiscal practices—they do not destroy freedom. The Victorian dissenter was not being compelled to go to church; having to contribute to aid for the third world abridges my freedom far less than being sent to fight in Vietnam.

If liberty is only one among many values, it may on occasion have to be compromised for the sake of something else, as when a man suspected of a grave crime is remanded to custody even though he may turn out subsequently to be innocent. In any case, we are always having to compromise one man's liberty in order to secure another's, and rather than assert, as Hayek does, that considerations

---

[13] *Constitution of Liberty*, p. 144 (but see also p. 375).

of liberty should generally override those of other values, we need to work out in detail how the requirements of liberty and other values can best be reconciled. In particular, we need to give weight to consideration of justice. Justice, like liberty, is a cardinal value. Many of the conclusions Hayek is anxious to establish can be buttressed better by arguments of justice than by arguments of liberty. And although I cannot help sympathizing with Hayek's distaste for admitting considerations of justice into economic arguments, both on account of the complexity of the concept and in view of the illegitimate extensions made of it by left-wing thinkers, nevertheless I shall maintain that it is wrong to exclude altogether considerations of justice from our account of men's business relations with one another.

Hayek in the Whig strands of his argument allows that we share values and are therefore not committed to merely pecuniary standards of success, and we are not under pressure to use the market for selfish ends. He distinguishes monetary rewards from social and moral esteem and argues that it is advantageous that they should be thus separated and that the market mechanism is entirely compatible with society as a whole having a definite moral *ethos*. Insofar as this is true, the market economy is acquitted of the charge of inherent selfishness. But it is still open to the objection that business transactions are shown to be essentially "nontuistic." When I do business with you, I may well not be animated by selfish motives—I may be acting for the sake of my children or my college or my country—but whether or not I am selfish, I am not taking *your* interests into consideration. That is for you to do. It is for you to decide whether the bargain is a good one from your point of view, and for me to mind my business on my side of the table. And yet this account falls far short of the realities of social life. Many people see themselves as serving the needs of others and pride themselves on taking the interests of others into consideration. Not only do they refrain from driving a hard bargain when a fortuitous combination of circumstances gives them the opportunity of doing so, but they regularly assess their services from the consumer's point of view and guide the consumer to the choice that is most in his interests even though not most in theirs. Often indeed the vendor is in a better position to assess the buyer's interests than the buyer himself, and the principle *caveat emptor* is far from being a necessary truth. This is not to say that the element of choice by the buyer can be eliminated. There are, as Hayek rightly insists,[14] some things that only the buyer knows, and only he can make up his own mind. But this curtain of ignorance is not as impenetrable as Hayek makes out. Contrary to what is often asserted, interests are what other people can sometimes know best, although necessarily not always so.[15] There is no epistemological reason, therefore, why a commercial transaction should be entirely non-tuistic. It may be, inasmuch as it is open to either party not to consider the other's interests at all, but it does not have to be, although each will naturally be specially solicitous of his own interests. We can reproduce in our approach to commercial negotiations the distinction Plato drew between πλεονεξία, self-aggrandizement, and τὸ τὰ αὑτοῦ πράττειν, each doing his own thing, or each minding his own business. But this is a distinction Hayek will not admit, and without it men are under pressure to see their workaday lives not as a service to their fellow men or a contribution to communal life, but as an exercise, usually not very successful, in profit maximization.

There are grave difficulties in giving each man his due in economics as in law. In our positivist age it is easy to pour skeptical scorn on something as vague as that attitude of mind portrayed by Justinian and Aquinas. But, as Hayek rejects positivism as a theory of law, so I reject it as the only possible theory of business transactions. The fact that many businessmen and most professional men are not chiefly concerned with profit maximization weighs heavily with me. I do not think it is good enough to brush aside the account given by the agents concerned with their own activities or to make out that it is only an imperfection or an inefficiency in the working of an ideal market system. Rather I want to offer a different elucidation of Hayek's *catallaxy*, the basic business transaction. In Hayek's analysis each party is entirely external to the other, and each asks himself only Is it to my advantage to accept the terms offered? and bargains with the other, trying to drive as hard a bargain as he can. The typical case is that of the itinerant trader exchanging amber for

---

[14] *Constitution of Liberty*, p. 371.
[15] See my *Democracy and Participation* (Baltimore: Penguin, 1976), pp. 86–96.

tin, or the rich vain man wondering whether to pay the exorbitant
fee demanded by the fashionable portrait painter.[16] These cases are
ones in which neither party is committed to the other, and each can
perfectly well afford to break off negotiations if the terms are too
steep. But this, surely, is untypical of a great many business transactions. A doctor and his patient, a retailer and a wholesaler, a manu-
facturer and his supplier have a continuing relationship. They are not
absolutely committed to each other. They may remove their custom
for good reason or after due notice. Still it would be wrong for a
doctor not to attend one of his patients just because he felt disin-
clined to do so, and it would be wrong also for him suddenly to
charge a very high fee for a particular visit. Even where there is no
continuing relationship, we think it reprehensible to charge an exorbitant price for a standard service to someone who happens to be
desperately in need of it—say a garage charging $100 a gallon for
gasoline to a motorist on his way to his dying mother. An analysis
which takes an entirely external view is inadequate. Instead, we
should see an exchange of goods or services as a special case of col-
laboration. Often we collaborate in some joint enterprise, and in
those cases where the enterprise yields divisible benefits, we think it
right to apportion them in accordance with the contribution each
party made to the success of the enterprise. There is room for dispute
over the exact quantitative assignments to be made, but the general
principle is widely understood and accepted. That is to say, we do
not all agree what exactly each man's ἀξία—as Aristotle would term
it[17]—is, but we do agree that this is the relevant criterion for dis-
tributing the fruits of the common enterprise. In most cases of col-
laboration the efforts of each party mesh together in a very complicated way to produce the end result, but in some cases a simple
exchange or provision of goods or services achieves all that is desired.
Each party could then view the transaction not as a bargain but as
a cooperative interchange to which each contributed and from which
each should benefit in proper proportion. They would see it primarily
as a two-person non-zero-sum game in which they were forming a
coalition and in which the division of the spoils was determined by
the nature of the coalition. This contrasts with the way in which

[16] *Constitution of Liberty*, p. 136.
[17] *Nicomachean Ethics*, V, 1131a 24 ff.

bargainers see their activity, which is essentially a competitive, not a cooperative, one, a zero-sum game, where my gain is your loss and I must seek to maximize my benefit at your expense; there is no common standpoint which we can both adopt and which will give us guidance about the apportionment of benefits that should be acceptable to us both.

Hayek's main argument against invoking considerations of justice does not apply here. We are not attempting to lay down an overall scheme of distribution of all benefits to all members of society. The catallaxy is limited, and therefore is not logically incapable of giving rise to principles of apportionment. Nevertheless, there are many difficulties in this account of commutative justice. It is vague. It lacks the clear-cut outline of the bargaining account. It is conventional. It has a tendency toward obsolescence—the just price or just wage of today seems often to be the economic price of sixty years ago. I admit all these objections but observe exactly the same difficulties in our concept of legal justice, which is the despair of lawyers on account of its vagueness, and of philosophers on account of its conventionality, and of radicals on account of its conservatism; and yet, however often we are told to abandon it, we find we cannot do without it. We are concerned to give each man his due, although we often know not what his due is. Very largely it is a matter of convention that determines the reasonable expectations of all the parties involved, and therefore we specify justice in terms of previously promulgated laws and decisions previously arrived at. The rule of precedents leads naturally toward ossification, and we are constantly complaining that the law is out of date. Nevertheless, our feelings for justice remain. We think it wrong to settle serious disputes by a flip of a coin or trial by combat, or by lynch law, or by a press campaign; we believe that they should be adjudicated by a judge who has listened to arguments on both sides and reached a rational decision, based on the facts of the case and the relevant statutes, precedents, and legal principles. A business transaction is seldom as serious as a legal action, but sometimes a similar sentiment shows itself inasmuch as we sometimes do not want the outcome to depend on the bargaining strength of the parties concerned and therefore seek some independent standard to assess a fair price. Occasionally we even obtain a valuation from a professional valuer, who arbitrates a price "as between willing buyer and seller"; more often we find out what the going price is, as settled by the impersonal mechanism of the market, and are guided by that. But however we settle it, the price is not reached by each side driving as hard a bargain as he can, and therefore such transactions need no longer be seen as essentially nontuistic.

The account just given of business transactions will strike most economists as incurably tender-minded, and so, of course, it is. After all, it was intended to meet the objections of the tender-minded to the market economy and show how it could be elucidated in terms of justice as well as of liberty. But so long as freedom remains, since some men are very selfish and we are all selfish sometimes, there will be a tendency for principles of commutative justice to be swept aside by determined bargainers who will not accept anything less than the most they can extort. It would be quite unrealistic to suppose that this will not happen. But provided it does not always have to happen, and provided it is not offered as a guide to what we ought to do, Hayek's libertarian defense of the market economy is cogent. The great merit of the market, so far as liberty is concerned, is that it safeguards freedom. Certain things cannot happen without my consent. On the decisions which concern me most—what job I shall take, where I shall live, whom I shall marry—I have a veto. Sometimes the veto will be costly to exercise—if I throw up my job I shall find it difficult to get another one, if I don't marry Jane, I shan't find any other girl who will have me—but I always can say no and am thus far better off than anyone living under a totalitarian regime. And often I have attractive alternatives to choose between. Equally, of course, other people may exercise their veto and may exercise it unreasonably and to my disadvantage. They can exploit their position at my expense. This is the unacceptable face of capitalism, but it changes its aspect when we see it in context. It can and does manifest itself on occasion but does not have to always. It can manifest itself because other men are, like me, free and therefore able sometimes to be awkward; it does on occasion manifest itself, because other men are, like me, selfish and inclined to disregard the interests of others. But complaints about original sin belong to theology, not political economy. As political economists, although we may seek to foster altruism, we cannot count on it always and must reckon on the possibility of men being moved solely by selfish considerations in arriving at decisions. And then, as an exercise in "damage control," the market economy is preferable to all available alternatives. Speculators who build office blocks and then keep them empty to obtain higher rents later on are, no doubt, inestimable creatures: but they are far less of a threat to my happiness than sensual pashas, Jew-baiting commissars, or empire-building civil servants. Businessmen may be bad, but they cannot be corrupt, as bureaucrats can. Better legitimize the profit motive and have some people honestly out to maximize their own profits than have them feather their own nests dishonestly in the course of official business.

The other merit of the market economy, in Hayek's eyes, is that it processes certain sorts of information and makes it available to each man considering what decisions to take. The market tells me other men's economic wants and how, therefore, I can dispose of my resources to the greatest economic advantage. Hayek makes much of this argument but fails, I think, to recognize its limitations. The market can deal only with certain sorts of information and, in processing it, homogenizes it and eliminates much relevant detail. It cannot register certain sorts of information, is highly imperfect in practice, and, with respect to a number of "prisoner's dilemma" situations, is in principle counterproductive. It is very good for dealing with cotton futures but not all that marvelous for allocating medical care or organizing public transport. Often the decision-maker has a lot of other information available besides that registered in market prices. An undergraduate discovers that he will be far better paid if he becomes an educational administrator, a chartered accountant, or a stockbroker, but he knows, not through the market but through the grapevine, that there is really much greater need for teachers, probation officers, or clergymen. The market is not the only source of information. Moreover, the information it does provide has been reduced to the one dimension of monetary terms. Much has been left out in expressing values in terms of £. s. d. In particular, neighborhood effects, both beneficial and adverse, are ignored. It is difficult to quantify the advantage, say, to a village of having a village school with a resident schoolmaster playing his part in village life as against busing the children to a large school in the market town, or the loss of amenity in constructing airports or motorways, but they are nonetheless real for that, and ought to be taken into consideration by any responsible man. Sometimes we can pass laws requiring decision-makers to pay due regard to some factors, but legislation lags behind social need, and there will in the typical case be some circumstances neither reflected in market values nor made mandatory by law which a man ought nevertheless to bear in mind in reaching his decision. We should not idealize the market too much. It does provide valuable information in a highly processed and convenient form, but it does not constitute our sole source of information and can impose its own distortions on the information it does provide. It is not sacrosanct. The responsible citizen ought not to ignore it in deciding how to use his resources, for it can constitute an indication of how other men would like him to act, but he is not bound to follow its guidance and ought to make up his mind on the basis of all the information at his disposal, which sometimes will indicate a course of action other than what purely economic considerations suggest.

I shall be slightly ungenerous in criticizing Hayek's philosophy of law as expounded in *The Constitution of Liberty*, for he has substantially modified it in *Law, Legislation and Liberty*, which gives an analysis of law as profound as H. L. A. Hart's *Concept of Law* and is in certain crucial respects preferable to it. In both statements of his position Hayek seeks to ground law on the basis of liberty alone and does not pay sufficient regard to considerations of justice. Hayek claims that the rule of law requires that laws be couched in general terms and have universal application and argues that only so can the individual know how the law bears on his plans and what he must do or abstain from doing, in order to be free of coercion or orders backed by threats of coercion. But the condition of universality is neither necessary nor sufficient. It is not sufficient, as Hayek's own example of the dappled cows shows.[18] With enough ingenuity we can frame laws in universal terms but so as, in fact, to have only very particular application. But quite apart from deliberate fiddling, legislators may pass oppressive laws, and the fact that they are to be themselves bound by them constitutes no adequate safeguard. Not only may Scottish sabbatarians impose Sabbath keeping on everyone,[19] but employees may restrict freedom in ways only the enter-

[18] *Constitution of Liberty*, p. 489.
[19] Ibid., p. 155.

prising mind knows about, and the poor may vote for steeply pro-gressive taxation.[20] Universality, although a safeguard, is not a com-plete safeguard, and although it is often a distinguishing feature of legislation in accordance with the rule of law, cannot be solely con-stitutive of it. The condition is also not necessary. Granted two con-ditions, to be elaborated later, a man can live under a common-law system and know where he stands with regard to the law and be able to mind his step and keep out of trouble. In his later work Hayek becomes increasingly conscious of the inadequacy of formulated rules to express all the know-how we have. Often we know how to behave although we have never been given a rule covering exactly the case in question. Even where laws are expressed in a legal code, difficult cases constantly crop up and have to be decided by a judge who is not merely applying a previously promulgated law in a purely me-chanical fashion. What we need is not that the rules should have been antecedently specified, but that the decisions of authority shall be reasonable, so that we can form a reasonable expectation of what they will be. This we can do, provided there is a shared understand-ing between the rulers and the ruled and provided also the point at issue does not depend on some convention not yet established. The demand for the laws to be promulgated often arose from distrust of the way in which the discretion hitherto vested in the judges was being exercised.[21] Rules are required because agreement is not other-wise to be had. Rules also are required when no matter how much we share the same rational understanding, what is at issue is some-thing that cannot be settled by reason alone. Sometimes we need legislation to lay down new conventions—about electricity or wire-less telegraphy,[22] for example—and sometimes we need to correct undesirable developments in the law and to give notice that expecta-tions which were reasonable in view of previous practice are no longer to be relied upon. Hence Hayek, somewhat reluctantly I think, allows in his *Law, Liberty and Legislation* that legislation is sometimes necessary. But the main drift of his admirable exegesis of the nature of law is that legislation is not generally necessary and

[20] Ibid., chs., 7, 8, 20.
[21] See, more fully, my *The Principles of Politics* (Oxford: Oxford Univer-sity Press, 1966), sec. 30.
[22] Hayek, *Law, Legislation and Liberty*, p. 109.

that we can live safely under a common-law system in which the laws are not fully formulated and in which, therefore, the rule of law cannot be characterized in terms of any strong principle of universality.

I want to take Hayek's subsequent modification of the doctrine of the rule of law a stage further. If we adopt his approach in *Law, Liberty and Legislation,* we shall ground the rule of law not only on liberty, important though that is, but also on the equally cardinal value of justice. And once we give considerations of justice their due, we shall find that they apply not only to law proper (*nomos*) the legal framework which governs the relations of one citizen with another, but also to administration and other activities of government (*taxis*), in which discretion has to be exercised in reaching decision about communal action.

The peculiar merit of the judicial process, according to Hayek,[23] is that the judge solves problems arising from conflicts of expectations by ratiocination, having listened to both sides of the case. Although inevitably he disappoints the expectations of one party, he does so reluctantly, only if the reasons for not so doing are overridden by weightier reasons on the other side. This is essentially different from an exercise of liberty or unfettered discretion. A girl in choosing a new dress, or deciding which invitation to accept, need not consider the financial expectations of owners of the boutiques or the hopes of aspiring males. A decision is justiciable when the question Why should I disappoint him? is pertinent and requires a cogent answer. This is why, as I argue elsewhere,[24] justice is essential if we are to identify with the community, and the alienation of present-day Britain is due to the unconcern in its decision procedures with respect to considerations of justice and freedom. Justice sympathizes, so far as it rationally can, with every party, and no one need feel that he has been ignored. His interests are not lightly disregarded. If they are ultimately overborne, it will be only for weighty reasons, whose force he can feel even if he does not fully endorse them. Although inevitably disappointed by an adverse decision, he will not be bruised by it, in virtue of the tender-mindedness manifested by authority towards him. If I can be confident—and it is a big IF—that the au-

---

[23] Ibid., ch. 5, esp. pp. 100–1, 115–17.
[24] *Democracy and Participation,* ch. 6.

thorities will be guided by considerations of justice in all their dealings with me, I can live safely under their suzerainty and can form my own plans without fear of their being arbitrarily frustrated. Justice gives me the security I want, and much of the freedom. It is not exactly the same as freedom, and we need a specific commitment to liberty too, and sometimes must compromise justice for the sake of liberty, but nevertheless it is really justice which underlies Hayek's revised concept of law and which alone can lead to a satisfactory doctrine of the rule of law.

Hayek maintains that his revised concept of law still leads to the general conclusions of *The Constitution of Liberty*. The argument comes in *Law, Legislation and Liberty*, and I quote the crucial passage:

> This implies a distinction between such "legitimate" expectations which the law must protect and others which it must allow to be disappointed. And the only method yet discovered of defining a range of expectation which will be thus protected, and thereby reducing the mutual interference of people's actions with each other's intentions, is to demarcate for every individual a range of permitted actions by designating . . . ranges of objects over which only particular individuals are allowed to dispose and from the control of which all others are excluded.[25]

I do not think this argument is entirely valid. Hayek is quite right in saying that we cannot be totally tender-minded, that we must take decisions adverse to some people's interests, and that therefore we must distinguish between protected interests and disappointable interests. And he is right also in seeing the institution of property as a method of enabling the distinction to be drawn. But it is not the only method, and although it works well in some cases, it does not do so in others, often failing to provide people with either the security or the liberty they need. Property works well with chattels, which are usually neither necessarily nor in fact unique. My having absolute rights over my car does not preclude your having a fairly similar car under your absolute sway.[26] But in general this solution is too absolute. First, there is not one single distinction between protected and disappointable rights, but rather a gradation. My life, limb, and liberty deserve—and get, in most legal systems—more protection than

[25] P. 107.
[26] See further my *The Principles of Politics*, sec. 44.

my property. I believe that there are many other interests which deserve some protection but do not get it because lawyers are misled by the concept of property, and, realizing that these interests are not property rights, reckon that therefore they are not any right at all. My passport is the property of Her Majesty's government. Fair enough. It is not my property, to leave to my children in my will or to sell to the highest bidder. But the right to leave the country is nonetheless an important right, not to be left to the arbitrary discretion of some executive-minded official. Property is too much an all-or-nothing affair, and if we rely exclusively on the institution of property, we leave people too much at the mercy of other men's—particularly government officials'—unfettered choices. This is not to deny its value. People need to have an absolute veto on the use of some things by others and an absolute choice in disposing of them themselves or they will not have room to develop their personalities properly, and these rights imply the possibility of their abuse. This can bear hardly on others, although, as Hayek keeps on reminding us, competition will tend to prevent the hardship being excessive. But often we need less than a complete veto of our own and would be glad not to be vulnerable to the unreasonable vetoes of others. Rather than be able to forbid absolutely every adverse decision within a certain range—which must therefore tend to be a fairly limited range—we should do better to have a much wider range of interests cherished and not overborne except for good reason.

Political debate in this century has been loud with various demands for various sorts of rights, and in consequence there has been a great increase in governmental activity to administer schemes to provide for these rights. These have been, characteristically, not subject to judicial control, and Hayek, in *The Constitution of Liberty*,[27] is vehement in his criticism of administrative discretion and decisions "taken on their merits." The logical criticism can no longer be sustained, once he has allowed that a decision can be rational although not syllogistically deduced from a previously promulgated law.[28] Instead, we should concentrate on the practical criticism that executive discretion tends in fact toward state tyranny, and we should seek to establish institutions which will ensure that decisions by public au-

---

[27] Chs. 14 and 16, secs. 5–6.
[28] Which he sometimes does in *Constitution of Liberty*, as on pp. 208–9.

thority are taken in a judicial frame of mind, with due regard to the interests of those affected. These can be arranged in some sort of order, ranging from the central ones of life, limb, and liberty, which are protected by elaborate legal procedures, to fairly peripheral ones, which deserve only a few seconds' consideration at most. It is the ones near, but not quite at, the center we need to think about most, because they are the ones where the danger of abuse by state officials is greatest and because failure to meet them is most likely to bring free institutions into disrepute. Hayek's remedy of having free markets is not enough. Although the market is marvelously flexible and enables people to do much to mitigate the adverse consequences of other men's decisions, it has some weaknesses of its own and cannot cater for all our needs, nor does it satisfy the desire some men have to see themselves primarily as serving their fellow men and to be contributors, rather than getters.

The attitude, therefore, I advocate our taking to the market is less enthusiastic than Hayek's, but consequently less vulnerable. It is an imperfect way of organizing cooperative enterprises, not only contingently so, as Hayek himself acknowledges, but necessarily so. Nevertheless, it is better than its alternatives. It secures to everyone some essential freedoms and gives us some safeguards against the worst excesses of our fellow men, who seldom are adequately altruistic and often are deeply selfish. It is the "system under which bad men can do least harm."[29] It also often works quite well in practice but does not always do so. It does not give us all the information we require and does not provide us with a rationale of our life's work. Rather, like the law, it furnishes us with a framework, on the basis of which we can concert our activities. Most of my professional life is lived in an informal personal setting. The law is very much in the background. I depend on its being there in the background, but it is importantly true that I have never sued my college or my colleagues, nor even consulted a solicitor about my legal rights against them. In something of the same way economic considerations may play a relatively subordinate part in a man's—or a college's or a hospital's or a church's—decision-making, setting limits to the options open and providing a sort of fallback should agreement be not otherwise forthcom-

[29] *Individualism and Economic Order* (Chicago: University of Chicago Press), p. 12.

ing, but not constituting the only sensible *raison d'être* for business activity. As often in political economy, we have to speak in two tones of voice at once. We have to take human imperfection seriously and allow for the fact that men—rulers, judges, businessmen, and minor government officials—are often selfish and sometimes downright bad, and therefore we have to lay down hard and fast distinctions that will enable us to break off relations with bad businessmen, punish transgressors, and sometimes depose rulers, if they should overstep the line. But we have also to take human aspiration seriously and address ourselves to men who mean well and do not take kindly to being regarded as rogues living among thieves. Hayek's low-key defense of law and liberty is deeply convincing, but his high idealistic note is too limited to strike responsive chords in many men's hearts. Individualism and liberty, although great themes, are not enough. We have many moral aspirations as well, and if we are really to identify with a free constitution, we need to see it as embodying not only liberty but justice as well.

7.

We Do Not Have a Right to Liberty

RONALD DWORKIN

LIBERTIES, NOT LIBERTY

Do we have a right to liberty?[1] Thomas Jefferson thought so, and since his day the right to liberty has received more play than his competing rights to life and the pursuit of happiness. Liberty gave its name to the most influential political movement of the last century, and many of those who now despise liberals do so on the ground that they are not sufficiently libertarian. Of course, almost everyone concedes that the right to liberty is not the only political right, and that therefore claims to freedom must be limited, for example, by restraints that protect the security or property of others. Nevertheless, the consensus in favor of some right to liberty is a vast one, though it is, as I shall argue in this essay, misguided.

The right to liberty is popular all over this political spectrum. The rhetoric of liberty fuels every radical movement from international wars of liberation to campaigns for sexual freedom and women's liberation. But liberty has been even more prominent in conservative service. Even the mild social reorganizations of the antitrust and unionization movements, and of the early New Deal, were opposed on the grounds that they infringed the right to liberty, and just now efforts to achieve some racial justice through techniques like the busing of black and white schoolchildren are bitterly opposed on that ground.

It has become common, indeed, to describe the great social issues of American politics, and in particular the racial issue, as presenting a conflict between the demands of liberty and those of equality. It may be, it is said, that the poor and the black and the

[1] I use *liberty* in this essay in the sense Isaiah Berlin called "negative."

uneducated and the unskilled have an abstract right to equality, but the prosperous and the whites and the educated and the able have a right to liberty as well, and any efforts at social reorganization in aid of the first set of rights must reckon with and respect the second. Everyone except the extremist recognizes, therefore, the need to compromise between equality and liberty. Every piece of important social legislation, from tax policy to integration plans, is shaped by the supposed tension between these two goals.

I have this supposed conflict between equality and liberty in mind when I ask whether we have a right to liberty, as Jefferson and everyone else have supposed. That is a crucial question. If freedom to choose one's schools, or employees, or neighborhood is simply something that we all want, like air conditioning or lobsters, then we are not entitled to hang on to these freedoms in the face of what we concede to be the rights of others to an equal share of respect and resources. But if we can say not simply that we want these freedoms, but that we are ourselves entitled to them, then we have established at least a basis for demanding a compromise.

There is now a movement, for example, in favor of a proposed constitutional amendment that would guarantee every schoolchild the legal right to attend a "neighborhood school" and thus outlaw busing. The suggestion that neighborhood schools somehow rank with jury trials as constitutional values would seem silly but for the sense many Americans have that forcing schoolchildren into buses is somehow as much an interference with the fundamental right to liberty as segregated schooling was an insult to equality. But that seems to me absurd; indeed it seems to me absurd to suppose that men and women have any general right to liberty at all, at least as liberty has traditionally been conceived by its champions.

I have in mind the traditional definition of liberty as the absence of constraints placed by a government upon what a man might do if he wants to. Isaiah Berlin, in the most famous modern essay on liberty, put the matter this way: "The sense of freedom, in which I use this term, entails not simply the absence of frustration but the absence of obstacles to possible choices and activities—absence of obstructions on roads along which a man can decide to walk." This conception of liberty is doggedly neutral among the various activities a man might pursue, the various roads he might wish to walk. It diminishes a man's liberty when we prevent him from talking or making love as he wishes, but it also diminishes his liberty when we prevent him from murdering or defaming others. These latter constraints may be justifiable, but only because they are compromises necessary to protect the liberty or security of others, and not because they do not, in themselves, infringe the independent value of liberty. Bentham said that any law whatsoever is an "infraction" of liberty, and though some such infractions might be necessary, it is obscurantist to pretend that they are not infractions after all. In this neutral, all-embracing sense of liberty, liberty and equality are plainly in competition. Laws are needed to protect equality, and laws are inevitably compromises of liberty.

Liberals like Berlin are content with this neutral sense of liberty because it seems to encourage clear thinking. It allows us to identify just what is lost, though perhaps unavoidably, when men accept constraints on their actions for some other goal or value. It would be an intolerable muddle, in this view, to use the concept of liberty or freedom in such a way that we counted a loss of freedom only when men were prevented from doing something that we thought they ought to do. It would allow totalitarian governments to masquerade as liberal simply by arguing that they prevent men from doing only what is wrong. Worse, it would obscure the most distinctive point of the liberal tradition, which is that interfering with a man's free choice to do what he might want to do is in and of itself an insult to humanity, a wrong that may be justified but can never be wiped away by competing considerations. For a true liberal, any constraint upon freedom is something that a decent government must regret and keep to the minimum necessary to accommodate the other rights of its constituents.

In spite of this tradition, however, the neutral sense of liberty seems to me to have caused more confusion than it has cured, particularly when it is joined to the popular and inspiring idea that men have a right to liberty. For we can maintain the idea that men have a right to liberty as such, in the neutral sense of liberty, only by so watering down the idea of a right that the right to liberty is something hardly worth having at all.

The term *right* is used in politics and philosophy in many different senses, some of which I have tried to disentangle elsewhere.[2] In order sensibly to ask whether we have a right to liberty in the neutral sense, we must fix on some one meaning of *right*. It would not be difficult to find a sense of that term in which we could say with some confidence that men have a right to liberty. We might say, for example, that someone has a right to liberty if it is in his interest to have liberty, that is, if he either wants it or if it would be good for him to have it. In this sense, I would be prepared to concede that men have a right to liberty. But in this sense I would also have to concede that men have a right, at least generally, to vanilla ice cream. My concession about liberty, moreover, would have very little value in political debate. I should want to claim, for example, that men have a right to equality in a much stronger sense, that they do not simply want equality but that they are entitled to it, and I would therefore not recognize the claim that men want liberty as requiring any compromise in the efforts that I believe are necessary to give other men the equality to which they are entitled.

If the right to liberty is to play the role cut out for it in political debate, therefore, it must be a right in a much stronger sense. In the article just mentioned I defined a strong sense of right that seems to me to capture the claims men mean to make when they appeal to political and moral rights. I do not propose to repeat my analysis here, but only to summarize it in this way. A successful claim of right, in the strong sense I described, has this consequence. If someone has a right to something, then it is wrong for the government to deny it to him even though it would be in the general interest to do so. This sense of a right (which might be called the antiutilitarian concept of a right) seems to me very close to the sense of right principally used in political and legal writing and argument in recent years. It marks the distinctive concept of an individual right against the state which is the heart, for example, of constitutional theory in the United States.

I do not think that the right to liberty would come to very much, or have much power in political argument, if it relied on any sense of the right any weaker than that. If we settle on this concept of a

---

[2] See "Taking Rights Seriously," *New York Review of Books*, December 17, 1970.

right, however, then it seems plain that there exists no general right to liberty as such. I have no political right to drive up Lexington Avenue. If the government chooses to make Lexington Avenue one-way downtown, it is a sufficient justification that this would be in the general interest, and it would be ridiculous for me to argue that for some reason it would nevertheless be wrong. The vast bulk of the laws which diminish my liberty are justified on utilitarian grounds, as being in the general interest or for the general welfare; if, as Bentham supposes, each of these laws diminishes my liberty, they nevertheless do not take away from me anything that I have a right to have. It will not do, in the one-way-street case, to say that although I have a right to drive up Lexington Avenue, nevertheless the government for special reasons is justified in overriding that right. That seems silly because the government needs no special justification—but only *a* justification—for this sort of legislation. So I can have a political right to liberty, such that every act of constraint diminishes or infringes that right, only in such a weak sense of right that the so-called right to liberty is not competitive with strong rights, like the right to equality, at all. In any strong sense of right, which would be competitive with the right to equality, there exists no general right to liberty at all.

It may now be said that I have misunderstood the claim that there is a right to liberty. It does not mean to argue, it will be said, that there is a right to all liberty, but simply to important or basic liberties. Every law is, as Bentham said, an infraction of liberty, but we have a right to be protected against only fundamental or serious infractions. If the constraint on liberty is serious or severe enough, then it is indeed true that the government is not entitled to impose that constraint simply because that would be in the general interest; the government is not entitled to constrain liberty of speech, for example, whenever it thinks that would improve the general welfare. So there is, after all, a general right to liberty as such, provided that that right is restricted to important liberties or serious deprivations. This qualification does not affect the political arguments I described earlier, it will be said, because the rights to liberty that stand in the way of full equality are rights to basic liberties like, for example, the right to attend a school of one's choice.

But this qualification raises an issue of great importance for liberal theory, which those who argue for a right to liberty do not face. What does it mean to say that the right to liberty is limited to basic liberties, or that it offers protection only against serious infractions of liberty? That claim might be spelled out in two different ways, with very different theoretical and practical consequences. Let us suppose two cases in which government constrains a man from doing what he might want to do: (1) the government prevents a man from speaking his mind on political issues; (2) the government prevents a man from driving his car uptown on Lexington Avenue. What is the connection between these two cases, and the difference between them, such that though they are both cases in which a man is constrained and deprived of liberty, his right to liberty is infringed only in the first, and not in the second.

On the first of the two theories we might consider, the citizen is deprived of the same commodity—namely, liberty—in both cases, but the difference is that in the first case the amount of that commodity taken away from him is, for some reason, either greater in amount or greater in its impact than in the second. But that seems bizarre. It is very difficult to think of liberty as a commodity. If we do try to give liberty some operational sense, such that we can measure the relative diminution of liberty occasioned by different sorts of laws or constraints, then the result is unlikely to match our intuitive sense of what are the basic liberties and what are not. Suppose, for example, we measure a diminution in liberty by calculating the extent of frustration that it induces. We shall then have to face the fact that laws against theft, and even traffic laws, impose constraints that are felt more keenly by most men than constraints on political speech would be. We might take a different tack, and measure the degree of loss of liberty by the impact that a particular constraint has on future choices. But we should then have to admit that the ordinary criminal code reduces choice for most men more than laws which forbid fringe political activity. So the first theory—that the difference between cases covered and those not covered by our supposed right to liberty is a matter of degree—must fail.

The second theory argues that the difference between the two cases has to do, not with the degree of liberty involved, but with the special character of the liberty involved in the case covered by the right. On this theory, the offense involved in a law that limits free speech is of a different character, and not just different in degree, from a law that prevents a man from driving up Lexington Avenue. That sounds plausible, though as we shall see it is not easy to state what this difference in character comes to, or why it argues for a right in some cases though not in others. My present point, however, is that if the distinction between basic liberties and other liberties is defended in this way, then the notion of a general right to liberty as such has been entirely abandoned. If we have a right to basic liberties not because they are cases in which the commodity of liberty is somehow especially at stake, but because an assault on basic liberties injures us or demeans us in some way that goes beyond its impact on liberty, then what we have a right to is not liberty at all, but to the values or interests or standing that this particular constraint defeats.

This is not simply a question of terminology. If I am right then the right to liberty is a misconceived concept that does a disservice to political thought in at least two ways. First, the idea of a right to liberty creates a false sense of a necessary conflict between liberty and other values when social regulation, like the busing program, is proposed. Second, the idea of a fundamental right to liberty provides too easy an answer to the question of why we regard certain kinds of restraints, like the restraint on free speech or the exercise of religion, as especially unjust. The idea of a right to liberty allows us to say that these constraints are unjust because they have a special impact on liberty as such. Once we recognize that this answer is spurious, then we shall have to face the difficult question of what is indeed at stake in these cases.

I should like to turn at once to that question. If there is no general right to liberty, then why do citizens in a democracy have rights to any specific kind of liberty, like freedom of speech or religion or political activity? It is no answer to say that if individuals have these rights, then the community will be better off in the long run as a whole. This idea—that individual rights may lead to overall utility—may or may not be true, but it is irrelevant to the defense of rights as such, because when we say that someone has a right to speak his mind freely, in the relevant political sense, we mean that he is entitled to do so even if this would not be in the general interest. If we want to defend individual rights in the sense in which we claim them, then we must try to discover something beyond utility that argues for these rights.

I mentioned one possibility earlier. We might be able to make out a case that individuals suffer some special damage when the traditional rights are invaded. On this argument, there is something about the liberty to speak out on political issues such that, if that liberty is denied, the individual suffers a special kind of damage which makes it wrong to inflict that damage upon him even though the community as a whole would benefit. This line of argument will appeal to those who themselves would feel special deprivation at the loss of their political and civil liberties, but it is nevertheless a difficult argument to pursue for two reasons.

First, there are a great many men, and they are undoubtedly in the majority even in a democracy like the United States, who do not exercise the political liberties that they have and who would not count the loss of these liberties as especially grievous. Second, we lack a psychological theory which would justify and explain the theory that the loss of civil liberties, or any particular liberties, involves inevitable or even likely psychological damage. On the contrary, there is now a lively tradition in psychology, led by psychologists like Laing, who argue that a good deal of mental instability in modern societies may be traced to the demand for too much liberty rather than too little. In their account, the need to choose, which follows from liberty, is an unnecessary source of destructive tension. These theories are not necessarily persuasive, but until we can be confident that they are wrong, we cannot assume that psychology demonstrates the opposite, however appealing that might be on political grounds.

If we want to argue for a right to certain liberties, therefore, we must find another ground, and there is only one plausible alternative. We must argue on ground of political morality that it is wrong to deprive individuals of these liberties, for some reason, apart from direct psychological damage, in spite of the fact that the common interest would be served by doing so. I put the matter this vaguely because there is no reason to assume, in advance, that only one kind of reason would support that moral position. It might be that a just society would recognize a variety of individual rights, some grounded on very different sorts of moral considerations from others. In what remains of this essay I shall try to describe only one possible ground for rights. It does not follow that men and women in civil society have only the rights that the argument I shall make would support, but it does follow that they have at least these rights, and that is important enough.

WHAT RIGHTS DO WE HAVE?

The central concept of my argument will be the concept not of liberty but of equality. I presume that we all accept the following postulates of political morality. Government must treat those whom it governs with concern, that is, as human beings who are capable of suffering and frustration, and with respect, that is, as human beings who are capable of forming and acting on intelligent conceptions of how their lives should be lived. Government must treat people not only with concern and respect, but with equal concern and respect. It must not distribute goods or opportunities unequally on the ground that some citizens are entitled to more because they are worthy of more concern. It must not constrain liberty on the ground that one man's conception of the good life of one group is nobler than, or superior to, another's. These postulates, taken together, state what might be called the liberal conception of equality, but it is a conception of equality, not of liberty, that they state.

The sovereign question of political theory, within a state supposed to be governed by the liberal conception of equality, is: What inequalities in goods, opportunities, and liberties are permitted in such a state, and why? The beginning of an answer lies in the following distinction. Citizens governed by the liberal conception of equality each have a right to equal concern and respect. But there are two different rights that might be comprehended by that abstract right. The first is the right to equal treatment, that is, to the same distribution of goods or opportunities that anyone else has or is given. The Supreme Court, in the Reapportionment cases, held that citizens have a right to equal treatment in the distribution of voting power; it held that one man must be given one vote in spite of the fact that a different distribution of votes might in fact work for the general benefit. The second is the right to treatment as an equal. This is the right, not to an equal distribution of some good or opportunity, but the right to equal concern and respect in the political decision about how these goods and opportunities are to be distributed. Suppose the question is raised whether an economic policy that allows unemployment to rise is in the general interest. Those who will be unemployed have a right that their prospective loss be taken into account in deciding whether the general interest is served by the policy. They may not simply be ignored in that calculation. But when their interest is taken into account it may nevertheless be outweighed by the interests of others who will gain from the policy, and in that case their right to equal concern and respect, so defined, would provide no objection. In the case of economic policy, therefore, we might wish to say that those who will be unemployed if inflation is reduced have a right to treatment as equals in the decision whether that policy would serve the general interest, but they have no right to equal treatment in the distribution of jobs that would prevent the policy even if it passed that test.

I propose that the right to treatment as an equal must be taken to be fundamental under the liberal conception of equality and that the more restrictive right to equal treatment holds only in those special circumstances in which, for some special reason, it follows from the more fundamental right, as perhaps it does in the special circumstance of the Reapportionment cases. I also propose that individual right to distinct liberties must be recognized only when the fundamental right to treatment as an equal can be shown to require these rights. If this is correct, then the right to distinct liberties does not conflict with any supposed competing right to equality, but, on the contrary, follows from a conception of equality conceded to be more fundamental.

I must now show, however, how the familiar rights to distinct liberties—those established, for example, in our Constitution—might be thought to be required by that fundamental conception of equality. I shall try to do this, for present purposes, only by providing a skeleton of the more elaborate argument that would have to be made to defend any particular liberty on this basis, and then show why it would be plausible to expect that the more familiar political and civil liberties would be supported by such an argument if it were in fact made.

A government that respects the liberal conception of equality may properly constrain liberty only on certain very limited types of justification. I shall adopt, for purposes of making this point, the following crude typology of political justifications. There are, first, arguments of principle, which support a particular constraint on liberty on the argument that the constraint is required to protect the distinct right of some individual who will be injured by the exercise of the liberty. There are, second, arguments of policy, which support constraints on the different ground that such constraints are required to reach some overall political goal, that is, to realize some state of affairs in which the community as a whole, and not just certain individuals, is better off by virtue of the constraint. Arguments of policy might be further subdivided in this way. Utilitarian arguments of policy argue that the community as a whole will be better off because (to put the point roughly) more of its citizens will have more of what they want overall, even though some of them will have less. Ideal arguments of policy, on the other hand, argue that the community will be better off, not because more of its members will have more of what they want, but because the community will be in some way closer to an ideal community, whether its members desire the improvement in question or not.

The liberal conception of equality sharply limits the extent to which ideal arguments of policy may be used to justify any constraint on liberty. Such arguments cannot be used if the ideal in question is itself controversial within the community. Constraints cannot be defended, for example, directly on the ground that they contribute to a culturally sophisticated community, whether the community wants the sophistication or not, because that argument would violate the canon of the liberal conception of equality that prohibits a government from relying on the claim that certain forms of life are inherently more valuable than others.

Utilitarian arguments of policy, however, would seem secure from that objection. They do not suppose that any form of life is inherently more valuable than any other, but instead base their claim that constraints on liberty are necessary to advance some collective goal of the community only on the fact that that goal happens to be desired more widely or more deeply than any other. Utilitarian arguments of policy, therefore, seem not to oppose but, on the contrary, to embody the fundamental right of equal concern and respect because they treat the wishes of each member of the community on a par with the wishes of any other, with no bonus or discount reflecting the view that that member is more or less worthy of concern than any other, or his views more or less worthy of respect than other views.

This appearance of egalitarianism has, I think, been the principal source of the great appeal that utilitarianism has had, as a general political philosophy, over the last century. In a recent article, however, I pointed out that the egalitarian character of a utilitarian argument is often an illusion.[3] I will not repeat, but only summarize, my argument here.

Utilitarian arguments fix on the fact that a particular constraint on liberty will make more people happier, or satisfy more of their preferences, depending upon whether psychological or preference utilitarianism is in play. But people's overall preference for one policy over another may be seen to include, on further analysis, preferences that are both personal, because they state a preference for the assignment of one set of goods or opportunities to him, and external, because they state a preference for one assignment of goods or opportunities to others. But a utilitarian argument that assigns critical weight to the external preferences of members of the community will not be egalitarian in the sense under consideration. It will not respect the right of everyone to be treated with equal concern and respect.

Suppose, for example, that a number of individuals in the community hold racist rather than utilitarian political theories. They believe, not that each man is to count for one and no one for more than one in the distribution of goods, but, rather, that a black man is to count for less and a white man, therefore, to count for more than one. That is an external preference, but it is nevertheless a genuine preference for one policy over another, the satisfaction of which will bring pleasure. Nevertheless, if this preference or pleasure is given the normal weight in a utilitarian calculation, and blacks suffer accordingly, then their own assignment of goods and opportunities will depend, not simply on the competition among personal preferences that abstract statements of utilitarianism suggest, but precisely on

[3] "The DeFunis Case: The Right to Go to Law School," *New York Review of Books*, February 5, 1976.

the fact that they are thought less worthy of concern and respect than others are.

Suppose, to take a different case, that many members of that community disapprove on moral grounds of homosexuality, or contraception, or pornography, or expressions of adherence to the Communist Party. They prefer not only that they themselves not indulge in these activities but that no one else do so either, and they believe that a community that permits rather than prohibits these acts is inherently a worse community. These are external preferences, but, once again, they are no less genuine, nor less a source of pleasure when satisfied and displeasure when ignored, than purely personal preferences. Once again, however, if these external preferences are counted in a manner that justifies a constraint on liberty, then those constrained suffer, not simply because their personal preferences have lost in a competition for scarce resources with the personal preferences of others, but precisely because their conception of a proper or desirable form of life is despised by others.

These arguments justify the following important conclusion. If utilitarian arguments of policy are to be used to justify constraints either on distributional inequalities or on liberty, then care must be taken to ensure that the utilitarian calculations on which the argument is based fix only on personal and ignore external preferences. That is an important conclusion for political theory because it shows, for example, why the arguments of John Stuart Mill in *On Liberty* are not counterutilitarian but, on the contrary, serve the only defensible form of utilitarianism.

Important as that conclusion is at the level of political philosophy, however, it is in itself of limited practical significance because it will be impossible to devise political procedures that will accurately discriminate between personal and external preferences. Representative democracy is widely thought to be the institutional structure most suited, in a complex and diverse society, to the identification and achievement of utilitarian policies. It works imperfectly at this, for the familiar reason that majoritarianism cannot sufficiently take account of the intensity, as distinct from the number, of particular preferences, and because techniques of political persuasion, backed by money, may corrupt the accuracy with which votes represent the genuine preferences of those who have voted. Nevertheless, democracy seems to enforce utilitarianism more satisfactorily, in spite of these imperfections, than any alternative general political scheme would.

But democracy cannot discriminate, within the overall preferences imperfectly revealed by voting, distinct personal and external components, so as to provide a method for enforcing the former while ignoring the latter. An actual vote in an election or referendum must be taken to represent an overall preference rather than some component of the preference that a skillful cross-examination of the individual voter, if time and expense permitted, would reveal. Personal and external preferences are sometimes so inextricably combined, moreover, that the discrimination is psychologically as well as institutionally impossible. That will be true, for example, in the case of the associational preferences that many people have for members of one race, or people of one talent or quality, over another, for this is a personal preference so parasitic upon external preferences that it is impossible to say, even as a matter of introspection, what personal preferences would remain if the underlying external preference were removed. It is also true of certain self-denying preferences that many individuals have; that is, preferences for less of a certain good on the assumption, or rather proviso, that if they have less, other people, equally deserving, will have more. That is also a preference, however noble, that is parasitic upon external preferences, in the shape of political and moral theories, and though we might resist this conclusion, such preferences may no more be counted in a defensible utilitarian argument than less attractive preferences rooted in prejudice rather than altruism.

I wish now to propose the following general theory of rights. The concept of an individual political right, in the strong antiutilitarian sense I distinguished earlier, is a response to the philosophical defects of a utilitarianism that counts external preferences and the practical difficulties of a utilitarianism that does not. It allows us to enjoy the institutions of political democracy, institutions which enforce overall or unrefined utilitarianism, and yet protect the fundamental right of citizens to equal concern and respect by prohibiting decisions that seem, antecedently, very likely to have been reached by virtue of the external components of the preferences democracy reveals.

It should be plain how this theory of rights might be used to support the idea, which is the subject of this essay, that we have distinct rights to certain liberties like the liberty of free expression and of free choice in personal sexual moralities. It might be shown that any utilitarian constraint on these liberties must be based on overall preferences in the community that we know, from our general knowledge of society, are likely to contain large components of external preferences, in the shape of political or moral theories, which the political process cannot discriminate and eliminate. As I have said, my present purpose is not to frame the arguments that would have to be made to defend particular rights to liberty in this way, but only to show the general character such arguments might have.

I do wish, however, to mention one alleged right that might be called into question by my general argument, which is the supposed individual right to the free use of property. I have elsewhere complained about the argument, popular in certain quarters, that it is inconsistent for liberals to defend a liberty of speech, for example, and not also concede a parallel right of some sort to property and its use. There might be force in that argument if the claim that we have a right to free speech depended on the more general proposition that we have a right to something called liberty as such. But, as I said earlier, that general idea is untenable and incoherent; there is no such thing as any general right to liberty. The argument for any given specific liberty may therefore be entirely independent of the argument for any other, and there is no antecedent inconsistency or even implausibility in contending for one while disputing the other.

What can be said, on the general theory of rights I offer, for any particular right of property? What can be said, for example, in favor of the right to liberty of contract sustained by the Supreme Court in the famous *Lochner* case and later regretted not only by the Court but by liberals generally? I cannot think of any argument that a political decision to limit such a right, in the way in which minimum-wage laws limited it, is antecedently likely to have given effect to external preferences and in that way offended the right of those whose liberty is curtailed to equal concern and respect. If, as I think, no such argument can be made out, then the alleged right may not exist; in any case, there can be no inconsistency in denying that it exists while warmly defending a right to other liberties.

8.

Legality as Privacy

GEORGE P. FLETCHER

THE prevailing view of legality is that conduct is legal if it conforms to authoritative rules. Depending on the indigenous rule of recognition, the rules might emanate from either the legislature or the judiciary; in either event they bind judges and citizens in their subsequent behavior. This is the popular view of maintaining a rule of law rather than of men. It is a view that unites the positivism of Hobbes, Hart, and Kelsen with the tradition of constitutionalism emanating from Montesquieu. For the sake of convenience, we shall refer to this theory as a formal theory of legality. The theory is formal because it holds that any form of conduct, regardless of content, might be legal if acted out in conformity with an authoritative rule.

The formal theory of legality may be restated as a particular type of judicial obligation. The obligation of judges, indeed of all citizens, is to observe the rules of law where they apply. Of course, where the current of the rules runs dry, the judge may turn to other springs for guidance in reaching a decision. These other sources might include legislative policies or principles of justice. Yet where the rules do control—in their core cases of application—these policies and principles are superfluous. To be bound by the law is to be bound by authoritative rules.

Restating the formal theory of legality as an obligation to follow authoritative rules invites us to consider an array of other obligations that guide judges in their deliberations. What should we say, for example, of a judicial obligation to ensure that all persons stand equally before the law? So stated, the principle of equality is ambiguous. It might mean that judges have the obligation to apply the law equally; in the process of interpretation and factfinding, they should not discriminate according to race, age, sex, or other standards unrelated to the dispute. This weaker reading of the demands of equality would permit a judge to apply legislation that was discriminatory on its face, so long as he did not exacerbate the discrimination in factfinding and interpretation. If, for example, a statute prevents bastards from obtaining driving licenses, the statute could presumably be applied in an evenhanded, nondiscriminatory way. Bastards and only bastards would be denied licenses. This sense of weaker obligation to apply the law equally, with prejudice to no one, is compatible with the formal principle of legality.

Yet a strong reading of the obligation to respect equality would intrude upon the formal principle of legality. If the judge's obligation were only to apply those laws that, as they were written, were nondiscriminatory, he could face a conflict between his obligation to apply all legislated rules and his obligation to treat all persons equally before the law. In the case of the above statute discriminating against bastards, the obligation to ensure equal treatment would presumably override the legislative command. Under those circumstances, it would be difficult to say that the legislated rule enjoyed the force of "law" in the particular legal systems. These, of course, are the types of decisions that American judges make routinely in interpreting the equal-protection clause of the Fourteenth Amendment. If the same mandate to ensure equality in the legal system were treated as an implicit obligation of judging, the effect would be to undercut the formal theory of legality. To know which rules should be followed, judges would then have to examine their potentially discriminatory content as well as their formal criteria of validity.

The argument thus far has been not to show that the stronger obligation to ensure equality is implicit in any particular legal system, but merely to demonstrate that the formal theory of legality is hostile to all judicial obligations except the obligation to follow formally valid rules. Stating the problem in this way helps us define a set of attacks that might be made against the formal theory of legality. If the judicial role entailed supplementary obligations that required attention to the content of legal rules, the theory of legality would no longer be formal. It would be substantive in the sense that the concept of judging according to law would presuppose an examination of the substance or content of formally valid rules.

A substantive theory of legality would not only mandate judges to disregard particular rules enacted by the legislature, it would also prescribe contours for the development of law in the courts. A formal theory of legality tells us nothing about the range of innovation permissible in the judicial development of the law. The formal theory of legality prescribes merely that one should follow rules already enacted; it tell us nothing about the constraints of enacting and refining rules. Yet a substantive theory, if it could be worked out, would provide a test for assessing the legality both of judicial application and of judicial development of the law. The reason that a substantive theory would provide this restraint is that it would recognize obligations on judges that went beyond the enacted rules. The substantive obligations would guide judges in their efforts to refine the law as well as to find it.

It is worth noting that approaching the problem of legality from the point of judicial obligation is different from asking about the makeup of the law. Professor Dworkin has argued eloquently that the "law" in any system consists of principles as well as rules, and I have no quarrel with this analysis.[1] Yet to give an account of what "principles" and "rules" are, Dworkin turns to the theory of judicial obligation. Judges are duty-bound to "apply" rules but to "take the measure" of principles. In the end what seems to matter is the set of obligations that judges bear, not the composition of the "law" as a material entity abstracted from the craft of deciding cases. If we concluded that judges were bound by the obligation to ensure equality in the strong sense discussed above, it would be a supplementary and arguably less interesting question whether the principle of equality was part of the "law." It seems plausible that judges might bear obligations to advert to criteria that were not part of the "law." And therefore, defining the contours of the law fails to settle the question of judicial obligation.

Now there might be many substantive theories of legality, or, more precisely, many obligations incumbent on judges in addition to the obligation to enforce formally valid rules. The obligation to en-

[1] See Ronald Dworkin, "The Model of Rules," *University of Chicago Law Review* 35 (1967): 14; for a revised version of the argument, see Dworkin, "Hard Cases," *Harvard Law Review* 88 (1975): 1057.

sure the equal treatment of all persons would provide one such theory. Another theory of particular prominence in the Western legal tradition is the liberal principle that judges should attempt to do corrective justice but should abstain from the broad issues of distributive justice. This means that in judging a tort or contract dispute, judges should consider the events that transpired and seek a just solution of the dispute, but they should not inquire into the past injustices suffered by the parties, probe their general moral desert, or ask whether a verdict would be good or bad for the classes or groups represented by the litigants. This is the principle of judicial restraint captured in the symbolic blindfold worn by the figure of justice. It obviously bears some connection to the broader principle of equal treatment as a basic obligation of judging.

It would be a work of some magnitude to explicate the structure of the plausible obligations that might require judges to examine the content of legal rules as a condition for recognizing their authority. As a preliminary effort, I shall attempt here to explicate a single substantive legal obligation that has received less attention than the obligation to ensure equality under the law. The stimulus to my argument comes from a number of puzzling, yet suggestive, aphorisms about the nature of law. It is often said, for example, that legal judgments pertain to external facts while moral judgments are directed to internal facts.[2] It is also thought to be a principle of justice under the law that no one should be punished for his thoughts alone.[3] These maxims are puzzling for we also know a just system of punishment attends to subjective criteria of culpability as well as objective criteria of behavior.

To make sense of these aphorisms about the external nature of law, we should think of them as an approximation of judicial obligation to follow a prescribed order in judging legal disputes. The prescribed order of analysis requires that judges resolve first those issues that are objective, external, and abstract, and second those that are

---

[2] See R. Stammler, *The Theory of Justice*, trans. Isaac Husik (New York: Macmillan Co., 1925), p. 41; G. Radbruch, *Einfuehrung in Die Rechtswissenschaft* (Stuttgart: K. F. Kochler, 1961), p. 16.

[3] See generally H. Morris, "Punishment for Thoughts," *Monist* 49 (1965): 342.

subjective, internal, and concrete. Following this prescribed order means that issues pertaining to the defendant—his intent, character, and psychological condition—may not be considered at the outset of a legal dispute. A judge may turn to these subjective and internal matters only after first establishing objective and external criteria that generate a prima-facie case of liability. Matters private to the defendant occupy a subsidiary position in the structure of legal analysis, and typically these personal matters come into play only by way of efforts to refute the incriminating implications of external public facts. The general relationship between the objective and the subjective factors of legal liability is that the objective factors generate an incriminating or prima-facie case against the defendant; the personal or subjective factors generate excuses that defang the incriminating bite of objective criteria.

I shall refer to this theory of legality by the general label "legality as privacy." The substantive obligation implicit in this theory of legality is that the privacy of the accused should be respected unless he is implicated by objective incriminating facts, such as observable behavior. It would follow from this principle of legality that judges should not interpret the law so as to dispense with the requirement of an objectively incriminating prima-facie case. If they are commanded to do so by the legislature, they would then face a conflict between this substantive theory and the formal theory of legality. Whether the legislative command should be nullified, either explicitly or by interpretation, obviously depends on the strength of judicial commitment to this theory of substantive legality.

The principles of legality as privacy, as I shall explicate them, have prevailed in varying degrees in the course of Western legal history. My examples to substantiate the theory will be drawn largely from criminal law and torts. It is possible therefore that the most we can show is a theory about cases in which someone is called to account for behavior causing or threatening harm to another. Though the argument will be primarily historical and conceptual, I shall turn in conclusion to an argument why, as a matter of principle, this historically prominent theory of legality merits our continuing loyalty.

It is interesting to note that in recent years Hayek too has moved from a formal conception of legality to a substantive theory close to the view that I shall advance in this paper. His earlier books focused on the importance of general, well-defined rules as the proper modes of protecting liberty from the encroachments of the regulatory state.[4] In *Law, Legislation and Liberty* Hayek concludes that the courts, generating the common law, have provided the bulwark of liberty in the English tradition.[5] The courts, he reasons, are less prone to the kind of rationalist, utilitarian reasoning that informs legislative decisions. As an historical matter, Hayek might be correct, but the argument needs the elaboration of a theory of legality that can withstand the contemporary pressure on the courts to rely on the kinds of policies and utilitarian goals that guide legislative judgments.

THE STRUCTURE OF CRIMINAL LIABILITY

The differences between moral and legal thought emerge in bold relief in the context of the criminal law. The same form of conduct—killing, stealing, betraying trust—is subject to both legal and moral assessment. Yet the way in which we analyze responsibility shifts as the inquiry changes from the moral to the legal. The assessment of legal responsibility is buffeted by conflicting forces. There is, on the one hand, a strong impulse to find out as much as possible about the criminal suspect. This drive toward knowing more about the man or woman in the dock is a response to our concern for punishing justly. For if we are concerned with the just distribution as well as the efficacy of criminal sanctions, then we have to attend to the question whether the criminal suspect deserves conviction and punishment. The question of desert leads us to an inquiry about his character, for presumably the question whether an actor deserves punishment depends on the kind of person he is. To assess the kind of person the actor is, we should certainly wish to know as much as possible about him. If juries sought to judge criminal defendants solely in response to this single impulse, they should presumably wish unbounded information about his past and present condition. The single act

---

[4] See F. A. Hayek, *The Constitution of Liberty* (Chicago: University of Chicago Press, 1960), pp. 153–54; Hayek, *The Political Ideal of the Rule of Law* (Cairo: National Bank of Egypt, 1955).

[5] F. A. Hayek, *Law, Legislation and Liberty* (Chicago: University of Chicago Press, 1973), vol. 1; For further exposition of this argument, see Fletcher, "The Individualization of Excusing Conditions," *Southern California Law Review* 47 (1974): 1269.

charged in the indictment would pale in contrast with the information gained by a survey of the suspect's life history.

The restraint upon this open-ended inquiry into character and
desert derives from the principle of legality as privacy. Though
courts and juries are interested in the accused's character, the principle of legality imposes a form of discipline in pursuing the kind of
person the defendant is. His character and desert must be established by reasoning from the implications of a single alleged criminal
act. Thus the principle of legality requires us to forgo knowing everything we can about the accused's past and present life and to limit
ourselves to the implications of a single criminal act.

In the typical case, the actor's deed generates an inference that
he is the type of person that engages in conduct of that sort—say,
robbing banks, raping, or mugging. Yet there are obviously unusual
situations in which the inference from act to actor proves unreliable.
These are the cases in which the conduct is more readily explained
as the product of circumstances than as an expression of the actor's
character. Cases in which the inference to character is unreliable are
typically known as cases of excused conduct. The typical cases are
those of necessity, duress, and insanity, where we say metaphorically
that the actor's will was overborne by circumstances beyond his control. A parallel excuse is mistake of law, where the actor's ignorance
prevents us from inferring the type of person he is from what he has
done. We say that an actor is culpable for his deed where the inference from act to actor appears to be reliable, but that the actor is
excused if the act appears to be attributable rather to circumstances
or ignorance than to character.[6]

This unconventional account of excuses and culpability has the
virtue of explaining why civilly disobedient actors are culpable under
the law. The civilly disobedient may appeal to conscience as a force
that compels them to act, say, to spill blood on draft cards or to write
death on military airplanes. Yet he is not compelled in the same way
that a bank teller is compelled when he opens a safe at gunpoint.
The bank teller's appeal to duress is a way of attributing the deed to
circumstances and thereby of challenging the inference from his deed

---

[6] Fletcher, "The Individualization of Excusing Conditions."

to the conclusion that he is a thief. The civilly disobedient does not claim that his deed is attributable to circumstances. Nor could we say on his behalf that his violation of the law fails to tell us what kind of person he is. Indeed, the acts of Berrigan or Gandhi bespeak the moral character of the actor; they are designed precisely to be personal statements to the rest of the world. Consequently, we have grounds for respecting and praising some civilly disobedient actors, but we have grounds neither to praise nor to blame the bank teller who opens the safe at gunpoint.

The more conventional way of talking about excuses is to invoke the concept of involuntariness. Cases of excused conduct are those in which the defendant could not avoid violating the law. Of course, the issue of voluntariness here is not strict physical involuntariness; it is linked with the normative question whether the defendant, faced with the pressure of circumstance, could be fairly expected to do otherwise. This normative question leads us back to the question whether the deed is attributable rather to circumstances than to the defendant's character. For our judgment whether the defendant could have been expected to do otherwise depends on the extent to which we see the act as an expression of character traits for which he is responsible.

Given our interest in the defendant's character, we might be puzzled by the restraints imposed by the principles of legality. Surely, we could make a sounder judgment of character and of desert by opening the field of inquiry to the actor's past acts as well. A series of robberies or rapes tells us much more about the actor than does a single deed. We know much more about the character of Adolf Eichmann than we do about a suspect whose past is cloaked in secrecy. Why then should the law adopt this artificial limitation?

The argument for this principle of legality would be that the accused is thereby protected against intrusive inquiries into his past behavior and present psychological condition. As an historical matter, however, it is difficult to say whether this respect for the accused's privacy is a beneficent side effect of legality or the very reason for the crystallization of this discipline in judging criminal cases. It may well be that legality as privacy should be seen, in Hayek's favored phrase, as the "product of human action, but not of human design."[7] Not every desirable institution is the product of rational choice. The reasons why it is desirable may have little to do with historical genesis. For example, the discipline of judging particular acts may derive from the courts' primordial concern with rectifying the desecration of the sacred by particular acts. Yet once abroad, the institution of legality may have found sustenance in its incidentally protecting the privacy of criminal defendants.

I should note that this discussion of excuses is based largely on German and French criminal practice. Common-law courts have balked at the theory of excuses and have tended, as I document elsewhere,[8] to convert excuses into claims of justification (duress, necessity), claims of special status (insanity), or denials of the intent required for conviction (mistake of law). The process of excusing in the common law tends to occur in the minimally visible corridors of prosecutorial discretion and plea-bargaining.

One might well object that even in a legal system that recognizes excuses, the protection of privacy is illusory. If the accused interposes an excuse such as insanity or duress, the inquiry immediately fans out to include all relevant data about the accused, his past conduct, and psychological condition at the time of the act. If the rationale for excusing objectively criminal conduct is that the accused could not help himself, we should presumably wish to know from all the facts whether this particular person had a fair chance of avoiding the deed. The trial of Patty Hearst is a dramatic case in point. It was not the principle of legality that precluded questioning every detail of her life in the ten months preceding her participation in a bank robbery. It was her raising the Fifth Amendment as a bar to questioning that was presumably relevant to her claim of duress. As the defense has alleged, there was no sensible choice but to try to find out whether the bank robbery was attributable to her coerced confinement or whether it was attributable to a change in her attitudes and beliefs.

Another defense that initiates inquiry into the accused's criminal past is the claim of entrapment, which, according to one interpreta-

[7] F. A. Hayek, *Studies in Philosophy, Politics and Economics* (New York: Simon & Schuster, 1967), ch. 6.
[8] Fletcher, "The Individualization of Excusing Conditions."

tion, functions as an excuse of beguilement or seduction.[9] The predisposed criminal cannot properly claim that he is seduced, and therefore proof of a prior disposition to commit the offense undermines the defense. With these defenses raising the prospect of a free-ranging inquiry about the accused's propensities, one wonders about the asserted protection of privacy implicit in the principle of legality.

In response to this objection, we should note two important and widely shared features of the criminal process. First, the suspect raises the excuse himself and thus remains in control of the inquiry into matters that go beyond the act charged against him. This point bears some qualification in the case of insanity, which may be raised by the common-law prosecutor as well as the defense.[10] Yet even apart from this qualification, the response is a weak refutation. It is little solace to the criminal defendant to know that he or she must choose between conviction and, as in the case of Patty Hearst, a wide-ranging inquiry into every corner of one's psyche and past behavior.

It is a point of greater weight that the process of accusation may not begin with an inquiry into the actor's character and criminal propensities. These questions are never raised, even by the accused, unless there is preliminary proof of an objectively incriminating act. Without proof of the bank robbery and the identification of Patty Hearst as one of the participants, it would have been impermissible to probe the extent to which she was influenced by her kidnapping and captivity. The principle of legality as privacy does not preclude these personal and often intrusive inquiries; it requires only that the inquiry be justified by the incriminating effect of public and objectively observable events.

LEGALITY IN RETREAT: DO WE JUDGE THE WHOLE PERSON?

When we speak of the substantive principle of legality, we should remind ourselves that we are talking about the classical ideal. Our own legal system is still nominally committed to the view that

---

[9] See *Sherman* v. *United States*, 356 U.S. 369 (1958).
[10] *Whalen* v. *United States*, 346 F.2d 812 (D.C. Cir., 1965).

a criminal trial should focus on a single alleged act of criminality. Guilt or innocence should turn on proof of that act and the availability of excuses, not on a generalized assessment of the actor as a malevolent or dangerous threat to society. Yet that nominal commitment has suffered erosion on a number of fronts. There are specially created offenses designed to punish multiple offenders more seriously than first-time offenders: the prior conviction becomes an issue to be established at trial.[11] There are rules of evidence that also covertly permit the consideration of past acts of the accused; these rules come dressed in a variety of doctrinal garbs, all of which conceal a latent function of proving the accused to be a criminal type. These are but minor instances of the principle of legality retreating in favor of a fuller consideration of the actor's character and criminal propensities.

The tendency to judge the whole person rather than the particular act finds its fullest expression in the institutions of prosecutorial discretion and sentencing. The institution of prosecutorial discretion is an ingenious mechanism of preserving the form, not the substance, of legality as privacy. The form is preserved because, when someone is brought to trial, the accusation and trial proceed on the assumption that guilt or innocence turns on the accusation of a particular act and its incriminating implications. The substance is lost because the decision to indict often turns on the prosecutor's view of the dangerousness and character of the accused as a whole person. The trial conforms to the classical ideal of legality; the pretrial processes realize all the advantages of open-ended inquiries into the dangerousness and character of suspects.

The prevailing view of sentencing is that a sound sentence requires an assessment of the convicted defendant's dangerousness and amenability to treatment. Relying on these factors tends to flout the widespread sentiment that punishment should be inflicted equally according to the desert of offenders. The latter view is an extension of the principle of legality that governs the question of liability. It stands in constant tension with the view that sentencing operates as an administrative process, akin in structure and criteria to the process of civil commitment.

[11] See, generally, Comment, *The Constitutionality of Statutes Permitting Increased Sentences for Habitual or Dangerous Criminals*, 89 Harvard Law Review 356 (1975).

As a general matter, the retreat of legality as privacy derives from the progressive melding in our legal culture of legal punishment with administrative confinement. A legal system with a strong commitment to the principle of legality would tend to distinguish rigorously between these two means by which the state may deprive an individual of his liberty. The usual distinction between the two institutions is that criminal punishment attaches to a past act and functions as a form of censure, while administrative confinement focuses on future dangerousness and applies without the stigma of condemnation. It may be more significant, however, that punishment is applied within the strictures of legality as privacy, while administrative confinement operates free of these restraints. In principle, nothing is irrelevant to the determination of dangerousness for the purpose of civil confinement. Everything about a potential confinee's past and present condition might bear on a decision to commit. Administrative processes transcend the discipline of legality; they proceed directly to an assessment of the whole person.

There are at least two determinants of the growing union of criminal punishment and civil commitment. In the United States the confusion of the two institutions has thrived on the liberal desire to extend constitutional guarantees to administrative processes. Minimizing the conceptual difference between punishment and civil confinement has contributed to a parity of procedural rights between the two forms of social protection. Of course, it would have been possible to extend the right to counsel and the right to the confrontation of witnesses to administrative hearings without muddying the difference between punishment and civil confinement, yet it was rhetorically far easier to secure this victory in the courts by maintaining that there was no essential difference between the two types of proceedings.[12]

Another reason for the progressive fusion of the two institutions has been the ascendancy of functional analysis in the law schools. From the vantage point of the potential confinee, it makes no difference whether he is confined in a jail or hospital. Why then should one retain two labels and seek to distinguish between functionally equivalent processes? It is a convincing argument, particularly as

[12] E.g., in re *Gault*, 387 U.S. 1 (1967).

applied to protecting the potential confinee in a juvenile court or a civil-commitment hearing. Yet the inverse implication of the argument is that the legal process should seek to integrate the advantages of administrative proceedings. This, as we have noted, is precisely what has happened to the critical stages before trial and after conviction. The tendency has been to view both the process of charging and that of sentencing as an administrative process, with all the advantages of free-ranging inquiry into the suspect's past.

There is no doubt that this process of assimilating legal and administrative processes has gained momentum from the reigning view that the criminal law is an instrument of social protection. Civil commitment is a far more rational system of social protection than the criminal process. It seeks to confine dangerous persons, not those who have done evil in the past (and may well not be dangerous now). Civil commitment aptly serves as the model for the transformation of the criminal law. As we shall see later, this process of transformation reaches to the substantive definition of particular offenses, such as the criminal law of attempts. The value lost in this transformation is precisely the value of legality as privacy. The quest for dangerous persons knows no discipline, no restraint, no privacy. It may be socially more effective, but at the cost of a value that was an intrinsic part of the legal tradition.

PRIVACY AND THE INQUIRY INTO INTENT

In the preceding section, I argued that the classical concept of legality restricted inquiries into the character and dangerousness of criminal suspects by requiring that a single act be taken as the locus of incriminating evidence. Upon refinement of the argument, we discovered that, at the level of excuses, the strictures of privacy are abandoned for the sake of refining the process of judgment. We were left with the conclusion that the act alone should serve the function of incrimination, while the process of exculpation might take on broader contours.

We encounter a similar phenomenon in the analysis of intent in the criminal law. Is intent a basis for incrimination? Or does nonintent function as a ground for defeasing the incriminating effect of external events? In this section, I shall argue that the classical conception of intent in the criminal law is that nonintent functioned as a ground of exculpation or excuse. It is only later in the history of the criminal law that one finds intent appearing as a basis for incrimination.

Harm as a Condition of Liability

The core offenses of the common law of crimes all presuppose harm as a condition of liability. The exception is treason, which takes the intent to kill the king to be a consummated offense. Yet homicide, rape, robbery, burglary—all of these are felonies that derive from the felon's leaving his mark on the external world. The harm-oriented offense par excellence is homicide. Death by human hand is so serious an event in Western culture that once even its accidental occurrence stigmatized both the actor and the instrument causing death. Biblical law required those who accidentally caused death to leave the community and take up residence in a city of refuge. The early law of the deodand required forfeiture of instruments used in causing death. These measures were designed to rid the community of the taint left by one man's killing another.

Legal excuses were first recognized in cases of homicide brought on by accident or mistake. The accident or the mistake defeased the incriminating implications of the death occurring by human action. We now think of accident and mistake as claims negating the intent required for murder, but this is a conceptual reordering of the issues that emerged as late as this century.[13]

The relationship of the victim's death to the problems of accident and mistake resembles the structure we noted earlier between acts and excuses. Death by a human agent is the incriminating event. The exculpating move is the proof of nonintent by way of showing accident or mistake. The conceptual reordering of the issues parallels the decline of structure we noted earlier in discussion of excuses based on external coercion. When accident and mistake are perceived as denials of the required intent, we are in a position to move intent

---

[13] The English courts confirmed the reconceptualization of the issue in *Woolmington* v. *Director of Public Prosecutions* [1935] A.C. 462. The prosecution argued in that case that defendant bore the burden of persuasion on the issue of accident; the court rejected the argument on the ground that the prosecution had to prove intent and accident was merely a negative condition of intent.

into a position of equal or superior definitional prominence to the causing of death. It is then no longer clear that essential criminality of homicide consists in death by human agency. It becomes more plausible to argue, as many moderns do, that the evil of homicide inheres in acting out an intent to kill. The fact of death then comes to be seen as a contingent fact retained by the force of tradition in the definition of the crime.

Legality as Privacy in the Absence of Actual Harm

It is easy enough to see how the law could impose a structuring of issues in cases in which an objective event—like death or the burning of a dwelling house—incriminated the actor. The problematic cases are those in which there is no harm that stands out with the same inculpatory effect as death by human hand. The primary examples are the crimes of attempt and larceny. Attempt by definition does not presuppose the occurrence of harm. Upon examination, larceny reveals similar features. The event of taking someone's property is a technical harm, but is is far from an incriminating event. Every time people buy, lease, or borrow goods, they engage in an act that is externally indistinguishable from taking goods against the owner's consent. It seems difficult in the cases both of attempt and of larceny to regard intent as a subsidiary issue. In the absence of an intent to commit a crime, there seems to be little basis for inculpating the accused.

Yet both crimes have witnessed a historic preference for an ordered approach to the issue of liability. This is less well marked in the field of attempts, for the crime of attempt did not emerge until the late eighteenth century. Therefore, I shall concentrate my remarks on the crime of larceny and try to show that the classical conception of the offense was based on an ordering we have already noted in the field of excuses and in the classical approach to homicide.

In ancient legal systems it was permissible in some instances to execute suspected criminals caught *in flagrante delicto*. The most notable instance of this private right of execution was the practice of executing nighttime thieves caught inside or breaking an enclosure. The thief subject to execution was known in Roman law as the *fur manifestus* ("manifest thief"). Private execution of the manifest thief could not have been tolerated in societies inclined toward blood feuds unless there was a ready consensus as to who was a thief and who was not. The *fur manifestus* was someone who was readily taken to be a thief, so readily that there was no need to verify the authenticity of appearances. In Roman and biblical law, other forms of larceny generated at most penalties in the form of multiple damages. Thieves were not subject to execution or corporal punishment unless they were manifest thieves.[14]

Though several changes occurred in the structure of larceny in the course of its evolution in Western legal history, the medieval crime was based essentially on the principle that thieving was an identifiable event in the external world. The event that incriminated the thief was not the taking of property, but the manner of his taking. The thief was someone who took "furtively" and by "stealth"— as the etymology of these words indicates. A variation of the crime, which came to be called robbery in many jurisdictions, required a taking that was open and violent. The classical conception of larceny was based, in short, on a shared image of the thief.

This consensus regarding the nature of thievery accounts for many practices of the common-law courts up to the end of the eighteenth century. It explains, for example, the appeal of the rule of "breaking bulk" as an exception to the principle that bailees could not be liable for taking goods already in their possession. By the late fifteenth century it was clear that if a bailee broke open the wrapping of a container and took the goods within, he would be liable for larceny. The act of breaking bulk was a manifestation of violence that brought his conduct within the shared conception of thievery. Merely absconding with the goods in his possession would not bring the actor's conduct within the pattern of stealthful or forcible conduct, and therefore the bailee could not be treated as a thief.

Within this system of thought, the issue of criminal intent functioned as a subsidiary ground for exculpation—not as a parallel condition for inculpation. The issue of intent arose by way of showing that the appearance of thievery did not provide a reliable indication that the actor was indeed a thief. The common-law term for intent

---

[14] For fuller development of this and other points discussed in this section, see Fletcher, "The Metamorphosis of Larceny," *Harvard Law Review* 89 (1976): 649.

to steal, *animus furandi*, is suggestive in this regard. To intend to steal was to have the spirit, the animus, of "someone thieving." In other words, it was to have the spirit of the type of person one appears to be. Intent in the common law of larceny was based on a monist rather than a dualist conception of acts and intent. The animus was conceptually derivative of the way of acting that had an identifiable external form.

Thus we find in the common law of larceny the same structural relationship that we noted generally in the theory of excuses and, in particular, in the law of homicide. There is the same ordering of objective and subjective considerations. While the objective issue in homicide was the fact of death by human hand, in larceny it was a manner of acting that conformed to a shared image of thieving. Proving the objective issue then legitimated the inquiry into possible grounds of excuse and exculpation. The foremost excuses in homicide were mistake and accident. In larceny, the issue of exculpation focused on the possible gap between appearance and reality. To check the inference from the objective to the subjective, the defendant could argue that he did not have the "spirit of one thieving."

A similar ordering of objective and subjective issues characterized the early stages of attempt liability. Both in Europe and in the United States, nineteenth-century courts insisted that the act of attempting, rather than the actor's intent, had to provide the grounds for incriminating the suspect. Yet the field of attempts lacked both an irredeemable event, like death, and a shared image of routine criminal conduct, like thieving. Holmes tried to work out the objective criteria for attempting by focusing on "the nearness of the danger, the greatness of the harm, and the degree of apprehension felt."[15] The New Zealand courts talked for a time of "overt acts which are sufficient in themselves to proclaim the purpose with which they are done."[16] There was at least this much of an effort to define the threshold of criminal attempts as objectively criminal conduct, subject to defeasance by proof of nonintent.

---

[15] O. W. Holmes, *The Common Law* (1881), p. 68.

[16] *King* v. *Barker*, 13 [1924] N.Z.L.R. 865; the same test is defended in Salmond, *Jurisprudence*, 7th ed. (London: Sweet and Maxwell Ltd., 1924), p. 404.

Further, there are many cases in the field of impossible attempts that seem to be explainable on the hypothesis that the courts convict when they perceive criminality in the objective facts of the defendants' conduct and acquit when they do not. This hypothesis explains the distinction between acquitting when the defendant has tried to kill someone by putting sugar into his coffee cup (thinking that the sugar was poison)[17] and convicting when he has tried to kill him by using too little poison (thinking that the dosage was sufficient).[18] Similarly, it explains the inclination to acquit when someone fires at a tree stump (thinking the stump to be his intended victim),[19] and the impulse to convict when the defendant tries to kill another by firing into the bed where the other usually sleeps (though he is not there at the time).[20] The mainspring of these close distinctions seems to be the assumption that crime is a publicly visible and disturbing event that occurs in the external world. Yet, on balance, it would be difficult to assert that the role of objective criminality ever became as important in the law of attempts as it was in the common law of larceny.

In the course of the past two centuries, the fields of larceny and attempts have witnessed a decline of structure in their respective definitions. In both cases, the decline is because of a loss of confidence in the coherence and reality of the objective element in the definition. Thieving as an event in the external world lost its grip on the minds of judges questing for precise rules of liability. The harm in larceny came to be thought of as the improper acquisition of the assets of another. Yet this was a harm that could be determined only upon examination of the actor's intent and the understanding between the parties. The intent to steal shed its conceptual dependence on a way of acting and emerged as an independent ground for incriminating suspected thieves. The same development has been taking place in the field of attempts in the last several decades. The intent to commit the act is now seen as the core of the attempt, and

---

[17] *State* v. *Clarissa*, 11 Alabama 57 (1847) (slave tried to kill master with harmless weed).

[18] *Commonwealth* v. *Kennedy*, 170 Mass. 18 (1897).

[19] Holmes, *Common Law*, p. 69.

[20] *State* v. *Mitchell*, 170 Mass. 633, 71 S.W. 175 (1902).

the problem of impossible attempts is resolved by asking whether the act would have been criminal "if the attendant circumstances were as [the actor] believes them to be."[21]

The emergence of intent as a basis for incriminating criminal suspects correlates with the tendency toward fusion of the criminal law with the practice of civil commitment. That tendency, as we noted above, accounts for the decline of legality as a restriction on the assessment of the dangerousness and moral character of criminal suspects. It also explains the ascendancy of intent as the central element of homicide, larceny, and attempts. Contemporary utilitarian theorists take intent to be the most reliable guide to the actor's criminal propensities. It is certainly a more reliable guide than the often fortuitous fact of harm and the appearance of criminality in the defendant's conduct. Thus the increasing focus on criminal intent tends effectively to serve the goal of isolating and confining dangerous persons—the primary objective of civil commitment. Further, the emphasis on intent seems not to depart from any of the traditional premises of the criminal law. After all, as the modern theorist might insist, is not the retributivist also concerned about intent? There is nothing suspect, he would insist, about the contemporary tendency to regard intent as the core of criminality.

Yet there is something troubling about the claim that an intent might render any act, however innocuous, a basis for just punishment. One is always punished for something. Now is that something the intent itself? If it were, one would be hard-pressed to demand (except for evidentiary reasons) that the actor take any steps to execute his intent. It seems that one is punished for causing harm or for acting in a particular way. But will any act suffice? Even an act of putting sugar into coffee or shooting at a cloud? Why should anyone be punished for acts like those? It is little help to say that the intent is wicked, for we just concluded that whatever one is punished for, it is not the intent. Classical criminal theory responds to this problem by introducing the concept of wrongdoing to supplement the concepts of intent and blameworthiness. One might engage in an act of wrongdoing by objectively violating a rule or by causing harm.

[21] Model Penal Code, sec. 5.01(1)(a) (Proposed Official Draft, 1962).

Either way, the wrongdoing would be manifested in the external world. And that is what one is punished for. The issues of blameworthiness, intent, and excusability arise only by way of seeking to determine whether the actor is responsible for the wrongdoing.

There admittedly is a dogmatic ring to the assertion that wrongdoing must take place in the external world, that others must be able directly to perceive the wrongdoing as acts of wrongdoing. This is a conclusion that needs some filling out. Yet if we do accept the point, we can see how pivotal the concept of wrongdoing was in the structure of reasoning implicit in the traditional approach to criminal liability. Objective issues correlate with the concept of wrongdoing, subjective issues with the analysis of responsibility for a wrongful act. The pattern of analysis always proceeds from objective to subjective, wrongful acts to personal responsibility.

Eliminating the concept of wrongdoing removes the pinion from the gears of the classical system. An interrelated set of ideas then collapses into the inquiry whether the defendant had the intent required for liability. The issue then is no longer responsibility for that act or harm for which one is to be punished. Responsibility and blameworthiness become issues disengaged from the question: Responsibility for what? Using the idiom of responsibility and blameworthiness forges a link with the past. Yet the link is one that harnesses a new chain to the old set of gears. While intent once served as the medium of assaying the issue of just punishment, it now serves as the vehicle for probing the dangerousness of the particular accused.

TORT THEORY AND THE DECLINE OF STRUCTURED THINKING

Lest we think that the practice of structured thinking is linked to criminal law, we should turn to the parallel phenomenon in the history of tort doctrine. The traditional approach to assaying liability under the writ of trespass was to inquire simply whether the defendant directly caused the injury to the plaintiff. The issue of direct injury made up the entire prima-facie case. The defendant's only recourse if he did directly but accidentally cause the injury was to plead the defense of "inevitable accident." Accident was an excuse to liability for trespass as it was an excuse to liability for homicide. Both in torts and in criminal law, the issue of the defendant's responsibility arose by way of an argument in confession and avoidance: the prima-facie case was conceded but it was maintained that despite the prima-facie case, there was a good reason for denying recovery. The good reason was, as the Kings Bench put it in the year 1616, that the defendant acted "utterly without fault."[22]

Modern tort theory has abandoned the concept of trespass as the criterion for stating a prima-facie right to recover damages for directly caused injury. The focus now is on the reasonableness of the defendant's risk or, in some cases, on the extrahazardous nature of the defendant's risk. The concept of risk, rarely mentioned in common law, has become the focal point of modern thinking about tort liability. Reliance on this abstract common denominator of tort analysis provides the modern substitute for the structure implicit in the writ of trespass. There are still defenses to liability as there are in criminal cases, but these defenses are not conceptualized as excuses. They are not seen as arguments in confession and avoidance that circumvent rather than challenge that plaintiff's grounds for recovery. The flattening out of tort theory has meant that all defenses have become denials of the plaintiff's right to recover.

THE ARGUMENT FOR LEGALITY AS PRIVACY

The point of bringing forth these examples from the law of crimes and torts is to show that in many contexts lawyers have tended to think in an orderly way about the issues bearing on criminal liability. The ordering always proceeds from objective to subjective, external to internal, general to particular. It is true that this method of ordered legal thought has declined in many areas; it has surrendered to a preference for perceiving the functional parallel of all issues bearing on liability.

This pattern of structured legal thought illuminates one difference between legal and moral thought. So far as I know, no style of moral thought, either utilitarian or deontological, insists upon an ordering of issues in the process of assessing the right and the good. Of

[22] *Weaver* v. *Ward*, 80 Eng. Rep. 284 (K.B. 1616).

course, Rawls generates principles of justice that are based on a lexical ordering comparable to the ordered structure of legal thought, but the process of moral analysis that generates these principles does not proceed on the basis of the ordering of issues.

If we have ferreted out a feature of legal thought, we are still a long way from the claim that judges today are bound by the principle of legality as privacy. The most we can say is that many judges in the evolution of Western legal thought have regarded themselves as so bound. What remains to be done is to clarify the argument that can be made on behalf of the principle's still influencing the judging of cases and the evolution of the law in the courts.

We shall resist making utilitarian claims about the value of privacy as contrasted with the value of isolating people with dangerous propensities. These arguments might be compelling, but they would not be faithful to the form of arguments about other judicial obligations. The assertions on behalf of the formal theory of legality are not couched in a calculus of costs and benefits. The argument of the formalists is not that, on balance, it is better in particular cases for judges to apply formally valid rules. The argument is that it is the nature of a legal system and of the role of judging that judges should follow the rules laid down by the legislature or prior decisions of the higher courts. Of course, there might be convincing utilitarian grounds for adopting the legal system as a whole, and one might even argue that on the whole it would be better, on utilitarian grounds, for judges to bear particular types of obligation. Yet when formalists argue that judges sitting in California should decide according to California law (including the California rules of choice of law) and judges sitting in Germany should decide according to German law, the argument hardly appeals to a contingent ranking of costs and benefits. The claim is that the nature of law requires that judges decide according to the law of the jurisdiction in which the court sits. Without denying the force of supplementary utilitarian arguments, I shall seek to argue against the formal theory of legality on its own terms. The argument will be that the obligation to respect privacy is implicit in the nature of law and the role of judging.

The argument will not be an overpowering one. But for that matter, so far as I can tell, the formalist hardly has an overpowering reason for limiting the obligation of judges to the application of formally valid rules. Yet there is a case to be made for legality as privacy, even though the principles of structured legal thought have suffered a decline over the past two hundred years.

ANARCHY AND SPONTANEOUS LEGALITY

The argument builds on a speculative theory of the emergence of the criminal law. One way to think afresh about the origins of the criminal law is to ask what kind of system of offenses and punishment we would generate if we found ourselves in a state of anarchy. Suppose there were no courts, no enacted rules, no police, and that everyone was armed and charged with the task of defining, identifying, and punishing criminal conduct. We today are so accustomed to coercive government that we might think anarchy of this sort would lead to incessant warfare and the death of the species. The Hobbesian tradition leads us to believe that life could not be secure in a state if everyone acted both as citizen and as legislator. Yet this is precisely the condition of the international community of sovereign states, and, though there are occasional wars, the community manages to survive.

If we found ourselves, then, in this state of anarchy, how would we be likely to behave? Would we never exercise our function of identifying and punishing criminal conduct? Would we be overly zealous? Self-protection would lead obviously to some use of our punitive powers. But how much? One fact of life that we would quickly notice is that punishing someone else, say by whipping or killing him, might be taken by others to be a criminal act. Therefore, we would confront an obvious limit to our punishing power. We would not punish if we ourselves were likely to be regarded as criminals inflicting harm. The question then becomes How could one convince other people that it was the person suffering the punishment, and not oneself, who was truly the criminal? In the interest of maximizing the safe and nonincriminating use of force, attention would turn to those facts that would be useful in convincing others that a person being harmed was a criminal and not a victim. What kinds of facts would these be?

They would obviously be highly public features of conduct. It would do no good to refer to the alleged culprit's intentions, because, if these intentions were not patent in conduct, no one would accept the accusation. If there were no consensus that the person being harmed was a criminal, the personal risks of punishing would be great, and one would obviously abstain. Personal security, then, would require that criminals be identified by appealing to public criteria. Let us see what these public criteria might be.

I should think that two different sorts of facts could generate a consensus about who was a criminal and who was not. One would be an act causing harm to an interest that the society took to be important. The obvious case in our tradition would be that of causing death, but it could as well be polluting a stream or violating a sexual taboo. The critical public facts would be the irreversible harm and the defendant's being the party clearly tied to its occurrence. It is hard to see, however, how causing the loss of property could constitute a crime in any society that freely traded goods. People part with their goods for manifold reasons; that fact alone could hardly be a basis for inculpating the recipient. Theft would, however, be covered by a second ground for public consensus about criminality. Given a society concerned about protecting personal security and property, one would expect a high degree of consensus that anyone manifestly threatening these interests would be acting criminally and would be summarily disabled. It would not be of primary importance whether this process of disabling was thought of as punishment; what would be significant is that one could intervene against a manifest threat without appearing, oneself, to be a criminal. Thus one arrives at the principle of manifest criminality that in fact informed the early law of larceny. Further, for the sake of avoiding ambiguous cases, the principle might emerge that only those thieves could be shot who were caught breaking into or already inside the protected sphere of another. Thus the law of larceny would gravitate toward those principles that are in fact recognized in all early Western legal systems.[23]

The law, as it is pictured in this scheme, is a composite of forcible assertions and self-restraint that would enable people to live together in a society without a constituted government. One would act in the name of the law when one could use force without appear-

---

[23] See Fletcher, "The Metamorphosis of Larceny," pp. 476–81.

ing to be a criminal. Though this sketch is limited to criminal law, I would not be surprised if the same perspective illumined some of our basic notions of private legal rights.

Now this model is speculative, but it is not meant to be a hypothetical state like Rawls' original position. The thought is that this is the way our criminal law might in fact have developed. Our concepts of law and legality may well have originated in the condition of anarchy, not in the state of a rule-enacting sovereign. At least this speculative account does dovetail with the origins, as we know them, of homicide and larceny as punishable conduct. And it also accounts for the widespread sentiment, particularly evident in German law,[24] that exercising violence in cases of self-defense is somehow a vindication of the legal order.

As a legal system moves from a state of spontaneous cooperation to a formal, centralized system, the most significant change is the refinement of the criteria of responsibility. Appearances sometimes deceive. People who act like thieves are not always thieves. Appealing solely to public facts, one has considerable difficulty distinguishing between culpable and nonculpable homicide. Every act of causing death is subject to punishment. Similarly, one is hard-pressed in a spontaneous system of justice to distinguish between threats that are real and those that are apparent, but false. Any person looking like a thief would be treated as a thief—appearance would form a basis for responding with legal force. For a system of excuses to emerge, one needs a formal deliberative factfinding process that goes beyond appearances. One also needs a theory of just punishment that acts as a restraint on the class of punishable acts defined by the principle of legality. Developing these theories has been an ongoing struggle in every legal system.

By beginning with a spontaneous order and then introducing a system of courts for the sake of clarifying excusing conditions, we have arrived at the structure of issues implicit in legality as privacy. The principle of legality is identified with those principles of coercive conduct that would emerge in a state of anarchy. The principle of

---

[24] A. Schoenke & H. Schroeder, *Strafgesetzbuch*, 16th ed. (Munich: Beck, 1972), p. 471 ("Die Notwehr dient der Bewahrung der Rechtsordnung im ganzen").

excusing reflects the refinement introduced by a centralized system of justice.

Thus the obligation to respect the privacy of citizens may be restated as the obligation to observe those restraints on the use of force that would emerge spontaneously in a state of anarchy. If judges did observe these restraints, they would adhere to the principle that legal responsibility presupposes a prima-facie case based on public, incriminating facts.

Of course, we do not live in a condition of anarchy and there are doubtless advantages to courts' making the required inquiries into personal culpability and the authenticity of appearances. The question is whether it is plausible also to expect judges to adhere to the restraints that would arise spontaneously if there were no centralized system of courts. The best argument for the continued recognition of these ancient restraints is that they invoke a theory of authority rooted in the equality and reciprocity of the person judged and person judging. By harking back to a principle of spontaneous legality, the requirement of objectively incriminating facts strips the judicial role of the taint of arbitrary power. The judge claims no more power over a citizen than a fellow citizen would claim in a condition of spontaneous legality.

It would be difficult to claim that this sense of humility and restraint actually generated the traces in the law of crimes and torts that we have invoked on its behalf. And there are considerable problems with the theory, particularly as applied to newly legislated crimes such as income-tax evasion, that could hardly arise in a condition of anarchy. Yet there is a point of moral appeal to any theory of justice that treats judge and accused as potentially interchangeable players in the drama of crime and punishment. That is enough to give us pause about the continuing decline of legality as privacy.

9.

Privacy, Liberalism, and the Role of Government

WALTER BERNS

I

IMPLICIT in the title of this paper is the assumption that a distinction may be drawn between what by nature is private and what by nature is public. Liberalism bases itself on the distinction, but before liberal regimes could be constituted it was necessary to demonstrate that the distinction existed; it could not be merely assumed. This was so because the regimes against which liberalism rebelled traditionally denied the distinction.

The highest claim to privacy has been made by philosophy, but as we know from Plato's *Republic* even the philosopher can be made to forgo his privacy—which is to say, even philosophy can be made public—in the theoretically best of all possible cities where he will rule as king. It followed as a matter of course that in his imaginary city where philosophers are kings, or kings are philosophers, all men will live only public lives, walking naked in the city and sharing meals, quarters, women, children, even happiness itself, by all of which means the potentially vicious will be forced to be virtuous, publicly defined in this city which is wholly devoted to virtue and where no doors are locked. There will be no conflict between the private and the public, or between private interest and public interest, because the private does not exist. Strictly speaking, this would be the most illiberal of cities. In practice, of course, this city cannot exist because the conditions permitting philosophers to rule cannot be, or will never be, met. As Leo Strauss said:

What is more likely to happen is that an unwise man, appealing to the natural right of wisdom [to rule] and catering to the lowest desires of the many, will persuade the multitude of his right: the prospects for tyranny are brighter than those for rule of the wise. This being the case, the natural right of the wise must be questioned, and the indispensable requirement for wisdom must be qualified by the requirement for consent. The political problem consists in reconciling the requirement for wisdom with the requirement for consent.[1]

The most illiberal cities in fact have been those governed by Hitler and Stalin, each of whom denied the private realm and each of whom claimed to be a philosopher but was not. In practice, rather than accept the limits imposed by the public, Socrates the philosopher accepted death. Either philosophy rules—but this is practically impossible—or it is entitled to what we would call the right of privacy. It was Socrates' task to demonstrate this. Liberalism, on the other hand, began with the attempt to demonstrate the private character of religious opinion. It was this that was traditionally denied, even in the West; after all, Socrates was executed in part for his impiety, and many a religious dissident followed him to the stake or the gallows or the block.

The liberal demonstration took the form of a denial of the natural existence of the public realm. It said that in the beginning was not the word ("and the Word was with God, and the Word was God"); according to the first liberals, in the beginning was the state of nature, which was a state of absolute liberty and no legitimate authority. The public realm came into existence only out of the private and only as the result of the contracting act of the private persons. Parallel to this was the attempted demonstration by Hobbes, Spinoza, and Locke, for example, that the biblical account of a providential God—on which Western rules had built their claims to rule —was false.[2] Liberalism is the political teaching that takes its bear-

---

[1] Leo Strauss, *Natural Right and History* (Chicago: University of Chicago Press, 1953), p. 141.

[2] To destroy the political power of revealed religion it was first necessary to destroy or displace the authority of revealed religion, which in the Europe of the seventeenth century meant the authority of Scripture, and especially of the New Testament wherein the proof of Jesus' authority is supplied by "the multitude of miracles he did before all sorts of people." This was necessary because "where the miracle is admitted, the doctrine cannot be rejected." Thus Hobbes wrote a critique of "miracles and their use" (*Leviathan*, vol. 3, ch. 37) and Locke a *Discourse of Miracles*, from which the passage quoted above is taken (*Works* [1812], vol. 9, p. 259), and Spinoza attempted to demonstrate

ings not from the word of God but, instead, from the rights of man. In the American Declaration of Independence this is stated as follows: all men are endowed with the unalienable rights of life, liberty, and the pursuit of happiness, and "to secure these rights, governments are instituted among men, deriving their just powers from the consent of the governed." To make it absolutely clear that government (or the public realm or the public authority) derived from the people and not from God, six states, as part of their acts ratifying the Constitution, called for various amendments to the Constitution. The first of these, which was not adopted because it was deemed redundant, provided that "all power is originally vested in, and consequently derives from, the people."[3] The third, which was adopted and is known to us as the First, provides in part that "Congress shall make no law respecting an establishment of religion or prohibiting the free exercise thereof." In this fashion, religion in America was consigned to the private realm, to the realm of private opinion, and Americans were free to worship as they pleased or not to worship at all. In doing this, and in carrying the whole of liberal theory into practice, the United States consigned to the private sector the care of those qualities it required to function well. This liberal dispensation is being sorely tested in our time.

II

The classic liberal statement delineating the private sphere was made by John Stuart Mill in *On Liberty*:

But there is a sphere of action in which society, as distinguished from the individual, has, if any, only an indirect interest; comprehending all that portion of a person's life and conduct which affects only himself, or if it also affects others, only with their free, voluntary, and undeceived consent and participation. When I say only himself, I mean directly, and in the first instance; for whatever affects himself, may affect others through himself; and the objection which may be grounded on this contingency, will receive consideration in the sequel. This, then, is the appropriate region of human dignity. It comprises, first, the inward domain of consciousness; demanding liberty of conscience in the most comprehensive sense; liberty

---

that "God cannot be known from miracles" (*Theologico-Political Treatise* [New York: Dover, 1951], p. 87).

[3] *Annals of Congress*, June 8, 1978, vol. 1, p. 451.

of thought and feeling; absolute freedom of opinion and sentiment on all subjects, practical or speculative, scientific, moral, or theological. The liberty of expressing and publishing opinions may seem to fall under a different principle, since it belongs to that part of the conduct of an individual which concerns other people; but, being almost of as much importance as the liberty of thought itself, and resting in great part on the same reasons, is practically inseparable from it. Secondly, the principle requires liberty of tastes and pursuits; of framing the plan of our life to suit our own character; of doing as we like, subject to such consequences as may follow: without impediment from our fellow-creatures, so long as what we do does not harm them, even though they should think our conduct foolish, perverse, or wrong. Thirdly, from this liberty of each individual, follows the liberty, within the same limits, of combination among individuals; freedom to unite, for any purpose not involving harm to others; the persons combining being supposed to be of full age, and not forced or deceived.[4]

The role of government is reduced to enforcing the rules governing the relations between men; or in Mill's terms, an individual's actions become public when they affect others. Professor Hayek has recently formulated this as follows:

This particular function of government is somewhat like that of a maintenance squad of a factory, its object being not to produce any particular services or products to be consumed by the citizens, but rather to see that the mechanism which regulates the production of those goods and services is kept in working order. The purposes for which this machinery is currently being used will be determined by those who operate its parts and in the last resort by those who buy its product [that is, privately].[5]

This is a subordinate role that is being assigned to government; in Hayek's formulation, the superior association, if I may call it that, is the "spontaneous order of society." Government exists within and as a part of this "overall order," and Hayek does not hesitate to say that it is "conceivable that the spontaneous order which we call society may exist without government," although he adds, "in most circumstances the organization we call government becomes indispensable in order to ensure that [the minimum rules required for the formation of the spontaneous order] are obeyed."[6] That the Constitution

[4] *On Liberty*, chap. 1.
[5] F. A. Hayek, *Law, Legislation and Liberty* (Chicago: University of Chicago Press, 1973), 1: 47.
[6] Ibid.

of the United States was built with these principles in mind is reflected in the political nomenclature that it engendered: Americans speak of the Ford administration, not the Ford government, whereas the British speak of the Churchill government. The reason for this is that in the decisive respects, Americans are not governed by government; they govern themselves—which is to say, what they do with their lives is their private business—and their interests are "represented" in the legislative bodies.[7] The role of an "administration" is, in principle, much more modest than the role of a "government," although it is one measure of our current troubles that Americans could be excused if they were unable to discern the difference in practice. Professor Hayek has stated this phenomenon of our times with his customary sobriety and moderation:

It is in connection with the second group of activities that the term "government" (and still more the verb "governing") carries misleading connotations. The unquestioned need for a government that enforces the law and directs an organization providing many other services does not mean, in ordinary times, that the private citizen need be governed in the sense in which the government directs the personal and material resources entrusted to it for rendering services. It is unusual today to speak of a government "running a country" as if the whole society were an organization managed by it. Yet what really depend on it are chiefly certain conditions for the smooth running of those services that the countless individuals and organizations render to each other. These spontaneously ordered activities of the members of society certainly could and would go on even if all the activities peculiar to government temporarily ceased. Of course, in modern times government has in many countries taken over the direction of so many essential services, especially in the field of transport and communication, that the economic life would soon be paralyzed if all government-directed services ceased. But this is so not because these services *can* be provided only by government, but because government has assumed the exclusive right to provide them.[8]

The most obvious instrument of government's intervention in the private realm is, of course, legislation—of all the "inventions of man the one fraught with the gravest consequences"[9]—and the most ob-

[7] Harvey C. Mansfield, Jr., "Hobbes and the Science of Indirect Government," *American Political Science Review* 65 (March 1971): 107.

[8] Hayek, *Law, Legislation and Liberty*, p. 131.

[9] Ibid., p. 72.

vious defender of the private realm against this intervention has been
the judiciary. That it no longer plays this role in the economic sphere
may be deplored, but I leave to others the description of the consequences of this; the courts continue to defend other aspects of privacy. In fact, in one sense privacy is better protected now than ever
before, although in some liberal circles—using the term *liberal* in the
contemporary sense—it is fashionable to deny this. The privacy of the
home and the person is better protected against unreasonable searches and seizures than ever in the past.[10] The viewing of films, however obscene, in the privacy of the home cannot be made a criminal
offense or forbidden by civil process.[11] The state may not forbid the
use of birth-control drugs or devices; although no specific clause of
the Constitution prohibits such laws, the Supreme Court found a
right to privacy in "penumbras, formed by emanations" from various
guarantees in the Bill of Rights.[12] Nor may a state, except during the
latter stages of a pregnancy, forbid abortions; the due-process clause
of the Fourteenth Amendment protects the right to privacy, which
includes this right to terminate a pregnancy.[13] I cite these cases
merely as recent examples of the privacy protected by the Constitution as enforced by the judiciary. The fact that I can cite no cases in
which the courts have prevented the sort of monstrous invasions of
privacy customarily suffered by Solzhenitsyn and Sakharov and other
citizens—or, better, subjects—of the Soviet Union, is because no
American legislature engages in such practices. The American Constitution was designed to secure the private sphere from governmental intrusions and, on those occasions when legislatures have violated the explicit or sometimes implicit constitutional provisions, the
judiciary has enforced them. Thus, there is a constitutional right of
association, even though the words themselves are nowhere to be
found in the document, and this right may be exercised to form labor
unions, trade associations, private religious schools, political parties,
churches, and even families.

The growth of government and of the techniques and devices

[10] *Katz* v. *United States*, 389 U.S. 347 (1967).
[11] *Stanley* v. *Georgia*, 394 U.S. 557 (1969).
[12] *Griswold* v. *Connecticut*, 381 U.S. 479, 484 (1965).
[13] *Roe* v. *Wade*, 410 U.S. 113 (1973).

available to government are sometimes seen as endangering privacy just so much, and there is, of course, some basis for this opinion. Whether the law of the Constitution will be able to keep pace with modern science and the utilization by government of its products remains to be seen. The problem is one that was induced by liberalism in the sense that among the human activities that were consigned to the private sphere and therefore left uncontrolled by government was science, and none has had so great a development since the advent of liberalism. In this connection it deserves mention that Mill's *On Liberty* was written primarily to protect the men of science, the talented few, from the inhibiting influence of the many, who, in democratic times, would gain control of the legislative power.

Recently the Supreme Court refused, by the narrowest of margins, to uphold the claim of newsmen to refuse to testify before grand juries with respect to information given them in confidence. This induced Justice Douglas, in dissent, to complain bitterly that the "intrusion of government into this domain is symptomatic of the disease in this society. As the years pass the power of the government becomes more and more pervasive. It is a power to suffocate both people and causes."[14] This is familiar libertarian rhetoric, and not necessarily foolish for being familiar, but it is, I submit, both misguided— because it is a liberal principle that requires everyone to testify—and misguiding, because it distracts our attention from the real enemy of privacy today, which is not government. However much all modern societies, whatever their theoretical origin—liberal, preliberal, or postliberal—tend with the passage of time to resemble each other in certain peripheral respects, the fact is that it is still possible in the United States to lead a self-determined private life. What is "symptomatic of the disease in [our] society" is that so many of us do not want to do so. For, notwithstanding inquisitive grand juries, intrusive policemen, electronic surveillance, tapped phones, computer data banks, and so-called administrative searches, and notwithstanding price freezes, planned economies, progressive taxation, and emission controls, our privacy has not been jeopardized by the coercion of governmental power nearly so much as it has by the misuse of the

[14] *Branzburg* v. *Hayes*, 408 U.S. 665, 724 (1972).

freedom to which we are entitled and with which we seem unable to contend. No judiciary, however imaginative in its discovery of "zones of privacy" in the Constitution, and no matter what it is willing to do to the Constitution in the course of these discoveries, can help us to lead private lives if we are bound and determined not to do so. We may have protected the right of privacy from governmental interference, but in certain major respects we seem unwilling to exercise it. There is something wrong in what Professor Hayek calls "the spontaneous order of society," and it cannot be fairly attributed to governmental action.

III

Two incidents serve to illustrate the change in the American attitude toward privacy, the first taking place almost a century ago and the second only yesterday. Samuel Warren was a proper Bostonian who in 1883 had married Miss Mabel Bayard, the daughter of a United States senator. They set up housekeeping in Boston's Back Bay section where they entertained their friends frequently. The Boston press reported this and their other activities, apparently in "lurid detail." This annoyed Warren, and he and his former law partner, Louis Brandeis, whom President Wilson would later appoint to the Supreme Court, took the occasion to write their famous *Harvard Law Review* article, "The Right to Privacy,"[15] published in 1890. It is said to be one of the most influential law-review articles ever published in the United States, but this is true only in a qualified sense. They argued that the press was exceeding the limits of propriety and decency, not, in the sense that concerned them, by defaming the subjects of its attention, which meant that the law of defamation provided no remedy against it, but by infringing the individual's right not to have his thoughts and sentiments made public without his consent. Warren wanted to be let alone, and to come into the public world, which for him was clearly distinguished from the private world, only at his own pleasure. One would have assumed that liberalism promised him this. But it was the press, and the in-

15 Vol. 4 (1890): 193–220.

satiably curious "public" for which it wrote, not the government, that threatened his private world. He and Brandeis wanted the law to protect that privacy.

The subsequent fate of their proposed legal right to privacy shows the difficulty it faces in a liberal regime. In 1903 the right was embodied in a New York statute but limited, out of consideration for freedom of the press, to protection against the unauthorized use of a person's name, portrait, or picture for commercial purposes. Thus, the baseball pitcher Warren Spahn (who also had a very successful career in Boston) managed to prevent the distribution of an unauthorized biography of himself,[16] but the Hill family, even with the legal services of a then private lawyer named Richard M. Nixon, could not recover damages from *Life* magazine for an article disclosing their unwilling participation in an event later dramatized by Joseph Hayes as "The Desperate Hours."[17] Privacy of the sort desired by Samuel Warren and the Hills seems to be incompatible with the liberal principle of freedom of the press. Yet Warren wanted the law to protect his home and his family life. The American family historically has been regarded, as ably expressed by Tocqueville, as a private institution that served a very important public function in a liberal society:

There is certainly no country in the world where the tie of marriage is more highly respected than in America or where conjugal happiness is more highly or worthily appreciated. . . . When the American retires from the turmoil of public life to the bosom of his family, he finds in it the image of order and peace. There his pleasures are simple and natural, his joys are innocent and calm. . . . While the European endeavors to forget his domestic troubles by agitating society, the American derives from his own home that love of order which he afterwards carries with him into public affairs.[18]

The second incident involves what can best be described as a caricature of the American family—or, at least, of the American family as it once existed—and constitutes a cruel mockery of Samuel Warren's hopes for his country. The occasion for these remarks was the American family portrayed in that television series of a few years

---

[16] *Spahn* v. *Messner*, 221 N.E. 2d 543 (1966).
[17] *Time* v. *Hill*, 385 U.S. 374 (1967).
[18] *Democracy in America* (New York: Knopf, Vintage Books, 1954), 1: 315.

ago entitled—perhaps not inaccurately—"An American Family." Rather than resent and vigorously resist the attention of the press, this American family, personified by Bill Loud (rhymes, we are told, with proud) and his wife, Pat, and their children, eagerly invited the attention of the press. In fact, it opened its home and its entire life to the press by welcoming the television cameras for an extended stay of seven months. It had nothing to conceal from anyone, nothing properly its own, and it therefore knew nothing of propriety. It even allowed the cameras to be set up in advance in a New York hotel room to record what ought to have been a very painful reunion between mother and son. What was especially significant was the reaction in the press to all this. Rather than be shocked, a novelist (Anne Roiphe), writing in the country's most influential newspaper, admired the way the mother "played the scene." She is said to have managed "to accept all the variety of choices in life [all, apparently, equally choiceworthy] and to act and become a worldly woman." The mother was recorded elsewhere as being of the opinion that her "best scene" was the one where she informs her brother and sister-in-law that she has decided on a divorce.[19] It was only after the series got a couple of bad reviews that Bill and Pat Loud are said to have had misgivings about having lived their lives on television. They could be likened to actors, except that even actors have some private lives, or used to during the past when there was a public opinion that led them to conceal some things.

What is disquieting here is that the Louds are probably not unique; they merely had a greater opportunity to "publicize" themselves than is given to most of us. Most of us can only hope to be picked out of a crowd by a camera during a pause in a game's action, or to be given the chance to be made ridiculous on "Candid Camera," or to have our reunions with our prisoner-of-war husbands filmed by television, and the last of these especially is a rare opportunity even for wives of prisoners of war. Justice Douglas to the contrary notwithstanding, it is not the intrusion of government into the domain of the press that constitutes the greater threat to privacy; it

---

[19] Anne Roiphe, " 'An American Family': Things are Keen but Could Be Keener," *New York Times Sunday Magazine*, February 18, 1973, pp. 8 ff.; *Newsweek*, March 12, 1973, pp. 48–49.

is our unwillingness to regard the press as an intruder, or publicity as an intrusion. One suspects the heirs of Samuel Warren have solved what they regard as his problem by hiring press agents.

IV

Liberalism denies that there can be knowledge of the principles of happiness, which is why the liberal state eschews any official position on its nature, but it does secure the inalienable right of everyone to pursue what he idiosyncratically defines as happiness. This was the position adopted by the United States at its beginning in 1776. In another sense, however, the United States began long before 1776. Regimes are not created out of nothing; even a regime that inscribes on its dollar bills the motto *Novus Ordo Seclorum* must be built with materials that were shaped, in part at least, in a past that preceded the creation of this "new order of the ages." As Professor Hayek reminds us, vestiges of this past will survive, and, if the United States is allowed to survive, far into the future. Americans were to some degree a religious people in 1776 and were Englishmen with English habits and tastes—the early visitors tell us they encountered many a rude house with copies of the Bible, Shakespeare, and Milton—and they continued to build churches and to worship and to form families and the other associations constituting the unlegislated "spontaneous order" present at the beginning. In these associations were bred the practices and habits congenial to a decent life in a liberal society. Liberal government depended on this. Forbidden to use the instruments needed to form the character of its citizens, it was also forbidden to interfere with the private world where, fortunately, good character was formed in time-honored ways. The rule of laissez-faire applied here as well as in the realm of economics, and just as the private economy produced wealth, the private society produced good citizens. George Washington would not have been displeased with Samuel Warren. The fact that he would have been appalled by Bill Loud is one index of our present situation and of what has happened to the private world that produces the Bill Louds. One is bound to wonder whether, in Professor Hayek's terms, it may not be necessary for organized government to do more than ignore (or not intrude upon) the spontaneous order. Stated more radically, is there not reason to believe that this order is not capable of generating spontaneously the kind of society appropriate to a liberal regime? In short, some of our troubles today may derive precisely from the tendency of liberalism to subordinate the political, to see it as merely a subordinate part of "this spontaneous *overall* order,"[20] a mere enforcer of rules between and among the members of society. There is good reason to believe that government cannot merely be one organization among many "existing within the Great Society"; instead, we ought to be able to see that the character of the so-called great society is ultimately dependent on government and its instrumentalities, primarily the law. This is illustrated dramatically by a recent event in America.

In 1966 the Supreme Court effectively put an end to the censorship of obscenity in the United States. It did this on the basis of what it understood to be sound liberal principles, principles that it learned from John Stuart Mill's *On Liberty*. If, in Mill's words, "the sole end for which mankind are warranted, individually or collectively, in interfering with the liberty of action of any of their numbers, is self-protection [and if] the only purpose for which power can be rightfully exercised over any member of a civilized community, against his will, is to prevent harm to others,"[21] on what basis may the law forbid anyone to offer to sell obscene materials to someone who wants to buy them? The Court could find none, and so it effectively abolished the censorship of obscene materials.[22] The effect —and the effect on the "spontaneous order"—of this *removal* of the law has been profound. Without the ultimate authority of the law, the spontaneous order of society proved unable to defend itself; both its vulnerability and its dependence on the political order are revealed by what has happened.

What has happened is sometimes called "the sexual revolution," and we have yet to enjoy—or to suffer—all the consequences of it. We are altogether unprepared for these consequences because, as liberals, we took it for granted that the American society that existed would continue to exist, changed, perhaps, in nonessential respects, but continuing to produce men and women who fell in love, formed

[20] Hayek, *Law, Legislature and Liberty*, p. 47 (emphasis supplied).
[21] *On Liberty*, ch. 1.
[22] *A Book . . . v. Attorney General of Massachusetts*, 383 U.S. 413 (1966).

families, exercised the customary restraints, eschewed the indulgence of every passion, and so on. In this connection it is interesting to notice that, until 1973, when the Court reversed itself, no Supreme Court justice, in any of the opinions in these obscenity cases, ever attempted to state the reasons in support of censorship. In the early cases, from 1896 to 1932, when the Court upheld the federal censorship statute, it took it for granted that obscene speech was not protected by the First Amendment; in the latter-day cases, it took it for granted that in a liberal society no argument in favor of censorship could be made.[23]

One aspect of the sexual revolution produced by the abolition of censorship is visible to everyone: sexual materials of the most explicit sort are now freely published, distributed, and displayed. This was anticipated, in some quarters appreciated, and in others accepted with considerable equanimity. Sex has been publicized. But, as I have said elsewhere,[24] there has also taken place a "publification" of sex, by which I mean that the erotic relationship has been made public. The appurtenances of what is called love are now sold in shops devoted exclusively to the subject; whores autograph their biographies in mainstreet bookstores and appear on TV talk shows; the works of "sexologists," hawking the discoveries of this newest of the sciences, are best-sellers; and men and women, and boys and girls, think nothing of watching pornographic films in each other's company. The sexual act has been transformed into an act that is not deemed inappropriate in the public sphere. But if, as I have argued in still another place,[25] human sexuality belongs naturally to the private sphere, its character will be transformed by allowing it to go public, so to speak: it is impossible to make love in public. It is no comfort to be reminded that in 1948 George Orwell portrayed the real horror of the totalitarian regime of *1984* to consist in the inability of the two lovers to find a place where they might be alone, concealed from Big Brother; in *1984* it turned out that not only philoso-

[23] See, e.g., *Rosen v. United States*, 161 U.S. 29 (1896).

[24] Berns, *The First Amendment and the Future of American Democracy* (New York: Basic Books, 1976), ch. 5.

[25] "Beyond the (Garbage) Pale or Democracy, Censorship and the Arts," in Harry M. Clor, *Censorship and Freedom of Expression* (New York: Rand McNally, 1971), pp. 58–60. This article has been reprinted in *Public Interest* (Winter 1971): 3–24.

phy, religion, and economics, but even erotic love were denied privacy. This does not appear so horrible to a world that does not seek privacy, the world where sex has been emancipated, which can only mean emancipated from the restraints that made it human: the modesty, delicacy, fidelity, and the shame that protected it and thereby made it distinguishable from animal sexuality in general. As Leslie Farber has complained, to an increasing extent these human qualities are seen as merely arbitrary interferences "with the health of the sexual parts."[26] Sex, emancipated and abstracted from its human context, has been made the measure of existence, and, of course, there is no reason why this sex should not be public.

These things have occurred and are occurring in society because of a change in the law, and the law was changed because liberals assumed society could take care of itself. But this is not the complete story yet. The sexual revolution is almost certain to have a profound effect on still another major institution of the private world, the family. In the absence of authoritative direction by church or state, liberals have depended on the family to instill the habits required by citizenship in a self-governing community. We Americans especially have depended on it to teach us to care for others, to moderate the self-interest that is not much moderated by love of God or love of country. And the democratic family, according to Tocqueville, unlike the aristocratic family, is not constituted by the laws; it is constituted, or characterized, by a "familiar intimacy" bred by equality instead of a "filial obedience" resting on authority. It is, he says, based on natural ties of affection. It seems, therefore, emphatically to belong to what Professor Hayek calls the "spontaneous order of society." Yet, as Tocqueville knew, it is not immune to changes in the laws. The American family he observed depended on an education of a certain kind; it depended on what I have called the domesticating of the sexual passion, so that there would be no disharmony between sexual desire and the family; it depended on "circumstances which render matrimonial fidelity . . . obligatory," and Tocqueville was able to identify circumstances in the America of his time that made this fidelity "easy."[27] It will not be so easy in our future, and the family is likely to prove a very fragile institution indeed. It would be fool-

[26] "I'm Sorry, Dear," *Commentary* 38 (November 1964): 48.
[27] *Democracy in America*, 2: 217.

ish to believe the loss of the family will have no effect on liberal democracy.

The crisis of liberalism is not primarily the result of governmental action; it is the result of events in society, the private sphere, which has been preserved in liberal regimes as a sanctuary for those activities that were regarded as essentially private. But, as Rousseau pointed out at the beginning of liberalism, what were relegated to the private sphere were qualities that liberalism needed even if it could not itself engender them. The United States began with Washington, Jefferson, Adams, Hamilton, Madison, Marshall, but it could not generate men of that quality, and it was understood at the outset that it would not be able to do so, hence the great care given by the founders to institutions. But it could reasonably hope to generate men of the quality of Samuel Warren and Louis Brandeis, and Woodrow Wilson and Charles Evans Hughes, if some attention were paid to the private sphere where their character would be formed. Washington recognized this in his Farewell Address when he, in effect, called for support for the churches. Reason and experience, he said, "both forbid us to expect that national morality can prevail in exclusion of religious principle." As is true in so many cases, Tocqueville provided salutary advice with respect to this: "When . . . any religion has struck its roots deep into a democracy, beware that you do not disturb it; but rather watch it carefully, as the most precious bequest of aristocratic ages."[28] He offered this advice not as a pious man, but as one of the most thoughtful political thinkers of modern times. He knew very well the civic virtues present at the beginning of the United States, but he also knew the obstacles—not the least of them imposed by the liberal principles embodied in the regime—standing in the path of any attempt to preserve them. Because it aims to liberate men and thereby to promote a privacy unknown in the regimes that preceded it, and especially in classical republics, the modern liberal state is limited with respect to the means it may adopt to achieve public ends. More than that, a government constituted to secure the private rights of man is limited with respect to the public ends themselves. It may not preach virtue because it may not give official recognition to any definition of it; it may not, out of a desire

28 Ibid., pp. 154–55.

to protect family life, forbid the dissolution of marriages; it is severely limited in the realm of censorship; it may not, for example, follow Rousseau and forbid the establishment of a theater; it may not forbid the dissemination of scientific knowledge—in fact, the Constitution requires the Congress to "promote the progress of science"; even the old-fashioned terms, such as moral education or the formation of character or the cultivation of tastes, seem inappropriate in the liberal American setting, although it might be agreed that some characters and some tastes are illiberal. In the event, we have taught civics, waved and saluted the flag, and sung the national anthem at sporting events. The public schools used to provide a modicum of moral education—122,000,000 copies of those moralistic McGuffey's Readers were sold to and used by earlier generations of schoolchildren—but the character of those schools today may be indicated in a recent report of a subcommittee of the Senate Judiciary Committee to the effect that 70,000 "serious physical assaults on teachers" occur each year.[29]

Liberalism created and liberal regimes have secured the greatest range of privacy known to history, but in doing so they consigned to the private sphere the care of those qualities that even liberal regimes require in its citizens. Our present difficulties derive from our belief that the private sphere that we call society could produce these "spontaneously."

[29] U.S., Congress, Senate, *Congressional Record* (daily edition), April 17, 1975, p. 6011.

10.

The Conservative Origins of Collectivism

STEPHEN J. TONSOR

It is a truism that the political extremes of Left and Right are more like one another than they are like the center. Why this should be the case is rarely explained. It seems to be assumed that the likeness of opposites is the consequence of a dialectical political geometry which contradicts the usual axioms. We know that from the end of the eighteenth century to the present, men have been moving from Left to Right and Right to Left with puzzling frequency.[1] Nor do they usually halt for a while at some liberal halfway house as they work their way to the polar opposite of their once firmly held political views. As a consequence of this ease of ideological movement and conversion, the suspicion arises that these extreme political positions share a body of common ideas and that they have developed out of a set of common notions.

In the past several decades, various elements in the mind set of Right and Left have been identified. However, these have usually stopped short of a discussion of the common origins of collectivist thought. Once the paramountcy and desirability of collective social forms were established, chiefly by conservative thinkers, it was almost a matter of course that these ideas were drawn on by the political, economic, and social theorists of both the Right and the Left. While the political and economic forms of this commonly held col-

---

[1] For a treatment of the German aspect of this phenomenon see Otto Ernst Schuddekopf, *Linke Leute von Rechts, National Bolshewismus in Deutschland von 1918 bis 1933* (Stuttgart: Kohlhammer, 1960).

lectivism are, of course, very important, more important still are the commonly held justifications for these collective forms.

Obviously, collectivist theory is not the only source of likeness in the doctrines of the Right and the Left. The chiliastic content of contemporary totalitarian movements has been elaborately studied. It is clear that a secularized millenarian tradition has been powerfully influential[2] in Western thought from at least the middle of the eighteenth century, that it was one of the constituent elements in the romantic world view,[3] and that its influence was felt in the political and social theory of both the Right and the Left. Ernest Lee Tuveson has demonstrated that a secularized millenarianism was a major source of the idea of progress,[4] and Eric Voegelin has repeatedly pointed to the close links between totalitarian enthusiasms and eschatology. The transformation of human nature, the repair of time's erosion, and the onset of the third age, whether it is the Third Reich or Moscow or the third and last Rome,[5] are a set of ideas closely linked to both the Right and the Left in their revolutionary efforts to restructure the totality of the way things are.

Equally important to both the Right and the Left has been the role of "scientism" in theories of revolutionary inevitability. F. A. Hayek, in *The Counter-Revolution of Science*, identified this misuse of science as one of the most influential elements in the evolution of "scientific socialism." Karl Popper, inspired no doubt by Hayek's initial insight, has treated this theme exhaustively. It is, however, not generally recognized that the totalitarian movements of the Right are hardly less "scientistically" oriented than those of the Left. When, in the 1830s, science became a word with which to conjure, both predictive historical analysis and racism cloaked themselves in the language of science. It is not often recognized that Comtean positivism

2 Norman Cohn, *The Pursuit of the Millennium: Revolutionary Messianism in Medieval and Reformation Europe and Its Bearing on Modern Totalitarian Movements*, 2d ed. (New York: Harper & Row, 1961).

3 M. H. Abrams, *Natural Supernaturalism, Tradition and Revolution in Romantic Literature* (New York: W. W. Norton & Co., 1971).

4 Ernest Lee Tuveson, *Millennium and Utopia: A Study in the Background of the Idea of Progress* (Berkeley: University of California Press, 1949).

5 Nicholas Berdyaev, *The Origin of Russian Communism* (Ann Arbor: University of Michigan Press, 1960).

is as rigid in its pseudoscientific categories as dialectical materialism. Both Marx and Comte insisted that progress was immanent in history and that the pattern of development and fulfillment might be divined and predicted through the use of science. Writing of Comtean positivism in *The History of European Liberalism*, de Ruggiero noted:

In a scientific and "organic" society there is no more room for liberty of conscience than there is in astronomy, chemistry, or physiology. Popular sovereignty is a meaningless phrase; the word *right* must be struck out of the political vocabulary as the word *cause* is deleted from the philosophical; the individual man is an abstraction; the only thing which exists is society, and the only form of government is a dictatorship exercised in its interests.[6]

The positivists were bourgeois men of the Right. The triumph of positivism in the Third Republic was not accidental and positivism must be seen as an ideological ancestor of the authoritarian forms of contemporary dictatorships of the Right. In the important matter of "scientism," Right and Left shared a faith which, if translated into political reality, would have created structures of remarkable similarity.

Neither chiliasm nor scientism, however, has provided contemporary collectivism with its distinctive note and content. Both the Left and the Right were in strenuous reaction in the late eighteenth century against the bureaucratic rationalism and the social-contract theory that had dominated Enlightenment thought. In this common rebellion by Right and Left against the theories and the forms of "enlightened" polity, the Left came increasingly to borrow the critical and scholarly inventions of the Right, shaping them to the purposes of revolution and social transformation. The direct debt of Marxism to German idealism is well known. It is less well known that conservative social and historical analysis provided the historical justification for collectivist visions of society and that Marx and Engels were particularly indebted to conservative thinkers for their vision of the unalienated and collectivist nature of primal society. Moreover, the very concept of alienation, both as a social stage and as a philosophical conception, had been invented by thinkers even more remote from Marx than Hegel. It was to have a career in German ro-

---

[6] Guido de Ruggiero, *The History of European Liberalism*, trans. R. G. Collingwood (Boston: Beacon Hill, 1959), p. 202.

mantic sociology, which reached down to the precursors of national socialism.[7] This common body of ideas has animated the collectivism of both the Right and the Left and has given their thought a sibling identity.

It is a mistake, of course, to assume that alienation as a consequence of the division of labor and the invention of property, or alienation as a dialectical stage leading to reconciliation and comprehensive identity, is the root cause of the conflict between traditional society and enlightened innovation. The source of the revolt against the eighteenth century went much deeper than the transformation of social institutions. The response of traditional society to the critique offered by enlightened rationalism, a response often termed conservative, is the response of premodern society to the metaphysic of modernity. To ignore the depth of the challenge is to misconstrue the intensity and the validity of the conservative critique.[8] The romantic quest was, at bottom, a "quest for order," and the social and institutional quest was but a reflection of a more profound metaphysical quest. That the means of ordering were often magical and based upon a false reconstruction of the historic past is today evident. Nonetheless, we in the contemporary world live with the categories and in the ambience created by the romantic conservatives. The conception of "community," which they created and which they advanced as the perfected social form of aboriginal society, dominates as never before the thinking of the Western intelligentsia.

No one reflecting now on the movement toward collectivism in the past half century, whether that collectivism is of the Left or the Right, can deny the compelling power of the conceptions of "alienation" and "community." Whether the new design is for a commune, a university, a church, or an industrial society as a whole, the same appeals to a dimly perceived past in which man lived in unalienated community are made. The youth movement, the ecological revolution, the movement of women's liberation, and participatory democracy, whether in an industrial or in a more narrowly political framework, adopt the language of romantic-alienation theory and pursue

[7] See Arthur Mitzman, "Anti-Progress: A Study in the Romantic Roots of German Sociology," *Social Research* 33, no. 1 (Spring 1966): 65–85.

[8] See Stephen J. Tonsor, "Gnostics, Romantics and Conservatives," *Social Research* 35, no. 4 (Winter 1968): 616–34.

the vision of the reestablishment of unalienated community. The most striking intellectual characteristic of this movement, Left and Right, is that it draws upon a body of thought which originated in traditional society and was formulated by "conservative" philosophers and social thinkers.

However, alienation and community, regardless of their present locations in the context of politics and society, have their roots in German idealist philosophy. The path by which development takes place is both significant and interesting.

That great Scotch contemporary of Hume, Smith, and Robertson, the man who succeeded Hume at the Advocate's Library and then became, in succession, professor of natural and then moral philosophy at Edinburgh University, played a larger role than is generally recognized in the development of Continental and particularly German theories of alienation. No doubt Rousseau's "Second Discourse" also had a determinative influence, but the initial impetus came from Adam Ferguson.[9]

One of the major debates of the eighteenth century was that which raged around the question of the decline of ancient society. The eighteenth-century idea of progress was tried by the fact of the collapse of classical civilization. Adam Ferguson, Montesquieu, and Gibbon were the leading discussants in this widespread inquiry. Central to the debate was the question of the causes of the decline of military spirit, aptitudes, and virtues in Roman society. Adam Smith, in lectures he delivered at Glasgow University in 1763—lectures which remained unpublished until 1896—had argued that although the division of labor was a necessity of industrial production, it nonetheless had a deleterious effect upon human well-being in that it contracted the mind of the workman and dampened courage and the martial spirit. When in 1767 Ferguson published *An Essay on the History of Civil Society* he deepened and intensified the argument concerning the effects of what he called the "separation of professions."[10]

[9] David Kettler, *The Social and Political Thought of Adam Ferguson* (Columbus: Ohio State University Press, 1965).

[10] Adam Ferguson, *An Essay on the History of Civil Society* (Edinburgh, 1767); see also William C. Lehmann, *Adam Ferguson and the Beginnings of Modern Sociology* (New York: Columbia University Press, 1930).

The impact of the division of labor on human society was clear to Ferguson:

In its termination and ultimate effects the separation of professions serves, in some measure, to break the bonds of society, to substitute form in place of ingenuity, and to withdraw individuals from the common scene of occupation, on which the sentiments of the heart, and the mind are most happily employed.[11]

One is struck by how contemporary the note is when Ferguson observes that in the commercial state,

man is sometimes found a detached and solitary being: he has found an object which sets him in competition with his fellow creatures, and he deals with them as he does with his cattle and his soil, for the sake of the profits they bring. The mighty engine which we suppose to have formed society, only tends to set its members at variance, or to continue their intercourse after the bands of affection are broken.[12]

Ferguson, moreover, was in agreement with Rousseau's contention that perfection in science and technical mastery may, in fact does, bring with itself a decline in true knowledge and virtue. Ferguson wrote in a vein not different from that of Rousseau's first discourse, "On the Moral Effects of the Arts and Sciences" (1750), when he observed:

It may even be doubtful whether the measure of national capacity increases with the advancement of the arts. Many mechanical arts, indeed, require no capacity; they succeed best under total suppression of sentiments and reason; and ignorance is the mother of industry as well as of superstition. Reflection and fancy are subject to err; but a habit of moving the hand or the foot is independent of either. Manufacturers, accordingly, prosper most, where the mind is least consulted, and where the workshop may with not any great effort of imagination, be considered as an engine, the parts of which are men.[13]

And like Herder, with whose argument he has so much in common, Ferguson was quick to see that the role of the state, quickened to life and growth by the necessities of modernity, led by way of bureaucratic rationalism to a new species of despotism:

When we suppose government to have bestowed a degree of tranquility

[11] Ferguson, *History of Civil Society*, p. 218.
[12] Ibid., p. 19.
[13] Ibid., pp. 182–83.

which we sometimes hope to reap from it, as the best of fruits, and public affairs to proceed, in the several departments of legislation and and execution, with the least possible interruption of commerce and lucrative arts; such a state, like that of China, by throwing affairs into separate offices, where conduct consists in detail, and in the observance of forms, by superseding all the exertions of a great or a liberal mind, is more akin to despotism than we are apt to imagine.[14]

We must recall that the Frederician state was at the height of its success and power in Prussia when Ferguson published his *Essay on the History of Civil Society*. The German response to "enlightened despotism" had begun. Herder was not alone in his rejection of bureaucratic rationalism; in fact, reaction to the alienating, centralizing, despotic tendencies of eighteenth-century German politics is the key to our understanding the growth of German conservatism.[15]

Little wonder then that a year after publication, *An Essay on the History of Civil Society* was translated into German and published in Leipzig (1768).[16] The impact of Ferguson on his German contemporaries was considerable. It was especially marked in the case of Schiller and Herder.

In Schiller's *On the Aesthetic Education of Man* (1795)[17] Letter Six is very nearly a paraphrase of passages in *Essay on the History of Civil Society*. In this letter Schiller discusses the unalienated individuality and community that existed in Greek society. He asks why the men of his own age fail to share this natural wholeness and nobility. Rousseau's "second discourse" and Ferguson are the source of his explanation:

It was culture itself that inflicted this wound upon modern humanity. As soon as enlarged experience and more precise speculation made necessary a sharper division of sciences on the one hand, and on the other, the intricate machinery of States made necessary a more rigorous disassociation of ranks and occupations, the essential bond of human nature was torn apart, and a ruinous conflict set its harmonious powers at variance. . . . That zoophyte character of the Greek States, where every individual en-

14 Ibid., p. 269.
15 Klaus Epstein, *The Genesis of German Conservatism* (Princeton: Princeton University Press, 1966).
16 See the discussion of this and associated matters in Abrams, *Natural Supernaturalism*, p. 508, nn. 16, 17.
17 Friedrich Schiller, *On the Aesthetic Education of Man*, trans. and introd. Reginald Shell (New Haven: Yale University Press, 1954).

joyed an independent life and, when need arose, could become a whole in himself, now gave place to an ingenious piece of machinery, in which out of the botching together of a vast number of lifeless parts a collective mechanical life results. . . . Man himself grew to be only a fragment; with the monotonous noise of the wheel he drives everlastingly in his ears, he never develops the harmony of his being, and instead of imprinting humanity upon nature he becomes merely the imprint of his occupation, of his science.[18]

Through Schiller the ideas of lost community and the alienation of the individual become the common property of German idealist philosophy. Through Schelling, Fichte, and Hegel the step is a short one to Marx and Engels. For Schiller the division of labor is the source of alienation and of bureaucratic tyranny. It is, however, only a dialectical stage through which humanity must pass, a part of the educational journal of the human race that will eventuate in reintegration and resolution at a higher level. Unity and the restoration of the age of gold stand at the end of this process of human development. The movement is threefold: from community through alienation to a higher unity. In this detail there is an anticipation of the historical dialectical movement in the system of Marx-Engels.

To these elements, all of which later reappear in Engels' *The Origin of the Family, Private Property, and the State*, Rousseau added an emphasis on equality as a determinative characteristic of primitive, unalienated community.[19] Unlike Hobbes, Rousseau recognized that man in the state of nature is in a state of inequality. Rousseau, however, distinguished between two kinds of inequality among men:

I conceive that there are two kinds of inequality among the human species; one, which I call natural or physical, because it is established by nature, and consists in a different age, health, bodily strength, and the qualities of mind or of the soul; and another, which may be called moral or political inequality, because it depends on a kind of convention and is established, or at least authorized, by the consent of men. This latter consists of the different privileges which some men enjoy to the prejudice of others; such as that of being rich, more honored, more powerful, or even in a position to exact obedience.[20]

18 Ibid., pp. 39–40.
19 Robert I. Nisbet, "Rousseau and Equality," *Encounter* 43, no. 3 (September 1974): 40–51; Roger D. Masters, *The Political Philosophy of Rousseau* (Princeton: Princeton University Press, 1968).
20 Jean-Jacques Rousseau, "A Discourse on a Subject Proposed by the

Moreover, Rousseau's state of nature is not an ideal condition; it is not an idyllic state. Such brute existence was not mankind at its best, and it was not to this condition that Rousseau sought to restore mankind through the reconstruction of human society he envisions in *The Social Contract.* Who wishes to live as Rousseau depicted man in the state of nature as living? Not even Rousseau cared for an existence that was less attractive and less communal than that of wild animals.

Rousseau then depicts for us the "revolution" by which mankind passes from a state of nature into rudimentary society. This primal culture Rousseau tells us was the true golden age:

The more we reflect on it, the more we shall find that this state was the least subject to revolutions and altogether the best man could experience; so that he can have departed from it only through some fatal accident, which for the public good, should never have happened. The example of savages, most of whom have been found in this state, seems to prove that men were meant to remain in it, that it was the real youth of the world, and that all subsequent advances have been apparently so many steps toward the perfection of the individual, but in reality toward the decrepitude of the species.[21]

What Rousseau depicts is the golden age of community in which unalienated men in innocence and virtue "confined themselves to such acts as did not require the joint labor of several hands" and "enjoyed the pleasures of mutual and independent intercourse." The devil's own work in this Eden is the invention of the division of labor. Rousseau writes:

But from the moment one man began to stand in need of the help of another; from the moment it appeared advantageous to any one man to have enough provisions for two, equality disappeared, property was introduced, work became indispensable, and vast forests became smiling fields, which man had to water with the sweat of his brow, and where slavery and misery were soon to germinate and grow up with the crops.[22]

Academy of Dijon: What Is the Origin of Inequality Among Men and Is It Authorized by Natural Law?" (hereafter referred to as "Discourse on the Origin of Inequality") in *The Social Contract and Discourses,* trans. with introd. G. D. H. Cole (London: J. M. Dent & Sons, 1913), p. 160.

  [21] Rousseau, "Discourse on the Origin of Inequality," p. 198.

  [22] Ibid., p. 199.

Far from the conceptions of Ferguson, Rousseau, and Schiller being revolutionary and a part of the eighteenth century's vanguard of modernity, they were a self-conscious part of the counterattack of traditional society. No doubt once the fall had taken place, once the division of labor was fact (*O felix divisio*), there was no turning back. The restoration of the happiness of mankind could take place only through a revolution, a dialectical moment which overcame alienation and restored community, and that moment was exactly what the social theorists of both the Right and the Left sought.

It could be argued that *Capital* is a far less essential expression of Marxism than the book which Marx failed to write but for which throughout his lifetime he gathered notes—notes which Engels was to work up into *The Origin of the Family, Private Property, and the State*.[23] That Ferguson, Rousseau, and the German idealists do not appear in this work is worth noting. However, they are there in fact even though they do not appear in citations. This work, second only to *The Manifesto* in importance, sounds again all the major themes that passed over to Marxism from German idealism. Robert Tucker makes this clear when he writes:

So Marx defined communism in his manuscripts as "transcendence of human self-alienation," and saw it as the real future situation that Hegel had depicted in a mystified manner at the close of his *Phenomenology*, where spirit, having attained absolute knowledge, returns to itself out of its alienation and is fully "at home with itself in its otherness." . . . Consequently, we are now able to see him far more clearly than anyone could have easily done a half-century ago, an heir and representative of the great age of German philosophy that started with Kant and ran its course through Schelling, Fichte, and Hegel to its diverse later outcomes.[24]

Rousseau, of course, was both a direct and an indirect influence. It is not accidental that Kant, the conservative revolutionary of Konigsberg, should have furnished his study with a large portrait of Rousseau or have translated the politics of "general will" into the

[23] Friedrich Engels, *The Origin of the Family, Private Property, and the State*, introd. Evelyn Reed (New York: Pathfinder Press, 1972); Engels, *Der Ursprung der Familie, des Privateigenthums und des Staats*, Im Anschluss an Lewis H. Morgan's Forschungen, Dreizenhnte Auflage (Stuttgart, 1910).

[24] Robert C. Tucker, *The Marxian Revolutionary Idea* (New York: W. W. Norton & Co., 1969), p. 217.

ethical language of the "categorical imperative." Moreover, Engels asserted that Rousseau's "Discourse sur l'origine et les fondements de l'inégalité parmi les hommes" was a "masterpiece of dialectics."

However, neither Rousseau nor the German idealists had provided a historical reconstruction of the state of nature, the development of alienation and inequality consequent upon the division of labor, and the origin of the state. Rousseau, in his "Discourse on the Origin of the Inequality among Mankind," specifically disavows that his essay is a historical description of the evolution of human society:

Let us begin then by laying facts aside, as they do not affect the question. The investigations we may enter into, in treating this subject, must not be considered as historical truths, but only as mere conditional and hypothetical reasonings, rather calculated to explain the nature of things than to ascertain their actual origin; just like the hypotheses which our physicists daily form respecting the formation of the world.[25]

With Rousseau as with Hobbes we have an admission that the reconstruction of the state of nature and primitive society is conjectural, hypothetical, and has something of the character of what we would today call an ideal type. In the century that separated Rousseau's "second discourse" from the *Communist Manifesto*, history came to play a much larger role as a source of certainty and the guarantor of social progress. Dialectical materialism is nothing if it is not a science of history, and until the primal stage of human development—that moment in which unalienated community was dissolved under the impact of the division of labor—can be historically illuminated, the whole structure of Marxist thought stands in jeopardy. We must think of scientific socialism as scientific in the broad sense of the word; science as *Wissenschaft* or *scientia*, that is, science as ordered inquiry rather than science as a positivist treatment of natural causality.

German idealism provided Marx and Engels with a philosophical explanation of the disruption of community and the creation of alienated individuality; German history provided them with an account of the stages of human development by which these philosophical insights had been translated into historical reality. But here,

25 Rousseau, "Discourse on the Origin of Inequality," p. 161.

as in the case of idealism, the new "science" of history was an elaboration of conservative minds.

The invention of the science of history went back to the opening years of the nineteenth century and was particularly associated with the foundation of the University of Berlin. Its most distinctive critical tool was philology. In the opening semester of the newly founded University of Berlin in 1810, Barthold Georg Niebuhr (1776–1831) gave a series of lectures on Roman history. Classical philology had since the day of Valla been employed as a tool of negative criticism in the study of historical documents. Niebuhr's lectures were revolutionary in that his philological criticism was "positive"; that is, it forced the language of past time to yield an account of the spiritual conceptions and social relationships of those forgotten eras. Even in the absence of documentary evidence, language itself could be forced to testify to the nature of the past. The bias of this new historical method was, of course, conservative. It emphasized continuity and development over enormously long stretches of time. It seemed to translate the "geological" principal of uniformitarianism into historical development and negate any hope of sudden revolutionary change.

Barthold Georg Niebuhr was the innovative genius who created the new method. Friedrich Carl von Savigny (1774–1861) took the new method, wedded it to romantic ideology, and demonstrated its potentialities for the historical study of the law and past social relationships. Through his marriage to Kunigunde von Brentano, Savigny came into close contact with the romantic poet Clemens von Brentano and Brentano's romantic circle. In 1808 Savigny was appointed professor at Bavarian University in Landshut and in 1810 was called to the chair of Roman law at the newly established University of Berlin. Few men have exerted such profound influence on both the study of history and the development of the law as Savigny.[26] It was Savigny who turned away from the natural law and insisted that the law was the historical creation of the folk community. It was Savigny who related the idea of community to its legal, social, and property arrangements. It was Savigny who concretized the idea of commu-

---

[26] Erik Wolf, "Friedrich Carl von Savigny," in *Grosse Rechtsdenker der deutschen Geistesgeschichte* (Tubingen: J. C. B. Mohr, 1963).

nity by calling attention to its legal expression. It was Savigny who, through Sir Henry Maine and particularly through his own student, Johann Jakob Bachofen (1815–87), directly influenced the development of conservative German sociology, a sociology that culminates in Tönnies, Sombart, and Michels.[27]

In 1836–37 Marx attended Savigny's lectures at the University of Berlin. He was unimpressed; or rather, unfavorably impressed. He saw clearly the antirevolutionary implications implicit in Savigny's ideas. In Marx's *Contribution to the Critique of Hegel's Philosophy of Right* there is a bitter attack on the German historical legal school. In fact, the historical legal school was much more revolutionary and collectivist than Marx thought. The historical legal school is the great nineteenth-century conservative counterattack against social atomism, the contract theory, laissez-faire economics, and individualism, all of which dominated eighteenth-century thought. Even when the historical legal school is used as a defense of nineteenth-century competitive social forms, as it was by Sir Henry Maine, it still pays glowing tribute to a time past in which the forms of unalienated community commanded the social scene.

Savigny had based the genesis of legal forms on Herder's equivalence of *Volk*, *Urpoesie*, *Naturmensch*, and *Kind*. He asserted that law cannot enforce what custom does not approve; that the source of law is the will of the folk community. He identified revolution with the dissolution of community and the substitution of arbitrary power over alienated individuals. The organic and integrated relationships of the folk community depend upon the common realization of a spiritual ideal.[28] The restoration of society was, for Savigny, dependent upon the restoration of community. The rejection of the revolutionary law of France, a law that could only encourage social dissolution and an intensification of egocentric privatism, and the substitution for it of a Germanic law that had developed historically out

---

[27] Arthur Mitzman, *Sociology and Estrangement: Three Sociologists of Imperial Germany* (New York: Alfred A. Knopf, 1973).

[28] Heinrich Ritter von Srbik, *Geist and Geschichte, vom deutschen Humanismus bis zur Gegenwart*, Band 1 (Munich: Bruckmann, 1950); Dieter Strauch, *Recht, Gesetz und Staat bei Friedrich Carl von Savigny* (Bonn: H. Bouvier & Co., 1960).

of the German folk community were fundamental, Savigny believed, to the recreation of the social order.

The distance from the belief that the historical community was the ultimate source of law to the belief that the community is the ultimate source of property rights is a short one. Sir Henry Maine, certainly a student of Savigny, drew that conclusion.[29] In the mid-1850s Maine had begun work on a manuscript dealing with the development of law in the ancient world. It was not published until 1861[30] although the bulk of it had been delivered previously as lectures at Cambridge dating possibly as far back as 1843. There can be no doubt that Maine was saturated with the thought of Savigny even though the direct connection between Maine and Savigny cannot be traced.[31] Maine sought an administrative post in India, and he cannot, in the period before 1862 when he received the appointment, have failed to notice the similarity between Rome's imperial position and England's. Certainly the translator of Savigny's *Das Recht des Besitzes*,[32] Sir Erskine Perry, chief justice of the Supreme Court at Bombay, called attention to the parallel in his translation of 1848. It seems to me quite unlikely that Maine did not know this book or that he was unaware of Erskine's comparison.

Sir Henry Maine's comparative method and his close attention to Savigny and the Roman law led him to denounce the customary treatment of a contract between individuals as the origin of the state, and to denounce the Lockean notion that property was the consequence of the individual's having mixed his labor in the common goods of the earth. Maine wrote:

It will be observed, that the acts and motives which these theories suppose are the acts and motives of individuals. It is each individual who for himself subscribed to the social contract. . . . It is the individual who, in the

[29] George Feaver, *From Status to Contract, A Bibliography of Sir Henry Maine 1822–1888* (London: Longmans, 1969).

[30] Sir Henry James Sumner Maine, *Ancient Law, Its Connection with the Early History of Society and Its Relation to Modern Ideas* (London: Murray, 1861).

[31] J. W. Burrow, *Evolution and Society: A Study in Victorian Social Theory* (Cambridge: University Press, 1966).

[32] Friedrich Carl von Savigny, *Possession; or the Jus Possessionis of the Civil Law*, trans. Sir Erskine Perry (London: S. S. Sweet, 1848).

picture drawn by Blackstone, "is in the occupation of a determined spot of ground, for rest, for shade, or the like." . . . But ancient law, it must be repeated, knows next to nothing of individuals. It is concerned not with individuals, but with families, not with single human beings but with groups. . . . The life of each citizen is not regarded as limited by birth and death; it is but a continuation of the existence of his forefathers, and it will be prolonged in the existence of his descendants.[33]

Not only did individualism not exist in ancient societies, but private property was lacking. Maine wrote: "It is more than likely that joint-ownership, not separate ownership, is the really archaic institution, and that the forms of property which will afford us instruction will be those which are associated with families and groups of kindred.[34]

The bias toward the primitive as the original and authentic expression of humanity and its institutions, which is so characteristic of mankind, found here a model that seemed to overthrow those models based on the natural law. Sir Henry Maine seemed to sweep away the arguments of the eighteenth century and to substitute for their rational-hypothetical state of nature a very different state of nature based upon comparative historical study. The historical antecedents of contemporary collectivism seemed written into the constitution of humanity.

This was not quite what Maine had anticipated. He argued a developmental pattern in human societies that passed through evolutionary stages in which the process of development was linear rather than dialectical. Individualism, private property, and contract stood at the end of the developmental pattern rather than at the beginning. Maine wrote:

The word *status* may be usefully employed to construct a formula expressing the law of progress thus indicated, which, whatever be its value, seems to me to be sufficiently ascertained. All the forms of status taken notice of in the law of persons were derived from, and to the same extent are still colored by, the powers and privileges anciently residing in the family. If then we employ status, agreeably with the usage of the best writers, to signify those personal conditions only, and avoid applying the term to such conditions as are the immediate or remote result of agree-

[33] Maine, *Ancient Law*, p. 214.
[34] Ibid.

ment, we may say that the movement of the progressive societies has hitherto been a movement from status to contract.[35]

Not surprisingly, Maine's impact was greatest on the Continent. There the quest for unalienated individuality and integrated, organic community intensified, if anything, as the nineteenth century wore on. Ferdinand Tönnies, the author of *Community and Society* and directly responsible for much of the nonsense currently written and believed concerning alienation and community, referred to Maine as "my teacher." It should not surprise us that Emile Durkheim also was influenced.[36]

Maine's ancient family, the family characteristic of archaic society, had been patriarchal. However, during the very years Maine was engaged in writing *Ancient Law*, Savigny's student Johann Bachofen, professor of Roman law at Basel, advanced a strikingly different conception of social organization. Bachofen was a colleague of the young Nietzsche and the older Jacob Burckhardt. Like Burckhardt, he was a member of an ancient patrician family of Basel. In 1861, the same year Maine published *Ancient Law*, Bachofen published *Das Mutterrecht*.[37]

Bachofen believed on the basis of the analysis of myth that the earliest forms of archaic society had been matriarchal rather than patriarchal. Whereas Maine had recognized only the patriarchal family as the archaic familial form, Bachofen and Lewis Henry Morgan advanced a daring thesis that seemed to cut completely across the structure of the patriarchal family, an organizational form which was so intimately related to capitalism. (That, of course, was because inheritance through the father was such an intrinsic part of the capitalist ethos; that is, accumulation, achievement, are passed on through the male line to one's blood descendants.)

To the submergence of the individual and the commonality of property that Maine asserted to be the condition of archaic society Bachofen added the notion that in primitive society promiscuous in-

[35] Ibid., p. 215.
[36] Feaver, *From Status to Contract*, p. 58.
[37] Johann Jakob Bachofen, *Myth, Religion and Mother Right*, trans. Ralph Manheim, Bollingen Series 84 (Princeton: Princeton University Press, 1973).

tercourse and the matriarchal family had been the norm.[38] With
Maine, Bachofen saw a developmental pattern through a series of
stages from primitive promiscuity to patriarchal Christian marriage.
No more than Maine did Bachofen anticipate that his reconstruction
of ancient society would lead to an attempt to recreate that society
at a higher stage of development. But such in fact was the fate of his
work, for not only did Marx and Engels seize on it as exemplary of
both primitive communism and the unalienated world that was to
come, but Ludwig Klages, right-wing fantasist in post–World War I
Munich, sought to realize Bachofen's theories.[39] Through Klages,
Bachofen's theories became an important intellectual ingredient in
the thought and art of the English novelist D. H. Lawrence and one
of the sources of Lawrence's *Lady Chatterly's Lover*. It does strike
one as odd, not to say laughable, that both Marx and Lawrence
would identify ideologically with the same unhappy professor from
Basel.

When Engels wrote *The Origin of the Family, Private Property,
and the State*, both Maine and Bachofen were cited: Bachofen indeed occupies a central position in Engel's historical analysis of archaic society. The real hero, however, of Engels' work was a then
obscure American, Lewis Henry Morgan (1818–1881).

Lewis Henry Morgan's[40] theories of primitive society depended
less on the speculative analysis of the histories of past societies than
on Morgan's direct observations of living primitive societies. Morgan
was by avocation an American Indian ethnologist. He discovered, to
his surprise, that the Iroquois Indians of New York State had a matriarchal society. He came to the same conclusion as Bachofen, that
matriarchy was the consequence of primitive promiscuity, and, like
Bachofen, he believed that the forms of society were an evolutionary
development and that the highest form was that of Christian patriarchal marriage. Even though Morgan suffered from a fuzzy-minded
agrarian socialism it had little in common with the dialectical fanta-

---

[38] Georg Schmidt, *Johann Jakob Bachofens' Geschichtsphilosophie* (Munich: C. H. Bech, 1929).

[39] Ludwig Klages, *Von Kosmogonischen Eros* (Munich: Georg Müller,
1922).

[40] Carl Resek, *Lewis Henry Morgan, American Scholar* (Chicago: University of Chicago Press, 1960); Bernard Joseph Stern, *Lewis Henry Morgan, Social
Evolutionist* (Chicago: University of Chicago Press, 1931).

sies of Marx and Engels. That fact did not prevent Engels from quoting with approval one of the concluding paragraphs in Morgan's *Ancient Society.*

Since the advent of civilization, the outgrowth of property has been so immense, its forms so diverse, its uses so expanding and its management so intelligent in the interests of its owners, that it has become, on the part of the people, an unmanageable power. The time will come, nevertheless, when human intelligence will rise to mastery over property and define the relations of the state to the property it protects, as well as the obligations and the rights of its owners. The interests of society are paramount to individual interests, and the two must be brought into just and harmonious relations. A mere property career is not the final destiny of mankind, if progress is to be the law of the future as it has been of the past. The time which has passed away since civilization began is but a fragment of the ages yet to come. The dissolution of society bids fair to become the termination of a career of which property is the end and aim; because such a career contains the elements of self-destruction. Democracy in government, brotherhood in society, equality in rights and privileges, and universal education foreshadow the next higher plane of society to which experience, intelligence and knowledge are steadily tending. It will be a revival, in a higher form, of the liberty, equality and fraternity of the ancient gentes.[41]

Those lines echo most of the hopes for the restoration of community so often voiced before and after in the course of the nineteenth and twentieth centuries. When Engels came to work up the notes Marx had left behind, he added little to the conception and the history of primitive society that conservative philosophers and social theorists had created. Any sober assessment of the intellectual development of the modern period leads to the inescapable conclusion that conservatives in quest of "community" have been even more influential in the creation of the ideas and language of collectivism than have the socialists. It is not accidental that Marx and Engels were influenced by Rousseau, Maine, Bachofen, and Morgan, for the quest for unalienated individuality and integrated community has been equally strong with both the Left and the Right.

[41] Lewis Henry Morgan, *Ancient Society*, ed. Leslie A. White (Cambridge, Mass.: Harvard University Press, 1964), p. 467.

11.

The Cognitive Basis of Hayek's Political Thought

EUGENE F. MILLER

I shall begin on a personal note so that I can express my appreciation to Friedrich Hayek as a teacher at the same time that I indicate the purpose of this essay. I met Hayek for the first time in 1957, when I enrolled for graduate study at the University of Chicago under the Committee on Social Thought. Hayek was one of the distinguished scholars who made up the committee's faculty. The Committee on Social Thought attempted to overcome the rigidity and narrowness of American graduate education by giving the student almost complete freedom to design and pursue a broad program of study. The student's primary responsibility, prior to the doctoral dissertation, was to study, either independently or in courses of his choice, selected great works of fundamental importance for Western thought. My own list of "fundamentals" included Hobbes' *Leviathan*, Smith's *The Wealth of Nations*, and Burke's *Reflections on the Revolution in France*, and Hayek readily agreed to tutor me in these works. In these tutorial sessions, I came to know firsthand the qualities of mind that are so manifest in Hayek's writings—the remarkable breadth of his intellectual interests, his concern for basic issues in moral and political theory, and his unfailing generosity. Many a teacher has been chagrined to discover that free inquiry does not lead necessarily

I wish to acknowledge that the preparation of this essay was supported in part by summer research grants from the Earhart Foundation and the Department of Political Science, University of Georgia. I am deeply grateful for this support.

to agreement, but Hayek knew that intellectual freedom is likely to produce instead a diversity of ideas. Thus he continued to offer his full help and encouragement when my inquiries led me to question some fundamental principles of his thought. He sought not to cultivate disciples but to challenge his students to face difficult issues with the same integrity and manliness that marks his own thought. I know, therefore, that Hayek will not regard the critical parts of this essay as indicating any lack of gratitude for his efforts to help this student to discover his true vocation.

My essay will examine what I take to be the foundation of Hayek's thought, namely, the account he gives of human knowledge. There is ample evidence that his work in the special sciences—logic, psychology, ethics, politics, and economics—is intended to rest on an epistemological foundation. As he observes on one occasion. "What Einstein once said about science, 'Without epistemology—insofar as it is thinkable at all—it is primitive and muddled,' applies even more to our subjects."[1] Hayek relates that as a young man, he had been uncertain whether to become an economist or a psychologist. In the course of his early studies in theoretical psychology, he formulated the principles that would be developed more fully thirty years later in *The Sensory Order*, a work which, although largely neglected by Hayek's interpreters, offers the most systematic and detailed formulation of his epistemology.[2] Hayek would become, for a time, "a very pure and narrow economic theorist," but difficulties which he encountered in pure economic theory forced him to consider "all kinds of questions usually regarded as philosophical."[3] The 1936 essay "Economics and Knowledge,"[4] which he points to as marking this turn to philosophy, deals directly with epistemological themes. Hayek's reliance on a theory of knowledge is quite evident in his mature writings, whose central theme is the importance for politics

[1] *Studies in Philosophy, Politics and Economics* (Chicago: University of Chicago Press, 1967), p. 131.

[2] *The Sensory Order: An Inquiry into the Foundations of Theoretical Psychology*, introd. Heinrich Klüver (Chicago: University of Chicago Press, Phoenix Series, 1963).

[3] *Studies in Philosophy, Politics and Economics*, p. 91.

[4] Reprinted in *Individualism and Economic Order* (Chicago: University of Chicago Press, 1948), pp. 33–56.

and for science of a correct understanding of the limits of human reason.

I agree with Hayek's contention that an adequate account of economics and politics must rest upon a proper understanding of the character of human knowledge. He argues persuasively that the sober estimate of man's rational capacities which underlies classical British liberalism and American constitutionalism is more sound in its political consequences than the extravagant rationalism which marks the opposing stream of radical and utopian thought. He gives wise counsel when he tells us that our primary task, if we are to find a defensible alternative to modern theories of politics and economics that endanger man's liberty, is to rethink the problem of knowledge. Nevertheless, I must take issue with Hayek's specific account of human knowledge, because I think that it is seriously defective.

The defects which I find in Hayek's epistemology will be discussed in the body of this essay, but their general character can be indicated briefly as follows: Hayek opposes the modern tradition of Continental rationalism by appealing to an "antirationalist" tradition of British thought, whose chief representative is Hume. He does not give sufficient consideration to the fact that both traditions are modern and, by virtue of this, have more in common with each other than either has with premodern or classical thought. Thus he fails to consider the possibility that the grave defects that he attributes to the rationalist tradition are intrinsic to modern thought as such. More serious, however, is the fact that his own account of knowledge does not simply reproduce the empiricism of eighteenth-century British philosophy, as one might assume. Instead, it is decisively influenced by the very latest tendencies in the tradition of Continental philosophy that he opposes. Hayek's account of knowledge thus culminates in a depreciation of reason that is more extreme than that found in the writings of British philosophers of the eighteenth century. Hayek opposes the contemporary epistemological position that he calls "extreme historicism" or "historical relativism," but he seems to have abandoned the ground on which reasoned opposition to this position can hope to succeed. By basing his political theory on an insecure epistemological foundation, Hayek endangers those very principles of liberty that he wishes to defend.

TWO KINDS OF RATIONALISM AND THEIR
POLITICAL CONSEQUENCES

In a number of his writings over the past three decades, Hayek discusses the close connection that has existed since the seventeenth century between theories of politics and theories of knowledge. In Hayek's view, the modern world has witnessed a fundamental conflict between two opposing theories of liberty, one genuine and one specious, which arose respectively in England and in France. These theories of liberty are based, in turn, on sharply different views of the nature and limits of human reason. When Hayek has primarily in mind the political side of this modern conflict, he speaks of two kinds of individualism,[5] or two traditions of freedom,[6] or two kinds of liberalism.[7] When he has primarily in mind the epistemological side of this conflict, he speaks of two kinds of rationalism or else of the struggle between rationalism and antirationalism.[8] An examination of Hayek's account of this great political-epistemological conflict will disclose his understanding of the proper relationship between politics and reason.

The two theories of liberty of which Hayek speaks were developed, for the most part, during the eighteenth century, although very important formulations of each theory have appeared since that time. The "British" theory of liberty emerged from the writings of men such as John Locke, Bernard Mandeville, David Hume, Josiah Tucker, Adam Ferguson, Adam Smith, and Edmund Burke. The "French" theory was developed primarily by the Encyclopedists and Rousseau and by the Physiocrats and Condorcet. Hayek emphasizes that these contrasting theories of liberty do not coincide strictly with national boundaries. The British theory was defended on the Continent by writers such as Montesquieu and, later, Benjamin Constant, Alexis

---

[5] See "Individualism: True and False," in *Individualism and Economic Order*, pp. 1–32.

[6] See *The Constitution of Liberty* (Chicago: University of Chicago Press, 1960), pp. 54–70.

[7] See "The Principles of a Liberal Social Order," in *Studies in Philosophy, Politics and Economics*, pp. 160–77.

[8] See "Kinds of Rationalism," in *Studies in Philosophy, Politics and Economics*, p. 85.

de Tocqueville, and Lord Acton. At the same time, Thomas Hobbes was, along with Descartes, an important forerunner of Continental liberalism; and many supporters of the French theory of liberty appeared in England during the French Revolution and afterward. Hayek understands the politics of the twentieth century in terms of this protracted struggle between two different traditions in the theory of liberty. It is from the social rationalism or constructionism of the French tradition that "all modern socialism, planning and totalitarianism derive."[9] Hayek warns that collectivist thinking threatens now to displace the old British principles of liberty even in the English-speaking world.

We may wonder why the eighteenth century should have produced such disparate theories of liberty. The answer, Hayek suggests, is to be found in the vastly different conditions that prevailed in England and in France. The British writers did not have to rely mainly on abstract speculation in order to formulate principles of liberty. Their contemporary England enjoyed a high degree of both economic and political freedom, resulting from an earlier imposition of limits on the powers of government and from the growth of commerce that came about as the undesigned and unforeseen byproduct of political freedom.[10] The British theory of liberty thus arose from efforts to understand and give a systematic account of the free institutions that had grown up in England over the course of several centuries. From their inquiry into the workings of a free society, the British writers were led to what Hayek regards as a momentous discovery regarding the source of order in human affairs, namely, that most order is the unforeseen result of individual actions and not of deliberate design. They came to recognize that man's reason is very limited and imperfect in its capacity to guide the processes of society. France, by contrast, had never enjoyed a tradition of political and economic freedom. French theorizing about liberty thus had much more of a speculative and utopian character than did British theorizing. In Hayek's view, the decisive influence on French Enlightenment political theory was the philosophy of Descartes, with its extravagant

---

[9] *Studies in Philosophy, Politics and Economics*, p. 85.
[10] See *The Constitution of Liberty*, pp. 54–55; *The Road to Serfdom* (Chicago: University of Chicago Press, 1944), pp. 14–16; and *Studies in Philosophy, Politics and Economics*, pp. 161–62.

assumptions about the powers of human reason.[11] Cartesian rationalism led to the belief that everything which men achieve, including
liberty, is the direct result of reason and should therefore be subject
to its control. It traced all order to deliberate human design and expressed contempt for institutions that were not consciously designed
or not intelligible to reason.

Let us look more closely at Hayek's account of the contrasting
views of reason that underlie the British and the French theories of
liberty. The French theory gives expression to a position that Hayek
calls "constructivist" rationalism. Hayek refers frequently to this view
of reason also as "Cartesian" rationalism, because its modern influence begins chiefly with Descartes. He observes, however, that the
tradition of constructivist or Cartesian rationalism goes back to Plato
and was carried forward after the French Enlightenment by Hegel,
Marx, and the philosophical and legal positivists.[12]

In either of his characterizations, constructivist or Cartesian rationalism may be said to reflect the following principles: (1) Everything good which man has achieved has been gained through the
power of his reason. Reason, which is always fully and equally available to all humans, enables man to understand and master the forces
of society as well as the forces of nature. There are virtually no
limits to the progress that men can make in the future if they rely
solely on reason for guidance in their actions.[13] (2) All discoverable
order in human society comes about from deliberate rational design.
It is both possible and desirable, therefore, that men should undertake the comprehensive direction of the processes of society toward
rational and preferred ends. Social institutions deserve approval only
insofar as they have been constructed in accordance with a precon-
ceived plan and can be shown to produce effects that are preferable
to the effects that an alternative arrangement might produce. Men
should refuse to submit to traditions or beliefs whose reasonableness
is not immediately evident to them.[14] (3) If social planning toward

[11] See *Individualism and Economic Order*, p. 4; *The Constitution of Liberty*, p. 56; *Studies in Philosophy, Politics and Economics*, pp. 84–88.

[12] See *Studies in Philosophy, Politics and Economics*, pp. 93–94.

[13] See *The Road To Serfdom*, pp. 165–66; *Individualism and Economic
Order*, p. 8; *The Constitution of Liberty*, pp. 59, 61; *Studies in Philosophy,
Politics and Economics*, pp. 92–93, 161.

[14] See *The Road to Serfdom*, pp. 20, 166, 203; *Individualism and Eco-*

deliberately chosen goals is to be successful, the political authorities must have discretionary power to organize and direct all social and economic activities. Human freedom must be circumscribed, because the results of free action are often quite unpredictable and thus are a hindrance to central planning. Government cannot afford to recognize an autonomous sphere in which the ends of the individual are supreme.[15]

Standing in opposition to constructivist or Cartesian rationalism is the position which Hayek himself defends. For many years, Hayek spoke of this position simply as "antirationalist."[16] More recently, he has declared that this is a dangerous and misleading expression that ought to be avoided, because it obscures the true purpose of the so-called antirationalists, which is to make reason more effective by establishing its proper limits. Thus he now distinguishes not between "rationalism" and "antirationalism," but between two kinds of rationalism: "constructivist" and "critical."[17] Critical rationalism is the view of reason that underlies British political thought of the eighteenth century, but like constructivist rationalism, its roots go back to classical antiquity, specifically to the thought of Aristotle and Cicero. According to Hayek, the tradition of critical rationalism was transmitted to the modern age mainly through the work of Thomas Aquinas. Among the adherents of this tradition after the eighteenth century, Hayek lists Immanuel Kant and Alexander Humboldt, although he does not believe that they wholly escaped the fatal attraction of constructivist rationalism, as well as Tocqueville, Lord Acton, the Austrian economist Carl Menger, and finally Karl R. Popper, whom Hayek credits for coining the term "critical rationalism."[18]

Critical rationalism, as Hayek describes it, stands opposed to the principles of constructivist rationalism at the following points: (1) Man is not a highly rational and intelligent being, but one whose individual reason is very limited and imperfect. Reason is not the omni-

nomic Order, pp. 8, 10; The Constitution of Liberty, pp. 57–59, 61; Studies in Philosophy, Politics and Economics, pp. 85, 92–93.

[15] The Road to Serfdom, pp. 19–21, 35–36, 56–57; Individualism and Economic Order, pp. 18–19.

[16] See Individualism and Economic Order, p. 11; The Constitution of Liberty, pp. 57, 63, 69.

[17] Studies in Philosophy, Politics and Economics, pp. 84, 94.

[18] Ibid., pp. 94–95.

potent source of all the good things that men enjoy. In fact, the role which reason plays in human affairs must be rated rather low. Man has achieved what he has in spite of the fact that he is only partly guided by reason. Far from being an autonomous force that can direct the processes of society, reason grows as part of a social process that reason itself can neither direct nor understand. Reason cannot be its own master and control its own development. Efforts to control the growth of society and thus of reason can only serve, in the end, to limit reason. The uncontrolled and nonrational forces of society provide the only environment wherein reason can grow and operate effectively. Men can know the immediate consequences of their actions, but not the significance of these actions for the whole of society. Reason can never comprehend more than a tiny part of the whole of society.[19] (2) Most of the order which we find in human affairs does not come about from rational design, but is the spontaneous and unforeseen result of individual actions. Reason thus has only a limited role to play in the construction of a complex social order. It can help to devise a suitable legal framework and to improve institutions which have grown spontaneously, but the part of our social order which can or ought to be made a conscious product of human reason is only a small part of all the forces of society. Civilization develops cumulatively by a process of trial and error. The successful institutions survive without the contrivance or design of men. The individual must be willing to submit to conventions which are not the result of intelligent design and which seem unintelligible and irrational. His proper attitude is one of humility toward processes which have enabled mankind to achieve much greater things than reason could have designed.[20] (3) No person or small group of persons can possibly know all that would have to be known in order for comprehensive social planning to be successful. The primary responsibility of government must thus be not the central direction of all activity, but the enforcement of universal rules of

[19] See *The Road to Serfdom*, pp. 165–66; *Individualism and Economic Order*, pp. 6–13, 32; *The Constitution of Liberty*, p. 69; *Studies in Philosophy, Politics and Economics*, pp. 86–87, 161.

[20] See *The Road to Serfdom*, pp. 14–16, 202–6; *Individualism and Economic Order*, pp. 8–13, 19–22; *The Constitution of Liberty*, pp. 56–57, 59, 61, 69; *Studies in Philosophy, Politics and Economics*, pp. 38–39, 91–93, 130–31, 161–62.

just conduct. The rule of law circumscribes the coercive power of government and provides each individual with an assured private sphere in which he can use his bit of knowledge for his own betterment. This freedom under law contributes to the growth of an undesigned, spontaneous order of human activities of much greater complexity and also of much greater benefit to man than ever would have been produced by deliberate arrangement.[21]

HAYEK'S CRITIQUE OF REASON

Hayek's discussion of the two kinds of rationalism and their political consequences provides us with a clear view of his objective, as he himself understands it. He wishes to discredit the tradition of constructivist rationalism, which stretches from Plato through Descartes to contemporary positivism. His strategy is to show that human reason lacks the vast power to know and control human affairs which the constructivists have attributed to it. Following in the footsteps of Hume and the British philosophers of the eighteenth century, Hayek sets out to undermine the extravagant claims made in behalf of reason by providing us with "a proper insight into the limits of the effective use of individual reason in regulating relations between many reasonable beings."[22] This insight into the limits of reason is needed to make reason safe for society: "Reason is like a dangerous explosive which, handled cautiously, will be most beneficial, but if handled incautiously may blow up a civilization."[23] Hayek does not contend that the view of reason which he sets forth is a novel one. He claims to be restoring a tradition of critical rationalism that goes back to Aristotle, Cicero, and Aquinas.

I propose to show that the outcome of Hayek's endeavors is something very different from what we are led to expect by this self-interpretation. I do not wish to question his account of the modern tradition of constructivist rationalism. Clearly there is such a tradi-

---

[21] See *The Road to Serfdom*, pp. 34–36, 72–87, 202–6; *Individualism and Economic Order*, pp. 16–19; *The Constitution of Liberty*, pp. 133–75; *Studies in Philosophy, Politics and Economics*, pp. 161–62.
[22] *Studies in Philosophy, Politics and Economics*, p. 84.
[23] Ibid., p. 94.

tion, although one may doubt that major philosophers such as Rousseau and Hegel belong to it in just the way Hayek suggests. Its adherents have indeed been led by an imprudent estimate of the powers of reason to undermine sound institutions and destroy decent traditions. The shape of Hayek's thought has been determined by a consistent opposition to this baneful stream of modern philosophy. What I do wish to question is Hayek's understanding of the character of his own critique of reason.

First of all, Hayek's critical rationalism cannot properly be understood as the continuation of a premodern, Aristotelian tradition in philosophy. A serious examination of ancient philosophy would have provided Hayek with a solid alternative to constructivist rationalism. That he did not undertake such an examination is suggested, for example, by his failure to see that Plato and Aristotle are much closer in their philosophical views to each other than either is to any of the moderns, such as Descartes or Hume. There is a fundamental difference between ancient and modern views of the character of human reason, and Hayek's account of reason falls unquestionably on the side of modernity.

In the second place, Hayek's critical rationalism cannot properly be understood even as a restoration of the early modern views of Hume and the British philosophers of the eighteenth century. It is true that Hayek shares Hume's desire to establish once and for all the limits of reason and thereby to discredit efforts to refashion society along perfectly rational lines. Yet Hayek goes much further than even Hume or Kant in calling into question reason's power to know the nature of things. These philosophers had continued to attribute to rational knowledge an essential constancy and stability, which was thought to be guaranteed by the uniformity of human nature or by the permanency of the mind's own structure. Hayek takes the fateful step of making reason a part of the historical process. Rather than returning to ancient or even to eighteenth-century thought, Hayek embraces the most recent and radical stream of modernity.

The problems that arise in Hayek's account of human knowledge are visible already in *The Road to Serfdom*. In this early work, as in all of his later writings, Hayek seeks to discredit the claim that the reason of individual men can plan and control the comprehensive processes of society for the common welfare.[24] His line of attack is to deny reason's independence or autonomy with respect to the social process. Far from being able to understand and guide the social process from above, "individual reason" is immersed in this process and shaped decisively by it. Hayek's position means, first of all, that there is an accumulation of wisdom in the social process which far surpasses the bits of knowledge that individual minds can attain; and no individual mind is capable of supervising this accumulation. As Hayek explains, "The growth of reason is a social process," based on the interaction of individuals with different knowledge and different views. It is only in the course of this social process that the individual errors of irrational and fallible men are corrected. We cannot plan or organize the growth of reason or even predict its outcome, because it is impossible to know in advance which views will or will not assist this growth.[25] The proper attitude of individual men is one of "humility toward the impersonal and anonymous social processes" by which they help to create things greater than they know.[26]

Hayek's principle that reason grows as a social process may imply more, however, than just the idea that the fund of knowledge available to man grows cumulatively or incrementally without conscious direction. He speaks, for example, of the need to recognize "the superindividual forces which guide the growth of reason."[27] What are these "superindividual forces" by which the growth of reason is guided? Are they rational in character and thus comprehensible to man, or does the growth of reason depend on forces that are essentially irrational? Is the reasoning of individual men determined by these forces in such a way that ways of viewing the world are relative to particular times and places? In recent decades, these questions have been debated under the general heading of *historicism*. Hayek takes up these questions directly in several essays that were prepared at more or less the same time as *The Road to Serfdom*.

[24] Collectivist doctrines "necessarily lead to the demand that the mind of some individual should rule supreme" (*The Road to Serfdom*, p. 166).

[25] *The Road to Serfdom*, pp. 165–66. See *Individualism and Economic Order*, p. 8.

[26] *Individualism and Economic Order*, p. 8.

[27] *The Road to Serfdom*, p. 166.

Hayek points out that the term historicism is often applied in a somewhat confused way to two quite different points of view. It is used, on the one hand, to refer to the "older historical school" in nineteenth-century German thought, whose fathers include Adam Smith and Edmund Burke. Hayek is mildly critical of the older historical school for its antitheoretical bias, but he applauds its suggestion that social institutions arise not as the product of conscious design, as eighteenth-century rationalists had held, but as the unintended result of the separate actions of many individuals.[28] The term historicism is used, on the other hand, to refer to the philosophies or theories of history that have been developed by writers such as Hegel, Comte, Marx, Sombart, and Spengler. Theoretical historicism regards historical complexes as given wholes, which develop through definite stages according to intelligible laws. According to this view, the human mind is always determined in its particular manifestations by a specific historical setting; and it develops as part of the comprehensive historical process according to laws that are accessible to theoretical understanding. Hayek is sharply critical of theoretical historicism on several grounds, especially its assumption that historical wholes are given to the observer rather than constructed by him and its belief that human reason can attain a direct insight into the laws of historical development and even predict its future course.[29]

Hayek is by no means the first to oppose the view that reason can discover laws of historical development and thus predict the shape of man's life in the future. By the early decades of the twentieth century, this grandiose claim on behalf of reason was under heavy attack in academic circles. Yet the repudiation of theoretical historicism raised a critical problem for its opponents, that is, the problem of historical relativism. Prior to the rise of historicism, philosophers had assumed that theoretical knowledge is constant from one time and place to another, either because the natural world was thought to have a permanent structure which reason could grasp or, in cases where the intelligibility of the external world was questioned, because the human mind itself was thought to operate according to invariant principles. Theoretical historicism had taught

[28] *The Counter-Revolution of Science: Studies on the Abuse of Reason* (Glencoe, Ill.: Free Press, 1955), pp. 64–65.
[29] *The Counter-Revolution of Science*, pp. 64–66, 73–74, 76.

that men necessarily hold different views of the world in different historical epochs, because the very categories or concepts of human thought are determined by conditions that are unique to each epoch. Nevertheless, it was able to save the possibility of theoretical understanding by maintaining that there is one privileged epoch in which men are able finally to understand the laws by which the historical process as a whole has developed. When opponents of theoretical historicism rejected its doctrine that reason can understand the laws of historical development but nonetheless retained its views on the variability of the human mind and the determination of thought by historical forces, historical relativism was the inevitable result. Historical relativism teaches that human thought is always based on concepts or presuppositions that vary from one time or place to another, so that men necessarily hold different world views in different historical epochs. Things have a different "meaning" for men at different times and places. Reason is unable to understand the forces that determine its own operations, because these forces are irrational and mysterious. The historical relativist concludes that there is no possibility of final truth about nature or history and thus no possibility of science or theory in the traditional sense of these terms.[30]

We must inquire now as to Hayek's success in avoiding the relativistic conclusions about human knowledge that follow upon the decay of theoretical historicism. Hayek offers a refutation of "the very fashionable doctrine of 'historical relativism'" in essays of his that first appeared in the early 1940s.[31] We must pay careful attention to the structure of this refutation, because it provides us with something of a standard for judging his success in overcoming historical relativism in what he says later about the character of human reason.

Hayek points out that a "consistently pursued historicism necessarily leads to the view that the human mind is itself variable."[32] All

[30] I have discussed these issues at greater length in "Positivism, Historicism, and Political Inquiry" and "Rejoinder to 'Comments' by David Braybrooke and Alexander Rosenberg, Richard S. Rudner and Martin Landau," *American Political Science Review* 66 (September 1972): 796–817, 857–73.

[31] See, in addition to the essays collected in *The Counter-Revolution of Science*, "The Facts of the Social Sciences," in *Individualism and Economic Order*, pp. 57–76.

[32] *The Counter-Revolution of Science*, p. 76.

concepts come to be regarded "as merely historical categories, valid only in a particular historical context."[33] This means that men must necessarily conceive of objects such as "price" or "monopoly" differently from one time and place to another. There can be no timeless generalizations or universal theories about society and its institutions. All social theory, according to a strict historicism, is "necessarily historical, *zeitgebunden,* true only of particular historical 'phases' or 'systems.' "[34] Hayek's refutation of historical relativism rests on the premise that man as man thinks in terms of certain invariable categories:

There is nothing paradoxical in the claim that all mind must run in terms of certain universal categories of thought, because where we speak of mind this means that we can successfully interpret what we observe by arranging it in these categories. And anything which can be comprehended through our understanding of other minds, anything which we recognize as specifically human, must be comprehensible in terms of these categories.[35]

Hayek argues as follows: Whenever we recognize or understand other men at all as human beings or human minds, we do so by analogy to our own mind. We explain their intentions and the meaning of their actions in terms of the familiar categories of our thought. We assume that the structure of their minds is not essentially different from that of our own mind. This analogical recognition of other minds is the basis on which we understand not only our contemporaries, but also men of other epochs and the signs and documents which they have left behind. History is accessible to us only on the assumption that the minds of men in the past reflect the same structure and the same categories as our minds. The historicist thus utters a "meaningless statement" when he contends that the human mind is variable or that mental categories change from one historical epoch to another. In Hayek's words, "to recognize something as mind is to recognize it as something similar to our own mind."[36] Again, "where we can no longer recognize categories of thought similar to those in

[33] Ibid., p. 75.
[34] Ibid.
[35] Ibid., p. 78.
[36] Ibid., p. 77.

terms of which we think, history ceases to be human history."[37] Hayek concludes that since certain invariable features are present whenever we find men, true theoretical statements or generalizations must be possible in the social sciences.[38]

With this refutation of historicism in mind, let us turn now to Hayek's account of human knowledge in *The Sensory Order*, which was published in 1952, and to his philosophical essays of the 1950s and 1960s, which are brought together in his *Studies in Philosophy, Politics and Economics*. As we have seen, Hayek's early case against a relativistic view of knowledge rests on the premise that the human mind is essentially invariable from one historical epoch to another and that it always thinks in terms of certain universal categories. We shall find that in Hayek's later writings, this very premise becomes questionable, so that we are compelled to wonder whether Hayek has surrendered the ground on which his case against historical relativism once rested.

Hayek's point of departure in *The Sensory Order* is the fundamental difference between the way the world appears to our senses and the way the world is described by modern science. Objects in the world appear to us as alike or different according to their sensory qualities, but "the progress of the physical sciences has all but eliminated these qualities from our scientific picture of the external world."[39] Science finds that our sensory classification of events in terms of qualities is inadequate to describe the regularities that exist in the physical world. To give a satisfactory account of these regularities, it must abandon the sensory classification and define objects instead in terms of observed relations between them. Thus it happens that the objects of the world around us are arranged or classified in two different orders: the "sensory" or "phenomenal" order of perceived qualities; and the "physical" order of events described exclusively in terms of their relations.[40]

At this point in Hayek's exposition, it might occur to someone to ask what order of things is real: the world as we perceive it or the world as it is described by physical science. Hayek disclaims any in-

[37] Ibid., p. 79.
[38] Ibid., pp. 70–72, 76–79.
[39] *The Sensory Order*, p. 2.
[40] Ibid., pp. 2–8.

terest in what things "really" are.[41] Nevertheless, his entire argument depends on his acceptance of the veracity of the scientific account of the world. Thus he observes that "we are not entitled to assume that the world appears to us as it does because it is like that."[42] Indeed, he speaks even of "the necessity of a belief in an objective physical world which is different from that presented to us by our senses."[43] Thus arises the central problem of *The Sensory Order*: If we cannot assume that the world appears to us as it does because it is like that, "the question why it appears to us as it does becomes a genuine problem."[44] This problem is one to which theoretical psychology must address itself: "Psychology must take the physical world as represented by modern physics as given and try to reconstruct the process by which the organism classifies the physical events in the manner which is familiar to us as the order of sensory qualities."[45]

Hayek's formulation of the problem of theoretical psychology permits us to make some very important observations about the philosophical basis of his thought. First, we see his decisive break with the ancient view that things themselves possess forms or natures, including the qualities perceived by the senses, which provide the basis for our qualitative distinctions and our classification of things according to their kinds. Hayek takes the view that science can account for things entirely in terms of their relations and effects, so that there is no need to assume that essential qualities or forms inhere in the things themselves. He is quite emphatic in denying that the mind's classification of things is ever based on the discovery of natural kinds or classes or qualities.

Second, despite his unqualified condemnation of Descartes' philosophy, Hayek's own distinction between the physical or material world and the world of the mind is a reflection of the Cartesian dualism that has permeated modern thought. Like Descartes and the philosophers who have preserved his dualistic viewpoint, Hayek insists on a radical difference between the phenomena, or the things as they appear to us, and the things as they subsist in the world ex-

---

41 Ibid., pp. 4–5; cf. pp. 173–74.
42 Ibid., p. 6.
43 Ibid., p. 176.
44 Ibid., p. 6.
45 Ibid., p. 7.

ternal to the mind. Insofar as the relation of cognition and reality is concerned, Hayek, like Descartes, stresses the deceptiveness and unreliability of the senses. There is an estrangement between the sensory order and the order of things. Hayek takes issue with Descartes primarily in regard to reason's capacity to overcome this estrangement and to know things as they are.

Third, Hayek is deeply influenced by the Kantian view that sense data are never accessible to consciousness in their original or pure state, but only as they are transformed by the mind's own apparatus of classification. For Hayek, the mind's sensory qualities function in much the same way as Kant's categories to predetermine the forms of sense experience: "All that we can perceive is thus determined by the order of sensory qualities which provides the 'categories' in terms of which sense experience can alone take place."[46] It follows that the mind's classificatory scheme or "frame of reference . . . can never be contradicted by sense experience and will determine the forms of such experiences which are possible."[47]

Finally, we must notice that this Kantian dimension of Hayek's thought leads him to break decisively with the empiricism of Ernst Mach and the Vienna Circle, to which he had once been attracted.[48] Viennese empiricism had been developed in conjunction with positivist efforts to claim for physical science an objectivity and reliability that could not be rivaled by traditional philosophy or metaphysics. The superiority of scientific knowledge of the world was said to derive from the fact that it is constructed from or tested by sense experience, while metaphysics is not grounded in experience. Sense experience must somehow be prior to conceptualization and theory if it is to serve as a standard for judging them. Accordingly, the Viennese positivists often argued that sense data are given to us by perception in a pure and uninterpreted form. These given data, which represent the facts of the external world, serve as the ingredients of reasoning without being essentially transformed by it.[49]

[46] Ibid., p. 167.
[47] Ibid.
[48] See *Studies in Philosophy, Politics and Economics*, p. 268; *The Sensory Order*, pp. 175–76.
[49] I discuss these points more fully in "Positivism, Historicism, and Political Inquiry," pp. 798–801; and "Rejoinder to 'Comments,'" pp. 864–67.

Hayek seems to have this empiricist theory of knowledge in mind when he speaks of "the traditional view," according to which

experience begins with the reception of sensory data possessing constant qualities which either reflect corresponding attributes belonging to the perceived external objects, or are uniquely correlated with such attributes of the elements of the physical world. These sensory data are supposed to form the raw material which the mind accumulates and learns to arrange in various manners.[50]

Hayek's argument in *The Sensory Order* is directed expressly against this viewpoint. He rejects the notion of an "hypothetical 'pure' or 'primary' core of sensation" which involves some direct communication of properties of the external objects or constitutes irreducible mental atoms or elements: "The conception of an original pure core of sensation which is merely modified by experience is an entirely unnecessary fiction."[51] We have taken notice already of the grounds on which Hayek denies that the data of sensation are given to consciousness in a pure form. He maintains that the forms of any possible sense experiences are predetermined by the mind's apparatus of classification: "Perception is thus always an interpretation, the placing of something into one or several classes of objects."[52] We can never perceive the unique properties of individual objects apart from the "categories" of this classificatory apparatus. If all that we know about the world from sense experience is of the nature of an "interpretation" or "theory," there must be a part of our knowledge that cannot be controlled by experience or contradicted by it.[53] Hayek thus calls into question the positivistic view that scientific theory can be conclusively tested, that is, either confirmed or falsified, by experience.[54]

Let us return to the issue that is of primary concern to us, namely, Hayek's success in upholding the possibility of genuine knowl-

[50] *The Sensory Order*, p. 165.
[51] Ibid., p. 42; see also p. 165.
[52] Ibid., p. 142.
[53] See ibid., pp. 169, 172.
[54] See ibid., p. 171: "Science thus tends necessarily toward an ultimate state in which all knowledge is embodied in the definitions of the objects with which it is concerned; and in which all true statements about these objects therefore are analytical or tautological and could not be disproved by any experience."

edge against the arguments of extreme historicism or historical relativism. As we have seen, Hayek adopts the Kantian view that sense
experience is accessible to consciousness only insofar as it is already
interpreted or classified by the categories of the mind. While Kant
had taught that the categories of thought are fixed and invariable,
historicists would later take the position that these categories vary
from one historical epoch or culture to another, so that men necessarily hold different interpretations of the world in different times
and places. Hayek, in his writings of the early 1940s, steadfastly opposes historical relativism on the grounds that the human mind is
essentially invariable and that "all mind must run in terms of certain
universal categories of thought." In *The Sensory Order*, however, he
seems to take the position that the mind and its framework of categories must vary in fundamental ways according to the formative
experiences of individuals and groups.

Beginning from stimuli defined in physical terms, Hayek attempts in *The Sensory Order* to reconstruct the physiological process by which the organism classifies physical events in the manner
familiar to us as the order of sensory qualities. His first point is that
"the difference of the sensory qualities is not due to the communication of a difference in the stimuli."[55] Physically different stimuli produce similar sensory qualities, and vice versa. Thus the sensory order
cannot be understood as simply the reflection of a corresponding set
of physical stimuli. Hayek explains the differential responses of the
organism to the various physical stimuli by reference to the ordering
of impulses that the stimuli produce in the fibers of the central nervous system. In the course of the development of the species or the
individual, a system of connections is built up, through which impulses can be transmitted from fiber to fiber. An individual impulse
or group of impulses owes its distinctive quality to its position in the
whole system of connections. This system of connections is structurally equivalent to what we know as the order of sensory qualities.
Moreover, this underlying physiological mechanism wholly determines the sensory or other mental qualities.[56]

We are concerned primarily with what Hayek has to say about
the stability and uniformity of the classificatory system—the system

[55] Ibid., p. 11.
[56] See ibid., pp. 52–53.

of sensory qualities or mental categories—that is created by these physiological processes. His emphasis throughout *The Sensory Order* is on the variability of the mind and its cognitive structure. Hayek denies that mind can be understood as a distinct "substance."[57] What we call mind is "a particular order of a set of events taking place in some organism and in some manner related to, but not identical with, the physical order of events in the environment."[58] We should not imagine that the network of physiological connections underlying the sensory order is something innate in the human organism. It is "acquired in the course of the development of the species and the individual" as a result of the organism's reaction to stimuli in its physical environment.[59] Thus the mind's apparatus of classification is "shaped by the conditions prevailing in the environment in which we live."[60] Since cognitive structure is determined by the organism's past "experiences," that is, its preconscious reactions to environmental stimuli, it is not surprising to find that these structures, while similar among individuals whose past experiences are similar, are not identical.[61] Again, it is not surprising to find that "the qualitative elements of which the phenomenal world is built up, and the whole order of the sensory qualities, are themselves subject to continuous change."[62] All of these implications of Hayek's position are brought out in the analogy he draws between the organism's physiological-mental classificatory system and a map:

This "map" of the relationships between various kinds of events in the external world, which the linkages will gradually produce in the higher nervous centers, will not only be a very imperfect map, but also a map which is subject to continuous although very gradual change. It will not only give merely some of the relations existing in the external world, and give in addition some which are different from those which exist objectively, but it will also not give a constant but a variable picture of the structures which it reproduces.[63]

The maps formed in different brains will be similar to each other be-

---

[57] See ibid., pp. 105, 177.
[58] Ibid., p. 16; this statement is italicized in the original.
[59] Ibid., p. 53; see also pp. 52, 106, 167.
[60] Ibid., p. 165.
[61] See ibid., p. 110.
[62] Ibid., p. 108.
[63] Ibid., p. 110.

cause they are determined by similar factors, but they will not be identical.

Complete identity of the maps would presuppose not only an identical history of the different individuals but also complete identity of their anatomical structure. The mere fact that for each individual the map will be subject to constant changes practically precludes the possibility that at any moment the maps of two individuals should be completely identical.[64]

The far-reaching epistemological implications of *The Sensory Order* should now be apparent. On the one hand, Hayek wants to retain the idea that science can give a reliable explanation of regularities in the objective physical world. Indeed, his account of human cognition presupposes the validity of his physiological explanation of the principles that underlie the cognitive processes. On the other hand, his general conclusions about the character of human cognition seem to undermine the very possibility of objective knowledge and to concede the basic premises of extreme historicism. He argues that all perception and reasoning are predetermined by a classificatory system or "map" that varies from one individual and group to another and changes over time. The categories of this classificatory system cannot be confirmed or falsified, because as the presuppositions of all cognition they give to sense perception and conceptual thinking their distinctive shape. We are sometimes forced to revise our apparatus of classification upon discovering that beliefs or expectations which result from it are disappointed or disproved. The process of "reclassification" leads not, however, to a "presupposition-free" grasp of the objective world, but to an understanding of the world in terms of a different frame of reference:

While the process of reclassification involves a change of the frame of reference, or of what is *a priori* true of all statements which can be made about the objects defined with respect to that frame of reference, it alters merely the particular presuppositions of all statements, but does not change the fact that such presuppositions must be implied in all statements that can be made.[65]

Hayek thus agrees with Kant that perception and reasoning always presuppose *a priori* categories of thought, but he embraces the view

[64] Ibid.
[65] Ibid., p. 169.

of extreme historicism that this *a priori* is neither constant nor universal but varies from one frame of reference to another. As Heinrich Klüver points out in his introduction to *The Sensory Order*, Hayek dissolves "substances" and "things" into changeable relations. Even "mind" for him has turned into a complex of relations. Not only are there no permanent or fixed objects: "The implication of the theory presented here is that even the ways of knowing 'objectively' are not stable, or only relatively stable, and that the ordering principles themselves are subject to change." [66]

Turning finally to Hayek's writings of the 1960s, we find that he continues to affirm the epistemological principles of *The Sensory Order*, although he restates them in the idiom of contemporary philosophy. Thus instead of speaking of a physiological mechanism of classification that underlies and determines all conscious mental operations, he speaks of implicit and unspecifiable "rules" that govern our perceptions and actions. These rules operate upon the contents of consciousness, but cannot themselves be made conscious. We are not aware of them and cannot test them. As the presuppositions of thought, they are "outside the range of what we can either state or reflect upon." [67] This framework of rules determines the "meaning" of conscious thought, but the framework itself is without meaning. Meaning depends on an order that is essentially meaningless: "If 'to have meaning' is to have a place in an order which we share with other people, this order itself cannot have meaning because it cannot have a place in itself." [68]

In *The Sensory Order*, Hayek had explained the acquisition of the categories of thought in physiological terms. Later, in keeping with the emphasis of contemporary philosophy, he suggests that the framework of categories or presuppositions on which thought depends might be acquired along with a language. The tradition of Scottish philosophy as well as the recent findings of social anthropology provide us with

the insight that even man's capacity to think is not a natural endowment of the individual but a cultural heritage, something transmitted not biologically but through example and teaching—mainly through, and implicit

[66] Ibid., p. xx.
[67] *Studies in Philosophy, Politics and Economics*, p. 61.
[68] Ibid., p. 61.

in, the teaching of language. The extent to which the language which we learn in early childhood determines our whole manner of thinking and our view and interpretation of the world is probably much greater than we are yet aware of. It is not merely that the knowledge of earlier generations is communicated to us through the medium of language; the structure of the language itself implies certain views about the nature of the world; and by learning a particular language we acquire a certain picture of the world, a framework of our thinking within which we henceforth move without being aware of it. As we learn as children to use our language according to rules which we do not explicitly know, so we learn with language not only to act according to the rules of language, but according to many other rules of interpreting the world and of acting appropriately, rules which will guide us though we have never explicitly formulated them. This phenomenon of implicit learning is clearly one of the most important parts of cultural transmission, but one which we as yet only imperfectly understand.[69]

This passage sheds light on Hayek's statement in *The Constitution of Liberty* to the effect that human reason has grown and can successfully operate only with and within a framework of institutions and morals, language and law, that has evolved by a process of cumulative growth.[70] This "evolutionary interpretation of all phenomena of culture and mind" leads to reverence for the tradition of civilization on which reason depends, but which reason cannot design or justify.[71] It appeals to men to see that if we are to use our reason intelligently, "we must preserve that indispensable matrix of the uncontrolled and nonrational which is the only environment wherein reason can grow and operate effectively."[72]

IN DEFENSE OF REASON

The view of knowledge that Hayek calls "constructive rationalism" has its roots in the understanding of theoretical science that was formulated in the seventeenth century by such founders of modern philosophy as Bacon, Hobbes, and Descartes. These philosophers specifically rejected the ancient notion of science as contemplative knowledge of eternal first causes or forms of being. They demanded

[69] Ibid., pp. 86–87.
[70] See *The Constitution of Liberty*, p. 57.
[71] *Studies in Philosophy, Politics and Economics*, p. 161.
[72] *The Constitution of Liberty*, p. 69.

a theoretical science that could be put to use for the relief of man's estate. Science could become useful by giving an account of nature at work, that is, a mechanics or dynamics of nature. It would seek the principles or causes not of permanent and unchangeable things, which the ancients had regarded as the highest and noblest objects of theoretical understanding, but of the common things, things that come into being or can be generated, things that men use. If we know how things come to be or the causes that produce them, we can, when the proper conditions come within our power, make things come to be or produce such effects as we desire. This knowledge of causes is useful knowledge. It enables man to conquer nature and subject it to his control. The difference between ancient and modern views of theoretical science has been stated concisely by Hans Jonas: "To put it in the form of a slogan, the modern knowledge of nature, very unlike the classical one, is a 'know-how' and not a 'know-what,' and on this basis it makes good Bacon's contention that knowledge is power."[73] As Jonas points out, the modern notion of science is technological by its very nature. It presupposes that knowledge is intended for practical use.[74] It leads perhaps more necessarily than Hayek recognizes to what he calls "the engineering type of mind."[75]

The search for a clear and fundamental alternative to "constructive rationalism" would seem to lead in one of two directions. First, we might adopt the critique of reason that emerges in modern thought itself and culminates in the extreme historicism of the past century. I have concluded that this is the path which Hayek eventually follows. His reformulation of classical liberalism "is based on an evolutionary interpretation of all phenomena of culture and mind and on an insight into the limits of the powers of the human reason." It is consequently "reverent of tradition and recognizes that all knowledge and all civilization rest on tradition."[76] The fact is, however, that "tradition" is not a single, unified phenomenon. What we call "Western civilization" is but one of many traditions of mankind; and in-

---

[73] Hans Jonas, *The Phenomenon of Life: Toward a Philosophical Biology* (New York: Dell Publishing Co., 1966), p. 204. This quotation appears in an essay entitled "The Practical Uses of Theory," from which I have drawn in discussing the difference between ancient and modern views of theoretical science.

[74] *The Phenomenon of Life*, p. 198.

[75] *The Counter-Revolution of Science*, p. 16.

[76] *Studies in Philosophy, Politics and Economics*, p. 161.

ternal to it are many divergent and conflicting strands. Hayek himself acknowledges that the tradition of constructivist rationalism is as old and as strong within Western civilization as the tradition of critical rationalism. What are we to do in the face of this conflict among and within traditions? Hayek leaves us only the option of submitting humbly to the tradition which makes the most forceful claim upon us or the option of choosing boldly but blindly among competing traditions. He eliminates the possibility that we can make a rational choice among traditions on the basis of what is true or good by nature. Reason cannot judge among traditions, because it can function only within such a matrix as tradition itself supplies; and this matrix is nonrational and devoid of meaning. Moreover, there are no permanent values by reference to which reason could make this judgment. All human values are the result of a long process of evolution, and they continue to change in the course of this process. Thus we are probably entitled to conclude that

our present values exist only as the elements of a particular cultural tradition and are significant only for some more or less long phase of evolution —whether this phase includes some of our prehuman ancestors or is confined to certain periods of human civilization. We have no more ground to ascribe to them eternal existence than to the human race itself.[77]

But if this is the case, what rational defense is there for those values or virtues on which the working of an individualist society depends, now that the collectivist tradition has virtually undermined them?[78] How are we to justify free institutions, if not on the ground that reason shows them to contribute most to man's well-being and happiness?

The second path that we might follow in searching for an alternative to the modern tradition of "constructivist rationalism" leads back to a premodern understanding of theoretical and practical science. In the view of Plato and Aristotle, theoretical science is neither

[77] Ibid., p. 38.
[78] See *The Road to Serfdom*, pp. 212–15; see also the chapter entitled "The Abandoned Road," pp. 10–23. If the individualist tradition has been supplanted by the collectivist tradition, as Hayek seems to concede, then the former cannot be justified merely by an appeal to tradition. It is necessary to argue, by reference to what is good for man and society, that the individualist tradition is better than collectivism.

inherently technological nor at the service of man's desire for power or control over common things. It aims instead at contemplative knowledge of the permanent forms of being. This rational activity ennobles the knower and reorients his life, but it neither equips him nor inclines him to bring about a radical transformation of the world of everyday life. One need not set strict limits to reason, as thus understood, or deny its capacity to know the nature of things in order to protect the sphere of practice, for this kind of theoretical reason is not likely to endanger the practical sphere. Genuine freedom, by this account, lies not in man's liberty to act for any purpose whatever, but in his ability through reason to escape the bonds of opinion, whether enforced by political authority or by the more subtle authority of tradition, and to see the order of nature as it is. By contrast to the modern notion of theory, this premodern notion leaves room for a due appreciation of the practical reason or prudence of nontheoretical men, that is, the capacity to figure out the best course of action in particular cases where things are contingent and uncertain. Hayek points to the need to restore the premodern notion of prudence when he emphasizes that there is no substitute for experience in teaching us how to act in the concrete affairs of life. He stops short of such a restoration in two fundamental ways: he elevates the prudence by which individuals manage their private affairs over political prudence, which plans for the common good; and he conceives of prudence as supplying knowledge of the best means not to the right ends of action, but to whatever ends the individual might choose.[79]

[79] I have treated these matters at length in an essay entitled "Prudence and the Rule of Law," which will be published in 1979 in *The American Journal of Jurisprudence*.

12.

Reason, Morality, and the Free Society

TIBOR R. MACHAN

DOES reason recommend freedom? Is the idea of a rational moral standard compatible with the free political order? There are both critics and advocates of the free society who answer these questions in the negative. Among those dismayed with the kind of support traditionally given to liberal political theory and institutions we find not only theorists of Marxist and other socialist positions, but also conservatives such as Thomas Molnar, Walter Berns, Marc F. Plattner, and Irving Kristol, who are concerned primarily with the spiritual and communitarian values in society. Frequent disavowal of moral values by classical liberals and utilitarian economists who defend the free society gives substance to the concern of these thinkers. Indeed, freedom is often caricatured as chaos by those who would have some people, "representing the state," establish order in a community. But more important is the argument of those who concede the point and then reject reason in favor of custom, habit, instinct, spontaneity, and liberty.

F. A. Hayek is among the latter. In this essay I will first outline Hayek's position, and then I will evaluate its worth as a theory. I desire to show that in terms of standards applicable either to any field of science or to the social sciences specifically, Hayek's thesis is defective.

Concerning the issue of when a theory is successful, I merely adopt the view that if such a theory consistently accounts for the

I wish to thank my wife, Marty Zupan, and my friend, Doug Den Uyl, for the valuable help I received from them as I developed the arguments of this paper. Of course, they are not responsible for the use I made of this help.

facts observed within the domain of inquiry at hand—including the commonsense facts of ordinary human experience, which philosophy aims to integrate into a comprehensive, coherent system—it is successful. When theories stand in competition with each other, this standard will be applicable for purposes of deciding how to rank them.[1]

Because I too have concluded that freedom is better than slavery, that the free society, with its emphasis on political and economic liberty, is superior to others, my paper includes an outline of a defense of conclusions I share with Hayek. I am all the more anxious to supply this alternative, given the eagerness with which some enemies of the free society have focused on Hayek's value-free case for liberty. Although several individuals throughout history have argued for liberty on moral grounds, the statists usually manage to ignore their case and focus instead on such defenses of liberty as Hayek's, dismissing it in the end for its lack of concern with virtue, justice, and morality in general.

From the ensuing discussion, critics of the free society may see just how compatible freedom is not only with reason but with virtue, justice, and morality as well.

SPONTANEOUS ORDER AND HUMAN REASON

The best sketch of Hayek's position is provided by the author himself in a recent work:

The preservation of a society of free men depends on three fundamental insights which have never been adequately expounded. . . . The first of these is that a self-generating or spontaneous order and organization are distinct, and that their distinctiveness is related to the two different kinds of rules or laws which prevail in them. The second is that what today is generally regarded as "social" or distributive justice has meaning only within the second of these kinds of order, the organization; but that it is meaningless in, and wholly incompatible with, that spontaneous order which Adam Smith called "the Great Society," and Sir Karl Popper called "the Open Society." The third is that the predominant model of liberal

---

[1] See my *The Pseudo-Science of B. F. Skinner* (New Rochelle, N.Y.: Arlington House, 1974), ch. 3.

democratic institutions, in which the same representative body lays down the rules of just conduct and directs government, necessarily leads to a gradual transformation of the spontaneous order of a free society into a totalitarian system conducted in the service of some coalition of organized interests.[2]

To begin an appreciation for Hayek's ideas it is evident that we must understand some of the central concepts in his analysis. Of these the concept of a spontaneous order is probably most crucial.

Hayek's conception of the spontaneous order seems at first simple enough to understand.[3] In certain circumstances individual entities of a given kind behave with no deliberate plan to give their behavior a definite purpose; nevertheless, the result is an orderly pattern. A number of illustrations of such circumstances are provided by Hayek. He notes:

There are in the physical world many instances of complex orders which we could bring about only by availing ourselves of the known forces which tend to lead to their formation, and never by deliberately placing each element in the appropriate position. . . . [Thus] iron filings on a sheet of paper are made to arrange themselves along some of the lines of force of a magnet placed below . . . [and] we can predict the general shape of the chains that will be formed by the filings hooking themselves together; but we cannot predict along which ones of the family of an infinite number of such curves that define the magnetic field these chains will place themselves.[4]

A spontaneous order has no designer but comes about through the operation of general rules or laws. These govern the behavior of the individual elements but do not determine the specific spatiotemporal

[2] F. A. Hayek, *Law, Legislation and Liberty* (Chicago: University of Chicago Press, 1973), vol. 1, p. 2.

[3] Hayek makes innumerable references to what he calls the spontaneous order and its opposite, deliberate organization. See especially *Studies in Philosophy, Politics and Economics* (New York: Simon & Shuster, 1967); and *The Confusion of Language in Political Thought* (London: Institute of Economic Affairs, 1968). Crespigny summarizes Hayek's idea of the former: "This type of order does not have a purpose since it has not been deliberately created, and to agree on its desirability it is unnecessary for us to agree on the concrete results it will produce" ("F. A. Hayek: Freedom for Progress," in A. de Crespigny and K. Minogue, eds., *Contemporary Political Philosophers* [New York: Dodd, Mead, 1975], p. 53).

[4] Ibid., pp. 39–40.

or otherwise relevant patterns of behavior of such individual elements.

For Hayek the same is true of social life: "It would be no exaggeration to say that social theory begins with—and has an object only because of—the discovery that there exist orderly structures which are the product of the action of many men but are not the result of human design."[5] Hayek's example from social life is, as we might expect, the commercial market. He points to Adam Smith's "invisible hand," a description "in the language of his time . . . [of] how man is led 'to promote an end which was no part of his intentions.' "[6] A crucial source of support for Hayek's updated version of the invisible-hand conception of the natural or proper mode of social existence is Darwinian evolutionary theory. Although Hayek makes it clear that he rejects the cruder versions of social Darwinism, he explains that "the basic conception of evolution is still the same in both fields [biology and social theory]."[7]

Often what we have to go on in understanding Hayek's characterization of human affairs is his assertion that his own ideas have been more or less well outlined by such thinkers as Bernard Mandeville and David Hume. He also acknowledges his debt to the epistemology of Immanuel Kant. His reliance on the former makes it crucial for Hayek to uphold a view of human behavior that accords with a variant of the evolutionist theory, so that he is anxious to defend the idea that "many of the institutions of society which are indispensable conditions for the successful pursuit of our conscious aims are in fact the result of customs, habits or practices which neither have been invented nor are observed with any such purpose in view."[8] In short, such institutions and practices evolve.

In the epistemological realm, Hayek's conception of how we are aware of reality manifests his basically Kantian framework (something he shares with his teacher Ludwig von Mises). Even at the basic level of perceptual awareness Hayek concludes that beings possess "the capacity to act according to rules which we may be able

[5] Ibid., p. 37.
[6] Ibid.
[7] Ibid., p. 23.
[8] Ibid., p. 11.

to discover but which we need not be able to state in order to obey them."[9] Indeed Hayek seems to construe the action of organizing sensory and perceptual data into a coherent structure (Gestalt) as quite automatic.[10]

The general idea is that our human way of viewing the world provides us with virtually instinctive guidelines which "are better seen as determining what an individual will not do rather than what he will do."[11] These rules are comparable to the Kantian categories and intuitions of the understanding, which are structurally innate for any human mind and are supposed to operate whether we are conscious of them or not. Hayek himself indicates his Kantian view when he tells us, "Abstraction is not something which the mind produces by processes of logic from its perception of reality, but is rather a property of the categories with which it operates—not a product of the mind but rather what constitutes the mind."[12]

To appreciate the significance of Hayek's epistemological position one would have to consider in detail the point of view with which it is contrasted, the background against which he develops his own position. Hayek wants to discredit what he identifies as a Cartesian view of rationalism, namely constructivism. Within the latter,

Reason was defined as logical deduction from explicit premises, rational action . . . came to mean only such action as was determined entirely by known and demonstrable truths. . . . Institutions and practices which have not been designed in this manner can be beneficial only by accident.[13]

According to this view, "Man's reason alone should enable him to construct society anew,"[14] but Hayek presents a position in which habit, custom, and practice have a far more prominent place than that of successful action based on logical deduction from explicit premises. Although Hayek notes the existence of a conception of rea-

[9] F. A. Hayek, *Studies in Philosophy, Politics and Economics*, p. 44.
[10] Ibid., p. 45; F. A. Hayek, *The Sensory Order* (Chicago: University of Chicago Press, 1952), pp. 52–54.
[11] *Studies in Philosophy, Politics and Economics*, p. 57.
[12] *The Confusion of Language in Political Thought*, p. 30.
[13] Ibid., p. 10.
[14] Ibid.

son different from the Cartesian one, he presents his analysis in terms of the above alternatives.[15]

In my criticism of Hayek I wish first to focus on the grounds he invokes for his own approach to social theory. He tells us:

If what is called the *Sprachgefühl* (the feeling for language, for correct versus incorrect language use) consists in our capacity to follow yet unformulated rules, there is no reason why, for example, the sense of justice (the *Rechtsgefühl*) should not also consist in such a capacity to follow rules which we do not know in the sense that we can state them.[16]

Yet consider also his point that the "scientistic" attitude "is decidedly unscientific in the true sense of the word, since it involves a mechanical and uncritical application of habits of thought to fields different from those in which they have been formed."[17]

If Hayek is right in his indictment of positivist scientism (except that one can hardly call all positivists uncritical), he nevertheless falls prey to a fault similar to theirs. For he clearly conflates the biological and social realms by his "application of habits of thought to" these two fields when he makes use of Darwinian evolutionary theory for the purpose of understanding the phenomena studied in each. Hayek protests that the Darwinian ideas had their origin in social theorizing. But that is irrelevant; he invokes the Darwinian approach as support for his conclusions about social affairs.

Even when Hayek invokes the ideas of students of human affairs such as Sapir, Lees, Polanyi,[18] he does not escape some decisive philosophical difficulties. The second main problem Hayek faces may be referred to as self-referential inconsistency. The standard in terms of which we can detect whether a theorist faces this problem is clearly stated by D. Bannister: a theorist "cannot present a picture of man

---

[15] *Studies in Philosophy, Politics and Economics*, p. 94; *The Confusion of Language in Political Thought*, p. 21.

[16] *Studies in Philosophy, Politics and Economics*, p. 45.

[17] F. A. Hayek, *The Counter-Revolution of Science* (Glencoe, Ill.: Free Press, 1955), p. 15.

[18] Ibid., pp. 43–65.

which patently contradicts his behavior in presenting that picture."[19]

Is Hayek self-referentially inconsistent? It seems to me that his conception of human action suggests such a problem. At the fundamental level Hayek appears to view human action as governed by general laws and rules that people do not invoke by choice. These laws and rules are just adopted or, later, just followed. As Hayek puts the point: " 'Learning from experience,' among men no less than among animals, is a process not primarily of reasoning but of the observance, spreading, transmission and development of practices which have prevailed because they were successful—often not because they conferred any recognizable benefit on the acting individual but because they increased the chances of survival of the group to which he belonged."[20] Aside from its dubious reference to what explains learning in human life, Hayek seems—at least on the surface—to deny any genuine freedom of choice for human beings. He does not explicitly treat the issue and he makes use of the concept "choice" when he refers to deliberate planning or selection from among alternatives. Still, a close look shows that nowhere in his analysis is there room for free will, man's capacity to initiate action. On the contrary, for Hayek, human behavior is mostly outside human control.

The crucial issue then is how Hayek conceives of human action in its most essential respects. The bulk of human affairs is viewed by him as governed by laws and rules that are not and cannot be of our choosing. People rarely if ever turn out to be agents of their actions in Hayek's framework. In accordance with the Darwinian model, human actions spring from a sort of evolutionary force that produces habits, customs, and practices which prevail (because they support group survival) over others as the driving factors in the lives of the members of any species of animals, including human beings. Even what Hayek calls conscious, deliberate choices must then be explained by reference to this Darwinian hypothesis; those which prevail must be those with survival value. Moreover the sort of choice involved in this conscious deliberative process seems to be a kind of selection, not an initiation. In other words, at the point where Hayek

[19] D. Bannister, in Borger and Cioffi, eds., *Explanation in the Behavioral Sciences* (New York: Cambridge University Press, 1970), p. 417.
[20] *Law, Legislation and Liberty*, p. 18.

admits the existence of human choice, the choice amounts to an act of selection from among alternatives one is aware of, along the lines of the "action" taken by computers, not an act of initiation or human causation that proponents of free will have in mind.

Hayek's use of Darwinian theory may itself be questionable in view of the many recent discoveries concerning the Darwinian method as opposed to Darwin's theories. I take it, however, that Hayek has in mind something that is not very complicated, namely, that nature somehow favors that which overcomes more effectively and lastingly the obstacles it faces. This same idea may be invoked for the purpose of understanding the relationship between sound and unsound, acceptable and unacceptable ideas. But more pertinently, the idea could serve to explain why individuals retain some beliefs and do not retain others, even which sensory data they have found worth employing and which they have rejected. In any of these instances we have a deterministic account of human actions, whether on the cultural or the individual level.

What we have here, if I am right, is a denial of man's capacity to initiate action, to exercise genuine choice, spontaneously to enter upon some behavior; and if so, then Hayek's own activities as a theoretician must be explained by reference to the same scheme. But the self-determinist free-will thesis seems to be indispensible for purposes of rendering intelligible the fact of human knowledge and rationality (including the distinguishability, on sound grounds, of truth and falsehood). According to this view, rational choice of selection from among competing theories is impossible if human beings are incapable of initiating action, and what Hayek proposes would thus appear to be internally inconsistent. I do not impose my own doctrine of free will on Hayek—his own theoretical activity theoretically presupposes that doctrine in that he surely regards what he proposes as true and demonstrable. Yet his own theory of human action appears to contradict this indispensable, even if only implicit, presupposition. Therefore, it is not acceptable.

Third, we should note that Hayek seems to draw a false dichotomy between spontaneous rule-obeying behavior and self-consciously planned conduct. Since the spontaneity which gives rise to a corresponding order is at least quasiautomatic, such behavior is not said to be guided by reasoning. Even though Hayek admits that conceptions of human rationality vary and do not at all rely on the Cartesian view, he does not leave room for reasoning in other than the domain of self-consciousness. In other words, only when someone knows that he is engaging in reasoning and is aware of his own rational processes, is he believed by Hayek to be rational. This is what his reference to deliberate, self-aware conscious process as the rational activity of the human mind is intended to emphasize. When we are simply thinking out our problems, ordering our experiences, doing our daily chores, or generally carrying on our living, we are not, by Hayek's account, either rational or nonrational. This is because in these matters we *follow* rules.

It seems to me that it is an inadequate examination to narrow reasoning or rational thinking down to self-conscious reasoning alone. Let me simply point to the way the criminal and the common laws conceive of the reasonable man, or how we conceive of ourselves when we distinguish between acting rationally and acting irrationally. There is no commitment in either of these instances to a view such as Hayek's. Of course when we examine whether we have carried on rationally, then we engage in a form of reasoning Hayek conceives of as rational, deliberative thought. When we have no special reason to think that we have gone astray with our thinking and acting, we might never reflect upon whether we have carried on rationally or not. Yet it is quite meaningful to characterize thinking and acting that are not self-conscious as either rational or not. Haphazard, hasty, sloppy, careless, jumbled, or erratic thinking and action could all be varieties of irrationality without it being the case that careful, attentive, prudent, and orderly thought and action must be self-conscious —monitored, as it were, by us as we perform it.

In his support Hayek draws on theories of language learning[21] that have noted the great facility we have for implementing rules of grammar with no self-conscious effort at rehearsing the rules. I am no expert in this field, so I cannot assess the merits of the many studies, nor pass judgment on the relative success of the many competing theories. Yet it seems that one could abandon a Darwinian explanatory scheme in these areas and plausibly accommodate the theories and facts Hayek invoked. One could turn to the competing

---

[21] *Studies in Philosophy, Politics and Economics,* pp. 43–65.

idea that human beings, from the time of infancy, can initiate the conceptual activity they are capable of, and without knowing that this is what they are doing, that is, without being able to state the nature of the capacities they are using, often do what is necessary for purposes of communication. Indeed, there are now students of psychophysics and neurophysiology who maintain that the human cerebral constitution renders plausible the suggestion that conceptual processes of consciousness are essentially self-generated.

Finally, Hayek's conception of human action, if I understand it, does not leave room for morality and normative political theory. If human action essentially follows rules which have emerged by (what I want to call) the impersonal process of natural selection, then the idea that some rules are to be obeyed or implemented, some to be avoided, or that some political systems are to be eschewed, others to be implemented—all these general ideas about what we should or should not do simply cannot make sense. If man cannot initiate these crucial forms of action, namely, those that are uniquely human, and if he is essentially guided by rules and laws outside his choice, then to call on him to act in one way as opposed to another is futile. He has no say in these matters. As the philosophical motto has it, "Ought implies can." The idea that we should eschew socialism in favor of a free market assumes that we have that capacity, that we *can* do things on our own, can choose to accept or reject customs, habits, and practices, however used to them many of us have become.

Although Hayek does not often employ normative concepts, he does freely call political liberty an ideal, a goal we should pursue. But his idea of human action does not appear to allow for such normative notions. On the one hand it is exclusive of self-determined action and on the other hand it is indeterministic. The indeterminism is basically epistemological, that is, based on the idea that complex phenomena cannot be fully known, rendering them incapable of prediction and effective centralized control. On the objective or ontological level, however, an underlying determinism emerges in Hayek's discussion of human perception and learning.

If ought does imply can, if ethical edicts make sense only if one has a genuine domain of choice where one either will or will not abide by such edicts, then Hayek's avoidance of normative issues at the ethical level is quite understandable. I take it for one of my many unproven but plausible premises that a moral principle or standard could not be sound if it were impossible for human beings to choose it as a guide to concrete conduct. In short, it is my view here that morality and some variation of the freedom-of-the-will thesis are logically linked—if the former is a real feature of human life, the latter must also be. Since Hayek's endorsement of any ideal is restricted to the domain of political theory, and since the ideal of liberty seems for him to grow out of his Darwinian belief that spontaneous order is the proper order for the biological entities we are, Hayek may be said to insist on the nonnormative treatment of political affairs on principle, by virtue of the implications of his own analysis. But if this is right, Hayek cannot do what he must want to do in the light of his vigorous advocacy of the free society—namely, recommend the free society, tell us that we ought to accept, and support it.

I have so far presented some of the difficulties I detect in Hayek's overall position. I will now turn to some of the historical facts that shed light on why Hayek takes the approach he does and ends with the views he advances. After that we shall consider an alternative analysis in support of the free society.

HAYEK'S KANTIANISM

Both F. A. Hayek and his teacher Ludwig von Mises admit their debt to Kantian epistemology. Some of the previous points already testify to this debt. It is possible also that Hayek's avoidance of the idea of natural law can be traced to the Kantian antimetaphysical stance. (However, Hayek does remark that the earlier Greek, as opposed to later Cartesian, idea of natural law is close to his own idea of habit, custom, or practice. He even refers to Locke as an exponent of the earlier idea of natural law. Nevertheless, he eschews the concept in his positive theory.) No doubt his general skepticism about knowledge of particular entities owes much to the Kantian rejection of the possibility of knowing things-in-themselves.

In modern philosophy "natural" has generally been used to refer to that which has sensory properties, that which can be perceived by sensory observation alone. In the bulk of philosophical discussions of naturalism—for example, when G. E. Moore and others speak of the "naturalistic" fallacy—it is accepted that a naturalist in ethics (or moral philosophy) believes that what is good or right must be something sensible and measurable, such as pleasure, economic welfare, and so forth. Thus natural does not have the meaning of "pertaining to its nature or essence" but "pertaining to that which is sensible, observable about it." Post-Cartesian and especially post-Kantian philosophy had rejected naturalism *qua* essentials but retained naturalism *qua* material components, phenomena, sensible properties.

I would like briefly to point out that the rejection of metaphysics as first philosophy can be traced most fruitfully and prominently to Descartes. In Hobbes, too, we find a nominalist epistemology which renders knowledge of nature or reality impossible. It might best be expressed by saying that the road to nature and arguments which rested claims on nature concerned nature *qua* material components, phenomena, sensible properties. What is decisive is that the idea that essential attributes can be identified by us, known by human beings, was rejected (mainly because the model of what counts as identifying or knowing something, deductive certainty, was very strict). Although this turn from the natural *qua* essential, to the natural *qua* sensible began with Machiavelli (perhaps because in his era the essential nature of things had been considered supernatural!), its epistemology is best expressed by David Hume and the twentieth-century positivists. More telling is Descartes' turn inward, toward consciousness as the primary datum of knowledge. The first truth, "cogito, ergo sum," is a truth of reason, a self-evident truth which requires no reference to a reality independent of the human mind. With this significant influence philosophy thereafter tended to focus on epistemology as its primary concern. It gained priority as the *fundamental* area of philosophical inquiry, displacing metaphysics, in the main, to our day. Not "What is there?" but "What is knowledge?" became the first question of philosophy.

Now it seems very likely that the empiricist ideas of Locke, Berkeley, and Hume, granting much diversity and originality, accommodated entirely this crucial turn made by Descartes. That many seventeenth- and eighteenth-century scientists continued to attest to a belief in an underlying substructure of reality is irrelevant. The grounds for such profession could be many. What is crucial is that the realm of reality capable of rational investigation was thought to be limited to the empirically confirmable or, in Kant, to the phenomenal. Empiricism first asks "How could we know?" Its answer is different from the rationalists', but the issue of what domain has priority is shared by these two major theories of knowledge. (Even Hegel, very often thought to be a powerful but nonetheless basically obscure diversion—especially by Anglo-American philosophers—took Mind or Spirit or Reason as prior to matter or content or the real. That is why Marx has to turn Hegel upside down in order to make use of the dialectic in a materialist scheme.) It is clear that Kant accepted the Cartesian order of priorities. We must again ask first how knowledge is possible, then see what we know.[22] The result in Kant—here unavoidably given short shrift—was that reality is derived from the structure of human understanding, with the admission in the end that knowledge of nature or reality (in the traditional sense) is impossible. The noumenon is fully indeterminate and unidentifiable.

I think it would be more precise to say that Kant's critique of (pure) reason amounted to what is often called philosophical skepticism: the view was derived that we cannot know whether knowledge of reality exists! Perhaps we know things-in-themselves, but we could never find out that we do (or do not). That is why Kant rejects all proofs for or against God's existence and counsels faith in the matter (i.e., in metaphysics).

In fairness, I should note that I believe Kant's conclusion also had a lot to do with the model of knowledge as formal, deductive certainty. For one to know reality as these philosophers wanted it (and then conclude that knowledge is impossible in such matters) one would have to be what one knows. To know the thing-in-itself (i.e., every entity as it is in itself), one would have to become the thing. Yet in a certain respect the demand is sound—metaphysical knowledge must have the degree of firmness these philosophers wanted. But here one might suggest that we do know the thing in itself (i.e., we know nature in itself, as it is essentially) by knowing our own being, by knowing ourselves as we are in ourselves.

So we come to Hayek. He has fought positivism with all his intellectual stamina for decades, yet he and the positivists owe a common philosophical debt to Kant. Both reject metaphysics as impos-

---

[22] Frederick L. Will, *Induction and Justification* (Ithaca, N.Y.: Cornell University Press, 1974).

sible—or, in the case of the positivists, as nonsense (since statements in the field are empirically unverifiable and have no predictive capacity). Both have the view that scientific methodology must be identical in all areas of science. Positivists seemed to have thought it enough to regard human affairs as complex manifestations of the components of all existent things, namely, sensory data. In Hayek's Kantian view, human affairs are still the complex phenomena of the simple sensory data of any form of existence, only now they must be understood in terms of the fixed categories of human understanding, something that logical positivists, at least, have abandoned as non-empirical. (For the logical positivists the categories are basically arbitrary constructs and are unsupported by either nature or the structure of the mind.)

The intellectual and philosophic history involved in the outline I have presented is extremely complex, yet without some indication of it we cannot appreciate Hayek's position. Any cursory glance at Hayek's works will indicate how prominent a place such historical (evolutionary?) considerations have in his analyses. So despite the necessary brevity of my outline, I have arrived at a point where we can at least attempt the presentation of an alternative to Hayek's position. I have shown that Hayek's idea of spontaneity is derived from his conclusion that our knowledge of the factors operative in human affairs is and must be limited. The nature of human understanding, including the structurally imposed limitations on knowledge of particular things, implies the view that human actions are not purposive (in the sense of freely chosen) or determinate (as the reductionists among positivists would in principle have it). If the problems I have outlined render this view crucially defective for purposes of understanding human affairs, we need a better alternative. I think Hayek's problems begin with his basically antimetaphysical approach to social theory, especially the theory of human action. With this in mind, I shall now begin an outline of the position which to me seems sound.

ALTERNATIVE CASE

That a certain position is defective does not imply that it has no valuable insights to offer or that there are any more satisfactory explanations available. What Hayek offers could indeed be the best among the numerous widely discussed approaches to political and economic affairs. My own criticism has thus far been internal, and it is not enough to answer the questions to which Hayek and others address themselves. So let me note that I regard Hayek's approach as valuable, better than most, even better than that offered by another widely respected school of free-market, libertarian-oriented thinkers, the positivists of what has come to be called the Chicago school. It is inappropriate here to discuss my reasons for this comparative evaluation but it may help to indicate some points that can legitimately occur to people considering the thesis of this paper.

In offering the outline of an alternative case for an essentially free social order I will mention where and how it differs from Hayek's position. First of all, my view takes metaphysics seriously and accords it a place of priority in an analytical scheme or a philosophical theory. For any claim of judgment whatever—about mind or society or knowledge—presupposes existence, and that fact pushes the metaphysical problem into the foreground. Descartes' thinking ego could not have been thinking had there been nothing to think about—the activity of thought not only requires some agent but also some object. Indeed, existence is an underlying fact in *any* inquiry and the attempt to deny it can lead only to nonsense. A proof of the nature of knowledge, for instance, that does not acknowledge existence cannot succeed as a proof—it is a nonstarter. The premises for a proof could not be obtained if reality itself is in doubt.

I cannot go further than to offer the above clues to the argument, but from that much it is possible to glimpse the direction I have in mind. The character of existence, or what it is essentially, is now a meaningful problem, and I am advocating an Aristotelian mode of approach to it.[23] For our purposes it is crucial that the Aristotelian scheme be a multispectival monism—a conception of reality as pluralistic in its manifestations but conforming to certain essential laws. Moreover, the idea of causation entailed by this metaphysics is naturalistic and necessitarian. Here a crucial difference between this and Hayek's scheme appears. No longer is cause to be construed either as a Humean regularity or as a Kantian category of human

---

[23] Tibor Machan, *Human Rights and Human Liberties* (Chicago: Nelson Hall, 1975).

understanding. Causes are real, part of nature, however difficult it may be for us to identify them and prove their existence in any given instance. Moreover, various kinds of causation may exist in nature, depending on what sort of things are involved in causal relationships. Unlike the Humean and Kantian conceptions of scientific causation, where the character of causes must be a function of the character of human knowledge, the present scheme proposes that the natures of the entities involved in causal encounters determine the identity of the causation.[24]

That such pluralism in causality is plausible may be appreciated by reflecting on the suggestion that thoughts, chairs, chemical compositions, and electrons are very different types of entities. They may thus interact with others in a variety of ways. When it is said that ideas produce consequences, is it warranted to expect the mode of production to be the same as when chairs produce backaches or pollutants produce eye irritation? Unless a reductionism is *built into* the methodology of studying these varied interactions—for example, by way of empiricism—the question of what *kind* of causation ensues can be left open to investigation.

We can now indicate how spontaneity emerges within the present schema. I am proposing that within the metaphysical framework hinted at above it is no longer necessarily unscientific to hypothesize the existence of genuine free will. Instead of the doctrine of spontaneity developed with the assistance of Darwinian evolutionary theory and other ideas about the complexity of human affairs, we have here the serious possibility that human beings can be first causes of some of what they do.

I am not claiming here that I have shown that people are first causes, only that there is no philosophical and scientific justification for thinking this impossible. We can go on to ask whether people are free—whether individual human beings have the capacity to make original choices, to take the initiative in producing some events in nature.

The usual attitude today is that the only way we could imagine this is by conceiving of nature as irrational; existentialists tend to move in that direction when they defend human freedom of choice.

[24] Milton Fisk, *Nature and Necessity* (Bloomington: Indiana University Press, 1973).

Theists do, of course, often defend free will, but if I relied on their approach I should be unable to offer an alternative to Hayek's position, one that is addressed to problems in a naturalistic, scientific manner (broadly conceived), in contrast to a supernaturalistic or mystical approach.

When free will is suggested to social scientists, the response is usually a dogmatic declaration that it is scientifically impossible. This, however, is not a scientific conclusion but a philosophical dogma.[25] It is worth noting why the rejection of free will is taken to be important within social science circles. Most of contemporary social science is either Humean or Kantian—broadly the division between positivists and Weberians. No doubt there are now other developments. But within these, it is required that each instance of a cause should have (in the last analysis) events or occurrences as its constituents. Any explanation of something in nature, including society, must end by citing some event as the cause. (The slight variation introduced by recent theorists indebted to positivism is the term *variable*. But a variable or a factor is still, in the last analysis, an event, some motion in time and space.) Human beings, however, are individual entities, not events (even if events take place within such entities). As human beings it would then be impossible to be a cause of anything. Thus to remain scientific as conceived in this philosophical framework, free will must be denied a priori.

Within the alternative scheme I am proposing it is an open question whether people are free or not, for on ontological or metaphysical grounds it is possible that they are. I shall not defend free will at length.[26] The basic argument for it is that the prospect of knowing what is true (including what is true about the free-will issue) and of distinguishing it from falsehood requires the freedom of the person making the evaluation. Rationality is itself inconceivable without freedom of the will. Furthermore, most of us are able to identify whether specific actions are free, forced, accidental, or unexplained for the time being. It may help here to reflect on the tortuous evi-

25 Machan, *The Pseudo-Science of B. F. Skinner*, pp. 26–28; 62–65.

26 Nathaniel Branden, *The Psychology of Self-Esteem* (Los Angeles: Nash, 1969); Machan, *The Pseudo-Science of B. F. Skinner*; Edward Madden and Rom Harre, "In Defense of Natural Agents," *Philosophical Quarterly* (April 1973): 117–32.

dential procedures required in criminal trials required to demonstrate that a defendant is not responsible for his actions. The defendant bears the burden of proof of lack of capacity, which indicates that in some institutions the causal efficacy of human beings is accepted as the norm, while incapacity is taken to be special. Hayek, incidentally, regards human causal efficacy as part of a deterministic view of human affairs which, however, lacks the needed scientific support. He does admit that there may be philosophical objections to determinism other than those he advances.

To deny the identification of free actions on a priori grounds would betray an unjustified loyalty to empiricism and the intersubjectivist doctrine of objective knowledge. This is not to say that to identify whether some behavior is self-determined or caused by some other agency is a simple matter. Sometimes it may be, although to prove that it is so could be difficult in any case. But that problem arises in any instance of identification. It needs to be noted that I have not made it my task here to demonstrate the existence of free actions on anyone's part, although I would also argue that a correct analysis of human action must regard the latter as free to be action at all, and if we have evidence of innumerable results of human action, then the case for freedom is overwhelming.

Now I want to suggest where a form of spontaneity enters the present scheme. In human affairs one can be free, fundamentally, in that one's mind is free to judge and guide conduct. But a judgment of the nature and the guidance of conduct would best be conceived along the following lines. The process of obtaining the grounds for the conclusion that something is so is an active not a passive one—a person might voluntarily or without external stimulus activate his capacity of being aware and form conceptual knowledge and understanding by means of that action. Or, to put it differently, one can look, see, and think things over, put two and two together. The process is active, not passive.

Human rationality, when exercised, is an activity conducted in accordance with valid reasoning, but it is not a static deductive process. So when it is argued that man is a rational animal, it is unwarranted to infer that human beings are therefore simply machines capable of performing calculations, however much that may be part of what they can do. It would be more accurate to think of human beings as capable of activating a faculty the operations of which are most fruitfully carried out in accordance with sound principles. I am talking in a philosophical vein, but in ordinary life we seem to think of people along these lines anyway. Even economists convinced that people act only to satisfy desires, or psychologists who conceive of human behavior as governed by laws of operant behavior, engage in arguments to try to persuade their colleagues, if not their wives, husbands, children, or political representatives. (Here we might recall the point made by Bannister!)

Again, if what I have said is right, then spontaneity and rationality are indeed very closely related. One could argue that since a free and rational person is one who engages in clear thinking, the imprisoned, rigid person is one who relies on what others say, on what his culture gives him, on what he has picked up—without ever paving his own way.

So we have here a conception of spontaneity and rationality that conflicts with Hayek's. Reason is on the side of freedom, indeed inextricably tied to it. And, contrary to Hayek, it is those who try to plan the individual's life who incur the burden of antirationalism: of stifling human reason, preventing the society's rational agents from actualizing their potential and creating rational solutions to problems, forming rational organizations, and developing a rational order —that is, one which is appropriate to man as a rational being.

FREEDOM AND VALUES

One problem with discussing values nowadays is that the majority of intellectuals and scientists (or those in fields aspiring to a scientific status) construe values as necessarily antinatural or supernatural. If there is a theory of value which appeals to social scientists, it is utilitarianism. But the utilitarian theory is embedded in the empiricist framework and has the resulting difficulties of locating value in that which is open to sensory observation. Pleasures, pains, economic need, and the like figure as plausible candidates for the assignment of value or disvalue within such a theory. But most people see this result as inadequate. The first objection is that while some of the obvious benefits and disadvantages that people possess or might acquire can be observed, others cannot. Empiricism does well with pain and pleasure, with profit and loss, with benefit versus cost, or with efficiency versus inefficiency—these have observable features within the various contexts in which they are discussed and treated. But from the early days of hedonism, of which utilitarianism is clearly a relative, identifying the higher profits and losses, goods and evils of human life raised epistemological problems. The finer pleasures, the profound pains—happiness and degradation—are not easy to locate by sensory observation, physical measurement, and the like.

Two stances have usually been taken in the face of these difficulties. Some have insisted that no higher or finer pleasures, no noble ideals or values, and no profound miseries or evils exist—instead we are facing mythical notions similar to "demon" or "witch" or "angel." Others have accepted a radical dualism and, while asserting that values exist, have rejected them as incapable of being rationally understood. I am not certain where Hayek stands on these alternatives— I suspect he falls between the two categories. His willingness to talk about values, his merely occasional or rare suggestion of specific instances, and his skepticism about anyone's capacity to identify any, give evidence of a disregard for values. Yet he also invokes the language of ideals and values in his writing, so it is not easy to place him.

These, however, are not the only alternatives. I have focused on them because they are prominent within the Anglo-American tradition as influenced by Hume and Kant. Humeans would, as I see it, take the alternative of explaining values away as objects of sociological inquiry, while Kantians would relegate them to the supernatural in the well-known Kantian dualism of the practical versus the rational.

When we depart from this tradition and turn to Continental philosophy after Kant, we see another alternative. This is to reconcile values with facts by way of Marxist scientific socialism. Marx wanted to incorporate values into his science, and he attempted this by way of dialectics. As in Plato, so in Marx dialectics points to perfection, to nature's fullest realization. But in Plato this remained at the epistemological level—dialectical reasoning led to knowledge of

perfect natures. With Hegel and Marx nature itself engaged in dialectical development, striving through revolutionary leaps for the
resolution of all strife and contradiction.

In Marxism values are what nature's end holds in store for us.
Communism is the fullest realization of mankind, so that at present
we must be conceived of as children moving toward maturity. The
greatest value in this culmination of the historical dialectic is equality—all human beings will fully exhibit the essential nature of man.
All Marxist-oriented criticism of present-day affairs rests on the future value of human equality. An understanding of that future yields
all of history's rationale as well.

The Marxist egalitarian scheme at least appears to provide a
satisfactory resolution of the fact-value dichotomy. Reason and good-
ness have merged, and the rational and good society is egalitarian.
Everything done to help history to achieve that goal is both rational
and good.[27] I am not holding, of course, that the Marxist scheme is
valid. What I am saying is that it fulfills a need for those interested
in solving a problem that actually faces us. It promises a solution of
the fact-value problem, and for that reason alone it gains attention.
Since it is also a comprehensive doctrine, covering all the bases with
metaphysical, epistemological, ethical, political, and aesthetic components, it has a staying power beyond that provided by positivism,
existentialism, or Hayekian systems.

One may say that nature abhors a vacuum and fools will rush
in where wise men fear to tread. There is a vacuum in value theory
in the current Anglo-American intellectual atmosphere, and Marxism
is rushing in to fill it. As with the thirsty who will drink poisoned
water rather than face sure death from thirst, so we may interpret
the clutching at the Marxist alternative as a sign of the philosophical
bankruptcy of our age. This is a large and ambitious point, but I am
confident that some of what I have said will call to mind evidence to
support it enough that we can reflect on the matter seriously.

Given the earlier considerations, I can now suggest that Marxism
is not the solution. The value-oriented approach is quite compatible
with Hayek's concern for liberty—even required for it. If we must
conceive of man as a naturally purposive being, and if his unique-

---

[27] Machan, *Human Rights and Human Liberties*, pp. 250–51.

ness consists, in part, in his having to choose to make his life conform with the proper goals of human life, then his political liberty becomes a necessary condition for his success in life as the sort of thing he is. This is naturalistic in that political liberty is somewhat like water to a fish, a need for the sort of life appropriate for the being involved. Liberty is a necessary but insufficient condition of human excellence. It is because each person should strive to succeed as the kind of being he is that each person must be free of other's interference with him. Liberty is indeed a value, man's political value, a good that each person in society requires by nature, a natural right.

Hayek has come close to saying that liberty and ethics are in opposition: "Isn't the idea that society or the political area is bound to ethics, a view of what is right for man, almost incompatible with the idea that a man ought to have freedom?"[28] This is a mistake, however. If there is a system of ethics that is naturally right for human beings, and if this system justifies political liberty for human beings in their social situations, then without the admission of that ethical system one is unable to give liberty normative support. As an instance, who could deny that in any society some people are destitute? Plans designed to remedy such situations may not be supported by the knowledge we should ideally like to have, but is this sufficient reason for giving up the plans? Even after a long history of ineffectual social planning, only with a sound normative objection to planning or social engineering can we rationally expect such programs to be abandoned. The mere limitation on human knowledge is not a sufficient ground for discontinuing the attempts to reach the goals of social engineering. In short, why should a political system admit liberty as a highest goal? Unless this can be answered with reference to an ethical system that is universalizable, the normative case for liberty is lost. And without it, there are the problems, discussed earlier, with something like Hayek's naturalistic evolutionary position.

Yet the worry of many defenders of the free society, Hayek among them, has been that reliance on an ethical system to justify liberty would necessarily undercut the latter. For if we know what is right for someone, must we not impose it upon him? From the fact, however, that human beings ought to live in such and such a manner,

---

[28] Hayek, "Economics, Politics and Freedom: An Interview with F. A. Hayek," *Reason* (February 1975): 4–12.

it simply does not follow that anyone is justified in forcing them to do so. Indeed, if the philosophical slogan "Ought implies can" is correct for ethical principles, as I think it is, then the imposition of conformity to moral edicts does not produce anything like moral conduct. Such conduct must be chosen. So the logical force of ethical skepticism as against authoritarianism vanishes, *pace* Hayek (and the Chicagoites).

Moreover, it seems that in certain contexts the skeptical defense of the free society can be an obstacle rather than a benefit to the realization of such a political situation. Leo Strauss points this out:

Generous liberals view the abandonment of natural right not only with placidity but with relief. They appear to believe that our inability to acquire any genuine knowledge of what is intrinsically good or right compels us to be tolerant of every opinion about good or right or to recognize all preferences or all "civilizations" as equally respectable. Only unlimited tolerance is in accordance with reason. But this leads to the admission of a rational or natural right of every preference that is tolerant of other preferences or, negatively expressed, of a rational or natural right to reject or condemn all intolerant or all "absolutist" positions. The latter must be condemned because they are based on a demonstrably false premise, namely, that men can know what is good. . . . But there is a tension between the respect for diversity or individuality and the recognition of natural right. When liberals became impatient of the absolute limits to diversity or individuality that are imposed even by the most liberal version of natural right, they had to make a choice between natural right and the uninhibited cultivation of individuality. They chose the latter. Once this step was taken, tolerance appeared as one value or ideal among many, and not intrinsically superior to its opposite. In other words, intolerance appeared as a value equal in dignity to tolerance. But it is practically impossible to leave it at the equality of all preferences or choices. If the unequal rank of choices cannot be traced to the unequal rank of their objectives, it must be traced to the unequal rank of the acts of choosing; and this means eventually that genuine choice, as distinguished from spurious or despicable choice, is nothing but resolute or deadly serious decision. Such a decision, however, is akin to intolerance rather than to tolerance. Liberal relativism has its roots in the natural-right tradition of tolerance or in the notion that everyone has a natural right to the pursuit of happiness as he understands happiness, but in itself it is a seminary of intolerance.[29]

---

[29] Leo Strauss, *Natural Right and History* (Chicago: University of Chicago Press, 1953), p. 65.

I believe that anyone aware of conditions prevalent in our culture and world today cannot fail to appreciate Strauss's point. It seems clear that the logic of the skeptical, relativist approach has allowed the victory of the antilibertarian political forces in our age. They are the serious, vehement, indignant masses and their intellectual representatives; they are the so-called radical professors, the third-world spokesmen, the Ralph Naders, the bombers, and the leaders of women's liberation rallies with their obvious disdain for liberty and their desire for power.

It seems to me then, that values and liberty are not in fundamental conflict. Quite the contrary. But more important, value and liberty are logically connected, since political liberty is the necessary condition of human beings' pursuit of correct values. Admittedly, it is only when individuals take the initiative to do so that we have both the necessary and the sufficient conditions of human excellence. But here is one of the most profound insights of the libertarian tradition—that people cannot be made good, and the state is the least capable agent for achieving that goal because it must demoralize culture whenever it wields power, it must rob people of the opportunity to exercise their capacity for being moral agents.

CONCLUDING POINTS

In the end the difference between Hayek's views and those offered for consideration here is negligible in respect of their conclusions. First, there is no denigration of science in my approach, but a suggestion that certain victories won the scientific way really may have been won by a combination of philosophical movements, science, politics, morality, and other developments in human history. It is arguable that the potential for the scientific revolution existed since the works of Aristotle were translated from the Arabic and that the real substance of that revolution was political. This political element in turn had to do with renewed confidence in man's capacity to improve life. Some unjustified conclusions may have been carelessly drawn from this, as Hayek himself points out in several places. But the self-assertiveness of human beings is not itself bad, nor something without which pure methodological advances could produce much in the way of progress.

To get to more specialized points, consider Hayek's case against planning. He rests it on the uncertainty about what suits individuals' lives and the lack of capacity to predict what individuals will do—in short, the lack of knowledge needed for a plan. All this may be so, but planners are notoriously willing to take risks, especially with the lives of others. Perhaps, they seem to say, just this once, we can succeed, even after years of failure. So let us charge ahead with another program of regulations and plans. Of course, we don't know enough, but isn't life itself a risk? Don't businessmen act in the face of uncertainty? Why should governments not do so?

The answer is that it is morally wrong, that it contradicts the value of liberty. Individuals should enjoy liberty because it is naturally right for them in a social context—their moral nature cannot flourish without it. Planners should plan their own lives, for here is where they have moral authority. Hayek's demonstration of the planners' incapacity supports this point. Obviously the prospects of living better are greater when people attend to their own circumstances, because they are in a better position to know what they require. The kind of conception of human mind I outlined earlier renders it highly probable though certainly not guaranteed that free individuals will make better decisions and the entire system will be more rational than one in which the few try to accomplish that which they cannot do—namely, learn the limits of suitable conduct and aspirations for all.

But it is wrong even to suggest that planning is the rational way while the lack of planning is somehow the result of skepticism. We know that a free system is better, more productive, more suitable for human beings. The planners have no idea what they are doing. Yet there are a few here and there who make a right decision once in a while—as when they look closely to find out, and order, like competent doctors, some remedy that works. From this the entire system is fed with confidence. Unless even that instance of good judgment is condemned as wrong because it results at the expense of liberty, the planners can go on with moral legitimacy on their side.

We might recall here Hayek's idea that deliberate planning should enforce very general laws. In short, his conception and endorsement of the rule of law also gain support from the present perspective. Human nature is such that each person is similar to others in some respects and differs from most in the rest. So human societies work when laws refer to general needs and capacities, those shared by all people. All are purposive agents and it is naturally right for them to have their freedom protected and preserved. Beyond that there should be greater and greater diversity. This does not mean that there is not something objectively good that each person ought to pursue, that there is not a simple conception of happiness that escapes Strauss's charge of relativism. It is simply that while one can know what another's happiness is, it is in the nature of the moral life that no one can *make* another happy in the strict and relevant sense of that phrase. One can even conceive of how another might achieve that happiness—one can write it down, dramatize it, even offer advice. But that is different from producing it for the other.

So here again Hayek's points are essential to showing the prospects of liberty, for indeed people are more favorably positioned to achieve their own moral self-realization and proper self-actualization that others would be, especially those who sit in governmental seats of power. But this does not mean that once in a while some people cannot know what is right.

It is to be hoped that these few points will show why I believe it important to study and understand Hayek's work. But what I have said also indicates that his work is insufficient. His case for liberty is not powerful enough to solve the problems which any political theory must face.

13.

Complexity, Change, and Control

ROBERT L. CUNNINGHAM

IN this essay I wish to explore certain of the implications ignorance and uncertainty have for our lives and institutions. As the world becomes more complex, our ignorance of the principles and facts relevant to rational prediction and to control over our welfare increases. Yet when social institutions operate in such a way that the knowledge possessed by others is put at the individual's disposal, ignorance is no block to the accomplishment of purposes. The scientific enterprise, for example, is characterized by increasing complexity and, if casual observation can be trusted, by increasing change. Nonetheless, competition and institutional controls over the dissemination of knowledge work, though imperfectly to be sure, to advance the growth of scientific knowledge.

A major problem of our times may thus be: How can we arrange our institutions so that others' knowledge can benefit each one of us as each one of us seeks his (changing) goals? How can our major social institutions, in particular the law, be structured so as to respond appropriately to the state of affairs characterized by the ignorance and uncertainty produced by complexity and change? How can institutions be arranged so that I can know how to make use of much of the knowledge possessed by others without knowing what they know?

As life becomes more complex, do we need more, or less, hierarchical control over it? Is the link between the growing complexity and interdependence of human relations, and the growing demand for centralized planning and control, a rationally justifiable link: "When life was simple, people could be left to do pretty well as they pleased; the more complex things became, the less autonomy people can be permitted, the more control must be exercised." I wish to explore the merits of the opposite view: the more complex the system, the less amenable to centralized hierarchical control it will prove to be.

As Leslie A. White has pointed out,

Primitive man could believe that he could control the weather only because he was ignorant; he knew virtually nothing of meteorology. And today it is only our profound and comprehensive ignorance of the nature of culture that makes it possible for us to believe that we direct and control it. As man's knowledge and understanding grew in meteorology, his illusion of power and control was dissipated. As our understanding of culture increases, our illusion of control will languish and disappear. As Durkheim once observed, "As far as social facts are concerned, we still have the mentality of primitives."[1]

Whitehead's dictum about civilization's advancing by extending the number of important operations we can perform without thinking about them might then be adapted to read: civilization advances by extending the number of ways in which the knowledge others have can be put at our disposal without our needing to learn what they know. I shall endeavor to counter the argument of those who suppose both that life is becoming more complex and that the more complex the system, the more hierarchical control must be exercised. The claim is not that one cannot ever by legislation accomplish social purposes—one can see to it that no one in the employ of another receives a wage below "minimal decency" (though accomplishing this purpose may entail increased unemployment or self-employment with smaller return than minimum wage)—but, rather, that this social purpose is very often accompanied by bad consequences which outweigh the good.

Civilization may be said to rest on two things: first, the conquest of our ignorance of the general laws of science—the knowledge may be possessed by relatively (even increasingly) few, so long as it is useful to many;[2] and second, increased access to particular facts en-

---

[1] See Leslie A. White, "Man's Control Over Civilization: An Anthropocentric Illusion," *Scientific Monthly* 66 (1948): 235–40.

[2] See John H. Schaar, "Some Ways of Thinking About Equality," *Journal of Politics* 26 (November 1964): 867–72: "We call ours a scientific age. What that really means is that a small handful of men have a tremendous scientific knowledge, while the rest of us are as ignorant of science as we have always been. So the gap widens: the distance between an Einstein or a Kepler and the

abling us to make use of what we are ignorant of, making widely dispersed knowledge useful to all. F. A. Hayek writes of the latter that our "necessary ignorance of most of the particulars [facts] . . . is the source of the central problem of all social order."[3] On this reading, the problem of social order is an enormously complicated problem of coordination: there are virtually innumerable bits of knowledge scattered about widely, and the problem is to arrange things so that this knowledge is used to serve all of our interests, to coordinate things so that what you know and act on will be of benefit to me when I act on what I know.

Under some circumstances complex orders develop spontaneously, the unintended order resulting from a myriad of individual activities. Hayek refers to such a social order as a "spontaneous order," James Buchanan calls it an "ordered anarchy," and Robert Nozick refers to it as an "invisible-hand order." Such an order or pattern of activities manifests intelligence, though that pattern was not the result of any single person's effective intelligent intervention; it is one that, like Topsy, just "growed."

It is of course not true that every such spontaneous order is a desirable one, that the independent and utility-maximizing behavior of individuals produces results which are efficient in the economic sense—the "problem of the commons" and some forms of the prisoner's dilemma bear witness to this.

Michael Polanyi, in his *Logic of Liberty*, develops the example of science and its progress as spontaneously ordered.

If the scientists of the world are viewed as a team setting out to explore the existing openings for discovery, it is assumed that their efforts will be efficiently coordinated if only each is left to follow his own inclination. It is claimed, in fact, that there is no other efficient way of organizing the team, and that any attempt to coordinate their efforts, by directives of a superior authority, would inevitably destroy the effectiveness of their coordination. . . . Early in life he [the scientist] specializes in certain branches of science which seem to fit his inclinations, and then through the years of his apprenticeship in research he keeps looking out for some problem especially suited to his gifts, by the pursuit of which he may

---

ordinary men of our day is far greater than the distance between a Newton or a Kepler and the ordinary men of their day."

[3] *Law, Legislation and Liberty* (Chicago: University of Chicago Press, 1973), p. 12.

hope to achieve important results. Since the credit for a new discovery goes to the scientist who first publishes it, each will be eager to publish his results as soon as he feels sure of them. This induces scientists to inform their colleagues, without delay, of their current progress. On the other hand, sharp sanctions are in operation against premature publication, and scientists whose conclusions have proved hasty suffer a serious loss in reputation; this guards scientific opinion from being confused by a flood of erroneous claims put in circulation by too ambitious investigators.[4]

In addition to inhibiting hasty conclusions, individual effort ultimately results in coordination, as Polanyi also points out:

The progress of science through the individual efforts of independent scientists is comparable in many ways to the growth of a higher organism from a single microscopic germ cell. Throughout the process of embryonic development each cell pursues its own life, and yet each so adjusts its growth to that of its neighbors that a harmonious structure of the aggregate emerges. This is exactly how scientists cooperate: by continually adjusting their line of research to the results achieved up to date by their fellow scientists.[5]

In what follows I attempt to consider characteristics of one such spontaneous order, the common law, with a view to improving our understanding of its merits and limitations. F. A. Hayek believes that the development of common law has occurred through a sort of evolution by natural selection. There is something comparable to the biological mechanism of reduplication with transmittable variations and competitive selection of those which prove to have a better chance of survival; and he appears to believe that this mechanism has in the course of time produced a great variety of structures adapted to continuous adjustment to the environment and to each other. He views the legal system as an almost incomprehensibly complex machine, almost a "black box," with which it would be rash and temerarious to tamper except under the most extraordinary circumstances. This attitude is comparable to that of the "negative utilitarian" who, fearing the unanticipated consequences of attempting to do good, attempts only to reduce obvious evil. So too Hayek fears using legislation to promote the good, and would legislate only

[4] Michael Polanyi, *The Logic of Liberty* (Chicago: University of Chicago Press, 1951).

[5] Ibid., p. 34; see also p. 163.

to reduce the evils of an order which has evolved in a way which is patently inefficient.

I first explore briefly the question of why it is that we find an explanation based on a spontaneous order difficult and unsatisfying. I then turn to the common law and consider the possibility of reconciling the "realist" position, that decisions made by common-law judges are innovative and arbitrary, with the position of those who strongly prefer common-law legislation to lawmaking by the legislature. After this I survey the problems raised by redistributionist public-policy decisions and programs, and close with a discussion of some aspects of the common law's power of adapting to change.

WHY ARE SPONTANEOUS-ORDER EXPLANATIONS UNSATISFYING?

Whenever one finds a complex pattern or order, one asks how such a pattern developed. If the answer is that it is a product of an intelligent being, then, in effect, the answer comes to asserting there is no reason for puzzlement, there is nothing to explain in any deep sense. (The only remaining problem might be: *Which* intelligent being produced this pattern?) We are familiar enough with our own intelligent attempts at planning to count "made by an intelligent being" as a basic pattern which does not itself call for explanation.

However, some "basic patterns which do not themselves call for explanation" may not always be recognized as such, as Warren Weaver, has pointed out:

No one, in any serious sense whatsoever, "understands" the law of gravitation. This law is, at least in the present state of science, an ultimate simplicity which we just accept. . . . [We] feel satisfied because of the compactness, simplicity, and universality of the laws which affect the explanation; we feel satisfied because we have an intelligent tool for predicting the future, as well as understanding the past. . . . It is not necessary that the old and familiar ideas be themselves understood; it is only necessary that they be so familiar that curiosity concerning them no longer exists. . . . The scientist, on the other hand, does not explain the unfamiliar in terms of the familiar; indeed he normally reverses the order as when he "explains" a chair or table in terms of electrons and protons.[6]

---

[6] Warren Weaver, "A Quarter Century in the Natural Sciences," *Rockefeller Foundation Annual Report 1958*: 41–42.

But if we find an intelligent order—a marvelously subtle and complex language, a complex legal system, an ecological system, a pattern of action which serves the interests of those who participate in complex and satisfying ways—but can find no maker, no planner, no orderer, then we are puzzled indeed. This puzzlement and frustration is illustrated clearly in the following reaction by a reviewer of Darwin's revolutionary *The Origin of Species*:

In the theory with which we have to deal, ABSOLUTE IGNORANCE is the artificer; so that we may enunciate, as a fundamental principle of the whole system, that IN ORDER TO MAKE A PERFECT AND BEAUTIFUL MACHINE, IT IS NOT REQUISITE TO KNOW HOW TO MAKE IT. This proof will be found, on careful examination, to express, in a condensed form, the essential import of the theory and to express in a few words all Mr. Darwin's meaning; who, by a strange inversion of reason, seems to think that ABSOLUTE IGNORANCE fully qualified to take the place of ABSOLUTE WISDOM in all the achievements of creative skill.[7]

In effect, an intelligent functional pattern must be the product of the same sort of intelligence that comprehends it. How could chance produce a pattern perceived as intelligent? Does not the "argument from design" (or conspiracy theories) lead us to search for a designer whenever we find intelligent order? Does not the "principle of sufficient reason" preclude an effect's being greater than its cause, and so preclude the possibility that chance could cause an intelligent pattern?

It is this line of thought that leads us to account for the order we find by appealing to gods and heroes. Such explanations, however, are not very enlightening: there are too few steps between the explanandum and the explanans; or, put another way, the similarity between explanans and explanandum is too great. To account for the order of the universe by appealing to an Orderer who does it all is less illuminating qua explanation, than an account which describes the coordinated steps and transformations to which the laws of nature and chance give rise. An explanation explains by breaking up the relationship we are puzzled about into a set of different relationships each of which we understand.

Another aspect of spontaneous orders that troubles us, by con-

---

[7] Quoted in Garret J. Hardin, *Nature and Man's Fate* (New York: Rinehart, 1959), p. 301.

trast with planned orders, is that they are relatively impervious to control. Their complexity is such that though understanding is often possible after the fact, predicting the effects of interventions is usually beyond our powers. When a crop fails, we cannot predict how other prices and resources will be shifted. When, for example, a new technology is developed, we cannot predict how the common law will deal with the new patterns of expectations which arise. This is not to say that prediction and control are much improved through planned interventions. The assumption that the more complex a system is, the more planning it calls for, flies in the face of the fact that the more complex the system, the less control we find ourselves able to exercise. If we wish to accomplish our purposes through intervention in the economic market, language, the scientific enterprise, judge-made law, a complex ecological system, we find we can do so successfully only if we can bring the system within our grasp by reducing its complexity. Even so, the problem of unexpected consequences looms so large in the social sciences precisely because, as Hayek, Popper, and Scriven have noted, the complexity of the social world puts prediction beyond our grasp.[8]

Such a spontaneous order, perhaps particularly the economic market, is deemed alien to man, an "order of necessity," as Engels put it, "imposed by nature and history," with man the victim of unplanned forces resulting from his activities. It is of course only under socialism that "the objective, alien powers, which until now ruled history, come under the control of men themselves," only then that "men will make their history themselves, with full consciousness; only from then on will the social *causes* they set in motion have in the main and in constantly increasing proportion, also the *results* intended by them. It is the leap of mankind from the realm of necessity to the realm of freedom."[9]

---

[8] F. A. Hayek, "The Theory of Complex Phenomena," in *Studies in Philosophy, Politics and Economics* (New York: Simon & Schuster, 1967); Karl Popper, "On the Sources of Knowledge and Ignorance," *Proceedings of the British Academy* 46 (1960); Michael Scriven, "A Possible Distinction Between Traditional Scientific Disciplines and the Study of Human Behavior," *Minnesota Studies in the Philosophy of Science* 1 (1956).

[9] *Entwicklung des Sozialismus von der Utopie zur Wissenschaft* (Berlin:

And is there under an order governed by the invisible hand any genuine freedom of choice for human beings? On some views of freedom it might seem not. Does not true freedom, as Marx thought, imply a sort of self-creation? "A being does not regard himself as independent unless he is his own master, and he is his own master only when he owes his existence to himself. A man who lives by the favor of another considers himself a dependent being." If I cannot initiate or genuinely choose actions which can be counted on to have their intended consequences, am I not committed to denying or restricting the scope of self-determining free will? Is one who participates in and contributes to the ordered anarchy of the scientific enterprise really a free human agent, freely choosing the problems to which he addresses himself; or is he not rather a plaything of forces of scientific progress whose direction he cannot even predict, much less control? And in what sense can such a scientist be said to be a moral agent, in what sense is it intelligible to speak about what he should or should not do? Tibor Machan writes, "If a man cannot initiate his own crucial forms of action, namely, those that are uniquely human, and if he is essentially guided by rules and laws outside his choice, then to call upon him to act in one way as opposed to another is futile. He has no say in these matters."[10]

Whatever the merits or limitations of such a view of human freedom, it seems clear that self-generating, complex, "purposeless," impersonal, rule-guided invisible-hand orders are, for a wide variety

---

Dietz, 1923), p. 5. See also H. B. Acton, "Tradition and Some Other Forms of Order," *Proceedings of the Aristotelian Society* 53, no. 1 (1952–53): 21: "Adam Smith and Rousseau thus seemed to be in search of a state of affairs in which no one is subservient to anyone else and in which when people are thwarted it is by something that does not thwart them for its particular satisfaction and it does not therefore injure their moral dignity. . . . Marx in his *Critique of Political Economy* wrote of men entering into 'definite necessary relations independent of their will.' He thought that men were often as it were imprisoned and depressed by such anonymous creations. Thus he deplored the very things that Mandeville and Adam Smith admired and believed that the anonymous creation would be replaced by 'human' arrangements corresponding to men's conscious desires."

[10] For an expression of anxiety about the possibility of reconciling free will with Hayek's view of human affairs as governed by evolutionary spontaneous orders, see T. Machan, "Reason, Values and the Spontaneous Order," herein.

of reasons, troubling when compared with orderings imposed by human reason and will.

LEGAL REALISM AND SPONTANEOUS ORDER

Gordon Tullock, in Essay Five, has argued that "our present system of having the details of our legal system generated as a sort of byproduct of judicial decisions [is] an extremely poor one. It developed rather by accident in Anglo-Saxon law at a time when judges thought they were not making new law, but finding or interpreting the existing law. Its continuance now is simply a matter of tradition."[11] The fact of the matter is that if a court is presented with a case in which the law is not clear, the court must make a decision, and this decision must be arbitrary. "The argument is simply that this is a rule which the parties before the court cannot have known before the court made its decision; hence, of necessity, it is arbitrary and there is therefore no need to invest a great many resources in determining which arbitrary rule will be used."[12]

Without denying that there is a certain arbitrariness (the product of human judgment but not of caprice) in the decisions made in novel cases, I should like to argue that the common-law system does nonetheless generate spontaneously a complex order which tends effectively to coordinate human purposes. I wish to agree with common-law critics that a judge, however earnestly he might wish to write a decision which suitably coheres with past decisions and the order of the law, may very well find it impossible to accomplish his purpose. The reason is a simple one: the law is too complex for him to manage; he is, that is to say, too ignorant to accomplish his purpose. Tullock notes that the new rule produced may indeed have expected interactions with other parts of the immense mass of legal rules, and that the certainty of the law may not be increased at all. This is analogous to adding a new instruction to a long computer program. Tullock points out that "anyone who has had anything to do with computers knows that very long programs have many unexpected interactions, with the result that the outcome is very hard to predict. Adding more instructions to such long programs is apt

[11] "Courts as Legislatures," p. 137.
[12] Ibid.

just to change the nature of the unexpected interactions, not to reduce them."[13]

Arbitrariness, chance, and fortune may well play a role in the development of the common law.[14] But is it possible that a coherent and coordinated system of judicial decisions would be produced if there were no way of telling ahead of time which decision was the best, which decision would maximize the coordination of human purposes? Is judicial wisdom a necessary condition for a common-law system which has the characteristics of a spontaneous order?[15]

Suppose that, within limits, decisions are made randomly. Suppose that some decisions prove to be successful. Suppose that "successful" decisions are imitated—*stare decisis* mandates the cheapest of all decision procedures: imitation. Suppose also that intention to imitate sometimes fails, thus introducing incremental innovation. In effect, if the decision could later be classifiable as a success or a failure in coordinating human expectations, then chance might produce spontaneously a legal order having all the characteristics of an invisible-hand ordering.

One might also look at some courts (higher courts, appellate courts) as "price searchers," while lower courts could be viewed as "price takers." In a price takers' market, each seller offers so small a part of the supply of goods that he has no effect on price. In a price searchers' market, an individual seller can affect the price by varying the amount he offers; in such a market it may appear, incorrectly, as if prices were arbitrarily set by sellers beyond the control of supply and demand.

Note that when it is said that a judge is searching for the right decision, what is implied is that the hidden treasure has a definite location, that he is playing in a two-person game versus nature. The fact of the matter is, though, that in law the judge is playing a multi-

[13] Ibid.

[14] See Deutsch and Madow, *Behavioral Science* (1969), for a brilliant account of how chance and fortune might produce a "military genius."

[15] The line of argument I make use of here was first applied by Armen Alchian to show how a modification of economic analysis which dispenses with "profit maximization" as a guide to conduct and embodies the principle of biological evolution and natural selection can lead to an improved explanatory and predictive economic schema; see "Uncertainty, Evolution and Economic Theory," *Journal of Political Economy* 57 (1950): 211.

person game: the location of the treasure shifts depending on the activities of other searchers (judges) and hiders (citizens) in a changing environment.

One might say that the changes proposed by the judges—the timid, the venturesome, and so on—can be thought of less as a process by which law adapts itself to change than as a process by which the system adopts the change it favors. The uncertainty as to which decision will best coordinate expectations arises from imperfect foresight and our inability to solve complex problems containing a host of variables. It is in such circumstances that ex post facto explanations of why a particular decision proved better than another are possible, though prediction was impossible. In sum, if the system adopts the best decision, it is not necessary to look very hard for profound wisdom on the part of the judges. All the judge needs to do is to come up with a relative best, not necessarily a terribly wise decision. If there is a satisfactory selection procedure, successful candidates may be produced by chance and the upshot will be rational. There are thus a number of factors which lead to imitation's playing so important a role in the development of a common-law system; among these are the absence of identifiable criteria for satisfactory decision-making, variability of the environment, the multiplicity of the factors calling for attention and choice, and the uncertainty attaching to all these factors.

In sum, then, there may be some reason to believe that the common law may be able to evolve in ways which effectively coordinate human actions, regardless of the presence or absence of wisdom, perspicacity, or high motivation on the part of the individual judges.

LEGISLATURE AND JUDICIARY

What is an appropriate division of labor between judiciary and legislature in making new law? Let us consider some of the more obvious characteristics of each. A legislature can establish committees to investigate issues in depth, and the scope of its investigation is not limited by well-defined rules of evidence; it can act on its own initiative and can deal with more aspects of a problem than can a court, which is limited by the live case and controversy provision and which can take judicial notice only of certain aspects of the case.

More or less comprehensive "solutions" to problems can be developed more quickly by a legislature than by a series of judicial decisions. Legislation is prospective, not retroactive; and legislatures have better means for promulgating statutes.

Among the disadvantages of legislative lawmaking is its tendency towards partiality and making law based on political considerations; this is particularly serious when the issue being decided is one on which political parties divide. The legislative process offers no satisfactory way of making sure that the positions of all interested parties will be effectively made known, especially when legislation is redistributive. Majority rule is the legislative watchword, but if government undertakes redistributive activities, special-interest groups (especially producer groups) impose costs on the general public (especially consumers, who are underrepresented in legislative halls because of free-rider problems) in excess of the benefits to the interest group; the upshot is that redistributive activities are undertaken which impose net costs on the public. This leads to a situation where all find themselves in a prisoner's dilemma: all would benefit from following a self-denying ordinance to refrain from using the political process for redistributive measures; but for each person there will be an advantage in making an exception for himself. The effective legislative power will be in the hands of the middle-class majority; but note that it is not necessarily true, and may well not be true today, that the greatest beneficiary is indeed a net beneficiary of redistributive programs.[16]

Though both judges and legislation can be said to make new laws, there is nonetheless a kind of "is" versus "ought" contrast in that the judge, to the extent he relies on precedent, works with law as it is, while the legislator is explicitly concerned with the future and with law as it ought to be. A sign of this contrast in emphasis is that retroactive legislation is far more objectionable than a judicial decision, even a novel decision. The judge's own sense of justice, unlike that of the legislator, is restrained by the necessity to give weight to "fair expectation": "Nothing is more common than the practice of

---

[16] See Robert Nozick, *Anarchy, State and Utopia* (New York: Basic Books, 1974), for an argument showing why the middle class is the greatest beneficiary of redistributive programs; and George J. Stigler, "Director's Law of Public Income Redistribution," *Journal of Law and Economics* 13 (1970): 1.

learned judges to say in rejecting some rule urged as being the law, that business could not be conducted as it actually is conducted if that were the rule. This is saying that the suggested rule does not conform to fair expectation."[17]

And the demands of fair expectation tend both to block judicial discretion, in the sense of the power to choose between two or more courses of action each of which is thought of as permissible, and also to block judicial decisions based on some supreme substantive principle. The holding of a court is not justified by being derived from some general standard, and that standard itself is not validated by being derived from some still more general standard and so on—as the leaf depends on the twig, and so on the branch, the limb, the single trunk of the tree; the structure of law is not hierarchical. The obligation of the judge is rather, as Sartorius has written, "to reach that decision which coheres best with the total body of authoritative legal standards which is bound to apply."[18] One might picture the set of authoritative legal standards which underlies fair expectation as a web or net stretched over growing, changing human wants; its principle of organization is that of maximizing strength by minimizing strain. Some strands in the net of legal standards are, for various reasons, stronger than others, and offer surer points to which a novel decision can be anchored; a bad decision is one that sets up an asymmetrical strain on the net—thereby weakening it or leading to substantial and unpredictable readjustment of its internal organization. "When looking for the *ratio decidendi* of a case we are not trying to discover the preexisting rule of law which was applied in the case. What we are trying to determine is the rule of law the decision will support when all other existing law-making decisions have been taken into account."[19] And if science and law can be compared as systems of spontaneous order that accommodate change,

total science is like a field of force whose boundary conditions are experience. A conflict with experience at the periphery occasions readjustments

---

[17] J. C. Carter, *Law, Its Origin, Growth and Function* (New York: Putnam's, 1907), p. 332.

[18] *Individual Conduct and Social Norm* (Encino, Calif.: Dickenson, 1975), p. 196.

[19] Harari, *Negligence in the Law of Torts* (Sydney: Law Book Company, 1962), p. 18.

in the interior of the field. . . . No particular experiences are linked with any particular statements in the interior of the field, except indirectly through considerations of equilibrium affecting the field as a whole.[20]

Does judge-made law develop too slowly? It is clear that if one does indeed know the substantive goal to which judicial efforts should be directed, then legislation would surely be more efficient and swift. And once the law has evolved significantly, it is clear we could have gotten there more expeditiously by legislation. But it would seem that if we have little experience with a problem or nest of problems, they should be wrestled with on a case by case basis, testing the rules that are gradually developed against social reality. Judges can thereby more easily modify basic law of their own making than they can modify statutory language. Further, it may be that the factors relative to a sound solution vary so much from case to case as to defy statutory formulation, as, for example, in negligence law.

Lon Fuller writes that "men's interests and desires form a complex network, and that to discover the most effective and least disruptive order within this network requires an intimate acquaintance with the network itself and the interests and desires of which it is composed."[21] So the judge legislates within the context of the particular actual case he has information about, information and guidance given by the interested parties only. The main focus of attention is on the instant case, not so much on future cases whose implications neither the judge nor the parties concerned can have confidence they fully understand. With his reliance on precedent,, and so on reasonable expectations, and with his focus on the particular case before him, and given the rules of evidence which exclude considerations relating to the relative merits of the parties, constraints are imposed on the ability of the judge to disturb settled expectations by making value decisions which have direct redistributive import; the redistribution which occurs is only a byproduct of transactions counted as voluntary within the context of settled law.

Fuller offers the helpful analogy of the father asked to decide a

[20] Quine, *From a Logical Point of View*, 2d ed. rev. (New York: Harper Torchbooks, 1961), p. 42.

[21] *The Problems of Jurisprudence* (Brooklyn: Foundation Press, 1949), pp. 706–7.

dispute between two of his children; he notes that there is a difference between making a decision after hearing both sides and laying down a rule for future conduct.

If, implored by the disputants to hear their arguments, . . . [the] father, at the conclusion of the evidence and arguments and without rendering any decision in the case before him, were to declare, "Well, now that I see what's going on around here, I announce that the following rule must be observed. . . ," it is fairly obvious that he would be sacrificing his moral position as judge for that of legislator. If he were then to decide the case before him, his ruling would not seem like a decision but an order.[22]

Judges do legislate. And judicial decisions are, to a degree, "arbitrary" because judges are ignorant of the consequences of their decisions and so cannot determine which decision is best; that is, has the best fit with the order of settled expectation, the legal order. It might be reasonable then for one who gives considerable weight to the implications of ignorance of the consequences of intervention in a complex order to favor only tentative, incremental judicial legislation and to deplore judicial activism. Posner points out that the

emphasis upon precedent and on small changes makes law more predictable than it would be if every case were decided afresh, on the basis of first principles. Predictability increases the settlement rate and thereby economizes on the costs of the legal system. Without predictability, moreover, property rights would be indefinite, which is the equivalent of saying there would be few property rights.[23]

There are two senses of certainty in the law which might be usefully distinguished here. In one sense, legislator's law, found as it is in a precise written text, might be more certain presently than the law found in a series of common-law precedents. But in another sense, a legal system which changes slowly and only at the margin is more certain prospectively, is a better basis for long-run personal planning, than a system which is subject to significant and quick changes. It is in this latter sense that precedent and *stare decisis* contribute to certainty, thus furthering private ordering by ensuring that if people comply with the announced law, they will not be en-

22 Ibid.
23 See Richard Posner, *Economic Analysis of Law* (Boston: Little, Brown & Co., 1972), pp. 328–32.

tangled in litigation; and, given that incentives to try to get from a different judge a different decision are minimized, the remedial processes of private settlement are encouraged.[24]

PUBLIC POLICY

Does legislation to promote public policy, or judicial decisions based on policy rather than on principle, tend to weaken or to strengthen an individual's attempt to accomplish his goals in a world of change, incomplete knowledge, ignorance, risk, and uncertainty?[25] Public-policy recommendations are aimed not so much at resolving disputes as at reallocating resources in the interest of what is argued for as a more just distribution—not at commutative but at (re)distributive justice. It would appear there is a degree of arbitrariness, an unpredictability, which would increase rather than reduce uncertainty in policy legislation or decisions. Consider, for example, compensation policies intended to reduce the impact of change.[26] It is clear that any sort of rule to compensate innocent victims of competition (or disaster) would have the effect of shifting to the general public the risk now borne by owners of productive resources, human and nonhuman. What justifies the private property system is that it encourages people to use resources most productively by requiring that they, rather than the general public, bear the risk of losses incurred as the price of retaining the profit which luck or skill sometimes brings. Under a compensation policy, what would otherwise have gone to some in the form of profits must be taxed away to provide compensation for those who sustain losses; the overall effect is

---

[24] See Henry M. Hart and Albert M. Sacks, *The Legal Process*, mimeographed (Cambridge, 1958), p. 587.

[25] Ronald Dworkin in "Hard Cases," *Harvard Law Review* 88: 1057, defines policy arguments (as contrasted with arguments of principle) as ones which "justify a political decision by showing that the decision advances or protects some collective goal of the community as a whole" (p. 1059). He goes on to note that the demand for "articulate consistency" is relatively weak when policies are in play and that "it need not be a part of a responsible strategy for reaching a collective goal that individuals be treated alike" (p. 1064).

[26] See *New York Times*, August 19, 1975, p. 48, for Edwin L. Dale, Jr.'s discussion of the "Adjustment Assistance Program" for workers who can make a case that imports have been an important cause of their loss of jobs—"now the government's fastest-growing program."

to stabilize society and it is not hard to see that it is the present pos-
sessors of wealth who would benefit at the expense of those un-
knowns who would have been successful.

Such policies are almost inevitably arbitrary, compensating some
but not others on irrelevant grounds, Lockheed but not Pan Am, the
faultless householder whose house burned down along with enough
others to qualify the area as a disaster area, but not the faultless
householder whose house was as completely destroyed by a fire not
in a disaster area. Here there is a clear violation of the principle of
treating like cases alike, by favoring some litigants over others if recovery by them promotes the favored policy, established, quite possibly, through political pressure. Such policies reduce efficiency by
dampening the incentive to use resources productively. Less knowledge will thus be employed. Such compensation policies render nu-
gatory the knowledge individuals have of particular circumstances,
opportunities, facts, or abilities.

Social purpose is defeated by complexity and change, and so
what has been called "the command society" must reduce the complex, spontaneously adapting society to a simpler one less subject to
change. It is possible to reduce uncertainty for some by depriving
others of the power to use their own knowledge and resources as
they see fit. And if one system is simpler than another (less knowledge is embodied in the system), then one can reduce uncertainty by
reducing the number of expectations but strengthening the grounds
for reliance on them, as is done in a status society.

If policy interventions so often do more harm than good, then
why is it that they prove politically possible? The answer lies in the
fact of an asymmetry between the costs and benefits of intervention
and the costs and benefits of nonintervention. The predictable benefits of intervention may be clear, at least in the short run; the evils of
intervention in a complex, spontaneous system may be unknown and
unpredictable, at least in detail; it is only seldom that one can be
quite confident that a particular group of people will be hurt by
an intervention, as one can in predicting the deleterious effect of
minimum-wage laws on teenage blacks. The upshot may well be that
since it may be known precisely who will be helped, but not precisely who will be hurt, the former may use the political process for
their own benefit while the latter, perhaps only a statistical group

whose identity and the extent of whose damage may never, in a changing society, be identified, are obviously in no position to lobby against the intervention. Opposition can be made, if at all, only on principle. If, for example, the tuition at a state university is lowered, a great many of those affected favorably can estimate fairly precisely the extent to which they benefited; what cannot be estimated, to mention only two of the most obvious losses, are the effect on taxpayers who cannot know exactly what goods would have been purchased by the dollars now taken away in taxes, and the effect on enrollment at private colleges. Thus, as Hayek has said, if we reject intervention only when evils are exactly predictable, too few will be rejected. Similarly, one might know very well who will be hurt by the workings of a spontaneous order—the shopkeeper who lost his customers because of foreign competition, or Lockheed—but not who would be helped.

Thus, when we compare the utilities of intervening and of not intervening, it is hard to believe that the political process operating on policy grounds is the appropriate vehicle for maximizing utilities. Perhaps Mill was right when he wrote that government "will interfere in the wrong place at the wrong time" because any such intervention, at least of the policy sort referred to above, will end up doing more (unspecifiable) harm than (specifiable) good. This would follow from the fact that we do not know enough to manage to do more good than harm in a system whose dominant order is spontaneous, one embodying so great a variety of ends and knowledge.

The very strengths of the common-law method of legal development through incremental change in "the law as it is" with the least possible disturbance of settled expectations—the focusing of attention upon a limited number of aspects of a particular case or controversy, and so on—may become liabilities when applied to changes recognized as more radical, whether these be justified on public-policy grounds or on the ground of radical expansion of standing, due process, or equal protection.[27] When the legislature and the

----

[27] Are the 1973 *Roe* and *Doe* abortion decisions based on "concordant practice" so that these decisions can be "provided with a consistent rationale in the sense of a systematic representation in terms of a network of interconnected rules and principles which may go well beyond the ground-level facts of concordant behavior, patterns of criticism and justification, etc., which are mani-

executive cannot or will not act to break what is recognized to be new ground in advancing what many deem to be the cause of human justice, should the judiciary properly exercise a degree of self-restraint? Or should the court be limited only after the fact, as it were, by constitutional amendment or statute when a decision is found to go "too far." Is there some danger that positions taken by the courts will be so far in advance of commonly accepted standards of right action that people will not be persuaded by the decision and will believe themselves to be ruled arbitrarily by virtually unreachable authorities? Nathan Glazer would counsel self-restraint:

> The legislature and executive have far more resources than the courts to determine how best to act. If they don't, it is because no one knows how to, or there is not enough money to cover everything, or because the people simply don't want it. These strike me as valid considerations in a democracy, but they are not considered valid considerations when issues of social policy come up as court cases for judgment. For example, no desegregation decision that I know of has been stayed by the fact that there is not enough money or that school or other educational resources will suffer, perfectly valid considerations for legislatures, executives, and administrators—but the kind of consideration that no judge considers worthy of notice.[28]

COMMON LAW AND CHANGE

Let us touch on certain aspects of the common law's power of spontaneous adapting to change. Is such a spontaneous order, an ordered anarchy, an invisible-hand order, inferior as an embodiment of reason to commanded orderings such as those which issue from legislatures? The central problem in a rapidly changing society is that of coordinating human expectations in such a way as to maximize the choice-options of independent decision-makers: it would be easy enough to coordinate by reducing options, as is done in a prison.

The importance of tradition, the status quo, or what David Lewis calls precedent, must not be overlooked.

---

fested within the community in question"? (Sartorius, *Individual Conduct and Social Norm*, p. 209).

28 "Towards an Imperial Judiciary?" *Public Interest* (Fall 1975): 118.

Precedent is . . . the source of an important kind of salience: conspicuous uniqueness of an equilibrium because we reached it last time. We may tend to repeat the action that succeeded before if we have no strong reason to do otherwise. . . . But suppose we are not given the original problem again, but rather that we are given a new coordination problem analogous to the original one. Guided by whatever analogy we notice, we tend to follow precedent by trying for a coordination equilibrium in the new problem which uniquely corresponds to the one we reached before. . . . The salience due to precedent . . . is uniqueness of a coordination equilibrium in virtue of its preeminently conspicuous analogy by means of shared acquaintance with a *regularity* governing the achievement of coordination in a class of past cases which bear some conspicuous analogy to one another and to our present coordination problem.[29]

James Buchanan has argued that the advantages of maintaining the existing legal constitutional rules, the status quo, are clear if one views law as public capital, which produces an "income flow" of conformity to the law. Changing the law will destroy the old income flow, which includes social cohesion, disalienation, and motivation to conform, and the higher yields possible in the form of conformity to an improved law may not be possible till the investment matures over time.[30] He has also noted that

there is an explicit prejudice in favor of previously existing rights, not because this structure possesses some intrinsic ethical attribute and not because change itself is undesirable, but for the much more elementary reason that only such a prejudice offers incentives for the emergence of voluntary, negotiated settlements among the parties themselves. Indirectly, therefore, this prejudice guarantees that resort to the authority of the State is effectively minimized. The State must adjudicate all conflicting claims, must take on all challenges to this and that, and, in the process, achieve the "unknown passing through the strange," a politico-legal setting that itself contributes to "future shock."[31]

Can a spontaneous order adapt to change in a satisfactory manner? Does not such an order need supplementing by explicit rational policies? We can get help in answering this question by considering Kenneth Minogue's contrast between two meanings of tradition. One

[29] *Convention* (Cambridge: Harvard University Press, 1969), pp. 36–41.

[30] James Buchanan, *The Limits of Liberty* (Chicago: University of Chicago Press, 1974), pp. 128–129.

[31] *Journal of Law and Economy* 15 (October 1972): 439–52.

involves doing things in a time-hallowed manner and refusing to countenance any kind of innovation. In the other sense of tradition, it is
development rather than repetition which is the central idea, and what leads such traditions into decadence is precisely the conscious operation of reason. For reason fragments a tradition into a set of policies, ends and means, and works in terms of principles . . . which are distorting fixed points outside the range of criticism.[32]

Why is it that the traditional is sometimes fixed and rigid and at other times, in language of the economic market, adapts freely and immediately to exogenous or endogenous change? The difference rests on failure or success in communication. If the changing knowledge and preferences of each participant in such a spontaneous order make a difference, then that order will be flexible; the other elements of the system will shift slightly to accommodate the new bit of information. If explanation is reduction to the comprehensible, then it is clear that the larger the role the traditional plays in modern life, the less puzzlement there will be. What is traditional does not call for explanation: there is no need to reduce the familiar to the familiar.[33] Expectations are always subject to slight and continuous modification, and make revolutionary change unnecessary. As Michael Oakeshott writes, "Revolutionary change is usually the product of the eventual overthrow of an aversion from change and is characteristic of something that has few resources of change."[34]

SUMMARY

I have been concerned in this paper with the argument that increasing complexity calls for increasingly centralized and coercive

---

[32] *The Liberal Mind* (New York: Random House, 1963), p. 62.

[33] "It is not necessary that the old and familiar ideas be themselves understood: it is only necessary that they be so familiar that curiosity concerning them no longer exists" (Weaver, "A Quarter Century in the Natural Sciences," p. 42).

[34] Michael Oakeshott, *Rationalism in Politics* (London: Methuen & Co., 1962); Oakeshott continues: "The more closely an innovation resembles growth (that is, the more clearly it is intimated in and not merely imposed upon the situation) the less likely it is to result in a preponderance of loss" (p. 172).

control. Without wishing to deny that the state functions not only as a referee or protector, but also as a producer of important public goods that are otherwise unobtainable; and without wishing to deny that common-law developmental logic may well lead to blind alleys from which extrication by the legislature is the only solution; and without wishing to deny that the pace and dimensions of technological development have combined to produce increasing interdependence and have consequently enlarged areas of potential conflict; I have wished to draw attention to some of the ways in which a spontaneous order merits being recognized as a nonstatic, dynamic, adapting principle of marginal change, and also to what I take to be the fact that legislative interventionism and judicial activism in the name of distributive justice have themselves introduced instabilities that accelerate change in unexpected ways, and so lead to a demand for still more legislative and judicial activism. As John Rawls has stated,

in designing and reforming social arrangements . . . ideally the rules should be set up so that men are led by their predominant interests and act in ways which further socially desirable ends. The conduct of individuals guided by their rational plans should be coordinated as far as possible and achieve results which although not intended or perhaps even foreseen by them, nevertheless are the best ones from the standpoint of social justice. Bentham thinks of this coordination as the artificial identification of interests; A. Smith as the work of the invisible hand. It is the aim of the ideal legislature in enacting laws and of the moralist in urging their reform.[35]

My central theme has been that complexity defeats control; that dealing with increasing complexity calls for increasing knowledge, and that the individual's incentive to acquire and use his own knowledge is stronger in institutions characterized by "ordered anarchy" than in what Hayek calls "constructive rationalist" institutions. The greater the scope and magnitude of change in society, the greater the unexpected consequences of our actions—and so the greater our ignorance of how best to promote our interests—and so the greater the importance of individual freedom to overcome that ignorance.

---

[35] John Rawls, *A Theory of Justice* (Cambridge, Mass.: Harvard University Press, 1971), p. 57.

An apposite coda to my variations on the Hayekian theme that human ignorance justifies human freedom is provided by Lao-tzu:

> If I keep from meddling with people,
>> they take care of themselves;
> if I keep from commanding people,
>> they behave themselves;
> if I keep from imposing on people,
>> they become themselves.

Conference Discussion

ROBERT L. CUNNINGHAM

INTRODUCTION

THE San Francisco Law and Liberty Conference in honor of F. A. Hayek was interdisciplinary, and the topics addressed and discussion were wide-ranging. What perhaps would be most valuable for readers of this book would be not a summary of all the discussions which followed the papers, but a summary of those parts of the discussion which contribute to the understanding of Hayek's position, whether by direct critical analysis of his writings, or by the development of themes which are central to his legal and political philosophy.

Among the questions discussed at the conference and touched on below are the following: Has Hayek significantly changed his position on the nature of the rule of law—is the analysis in *Law, Legislation and Liberty* different from that in the *Constitution of Liberty*? Hayek has a good many favorable things to say about spontaneous order, as opposed to planned order; but does his system permit, without contradiction, an independent criterion of "betterness" and of progress? What grounds Hayek's preference for freedom over justice, and his hesitation over trading some freedom for more justice? Do Hayek's skepticism about the possibility of knowing final truth, his moral and historical relativism, and his determinism weaken the rationality of his preference for freedom and reliance on spontaneous order? In what sense is Hayek a utilitarian? Is Hayek's notion of freedom adequate to permit him to distinguish permissible from impermissible government interventions? From where does the principal threat to freedom come—from too much government intervention, or from a failure of government to inculcate liberal principles such as respect for privacy?

HAYEK AND THE "RULE OF LAW"

In the *Constitution of Liberty*, law was thought of as a universally applicable rule. It was the fact that law must be such as to apply to everyone which ensured against tyranny. Law is, by its nature, inherently restrictive of liberty, and so law can best be kept within its proper bounds, and dangerous discretionary power avoided, if the law is general and is such as to apply to everyone alike, including the legislator. By contrast with this Benthamite view of law as instructions by government to the governed, Hayek in *Law, Legislation and Liberty* sees law not in opposition to liberty but as a sort of enfranchisement. Freedom is not the absence of law but the presence of enfranchising law which makes it possible for each of us to do the maximum while, in effect, respecting the rights of others also to do the maximum. Law is a guide to behavior, and Hayek is now far more sympathetic to piecemeal growth, to rational particularistic judging. Such law, *nomos*, in great part the formulation of a tradition expressing the common understanding of people, grows out of the community and so is not a restriction on activity imposed on us from outside. Such law grows in response to new circumstances by throwing up a decision which disturbs settled expectations least, a decision created by and embodied in existing law, one which harmonizes best with existing law. What was lacking in the earlier analysis was the recognition of the fact that law is a social phenomenon, that "growing law" has deep social roots. A rule, *taxis*, can be laid down by a lawgiver for any particular reason, to accomplish some social purpose; a law, *nomos*, necessarily serves a multiplicity of purposes. And this logical analysis of the difference between nomos and taxis is reflected in the genesis of the two: taxis is generated by legislators, nomos by common-law judges. Law, which is the product of something like social evolution, is, by contrast with taxis, more a government by laws than by men. Though it is Hayek's position that the "grown law" must be respected, he does not accept the conclusions of the organic school without reservation, for he grants that at times the common law got itself into blind alleys from which it had to be extricated through legislation.

Some attention was given to exploring the connection between the concept of legal system and the concept of rule of law. The positions of Lon Fuller and Joseph Raz were compared, Fuller holding that the requirements of the rule of law are properties of law itself, Raz maintaining that these requirements are better conceived as properties not of law but of good law. It is not true that if there is no violation of the formal rule of law, the law is therefore good; only that if there is a violation, a law is to that extent bad; the requirements of the rule of law are not the only virtues of law.

Attention was also given, in particular by Letwin, to the way in which not only the executive and judicial branches of government, but also the legislative branch must be subject to the rule of law. There is, though, some reason for less worry about the legislature's violating the rule of law than about violations by the judiciary. For in general, and this line of argument is reminiscent of Hayek's *Constitution of Law* analysis, the legislature can be given a relatively free hand because legislation applies to large numbers of people and any burden imposed will be carried by many, the many who are also the electorate. The impact of judicial or executive decisions may well be more restricted: since it deals with individuals, it has greater impact. Legislation which imposes heavy burdens on large numbers of people is not likely to get very far, whereas a judge might impose a severe burden on a few without generating a great hue and cry. But now, as Hayek has written in *Law, Legislation and Liberty*, a legislature often acts in ways which put burdens on a few or which restrict the activities of many in a small way to help a few in a big way. The upshot is that at a time when the legislature uses its powers to justify policy interventions on narrow utilitarian grounds, there is increasing need for recognition that the rule of law binds the legislature no less than it binds the executive and judicial branches of government.

Hayek's earlier views on the rule of law are shared by Tullock to the extent that both look on law as something government does to people, and like most other economists, both have a deep faith in the fact-value distinction and are skeptical about the usefulness of "justice" as a key socioeconomic or political concept. Tullock, it was suggested, does not share the ordinary conception of a court as committed to doing justice to people, and so he sees a bureaucratic agency as preferable on the grounds of efficiency to a court, with its obfuscating mystique, for the settlement of disputes. Hayek's later view, which sees law rather as a shared possession generated by the community, guiding us in ways that only occasionally and on the margin need judicial determination, is hardly reconcilable with Tullock's frankly prospective and stringently utilitarian view.

Tullock comes close to concluding that from the fact that judges disagree, one cannot say that a particular decision is better than some other would be. If people generally, and if judges more particularly, held Tullock's views about law, the institution of law would change drastically, or judges would no longer be always bound, at least in principle, to try to reach decisions which best cohered with the body of applicable law, and to defend that decision as the more reasonable to the one whose expectations were disappointed. Here is a conception of courts which denies that an independent judiciary has a responsibility to defend and vindicate decisions, a notion of courts in which, since there is no applicable law in hard cases, it would be nonsensical to ask the judge to make the best decision.

Fletcher's paper triggered discussion of what appears to be a change in emphasis in criminal law from concern with punishment of criminals to concern with protection from those judged to be threats to good order. Just as on Hayek's view in *Law, Legislation and Liberty* the judge must refrain from basing his judgment on policy grounds, so legality demands a similar self-denial in the use of evaluations of intent in criminal law. In a family or in the confessional, everything ought to be taken into account; in the state, though, one's privacy ought to be respected. This has the consequence that one should be treated impersonally, less as an individual than as a "case": if people are to be free, and their dignity respected, a veil of ignorance should initially be drawn over their mental processes. Criminal justice is retributive rather than distributive, and the blindfold that justice wears should prevent it from focusing too early on issues of intent or motivation. Judicial inquiry is thus quite different from moral or administrative inquiry; in the latter, one may very properly attend not only to guilt but to dangerousness, and so one may give weight to past acts in ways inappropriate in criminal law. It follows from this view of legality that a whole class of acts should be decriminalized. Crossing a state line, for example, is not in itself a wrongful act, and since intent should not be attended to unless a wrongful act has been done, crossing a state line with criminal intent should not be made a crime. Or borrowing money with the intent not to repay should not be a defined crime; there must be objective evidence that a wrongful act has been done before probing intent—for example, leaving a bank with money given by mistake would trigger investigation of whether intent to defraud was present. If, as was argued, the acceptance of legality as privacy would lead to a good deal of decriminalization, it would then be possible to reduce prosecutorial discretion; though whether this upshot would be on balance desirable was disputed.

SPONTANEOUS ORDER

The issue of the nature and role of Hayek's "spontaneous order" was considered in a number of papers and elicited considerable discussion.

The reasons for Hayek's reliance on spontaneous order for the organization of human affairs was explored at length. What justifies this reliance? One answer is that spontaneous order promises to produce better results. But how avoid tautology in defining "betterness of results" produced by spontaneous order against the results produced by planning? Is there something analogous to Darwinian survival involved? But how would this analogy help? So long as the species survives in some form, there is still a question whether the species is in a better state than before; and of course the number of survivors is not the crucial issue since survival may call for a reduction in the size of the population. Is Hayek a Burkean, one who holds that the reasoning of many is likely to be more fruitful, "better," than the reasoning of one? Is it the case that his criterion for preferring spontaneous order to other organizing principles is confidence that it makes self-actualization more likely, or makes more likely the attainment of individuals' goals and purposes?

When one recommends spontaneous order as an organizing principle for a community, given the inevitability that the goals of some must give way to the goals of others, the question "What is the better order?" cannot be answered by specifying what it is that people initially want. Efficiency in getting people what they want at some point may block the attainment of more, or more important, wants at a later time. Efficiency in the short run does not necessarily lead

to efficiency in the long run. If spontaneous order effectively coordi-
nates peoples' desires, so that people have to give up less in order to
live with others, then spontaneous order is justified for that time and
place—but what justifies it generally? One needs also to be able to
show that this is the kind of order which best adjusts to changing
circumstances. Of course, if one rejects the view shared by Aristotle
and Mill that it is good to satisfy individual desires for happiness,
the short-run versus long-run efficiency argument will not be satisfactory. Or if one somehow knows what it is that the future indeed
holds for mankind—Marxist revolution, for example, leading to the
abolition of the state—then the efficiency argument will hardly be
telling. We do need to distinguish, as Hayek perhaps sometimes fails
to do as carefully as desirable, between spontaneous order as the
principle for ordering the actions of members of a community at
some one time, and history itself as a spontaneously ordered se-
quence of affairs.

The argument from utility is also open to the objection that we
have no way of knowing what the alternatives would have been, and
so no grounds for preferring this organizing principle to some other.
There was, to be sure, no control group. One might respond that
there are nonetheless good grounds for putting one's confidence in
spontaneous order. For there is a great deal of experience to show
that when spontaneous orders have been tried in roughly comparable situations, spontaneous order has proved superior. If the case
can be made that spontaneous order is superior in science as an organizing principle for promoting scientific progress—the ground being that our necessary ignorance of the truths science will reach in
the future makes planning, which presupposes knowledge of the direction in which truth will be found, counterproductive—then to the
extent that human wants (or human needs, human nature) change in
unpredictable ways, progress in science can be seen to offer a problematic analogous to progress, or at least adaptability, in social affairs.

Further, if one emphasizes the rule-utilitarian grounds of Hayek's
political philosophy, one can still raise the question which sort of rule
works best, for example in law, a Benthamite rationalistic positivism
favoring legislation, or a Hayekian reliance on coordination by a
common-law judiciary. Hayek needs a firmer foundation to rely on

than our common experience that any one of us is likely to make mistakes, and that there is some pressure leading us to better answers over time. But if, as a matter of historical fact, large-scale rationalistic constructions have proved inferior to the small-step dialectical approach of intellectual criticism, then it is clear that liberty, as a condition of having values we are not at all sure about, needs to be given an important role.

If one believes that truth is best attained through a winnowing-out process engaged in by independent ratiocinators, and that error or inferior values are more likely to be thrown out than truth or superior values, then there are some grounds for preferring spontaneous order. Such a preference, one might say, is grounded on a theory of imperfect rationality: man is ignorant, but not totally so. One needs to know some criteria for evaluating the success or failure of programs, policies, and institutions; otherwise the last thing is the best thing, and surely this is far from being the position of a theorist like Hayek, who not only has vigorously criticized the direction human history has taken, but also has offered suggestions for appropriate radical changes. A question was raised in this connection about Hayek's determinist position and its relation to the distinction he makes between spontaneous order and deliberate action: How can he distinguish these two satisfactorily if he is a determinist? One suggestion was that though he is a determinist, Hayek also holds that our ignorance of human affairs is of such a nature and quality that it is impossible for us to predict human actions, and so we must, in effect, act as if we were free.

Some concern was expressed about the weight Hayek gives, or fails to give, to the need for communal, legal, and institutional support required to promote a liberal individualism which avoids the extreme of atomism. Is there adequate appreciation of the legitimate criticism of pure individualism made by the Scottish philosophers of common sense, Hayek's allies in analyzing and criticizing Cartesian rationalism? Is sufficient attention given to the importance of communal feelings in forming a civil community, and to those areas in human life in which people share purposes and feel no need to compete? It was urged that Hayek assumes a great deal when he assumes that one can trust the spontaneous orders subsidiary to the state to foster the growth of community at various levels. Some suggested that the principal threat to the free and liberal society comes from the state's failing to take steps actively to promote the inculcation of values and attitudes crucial to the very maintenance of a liberal society. If only certain kinds of character will make the liberal state viable, as both Mill and Hayek have suggested, and if, as seems to be the case today, the various subsidiary institutions—family, locality, church—fail to promote civic virtue, the state must intervene to supply this need, to inculcate the virtues necessary to preserve civility.

The dangers, though, of government intervention for such a purpose were stressed, for the power to control moral (re)education is perhaps too dangerous to entrust to the state. Though one may fully recognize the importance of civic virtue, one might maintain that it is too important to entrust to the coercive state. Perhaps we have reached a time when we must be willing to pay the cost of living in a society which lacks many highly valued qualities, privacy for example, if we are not to lose the more important value of freedom.

In another suggested analysis, many of the features of modern liberal society which displease us are due not to failure of the government to intervene beneficently, but to the failure of government to live up to its obligations to protect the individual from other individuals. The lack of self-control and self-responsibility comes more from an increase in state activity in the name, usually, of egalitarian justice, than from a lack of government activity. If we are presumed to know exactly what human values and amenities are worth preserving and fostering, then of course our subscription to liberalism is our subscription to a means, an instrument, to independently desired ends. Hayek's own support of the liberal state is rather to the liberal state as an end, as the politically achievable end, though not, of course, as the end of individuals.

There was considerable discussion of planning as a means of inducing order as contrasted with spontaneously generated order. Here one needs to distinguish the thesis that government policies often do not work—the thesis supported by evidence that the more a government tries to achieve equality of result the more it hurts those it wishes to help—from the thesis that government policies cannot work at all. Further, the problems one encounters in evaluating the success of a public housing policy, for example, are in essence the same as those encountered in evaluating one's own actions in furtherance of some private policy.

When two people disagree about whether some policy or other will promote the "common good" or the "general welfare" or the "public interest," the disagreement is not merely verbal, or, usually, one that can be resolved by further analysis or explication of the concept. It is not that the term is ambiguous or objectionably vague or remediably imprecise, but, rather, that "general welfare" is an essentially contested concept, a concept shared by the disputants though there is disagreement about its correct instantiation. To make unanimity of reference a condition of the success of a concept is to miss the point of concepts like "general welfare," and "due process," and to make useful discussion and debate impossible.

RELATIVISM

Hayek's skepticism about justice received critical consideration. It was suggested that Hayek failed to distinguish an end-state conception of justice (for instance, income should exist in a certain pattern) from justice per se; and so, although Hayek gives good reasons for denying the relevance of static, end-state justice to political and legal theory, he has not really denied the relevance of other alternative, procedural conceptions of justice. On this analysis Hayek's position is that liberty is everything, whereas (end-state) justice is nothing; and other views of justice are not adequately discussed. Perhaps there is also an element of antiutopianism, most emphatically expressed in *The Road to Serfdom*, involved in his distaste for arguments based on considerations of justice. Thus instead of saying there are some arguments of justice which favor laissez-faire, and also some arguments of justice which favor socialism, and that since freedom and justice are the major political goods, which, however, cannot be achieved satisfactorily this side of utopia, some liberty will need to be traded for some justice—instead of needing to deal with problems of trade-off, Hayek's (oversimplified) position calls merely for favoring freedom over justice.

As regards Hayek's skepticism about the human mind's ability to capture the truth, a case was made for the view that the issue of relativism, of whether all minds are the same or different, is not the crucial question. More important than variability is determinism, for even if all minds are the same but are determined to reach error, there is no mind that will penetrate to the truth of things.

Hayek's value-relativism came in for discussion. If his view can be fairly summarized by saying he holds that no matter what a person's values, that person can do best in an open society, then there is no need for him to concern himself with defining what man is or ought to be, since in his society everyone will get more of what he wants no matter what he wants.

An objection that was raised against Hayek's utilitarian value-relativism argues that the liberal, open society cannot maximize certain values, for example, values characteristic of a religious and aristocratic society. If these values cannot be accommodated, then to be in favor of a liberal, open society is implicitly to claim to know what is good for man, to claim that getting life, liberty, and property is better for man than getting, for example, religious and aristocratic goods. Thus since not all values can really be maximized in a liberal society, a choice must be made between a liberal society and some variant of a closed society. Further, if collectivism is increasingly victorious, as appears to be the case, one can justify the claim that it is not the comparative merits of collectivism which ground its victory only if one can somehow know what is indeed good for man. We can fault a historical development as a blind alley only if we can find an objective, ahistorical ground to stand on when contemplating and criticizing the developments which actually took place.

FREEDOM

A good deal of attention was given to the analysis of the notion of liberty. Certain liberties are believed to be more important than others, to be protected from government interference more carefully than others. Freedom of speech and freedom of contract and freedom to drive up Lexington Avenue are all cases of freedom, but most believe freedom of speech more important than freedom of contract, and freedom of contract more important than freedom to drive without certain restrictions. But can one, on the basis of an analysis of the notion of freedom itself, say which of two freedoms is more important, or which is the greater and which the lesser freedom?

It was argued, principally by Dworkin, that such an analysis would be possible only if a coherent notion of quantity of liberty or of liberty as a fungible good could be developed; but that no such coherent notion could be found. One need not say that "right to a fair trial" must be analyzed into sets of various *rights* to a fair trial, though fairness in a criminal trial is different from fairness in a civil proceeding: for here we need not speak of one right being more a case of fairness than another—fairness is simply instantiated in different ways. But we do say that of freedom—we do say that one freedom is a greater or more important freedom than another. And so, it was concluded, if we are to focus analytically on freedom, rather than synthetically on freedoms, we must produce a satisfactory operational notion of quantity of freedom; but none seems available.

Some argued the contrary, that a viable notion of freedom could be developed by making use of the resources of the libertarian tradition, which views the right to liberty as including the right to property; such a conception might well be rich enough to ensure that problems like the Lexington Avenue driving problem would not arise. If Lexington Avenue were privately owned, no one's rights would be infringed if the owner made Lexington Avenue a one-way street; the issue of the utilitarian justification, whereby a lesser right of a minority is trumped by a greater right of a majority, would not arise. Such a right to property would need, though, to be developed as a separate basic independent right, and not as a consequence of a more basic right of liberty; otherwise the problem of comparing quantities of liberty would arise all over again.

If one takes the position that individual freedom is primary and the burden of proof is on those who would interfere, disagreement will still arise over what a good reason for interfering would be—and one would need a better reason for interfering with some freedoms than for interfering with others. Developing such a view would presuppose a view of the nature of man and his good; only then could one give a satisfactory account of when equality or justice ought to be trumped by freedom.

Notes on Contributors

WALTER BERNS is professor of political science at the University of Toronto, Toronto, Ontario, Canada.

ROBERT L. CUNNINGHAM is professor of philosophy at the University of San Francisco.

GOTTFRIED DIETZE is professor of political science at Johns Hopkins University.

RONALD DWORKIN is professor of law at Oxford University, England.

GEORGE P. FLETCHER is professor of law at the University of California, Los Angeles.

WILLIAM LETWIN is professor of political economy at the London School of Economics.

JOHN R. LUCAS is Fellow and tutor of Merton College, Oxford University, England.

TIBOR MACHAN is associate professor of philosophy at State University of New York College, Fredonia.

EUGENE MILLER is professor of political science at the University of Georgia, Athens.

JOSEPH RAZ is Fellow of Balliol College, Oxford University, England.

ROLF SARTORIUS is professor of philosophy at the University of Minnesota, Minneapolis.

STEPHEN J. TONSOR is professor of history at the University of Michigan, Ann Arbor.

GORDON TULLOCK is university professor of economics and public choice at the Virginia Polytechnic Institute and State University, Blacksburg.

Index

abortion, 213
accident: and liability for homicide, 195–196; and liability in tort, 201–202
Acton, H. B., 301n, 147–148
Acton, Lord, 81, 246, 248
Adams, John, 82, 222
Adkins v. *Children's Hospital*: and freedom of contract, 60–61, 62, 66; and minimum wage, 60–62; and occupational safety, 61–62; overturning of, 62–64, 65; and police power, 60, 61; and status of women, 60–61, 62
administration. *See* executive
administrative boards: abuse of discretion by, 148, 164; writing of prospective law by, 138–139
Alchian, Armen, 303n
alienation: of community, 229, 230–231, 232; concept of, in collectivist thought, 226–228; and division of labor, 228–233; and progress, 228–233; transcendence of, 233
American Revolution: moderation of, 85
"An American Family," 217
anarchism: and minimal state, 87, 89, 110, 116, 129
anarchy: emergence of law from, 204–207; and liberty, 80, 85. *See also* nature, state of; spontaneous order
Anarchy, State, and Utopia (Nozick), 87
Ancient Law (Maine), 239
Ancient Society (Morgan), 241

Anglo-Saxon law: anticipation of contingencies under, 143–144; determination of laws under, 144–145; enshrinement of precedent under, 144; function of courts in, 132–134, 141–143, 302–303
"antirationalism," 244, 245, 248, 286
appeals process: determination of future cases in, 144; in European law, 141, 143; and explanatory essays, 134; in parole law, 138–140
Aquinas, Thomas, 155, 248, 250
arbitrary power: application of, to economy, 20–21; constitutional restriction of, 22, 23; of courts, 207, 302, 308, 312; definition of, 12–13; distributive justice as, 309–310; in licensing procedures, 47; regulation of working hours as, 59; restraint of, as morality, 16, 17; revolution as, 236; and right of contract, 49; and rule of law, 12, 13; violation of due process by, 69, 72, 73
Aristotle, 147, 156, 248, 250, 251, 266, 282, 291, 322
association, right of, 211, 213
attempts: determination of liability in, 196, 198–200, 206
auctoritas, 81

Bachofen, Johann Jakob, 236, 241; on archaic society, 239–240
Bacon, Francis, 264, 265
Bannister, D., 273–274, 286
Barry, Brian, 93
Bayard, Mabel, 215

tionality, 246, 252n; diverse appeal of, 224–225; rational appeals against, 266; scientism of, 225–226; and unalienated community, 226–228, 241
command society, 310
common law: decision making under, 142; definition of private business in, 38; definition of public interest in, 35–36; evolutionary development of, 297, 311; excusing circumstances under, 190; harm v. liability in, 195; larceny in, 197–198; precedents in, 308; protection of liberty by, 187; and regulation, 37, 39; spontaneous development of, 302–304; sufficiency of, 161, 162; view of reason by, 276
communism, 233, 240, 288
Communist Manifesto (Marx and Engels), 233, 234
community: alienation in, 229, 230–231, 232; basis of law in, 235–237, 318, 320; basis of property in, 237–238; circumscription of liberty by, 64, 65; in collectivist thought, 227–228, 241; interests of, v. individual, 177; and motivation of collective action, 93; personal v. external preferences of, 178–180, 181; principle of justice in, 162; restoration of, 236–237, 241; shared values in, 323–324; utilitarian policy in, 177–180
Community and Society (Tönnies), 239
competition: legislative restriction of, 51–52. *See also* free market
Comte, Auguste, 225, 253
Concept of Law (Hart), 160
concordant practice, 311n–312n
Condorcet, Marquis de, 245
consent: and collective action, 108–109; government by, 19–20, 210; and minimal state, 111, 127–128; and protection, 115, 116–117
Constant, Benjamin, 82, 245
Constitution, U.S.: and derived powers of government, 210; and economic due process, 22–73 *passim*; liberties safeguarded by, 176; and majority

opinion, 55; mandate for rule of law in, 22–23; mandate for science in, 223; protection of privacy by, 213, 214, 215; restraint of democracy by, 85; and spontaneous order of society, 211–212
constitutionalism, 244
The Constitution of Liberty (Hayek), 75, 80, 81, 83, 84, 86, 87, 147, 160, 163, 164, 264, 317, 318, 319
constitutions: guarantee of liberty by, 80, 82, 85; self-enforcing mechanisms in, 143; stabilizing influence of, 313; values embodied in, 166
constructive grant, 39
contracts, 123, 126; v. antiutilitarian view of rights, 181; constitutional limitations on, 64, 65–66; and economic due process, 72; immunity of, to legislation, 37; just settlement of, 185; validity of, 25. *See also* social contracts
—freedom of, 326; v. police power, 33, 42, 44, 46, 49–54; for women, 61; v. working conditions, 62
Contribution to the Critique of Hegel's Philosophy of Right (Marx), 236
cooperation. *See* collective action
corrective justice, 185
Corwin, E. S., 30, 56
The Counter-Revolution of Science (Hayek), 225
courts: accessibility of, 10–11; activism of, 312; application of due process clause to, 23, 48; and arbitrary power, 12; as author of authoritative rules, 182; and common law, 318; decision making by, 319–320; defense of privacy by, 213; destabilizing influence of, 315; development of law by, 77–78; and doctrine of presumed constitutionality, 34, 35; under European law, 140, 143; explanatory essays of, 133–134; function of, in Anglo-Saxon law, 132–134, 141–143, 302–303; independence of, 10; interpretation of particular cases by, 133, 134, 135, 136, 140, 141–142, 144–145; law-

making aptitude of, 304–309; law-making function of, 10, 132, 134, 135–136, 138, 302–304; and nullification of state legislation, 26; and occupational safety, 45; regulation of prices by, 41; rendering of justice by, 162; review powers of, 10, 11; ruling of future cases by, 132–133, 134, 142–143; upholding of police power by, 42; violation of due process by, 69; violation of rule of law by, 319. *See also* Supreme Court

—obligations of: to corrective justice, 185; to equality, 182–183, 184; to formal rules, 161, 182–184, 187, 203–204; to privacy, 185–187, 191, 203, 207

courts, state: discrimination by, 43; upholding of due process by, 27–30

crime: deterrence of, by minimal state, 123, 125–126; discretionary treatment of, 11

criminal law: assessment of liability in, 187–191; diminution of liberty by, 172; emergence of, from anarchy, 204–207; erosion of privacy under, 191–194; intent in, 194–201; and legality as privacy, 186, 188, 189–190, 320–321; objective-to-subjective ordering of, 202–203; responsibility in, 285; view of reason by, 276

Critique of Political Economy (Marx), 301n

Dale, Edwin L., Jr.: on compensation, 309n

Darwin, Charles: evolutionary theory of, 271–278 *passim*, 289, 299, 321

Day-Bright Lighting case, 71–72

decision making: in collective action, 107–109; in free market, 158–160, 165–166; in free society, 292–293; in minimal state, 128; and particular laws, 9; and rule of law, 8, 13, 14, 15, 160–161

Declaration of Independence, 210

dedication of private property, 39–40

defamation, law of, 215

democracy, antiutilitarian concept of, 180–181; compatibility of, with liberty, 79–80; confusion of, with rule of law, 4, 7; corruption of spontaneous order by, 270; inhibition of science by, 214; and interest group politics, 70–71; legislation as centerpiece of, 78; policy change in, 312; preferences measured by, 179–180; reproduction of values of, 221–223; restraint of, 85

Democracy in America (Tocqueville), 79

Descartes, René, 250, 251, 264, 282; dualism of, 257–258; on nature of knowledge, 279, 280; rationalism of, 246–248, 272, 273

desert: assessment of, in criminal law, 187–188; assessment of, v. legality as privacy, 188, 189–190; v. excusing circumstances, 188, 189

dialectical materialism. *See* Marxism

Dicey, Albert Venn, 11n; on lawmaking, 76

dignity: and concept of equality, 175; confusion of, with rule of law, 4; identification of, with privacy, 210–211; and legality as privacy, 320; protection of, by rule of law, 14–15

"Discourse on the Origin of the Inequality among Mankind" (Rousseau), 234

discrimination: v. 14th Amendment, 43, 46, 48; and generality of law, 9; legal proscription of, 17, 74–75; and occupational safety, 44, 45–46; regulation as, 52–53; special protection of women as, 57

distributive justice: v. acquisition of natural resources, 118; avoidance of, by courts, 185; correlation of, with organization, 269; desirability of, 147–148; liberal commitment to, 324; and state-worship, 149; unpredictability of, 315

Douglas, Justice William O.: *Day-Bright Lighting* opinion of, 71–72;

racy by, 270; creation of, 107; pressure of, on government, 70–71; and redistributive legislation, 305
International Congress of Jurists (1959), 3–4
interstate trade, 67
invisible hand, 312, 315; and consolidation of protective agencies, 114; and creation of ultraminimal state, 114, 129; limitation of free will by, 301–302; manifestation of intelligence by, 296; and origin of minimal state, 112–113, 129; provision of public goods by, 88, 104; of spontaneous order, 271
involuntariness, 189
Iroquois Indians, 240
isonomia, 78

Jefferson, Thomas, 55, 82, 222; on right to liberty, 167, 168
Jehovah's Witnesses, 71
Jonas, Hans, 265
Journeymen's Bakers Union, 52
judicial obligation: to corrective justice, 185; to equal protection, 182–183, 184; to formal rules, 182–184, 187, 203–204; to privacy, 185–187, 191, 203, 207
judicial review, 10, 11
judiciary. *See* courts
justice: in business transaction, 155–158; as cardinal value, 154; and collective decision making, 107–108, 128; compatibility of, with liberty, 325, 327; confusion of, with rule of law, 4, 7; and enforcement of laws, 85; legislation of, 78; as motive for collective action, 101–103, 104, 106, 120; as motive for national defense, 120; as motive for organizing, 107; v. order, 81; protection of, by rule of law, 5; in rule of law, 162–163, 166, 319–320; rules of, 273; in spontaneous order, 315; in state of nature, 111–112, 113. *See also* corrective justice; distributive justice; natural justice
Justinian, 155

Kant, Immanuel, 95–96, 233–234, 248, 251, 258, 260, 262–263, 271, 272, 282, 283, 284, 287; on nature of knowledge, 278, 280–281
Kelsen, Hans, 78, 182
Klages, Ludwig, 240
Klüver, Heinrich, 263
knowledge: accessibility of, 294–296; capacity of reason for, 251–252, 267; complexity of, 294–295; concentration of, 295n–296n; coordination of, 296; detachment of, from experience, 259; devaluation of, by compensation policy, 310; empiricist theory of, 258–259; and free will, 284; guidance of, by extraconscious forces, 263–264; of human action, 281; incentive to, 315; in intellectual activity, 275; and mutability of tradition, 314; and planning, 289, 292; and presupposition of existence, 282; of reality, 279–280; variability of, 253–254, 262–263
Koran, 132
Kristol, Irving, 268

labor, division of, 228–233
labor law, 52–53
Lady Chatterly's Lover (Lawrence), 240
Laing, R. D., 174
laissez-faire, 32, 40, 218, 236. *See also* free market
language: rules of, 273, 276; and thought, 263–264
Lao-tzu, 316
larceny: determination of liability in, 196–200, 206; in system of spontaneous legality, 205
law: anticipation of contingencies by, 136–138, 143–144; application v. development of, 184; as arbiter of social processes, 249–250; basis of, in community, 235–237; concept of justice in, 157; concepts of, 6; correction of, by legislation, 76–78; enfranchisement of liberty by, 318; guidance of behavior by, 6–8, 9,

www.ingramcontent.com/pod-product-compliance
Lightning Source LLC
Chambersburg PA
CBHW021847020426
42334CB00013B/222